Teacher Edition

W9-AVT-169

G.U.M.

Grammar, Usage, and Mechanics

ZB Zaner-Bloser

The Language Arts and Reading Company

Grade Level Consultants

S. Elaine Boysworth
Lincolnton, North Carolina

Linda Crawford
Calhoun, Georgia

Martha Swan Novy
Florissant, Missouri

Heather Stanton
Colorado Springs, Colorado

Jaqueline Xavier
Cleveland, Ohio

Developed by Straight Line Editorial Development, Inc., and Zaner-Bloser, Inc.

Cover photo: Rycus Associates Photography

Book Design: Dominion Design

Illustration: Tom Kennedy, Tracy Greenwalt

ISBN: 978-0-7367-5747-8

Zaner-Bloser, Inc., P.O. Box 16764, Columbus, Ohio 43216-6764 (1-800-421-3018)

Printed in the United States of America   08 09 10 11 12 997 5 4 3 2 1

Teacher Edition Table of Contents

G.U.M.
Grammar, Usage, and Mechanics

Levels A–F
Recommended
for Grades
3–8

- Focuses on grade-level appropriate skills important for writing
- Provides self-directed instruction and practice
- Complements any curriculum with easy-to-follow lessons
- Prepares students for high-stakes tests

A Full Pack of Practice Options!

Student Edition
- Proofreading practice and checklists
- Activities to involve families and communities
- Comprehensive G.U.M. Handbook
- Flexible testing options and practice with standardized test formats

Teacher Edition
- Quick and easy instruction at a glance
- Strategies to help English Language Learners
- Speaking and Listening activities
- Activities for assessment and remediation
- Annotated student edition

Themes with Long-Lasting Flavor!

Contemporary high-interest themes hold students' attention, increase their content-area knowledge, and make learning fun all year long.

Looking Back
Connects to history and social studies.

Unforgettable Folks
Focuses on heroes, athletes, inventors, and world leaders—past and present.

Grab Bag
Explores different cultures, fashion, cars, technology, movies—anything goes!

The World Outside
Connects to science—volcanoes, glaciers, weather systems, and more.

Beasts and Critters
Puts the spotlight on remarkable birds, reptiles, insects, mammals, and sea creatures.

Timeless Tales (Levels E and F only)
Highlights a variety of folktales, myths, and legends.

Great Getaways (Levels E and F only)
Explores rivers, islands, and near-islands around the world.

Each two-page lesson targets important skills and helps students transfer them to their writing. Our five-step format makes it easy.

STEP 1

Provides an example of the targeted skill in context

STEP 2

States skill information

STEP 3

Offers practice of the skill

STEP 4

Helps students apply their knowledge in writing

STEP 5

Reinforces learning through writing activities, puzzles, and technology connections

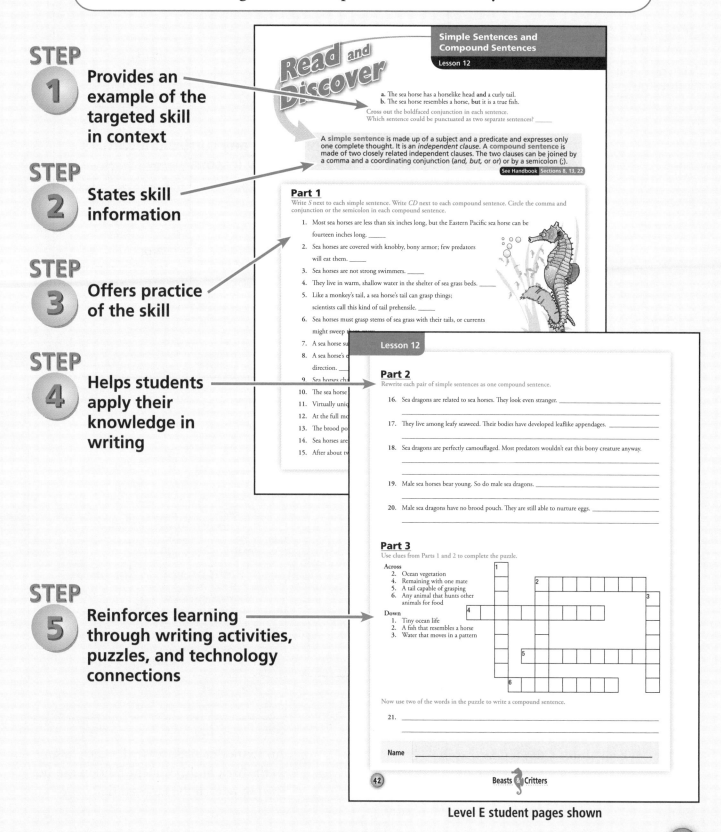

Read and Discover

Simple Sentences and Compound Sentences
Lesson 12

a. The sea horse has a horselike head **and** a curly tail.
b. The sea horse resembles a horse, **but** it is a true fish.
Cross out the boldfaced conjunction in each sentence.
Which sentence could be punctuated as two separate sentences? _____

A **simple sentence** is made up of a subject and a predicate and expresses only one complete thought. It is an *independent clause*. A **compound sentence** is made of two closely related independent clauses. The two clauses can be joined by a comma and a coordinating conjunction (*and, but,* or *or*) or by a semicolon (;).

See Handbook Sections 8, 13, 22

Part 1
Write *S* next to each simple sentence. Write *CD* next to each compound sentence. Circle the comma and conjunction or the semicolon in each compound sentence.

1. Most sea horses are less than six inches long, but the Eastern Pacific sea horse can be fourteen inches long. _____
2. Sea horses are covered with knobby, bony armor; few predators will eat them. _____
3. Sea horses are not strong swimmers. _____
4. They live in warm, shallow water in the shelter of sea grass beds. _____
5. Like a monkey's tail, a sea horse's tail can grasp things; scientists call this kind of tail prehensile. _____
6. Sea horses must grasp stems of sea grass with their tails, or currents might sweep them away.
7. A sea horse su
8. A sea horse's e direction. _____
9. Sea horses cha
10. The sea horse
11. Virtually uniq
12. At the full mo
13. The brood po
14. Sea horses are
15. After about tw

Lesson 12

Part 2
Rewrite each pair of simple sentences as one compound sentence.

16. Sea dragons are related to sea horses. They look even stranger. _____
17. They live among leafy seaweed. Their bodies have developed leaflike appendages. _____
18. Sea dragons are perfectly camouflaged. Most predators wouldn't eat this bony creature anyway.
_____
19. Male sea horses bear young. So do male sea dragons. _____
20. Male sea dragons have no brood pouch. They are still able to nurture eggs. _____

Part 3
Use clues from Parts 1 and 2 to complete the puzzle.

Across
2. Ocean vegetation
4. Remaining with one mate
5. A tail capable of grasping
6. Any animal that hunts other animals for food

Down
1. Tiny ocean life
2. A fish that resembles a horse
3. Water that moves in a pattern

Now use two of the words in the puzzle to write a compound sentence.

21. _____

Name _____

42   **Beasts & Critters**

Level E student pages shown

T7

Proofreading Practice

At the end of each unit, students proofread for errors. A **Proofreading Checklist** helps students apply targeted skills to their own writing.

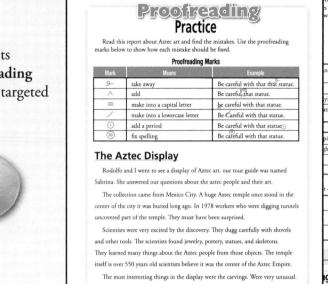

Proofreading Practice

Read this report about Aztec art and find the mistakes. Use the proofreading marks below to show how each mistake should be fixed.

Proofreading Marks

Mark	Means	Example
⟋	take away	Be careful with that that statue.
∧	add	Be careful that statue.
≡	make into a capital letter	be careful with that statue.
/	make into a lowercase letter	Be Careful with that statue.
⊙	add a period	Be careful with that statue⊙
⑨	fix spelling	Be carefull with that statue.

The Aztec Display

Rodolfo and I went to see a dissplay of Aztec art. our tour guide was named Sabrina. She answered our questions about the aztec people and their art.

The collection came from Mexico City. A huge Aztec temple once stood in the center of the city it was buried long ago. In 1978 workers who were digging tunnels uncovered part of the temple. They must have been surprised.

Scientists were very excited by the discovery. They dugg carefully with shovels and other tools. The scientists found jewelry, pottery, statues, and skeletons. They learned many things about the Aztec people from those objects. The temple itself is over 550 years old scientists believe it was the center of the Aztec Empire.

The most interesting things in the display were the carvings. Were very unusual. Snakes and flowers were carved on one flat peace of stone Another carving looked like a huge shell. We also saw a tiny statue of a person carved from jade.

Looking 🏠 Back 27

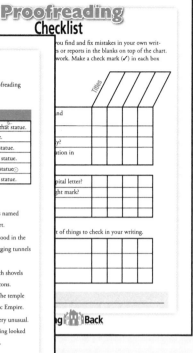

Proofreading Checklist

...you find and fix mistakes in your own writ-...es or reports in the blanks on top of the chart. ...work. Make a check mark (✓) in each box

Looking 🏠 Back

Connections Beyond the Classroom

Send the **School Home Connection** (Levels A–D) or **Community Connection** (Levels E–F) activities home anytime during the unit to reinforce unit skills and to involve families and the community in student learning.

School 🏠 Home Connection

In Unit 2 of *G.U.M.* students are learning about the jobs different words have in sentences. They are learning that **nouns**, such as *dog* and *planet*, name people, places, and things, and that **verbs** tell about actions. The activities on this page give extra practice with some of the concepts they are learning. You can help your child use the information he or she is learning in school by choosing one or more activities to complete together at home.

Twenty Questions (Nouns)

This guessing game can be played by two to eight people. One person thinks of a person, place, or thing but keeps it a secret. The other players try to guess what noun the person is thinking of by asking questions that can be answered "yes" or "no." Guessers can ask up to twenty questions before the mystery noun is revealed.

Dream Trip (Proper Nouns)

Work with your child to plan a dream trip he or she would like to take. The trip can be to anywhere in the world, and your child's guests can include friends, sports or movie stars, relatives, and others your child might like to invite. Help your child write a plan for the trip on a large sheet of construction paper. Include departure and return dates. Remind your child to capitalize proper nouns such as the names of cities, states, and people.

Unforgettable 🧠 Folks 57

Community ✦ Connection

...different kinds of nouns, pronouns, and adjectives ...own writing. The content of these lessons focuses on ...s. As students completed the exercises, they learned ...ds of challenges. These pages offer activities that ...unit. They also provide opportunities for the ...terials in the lessons and the community at large.

...enges are available in your community. Look for ...ers, shelters, immigrant resource centers, help ...Contact the organizations to find out what ...n create a descriptive list of helpful organizations. ...ization, its phone number and address, and how ...you have finished, decide whether you think your ...on or if other services should also be offered. Add

...that helps people overcome challenges, such as a ...nded veterans. Visit or call the organization to find ...he organization as a volunteer. If possible, spend ...Then write an advertisement to convince others to ...de what services the organization offers, what jobs ...mportant. You may also want to invite a representative ...ut community needs and the value of volunteers.

...or state who have overcome challenges of various ...book of local heroes. In your scrapbook, include a ...nd. Or, choose two or three of the people and write a

...raises money for a good cause. Answer each of these

...rain?

...e money go to?

...ds raised?

...tion get people interested in participating? ...s for their participation? If so, what? ...report.

...ttable 🏃 Folks 97

Extra Practice

An **Extra Practice** activity for each lesson in the back of the Student Edition can be used to reteach the targeted skill.

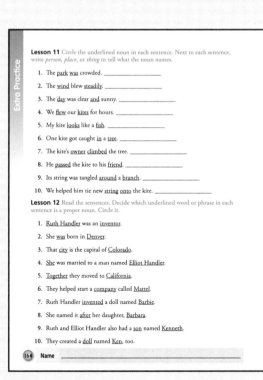

Lesson 11 Circle the underlined noun in each sentence. Next to each sentence, write *person, place,* or *thing* to tell what the noun names.

1. The <u>park</u> <u>was</u> crowded. _____
2. The <u>wind</u> blew steadily. _____
3. The <u>day</u> was clear <u>and</u> sunny. _____
4. We <u>flew</u> our <u>kites</u> for hours. _____
5. My kite <u>looks</u> like a <u>fish</u>. _____
6. One kite got caught <u>in</u> a <u>tree</u>. _____
7. The <u>kite's</u> <u>owner</u> climbed the tree. _____
8. He <u>passed</u> the kite to his <u>friend</u>. _____
9. Its string was tangled <u>around</u> a <u>branch</u>. _____
10. We helped him tie new <u>string</u> <u>onto</u> the kite. _____

Lesson 12 Read the sentences. Decide which underlined word or phrase in each sentence is a proper noun. Circle it.

1. <u>Ruth Handler</u> was an <u>inventor</u>.
2. <u>She</u> <u>was</u> born in <u>Denver</u>.
3. That <u>city</u> is the capital of <u>Colorado</u>.
4. <u>She</u> was married to a man named <u>Elliot Handler</u>.
5. <u>Together</u> they moved to <u>California</u>.
6. They helped start a <u>company</u> called <u>Mattel</u>.
7. Ruth Handler <u>invented</u> a doll named <u>Barbie</u>.
8. She named it <u>after</u> her daughter, <u>Barbara</u>.
9. Ruth and Elliot Handler also had a <u>son</u> named <u>Kenneth</u>.
10. They created a <u>doll</u> named <u>Ken</u>, too.

164 **Name** _____

Sentence Diagraming

A sentence diagram is a "picture" of a sentence's structure. Model diagrams and diagraming activities help students understand the relationships between words and phrases within sentences.

Writing Sentences and Writing a Paragraph

At the end of each unit, students use the skills they have studied to revise poorly constructed sentences, to craft those sentences into a paragraph, and to write an original paragraph. Different types of paragraphs and a variety of sentence constructions provide learners with the tools to become successful writers.

(you) | Diagram | sentences

See Handbook Section 40

Diagraming Understood *You*

Imperative sentences (commands) usually contain the understood *you* as the subject. When the subject is understood, write *(you)* in the sentence diagram, like this:

Light the candle.   (you) | Light | candle
the

Try diagraming these sentences.

1. Set the table.

2. Light the fire.

3. Slice the cake.

Diagraming Possessive Pronouns

Look at the way the possessive pronouns *my* and *their* are diagramed in these sentences.

My neighbors celebrated May Day.   neighbors | celebrated | May Day
My

We decorated their garden.   We | decorated | garden
their

Now diagram these sentences.

4. My sister made a salad.

5. Alex brought his guitar.

6. Your lasagna and my chili fed the group.

7. Our celebration pleased us.

Unforgettable Folks

Diagraming Demonstrative Pronouns

You have learned that the demonstrative pronouns *this, that, these,* and *those* take the place of nouns. Look at how the demonstrative pronouns in these sentences are diagramed.

My grandfather carved this.   grandfather | carved | this
My

That demands courage.   That | demands | courage

8. Based on these diagrams, which sentence below tells where to place a demonstrative pronoun in a sentence diagram? _____
   a. Always place it where the subject belongs.   b. Always place it where the direct object belongs.
   c. Put it wherever the noun it replaces would go.

Now diagram these sentences.

9. These need repair.

10. We ate those.

11. This works better and costs less.

Diagraming Indefinite Pronouns

Indefinite pronouns include *anybody, somebody, both,* and *no one.*

12. Where do you think an indefinite pronoun belongs in a sentence diagram? _____
   a. where the subject goes   b. where the predicate goes
   c. wherever the noun it replaces would go

Try diagraming these sentences.

13. Everyone liked your song.

14. The music bothered no one.

15. Somebody ate my sandwich and drank my juice.

Name _____

90   Unforgettable Folks

Writing Sentences

The writer of these sentences has tried to include too many ideas. Rewrite each sentence shorter, clearer sentences. Make sure each sentence you write is complete.

1. Due to the great energy they expend, otters eat tremendous amounts of food, of their day diving for shellfish such as abalone and sea urchins, which they cra a rock which they lay on their stomachs and use as an anvil.

2. Otters seem to smile as they eat the meat from the shellfish they have broken w lips away from their teeth because the broken shells often have sharp edges.

There are four kinds of sentences—a statement, a question, a command, and an excla these sentences may be simple, compound, or complex. Notice the different types of model paragraph.

question —— Have you ever wondered what life is like bottom of the ocean? Last month I had a cha find out by studying it with my own eyes. I ro
statements —— submersible to explore an oceanic trench off
complex sentence —— Coast. *Because the bottom of the trench is so sunlight reaches the creatures there.* Several fis
command —— saw glow through a process called biolumines Imagine seeing an anglerfish use its glowing
exclamation —— attract prey. *Wow, that was impressive!*

Beasts & Critters

Writing a Paragraph

The sentences you repaired on page 61 can be used to make a paragraph. Decide what order the sentences should be in. Then revise at least two of the sentences so your paragraph has a variety of sentence types. Use the model on page 61 as a reference. Write the paragraph on the lines below.

Imagine that you are an ocean diver. You have just returned from a dive during which you saw many unusual creatures. Write a paragraph about your experience. Vary the types of sentences you use, and include different types of phrases to add variety and interest to your paragraph.

Read your paragraph again. Use this checklist to evaluate your writing.

☐ Does my paragraph have a topic sentence?
☐ Have I used at least two of the four kinds of sentences?
☐ Have I included at least one compound or one complex sentence?
☐ Do my sentences have correct punctuation?
☐ Does my paragraph have a concluding sentence?

Name _____

62   Beasts & Critters

Assessment Options

Diagnostic, Formative, Summative

> *G.U.M.* includes a variety of assessments that can be used to guide teaching, provide feedback on student learning, indicate when reteaching is needed, and evaluate student achievement.

- **Diagnostic Assessment**
  Unit Assessment: When used as a pretest, the **Unit Assessment** helps you determine your students' strengths, weaknesses, knowledge, and skills.

- **Formative Assessment**
  Unit Assessment: When used as a posttest, the **Unit Assessment** provides feedback that you can use to guide further instruction.

- **Formative Assessment**
  Unit Review: This activity checks students' progress and determines when reteaching is necessary.

- **Summative Assessment**
  Unit Test: This assessment evaluates students' achievement while providing valuable practice for high-stakes tests.

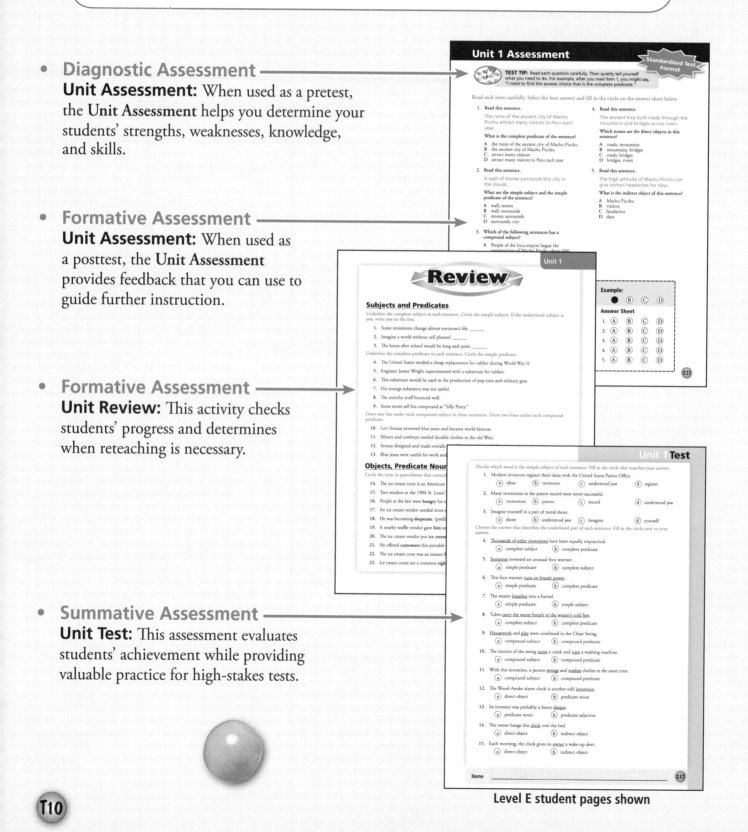

Level E student pages shown

G.U.M. offers two options for using assessment to differentiate instruction. The lessons are versatile and can be used regularly or as needed to address students' specific skill needs.

Option 1: Whole Class Instruction

Step 1	Instruction and Review	Teach all of the **lessons** in the unit and assign the **Unit Review.**
Step 2	Formative Assessment	Administer the **Unit Assessment** as a **posttest** to check students' progress. Use the results to determine which lessons require additional instruction.
Step 3	Reteach	Use the corresponding **Extra Practice** activity to reteach the targeted skill.
Step 4	Summative Assessment	Administer the **Unit Test.**

Option 2: Targeted Instruction

Step 1	Diagnostic Assessment	Administer the **Unit Assessment** as a **pretest** before teaching the unit. Use the results to determine which lessons to teach.
Step 2	Instruction and Review	Teach the appropriate **lessons** in the unit.
Step 3	Formative Assessment	Assign the **Unit Review** to check students' progress and to guide further instruction.
Step 4	Reteach	Use the **Extra Practice** activity for reteaching as necessary.
Step 5	Summative Assessment	Administer the **Unit Test.**

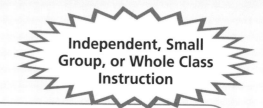

Independent, Small Group, or Whole Class Instruction

Each book contains a year's worth of study lessons. Additional options for differentiating instruction appear throughout the Teaching Notes for each lesson and are highlighted below the chart.

Three-Day Plan (2 lessons a week)		
Day 1	**Day 2**	**Day 3**
Do **Part 1** in class. Assign **Parts 2** and **3** as homework, or have students complete them cooperatively in class.	Go over **Parts 2** and **3** in class. Complete the **Speaking and Listening** activity in the teacher edition. Assign the **Extra Practice** activity, if necessary.	Do **Part 1** as a group. Have students complete **Parts 2** and **3** cooperatively. Assign the **Extra Practice** activity as homework, if necessary.

Five-Day Plan (2 lessons a week)				
Day 1	**Day 2**	**Day 3**	**Day 4**	**Day 5**
Do **Part 1** in class. Assign **Part 2** as homework, or have students complete it cooperatively in class.	Go over **Part 2** in class. Have students complete **Part 3** cooperatively.	Complete the **Speaking and Listening** activity in the teacher edition.	Do **Part 1** in class. Assign **Parts 2** and **3** as homework, or have students complete them cooperatively.	Go over **Parts 2** and **3** in class. Complete the **Speaking and Listening** activity in the teacher edition. Assign the **Extra Practice** activity, if necessary.

Scaffolding for English Language Learners
Teaching suggestions provide options to meet the needs of students with different language and cultural backgrounds.

Speaking and Listening
Specific **Speaking and Listening** activities in the teaching notes reinforce lesson concepts.

 Speaking Alert The megaphone signals specific skills that relate to both oral and written communication. When the megaphone appears, encourage students to discuss how the lesson topic will help their spoken language. Remain sensitive to dialects and regional usage.

Technology
Connections to technology offer students opportunities to apply the grammar, usage, and mechanics skills in today's high-tech world.

Note: Internet use should always be closely monitored. The listed Web sites have been carefully researched for accuracy, content, and appropriateness. However, Web sites are subject to change.

 Use *G.U.M.* with Zaner-Bloser's *Strategies for Writers,* a research-based program that explicitly teaches every step of the writing process. *Strategies for Writers* integrates the six traits of effective writing with instruction and assessment.

Levels	A	B	C	D	E	F
Sentence Structure						
subjects						
subject	•	•	•	•	•	•
simple and complete subjects		•	•	•	•	•
understood *you*				•	•	•
compound subject			•	•	•	•
predicates						
predicate	•	•	•	•	•	•
simple and complete predicates		•	•	•	•	•
compound predicate		•	•	•	•	•
predicate noun		•	•	•	•	•
predicate adjective		•	•	•	•	•
sentences						
basic (simple) sentences	•	•	•	•	•	•
statements and questions	•	•	•	•	•	•
commands and exclamations	•	•	•	•	•	•
compound sentences	•	•	•	•	•	•
complex sentences		•	•	•	•	•
word order in sentences						•
parallel structure						•
clauses and phrases						
dependent and independent clauses			•	•	•	•
adjective and adverb clauses					•	•
noun clauses						•
prepositional phrases	•	•	•	•	•	•
adjectival and adverbial prepositional phrases					•	•
infinitive phrases					•	•
participial phrases					•	•
gerund phrases					•	•
appositives						
appositives				•	•	•
restrictive vs. nonrestrictive					•	•
correcting sentences						
sentence fragments	•	•	•	•	•	•
run-on sentences	•	•	•	•	•	•
comma splice		•	•	•	•	•
making sentences say more	•	•			•	•
ramble-on sentences				•	•	•
misplaced subordinate clauses					•	•
objects						
direct object		•	•	•	•	•
indirect object			•	•	•	•
object of the preposition			•	•	•	•
object complement						•

Parts of Speech	A	B	C	D	E	F
nouns						
common nouns, proper nouns	•	•	•	•	•	•
singular and plural nouns	•	•	•	•	•	•
irregular plural nouns		•	•		•	•
possessive nouns	•	•	•	•	•	•
collective nouns					•	•
verbs						
action verbs and linking verbs	•	•	•	•	•	•
present tense	•	•	•	•	•	•
regular past tense verbs	•	•	•	•	•	•
irregular past tense verbs	•	•	•	•	•	•
future tense			•	•	•	•
present perfect tense			•	•	•	•
past perfect tense				•	•	•
future perfect tense					•	•
progressive forms (present, past, future)				•	•	•
main verbs and helping (auxiliary) verbs		•	•	•	•	•
transitive and intransitive verbs					•	•
active and passive voice				•	•	•
pronouns						
personal pronouns	•	•	•	•	•	•
compound personal pronouns				•	•	•
demonstrative pronouns	•			•	•	•
interrogative pronouns		•		•	•	•
subject pronouns and object pronouns	•	•	•	•	•	•
possessive pronouns	•	•	•	•	•	•
indefinite pronouns				•	•	•
pronouns and antecedents			•	•	•	•
relative pronouns					•	•
adjectives						
adjectives	•	•	•	•	•	•
demonstrative adjectives		•	•	•	•	•
proper adjectives			•	•	•	•
comparative adjectives and superlative adjectives	•	•	•	•	•	•
absolute adjectives					•	•
adverbs						
adverbs		•	•	•	•	•
comparative adverbs			•	•	•	•
superlative adverbs			•	•	•	•
conjunctions						
coordinating conjunctions	•	•	•	•	•	•
subordinating conjunctions			•	•	•	•
correlative conjunctions					•	•
prepositions		•	•	•	•	•
interjections				•	•	•
Usage						
homophones						
your and *you're*	•	•	•	•	•	•
their, they're, there	•	•	•	•	•	•

Levels	A	B	C	D	E	F
Usage (continued)						
its and *it's*	•	•	•	•	•	•
whose and *who's*		•		•	•	•
to, two, too		•		•	•	•
than and *then*					•	•
comparatives						
good and *bad* (*better/worse, best/worst*)	•		•		•	•
less and *least*					•	•
-er, -est	•	•	•	•	•	•
more and *most*		•	•	•	•	•
irregular verbs						
bring, sing, and *ring*	•					
come and *go*	•					
eat and *sleep; give* and *take*	•					
forms of *be*	•	•	•	•	•	•
know and *grow*			•			
run, fly, and *swim*				•		
throw and *catch*		•				
irregular verbs (general)					•	•
problem words						
very and *real*	•		•			
good and *well*		•		•		
who and *whom*				•	•	•
doesn't and *don't*		•		•	•	
learn and *teach*			•			
set and *sit*			•		•	•
like, you know, go, and *all*			•	•	•	•
who, which, and *that*			•	•	•	•
leave, let, rise, and *raise*				•	•	•
lie and *lay*					•	•
less and *fewer; over* and *more than*						•
articles						
a and *an*	•	•	•	•	•	•
the		•	•	•	•	•
Grammar						
pronouns						
subject and object pronouns	•	•	•	•	•	•
pronouns in pairs	•	•	•	•	•	•
avoiding extra pronouns	•					
I and *me*	•	•	•		•	•
pronoun antecedents			•	•	•	•
verbs						
subject-verb agreement (forms of *be*)	•	•	•	•	•	•
subject-verb agreement (regular verbs)	•	•	•	•	•	•
subject-verb agreement (special cases)					•	•
choosing verb tense	•	•	•	•	•	•
using helping (auxiliary) verbs	•	•	•	•	•	•
agreement with compound subjects				•	•	•

Scope and Sequence (continued) Levels	A	B	C	D	E	F
Grammar (continued)						
negatives						
avoiding double negatives	•	•	•		•	•
modifiers						
dangling and misplaced modifiers					•	•
Mechanics						
punctuation						
end marks (question mark, period, exclamation point)	•	•	•	•	•	•
titles						
books	•	•	•	•	•	•
movies, songs, stories, poems, CDs, DVDs		•	•	•	•	•
newspapers and magazines					•	•
capitalization						
names	•	•	•	•	•	•
places	•	•	•	•	•	•
titles of respect	•	•	•	•	•	•
sentences	•	•	•	•	•	•
titles of works		•	•	•	•	•
proper adjectives			•	•	•	•
proper nouns	•	•	•	•	•	•
abbreviations of proper nouns	•	•	•	•	•	•
direct quotes	•	•	•	•	•	•
month, day			•	•	•	•
abbreviations						
titles of respect, initials	•	•	•	•	•	•
streets, cities, states, countries	•	•	•	•	•	•
month, day					•	•
kinds of business			•		•	•
acronyms						•
commas						
in a series	•	•	•	•	•	•
after introductory words and nouns of direct address	•	•	•	•	•	•
in compound sentences	•	•	•	•	•	•
in direct quotations	•	•	•	•	•	•
in greetings and closings (letters and e-mails)			•	•	•	•
to separate adjectives of the same class					•	•
after introductory adverb clauses					•	•
semicolons						
in compound sentences			•	•	•	•
colons						
to separate independent clauses				•	•	•
before lists				•	•	•
in dialogue					•	•
after an introductory phrase					•	•
in business letters				•	•	•
in expressions of time					•	•
in a bibliography entry					•	•
quotations						
direct	•	•	•	•	•	•
indirect	•	•	•	•	•	•

Levels	A	B	C	D	E	F
Mechanics (continued)						
apostrophes						
in possessive nouns	•	•	•	•	•	•
in contractions	•	•	•	•	•	•
hyphens and dashes						
to separate syllables in a word break					•	•
to link some compound words					•	•
to link word pairs or groups of words that precede nouns					•	•
to link the parts of some numbers					•	•
parentheses						
letters and e-mails						•
friendly			•	•	•	•
business					•	•
e-mails			•	•	•	•
Writing Paragraphs						
varying sentence length and type					•	•
writing a topic sentence					•	•
writing supporting details					•	•
writing a concluding sentence					•	•
using time-order words					•	•
using correct verb tense					•	•
writing to support an idea					•	•
writing a description					•	•
writing an informative paragraph					•	•
writing a comparison					•	•
writing a persuasive paragraph					•	•
writing a personal narrative					•	•
writing a friendly letter						•
Research						
Internet searches	•	•	•	•	•	•
library research	•	•	•	•	•	•
bibliography entries					•	•
Diagraming Sentences						
subjects and verbs					•	•
adjectives, articles, and adverbs					•	•
direct objects					•	•
predicate nouns and predicate adjectives					•	•
compound subjects and predicates					•	•
compound sentences					•	•
prepositions and prepositional phrases					•	•
indirect objects					•	•
sentences beginning with *there*					•	•
adjective clauses					•	•
adverb clauses					•	•
inverted sentences						•
complex sentences						•
participial phrases						•
infinitive phrases						•
gerund phrases						•
appositives						•

Looking Back

Unit 1 Sentence Structure

Pretest Option

You may use the **Unit Assessment** as a pretest. See pages T10 and T11.

Building Sentence Awareness

Write these groups of words on the board and ask a volunteer to read them aloud:

The invention of the printing press.
The printing press was invented in 1440.

Ask students to identify the group of words that does not tell a complete thought. (first group) Then have students add words to create a sequence of words that makes sense. (Example: The invention of the printing press changed the world.) Explain to students that in Unit 1 they will learn about the different parts that make up a sentence. They will also learn how to combine different parts of a sentence to create sentences that give clear information. Point out that knowing what a sentence is and how to construct sentences will help students become better readers and writers.

Introducing "Looking Back"

Innovations That Changed History

Explain that Unit 1 gives information about some important inventions in history. Invite students to name inventions they think were especially important. List their ideas in a word web with the word INVENTIONS in the center. Encourage students to tell why each invention is important and to speculate about how that invention was created.

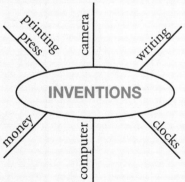

Lesson 1 (student pages 9–10)
Complete Subjects and Complete Predicates

Objectives

- To learn that every sentence has a subject and a predicate
- To learn what words make up the complete subject and what words make up the complete predicate
- To identify the complete subject and the complete predicate in sentences
- To complete sentences by adding a subject or a predicate
- To write original sentences using literature as a model for long or short subjects and predicates

Options for Organizing and Differentiating Instruction

See pages T11 and T12.

Scaffolding for English Language Learners

Invite students to share what they know about how crops are grown. Introduce the words *agriculture, production,* and *irrigation,* using sketches or photographs to clarify meanings.

Read the sentences in **Part 1** aloud and invite volunteers to paraphrase the information. Then reread each sentence, one at a time, and ask students to identify the complete subject and complete predicate in each by asking Whom or what is this sentence about? to identify the subject and What happened? or What did the subject do? to identify the predicate.

Read the phrases in **Part 2** aloud, and ask volunteers to suggest a subject or predicate that could complete each phrase. (Example: item 20: Prehistoric people hunted bison and mammoth.) Pair students with English-proficient partners to complete the activity.

For **Part 3,** read the two examples from literature aloud and model writing very short and very long sentences. Have students compose their sentences orally before writing them.

Speaking and Listening

Invite volunteers to read aloud the sentences they wrote in Part 3. Have listeners identify the complete subject and complete predicate in each. Then write two students' sentences on the board, one long and one short. Invite students to suggest shorter versions of the long sentence and longer versions of the short sentence. Listeners should verify that each suggested sentence is complete.

Reinforcement and Reteaching

Review **Read and Discover** and the rule statement, refer students to the **G.U.M. Handbook,** or use the **Extra Practice** activity on page 251.

Simple Subjects and Simple Predicates

Objectives

- To learn that the simple subject is the most important word or words in the complete subject and that *you,* the understood subject in imperative sentences, is not named
- To learn that the simple predicate is the verb that tells what the subject did, or links the subject to information about it
- To identify simple subjects, the understood subject *you,* and simple predicates in sentences and to write them in original sentences
- To solve rebus puzzles to identify simple subjects

Options for Organizing and Differentiating Instruction

See pages T11 and T12.

Scaffolding for English Language Learners

Read **Part 1** aloud. Clarify the word *symbol* by drawing a symbol on the board. Discuss why symbols were difficult to use as the foundation of a writing system. Make sure students understand the difference between a written language based on symbols and one based on sounds.

Reread Part 1. Have students identify the complete subject and predicate in each sentence and then find the simple subject and predicate. Read the sentences that contain understood *you* (2, 10, 12) aloud with the *you* in place to help students recognize them as commands. Point out that sometimes a simple predicate contains a helping verb, such as *could,* and a main verb. Ask students which sentences have both a helping verb and a main verb. (8, 11, and 16) Then have students circle the helping verb and underline the main verb.

For **Part 2,** have each student say sentences orally before writing them with the help of an English-proficient partner.

Have students complete **Part 3** with a partner. They should begin by saying aloud the English word for each symbol and then blending the sounds to form words that fit the sentences.

Speaking and Listening

Write ten action verbs, five nouns, and five instances of the word you on separate index cards. Place the verb cards and the subject/*you* cards facedown in separate piles. Have students draw a card from each pile and construct a sentence. When a *you* card is picked, ask students to compose a sentence with the understood *you.*

Reinforcement and Reteaching

Review **Read and Discover** and the rule statement, refer students to the **G.U.M. Handbook,** or use the **Extra Practice** activity on page 251.

Compound Subjects and Compound Predicates

Objectives

- To learn that a compound subject is two or more subjects joined by a conjunction and that a compound predicate is two or more verbs joined by a conjunction
- To identify the simple subjects in each compound subject and the simple predicates in each compound predicate in sentences
- To combine phrases to form sentences with compound subjects or predicates
- To understand that in a sentence containing both a compound subject and a compound predicate, both parts of the subject must perform both actions in the predicate

Options for Organizing and Differentiating Instruction

See pages T11 and T12.

Scaffolding for English Language Learners

Discuss the ways we measure time, including clocks, calendars, and the sun's position in the sky.

Read aloud **Part 1** as students listen. Clarify the words *cycles, celestial, astronomers, inaccuracies,* and *physicists.* Then help students identify the compound subject or predicate in each sentence. Explain that the conjunctions *and* and *or* are signals to the presence of a compound subject or compound predicate. Have students confirm their responses by restating each sentence as two simple sentences. (Example: item 1: The concept of time fascinates humans. The concept of time perplexes humans.)

For **Part 2,** help students identify which part of each pair of sentences is the same, the subject or the predicate, before determining how to rewrite each pair as a single sentence.

Rewrite the sentences in **Part 3** on the board, breaking each down into simple sentences to help students figure out which one is incorrectly written. (Example: The sun lights up the day./The moon lights up the day./The sun shines at night./The moon shines at night.)

Speaking and Listening

List words such as these on the board: NOUNS— astronomers, cycles, calendar, festival, stars, clock. VERBS—measure, invent, rise, set, carve, move, occur. Encourage students to use these and other words in oral sentences that contain compound subjects or compound predicates.

Reinforcement and Reteaching

Review **Read and Discover** and the rule statement, refer students to the **G.U.M. Handbook,** or use the **Extra Practice** activity on page 252.

Objectives

- To learn that a direct object is a noun or pronoun that receives the action of a verb and that in a compound direct object more than one word receives the action of the verb
- To identify the direct object or compound direct object in sentences and to complete sentences using direct objects
- To learn that a transitive verb requires a direct object, while an action verb without a direct object is intransitive
- To identify transitive and intransitive verbs in sentences

Options for Organizing and Differentiating Instruction

See pages T11 and T12.

Scaffolding for English Language Learners

Brainstorm the names of various metals with students. Then help students list them on the board from softest to hardest. (Example: gold, copper, bronze, steel) Ask students how the invention of harder, stronger metals might have helped people long ago. Explain that Lesson 4 is about the invention of bronze.

Read **Part 1** aloud and call on volunteers to summarize the information. Point out the compound words *craftspeople, metalworkers,* and *widespread* and help students understand the meanings. Then help students find the direct object in each sentence by saying the sentence and repeating the verb followed by *whom?* or *what?*

Read aloud each incomplete sentence in **Part 2** and help students decide which word fits the blank. Sketch a simple picture of the Trojan horse on the board to help students understand the trick the Greeks played on the Trojans.

Read aloud the explanation of transitive and intransitive verbs in **Part 3**. Have students circle the action verb in each sentence and determine which verbs have a direct object by saying the verb followed by *what?* (Example: Work what?) Those questions that cannot be answered with a noun indicate intransitive verbs.

Speaking and Listening

Write this sentence frame on the board: We made _____. Call on volunteers to complete the sentence by using a variety of direct objects. Then call on volunteers to suggest other action verbs and follow a similar procedure with a different sentence.

Reinforcement and Reteaching

Review **Read and Discover** and the rule statement, refer students to the **G.U.M. Handbook,** or use the **Extra Practice** activity on page 252.

Objectives

- To learn that an indirect object is a thing or person to whom something is given, told, or taught and that it comes before a direct object
- To identify indirect objects in sentences
- To rewrite sentences, changing prepositional phrases into indirect objects
- To complete sentences using indirect objects and to use number clues to solve a puzzle

Options for Organizing and Differentiating Instruction

See pages T11 and T12.

Scaffolding for English Language Learners

Invite students to describe trades they have made with friends. Explain that before the invention of money, people traded for the things they needed, including food and clothing. Inform students that this lesson tells about this system.

Read the sentences in **Part 1** aloud. Ask students why the trade system might have caused problems for people. (It was complicated; it was hard to agree on the value of different things.) Have volunteers reread each sentence, one at a time. Call on other volunteers to identify the verb and the direct object and then to identify the indirect object. Help students test whether a word is the indirect object by moving it after the direct object and putting the word *to* in front of it. (Example: item 1: In ancient times, farmers traded their crops *to others...*)

Have students complete **Part 2** in pairs. Model how to respond correctly by using item 17 as an example.

Students can complete **Part 3** with their partners. Provide help as necessary with unfamiliar vocabulary.

Speaking and Listening

Write this sentence frame on the board:
_____ gave _____ (a/an/some/the) _____.
Have students create oral sentences about trading by filling in the blanks. (Example: The farmer gave the baker some tomatoes.) Have volunteers identify the indirect object in each sentence.

Reinforcement and Reteaching

Review **Read and Discover** and the rule statement, refer students to the **G.U.M. Handbook,** or use the **Extra Practice** activity on page 253.

Objectives

- To discover that predicate nouns follow linking verbs and tell more about who or what the subject is, and that predicate adjectives follow linking verbs and describe the subject
- To identify linking verbs, predicate nouns, and predicate adjectives in sentences
- To add predicate nouns or predicate adjectives to complete sentences
- To identify predicate nouns that are misspelled and unscramble them

Options for Organizing and Differentiating Instruction

See pages T11 and T12.

Scaffolding for English Language Learners

Write the word type on the board and ask students to give two meanings for this word. ("kind"; "letter stamps") Point out that the letters in books are printed type.

Have students read **Part 1** silently. Remind them that a noun names a person, place, thing, or idea, while an adjective describes someone or something. Reread each sentence aloud, one at a time, and ask students whether each boldfaced word *names* or *describes*. Tell students that the naming words are predicate nouns and the describing words are predicate adjectives. Also explain that a linking verb does not show action; the linking verbs *become, is, are, was,* and *were* help give more information about the subject. Then have students draw a box around the linking verb in each sentence.

For **Part 2**, have students describe a book the class has read before they write their responses.

Students can work with partners to unscramble the predicate noun in each sentence in **Part 3**. Model the process using item 30 as an example.

Speaking and Listening

List these linking verbs on the board: is, are, was, were, feel, become, seem. Then display a picture, poster, or painting that shows people in a scene. Encourage students to compose oral sentences about the scene using a linking verb and a predicate noun or a predicate adjective. (Examples: The man is a musician. He seems happy.)

Reinforcement and Reteaching

Review **Read and Discover** and the rule statement, refer students to the **G.U.M. Handbook**, or use the **Extra Practice** activity on page 253.

Objectives

- To learn that a prepositional phrase can tell *how, what kind, when, how much,* or *where*
- To identify prepositions, prepositional phrases, and objects of prepositions in sentences
- To add prepositional phrases to make sentences give more information
- To solve a maze puzzle using prepositional phrases as clues

Options for Organizing and Differentiating Instruction

See pages T11 and T12.

Scaffolding for English Language Learners

Draw on the board a simple sketch of a three-masted ship with triangular sails. (You may wish to use the picture on page 21 as a model.) Introduce these words as you point to different parts of the ship: **rudder, mast, triangular sail, compass**.

Read the sentences in **Part 1** aloud. Clarify the meaning of *uncharted* (unmapped). Explain that the Iroquois League was an association of Native American groups who voted for leaders and solved problems by working together. Then reread each sentence and call on volunteers to identify the prepositional phrase, the preposition that begins the phrase, and the object of the preposition.

Read the sentences in **Part 2** aloud. Point out that there is more than one way to rewrite each item. Suggest that students work in pairs to select a prepositional phrase for each sentence and then write their responses.

Have the same pairs complete the maze activity in **Part 3**.

Speaking and Listening

Write these prepositional phrases on the board.

through the waves
in the wind
to the shore
after the voyage

Ask students to incorporate these phrases in oral sentences about sailing ships. (Example: The schooner sailed gracefully through the waves.)

Reinforcement and Reteaching

Review **Read and Discover** and the rule statement, refer students to the **G.U.M. Handbook**, or use the **Extra Practice** activity on page 254.

Objectives

- To discover that an adjectival prepositional phrase tells more about a noun or a pronoun and comes after the noun or pronoun it modifies
- To identify adjectival prepositional phrases in sentences
- To complete sentences using adjectival prepositional phrases
- To identify the adjectival prepositional phrases in an excerpt of literature

Options for Organizing and Differentiating Instruction

See pages T11 and T12.

Scaffolding for English Language Learners

Invite students to discuss what they know about photography and cameras. Ask them when and where photographs are often taken.

Read the sentences in **Part 1** aloud. Clarify the meanings of *miniature, chemical processes,* and *preserved.* Reread each sentence and ask a volunteer to identify the adjectival prepositional phrase or phrases. Call on others to name the preposition that begins the phrase as well as the noun it tells about.

For **Part 2,** read aloud the sentences and clarify the meanings of *telephoto lens* and *digital files.* Suggest that students match each prepositional phrase with an incomplete sentence and then read it for sense.

Read aloud the excerpt in **Part 3.** Clarify unfamiliar vocabulary and terms. Students should work with an English-proficient partner to list the eleven adjectival prepositional phrases.

Speaking and Listening

Write these adjectival prepositional phrases on the board.

> of the classroom
> for my camera
> from my window
> near our house

Have students use these phrases to create oral sentences that tell about photographs they or their families have taken. (Example: I took a great picture of a bird at the park near our house.)

Reinforcement and Reteaching

Review **Read and Discover** and the rule statement, refer students to the **G.U.M. Handbook,** or use the **Extra Practice** activity on page 254.

Objectives

- To discover that an adverbial prepositional phrase tells more about a verb, an adverb, or an adjective
- To learn that adverbial prepositional phrases usually tell *when, where, how,* or *how long*
- To identify adverbial prepositional phrases in sentences
- To revise sentences by adding adverbial prepositional phrases
- To identify adverbial prepositional phrases in two stanzas of poetry

Options for Organizing and Differentiating Instruction

See pages T11 and T12.

Scaffolding for English Language Learners

Discuss with students how they use computers at home or at school. Tell them that fifty years ago, computers were big, complicated machines that were almost the size of rooms.

Read aloud the sentences in **Part 1.** Clarify unfamiliar terms such as *rear admiral, computer compiler,* and *national security.* Call on volunteers to reread each sentence and identify the adverbial prepositional phrase. Students can verify their responses by asking the questions *when, where, how,* or *how long.* (Example: item 1: in 1952 answers the question When?) Note that in item 12 the phrase *because of* is the preposition.

For **Part 2,** have students work with partners to create an adverbial prepositional phrase to add to each sentence. Remind them to be sure that the completed sentence answers the question in parentheses.

Read aloud the two stanzas in **Part 3.** Then have students work with an English-proficient partner to find five adverbial prepositional phrases. Be sure that students do not include the infinitives *to praise* and *to love.* Point out that the phrases *of Dove* (line 2) and *by a mossy stone* (line 5) are adjectival prepositional phrases modifying the nouns *springs* and *violet,* respectively.

Speaking and Listening

Have students work in small groups to create sentences that tell about how they like to use the computer. Ask them to include adverbial prepositional phrases in their sentences. Have groups share their sentences with the class. (Example: We wrote this story on the computer. We created this picture with the graphics program.)

Reinforcement and Reteaching

Review **Read and Discover** and the rule statement, refer students to the **G.U.M. Handbook,** or use the **Extra Practice** activity on page 255.

Objectives

- To discover that an appositive is a phrase that identifies or means the same thing as a noun
- To learn that an appositive follows the noun it identifies and is usually set off by commas
- To identify appositives in sentences and to rewrite sentences using appositives
- To learn that appositives that are needed to explain who or what a noun is should not be set off by commas

Options for Organizing and Differentiating Instruction

See pages T11 and T12.

Scaffolding for English Language Learners

Ask students to name some things that are made in factories. Then explain the term *Industrial Revolution*. Discuss with students how the Industrial Revolution changed the lives of people who made goods, and of people who used them.

Read the sentences in **Part 1** aloud and invite students to summarize the information. Have a volunteer reread the first sentence, identify the appositive, and tell which noun it identifies. (a vast change in working methods; Industrial Revolution) Follow a similar procedure for the remaining items. Have students note that each appositive gives additional information about the noun it refers to.

Have volunteers read the sentence pairs in **Part 2** aloud, and ask other volunteers to tell which words in the underlined sentence give more information that could be added to the other sentence. Have students say the revised sentence aloud with the appositive in place before writing it.

Read aloud the explanation at the beginning of **Part 3** and help students see that the underlined phrase is necessary in the second sentence but not in the first. Have them determine whether item 21 or 22 should have commas around the appositive, and explain why.

Speaking and Listening

Invite each student to briefly describe a friend or a favorite relative for the class, using appositives. (Example: My uncle Rick, *my mother's brother,* wrote me a letter.)

Reinforcement and Reteaching

Review **Read and Discover** and the rule statement, refer students to the **G.U.M. Handbook,** or use the **Extra Practice** activity on page 255.

Objectives

- To learn that a sentence diagram is a picture of a sentence that shows how the parts of a sentence fit together
- To place subjects, predicates, adjectives, articles, and direct objects in a sentence diagram

Diagraming Subjects and Verbs

Have students read the information in the box at the top of page 29. Then draw their attention to the first sentence, *Gold melts.* Have them use the diagram of this sentence to answer questions 1–3. Before students diagram sentences 4–6, help them identify the simple subject and the simple predicate (verb) in each sentence.

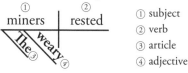

① subject
② verb

Diagraming Adjectives and Articles

Ask students to read about where articles and adjectives belong in a sentence diagram. Then have them explain why the words *the* and *weary* are placed under the word *miners* in the example. (because *the* and *weary* both modify *miners*) Have students work independently to complete the sentence diagrams.

miners | rested

① subject
② verb
③ article
④ adjective

Diagraming Direct Objects

Invite students to read this section and to answer the question. If necessary, point out that the line that separates the direct object from the verb does not cross the horizontal line. Student pairs can diagram the remaining sentences. Remind them to look back at earlier sections, if necessary, to recall where adjectives, articles, subjects, and predicates belong in the diagram. Suggest that students use a ruler to draw the diagrams for the sentences at the bottom of page 30.

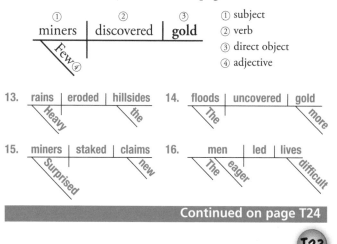

① subject
② verb
③ direct object
④ adjective

13. rains | eroded | hillsides

14. floods | uncovered | gold

15. miners | staked | claims

16. men | led | lives

Continued on page T24

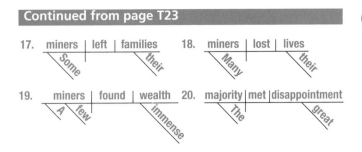

17. Some miners left their families
18. Many miners lost their lives
19. A few miners found immense wealth
20. The majority met great disappointment

Writing Sentences (student page 31)

Explain to students that on this page they will practice rewriting sentences that are poorly written. Ask students to read the directions at the top of the page and then work in pairs to identify the problem in each of the five sentences. Point out that there is more than one way to revise each sentence.

After students have rewritten the sentences, call on several volunteers to read aloud the new sentences. Encourage students to compare and comment on the different solutions.

Direct them to read the description of a paragraph at the bottom of the page. Point out that the kind of paragraph described here is a paragraph of information; paragraphs that appear in narratives (stories) do not always need to follow the format described here. Call on volunteers to identify the topic sentence, the supporting sentences, and the concluding sentence in the model paragraph.

Writing a Paragraph (student page 32)

Work with students to define what a paragraph is. Then work with students to reorder the sentences they wrote on page 31 so that they form a paragraph with these same elements. Students may want to make additional revisions to the topic sentence so that it tells what the whole paragraph is about. After students have written their paragraphs, encourage them to share the finished products.

Students can work independently to write their original paragraphs. Remind them to use the checklist at the bottom of page 32 to evaluate their paragraphs.

Proofreading (student pages 33–34)

Scaffolding for English Language Learners

Have students work with a partner who is fluent in English for the proofreading activities.

Proofreading Practice

Ask students to identify the topic of the report on page 33. (obtaining a patent) Explain to students that the report contains several errors and that as they read, they should look for these.

Review the **Proofreading Marks** chart and the examples. Remind students that these marks are used by professional writers to correct their work before publication. Read the first sentence aloud. Discuss the error (*finishing* is spelled incorrectly), how it should be marked, and how that word should be spelled. Ask students (in pairs or independently) to mark how the errors should be corrected with proofreading marks. You may wish to have students correct the spelling errors.

After students have completed the activity, ask volunteers to read each sentence aloud and to identify any errors. Ask students to mark overlooked errors in another color. **Note:** Some errors can be corrected in more than one way.

Proofreading Checklist

Ask students to select a recent piece of their own writing and to write the title of that piece at the top of the chart. Have them put a check mark next to each item in the checklist after they have checked it in their work. Students might first work independently and then trade papers with a partner to double-check each other's work. You might model, or ask a student to model, using the **G.U.M. Handbook** (beginning on student page 303) to clarify a concept or rule.

Also Remember...

Remind students that capitalization and punctuation are important for clear writing. If necessary, help students use the **G.U.M. Handbook** to clarify when commas should be used and to review the use of capital letters.

Your Own List

Suggest that students look at the errors they did not find in the proofreading activity and add them to the checklist. Ask students to think about other kinds of errors they sometimes make and to add these to the checklist.

Ask students to place this page in their writing portfolios. These pages may be used to assess students' progress over the course of the year.

Assessment Options

See page T11 for ways to use *G.U.M.* assessments to differentiate instruction.

Unit Review

The **Unit Review** (pp. 35–36) allows you to check students' progress and determine when reteaching is necessary. The review pages may be completed in class or as homework. If a student responds incorrectly to two or more items involving the same skill, you may want to work directly with the student to review the relevant lesson. The lesson number to which each review item relates appears in parentheses on the review pages in the Teacher Edition.

Assign the **Extra Practice** activities (pp. 251–255) to reteach targeted skills in a more focused way.

Unit Assessment

The **Unit Assessment** (pp. 221–224) is intended to (1) familiarize students with standardized testing procedures, (2) check students' ability to apply key unit concepts in a different format, and (3) serve as an indicator of student progress.

- When used as a **pretest,** the Unit Assessment helps you determine, prior to instruction, your students' strengths, weaknesses, knowledge, and skills.
- When used as a **posttest,** the Unit Assessment provides feedback that you can use to guide further instruction.

Follow this procedure for administering the Unit Assessment.

1. Read aloud the Test Tip and the test instructions. (**Note:** For additional scaffolding, you may wish to read the test questions and answer choices aloud.)
2. Tell students that they will have 20 minutes to read and answer the questions independently.
3. When time is up, collect and correct the tests. Use the results to measure student progress and guide reteaching.

Assign the **Extra Practice** activities (pp. 251–255) to reteach targeted skills in a more focused way.

Note: The **Unit Review** may be reused after reteaching to check students' understanding of the lesson concepts.

Unit Test

The **Unit Test** (pp. 287–288) helps you judge students' achievement while providing them with valuable practice for high-stakes tests. When you are ready to administer the test, ask students to carefully tear it out of their books. (**Note:** If the test has already been removed, distribute it to students.) Read aloud the directions for each section and make sure students understand how to answer the questions. Ask students to work independently to complete the test.

Students who miss two questions focusing on the same grammar element may need additional help understanding the concept. Reteach the concept, following this procedure:

1. Review **Read and Discover**.
2. Review the rule statement for the concept.
3. Guide students through items a second time. Ask the students to explain why each correct answer belongs in each sentence.
4. Refer students to the **G.U.M. Handbook** for further reinforcement.

Community Connection (student pages 37–38)

These two pages provide interesting activities that reinforce the skills and concepts students learned in Lessons 1 to 10. These activities provide opportunities for students to share what they have learned with their families and to make connections between the content of the lessons and their own communities. You might utilize the **Community Connection** pages in one of the following ways:

- Ask students to take the pages home, select one activity to do, and then share the results of that activity with the class.
- Have pairs of students select one activity to complete together.
- Preview the activities as a class, and then assign the activities to small groups of students to complete cooperatively. Set aside a time for groups to share the results.

When you are ready to have students select activities, direct them to pages 37–38. Explain that the activities on page 37 will give them an opportunity to learn about inventions and inventors on their own by exploring their own community and other communities. Point out that page 38 includes a planning guide that will help them learn more about the process of obtaining a patent. Then ask students to carefully tear the pages out of the book, and explain how you wish students to use them.

Beasts & Critters

Unit 2 Sentence Structure

Pretest Option

You may use the **Unit Assessment** as a pretest. See pages T10 and T11.

Building Sentence Awareness

Write these words in a single line on the board: are creatures water many most in live breathe under unusual sea the. Ask students if the words make sense as a complete thought. (no) Then invite students to choose and arrange some of these words to form sentences. (Examples: Many unusual creatures live in the sea; Many sea creatures are unusual; Most sea creatures breathe under water.)

Point out that word choice and word order are important in forming sentences. Tell students that in Unit 2 they will learn more about sentences: different kinds of sentences; the words and phrases that make up sentences; and how to write clear, descriptive sentences that are free of the errors writers often make.

Introducing "Beasts and Critters"

Sea Creatures

Ask students to describe sea creatures they know or want to know more about. Record their responses in a chart with the words Sea Creatures at the top and the words Mammals and Fish in separate columns beneath. Explain that Unit 2 describes some of the most unusual, dangerous, and fascinating creatures found in the world's oceans.

Sea Creatures	
Mammals	Fish

Objectives

- To learn that every sentence begins with a capital letter and ends with an end mark
- To learn that a declarative sentence makes a statement and ends with a period, an interrogative sentence asks a question and ends with a question mark, an imperative sentence gives a command and ends with an exclamation point or a period, and an exclamatory sentence shows excitement and ends with an exclamation point
- To identify kinds of sentences and to add end marks
- To rewrite each kind of sentence as another kind of sentence
- To recognize the four kinds of sentences in literature and to evaluate their effect in writing

Options for Organizing and Differentiating Instruction

See pages T11 and T12.

Scaffolding for English Language Learners

Elicit descriptions of whales and sharks. Tell students that this lesson is about a huge sea creature called a whale shark, which is a fish (picture on page 39), not a mammal.

Read the sentences in **Part 1** aloud. Call on volunteers to describe the whale shark's appearance and eating habits. Then have students work in pairs to identify each kind of sentence. Remind them that commands contain the understood *you* and therefore often begin with a verb. Help students see that items 1, 7, 9, and 15 are commands by identifying the verb that begins each sentence.

Read aloud each item in **Part 2** with vocal expression that helps show what kind of sentence it is. Have students work in pairs to rewrite each sentence as the type indicated. Then call on volunteers to read aloud each sentence with the inflection indicated by the end punctuation—once as it is originally stated and then as they have rewritten it.

Read aloud the passage for **Part 3**. Clarify unfamiliar terms and vocabulary. Students can work with a partner to identify each kind of sentence in the passage and then write three sentences.

Speaking and Listening

Have students imagine that they have just spotted a whale shark while swimming in the ocean. Invite students to say aloud some sentences that show surprise, ask questions, give commands, and make statements. (Examples: What was that? Get out of its way! It's harmless. What a huge head!) Listeners should identify each kind of sentence and tell what punctuation mark belongs at the end.

Reinforcement and Reteaching

Review **Read and Discover** and the rule statement, refer students to the **G.U.M. Handbook**, or use the **Extra Practice** activity on page 256.

Simple Sentences and Compound Sentences

Objectives

- To learn that a simple sentence (or independent clause) is made up of a subject and a predicate and expresses one thought and that a compound sentence is made up of two closely related independent clauses joined by a comma and a coordinating conjunction or by a semicolon
- To identify simple and compound sentences and the conjunction or semicolon that joins compound sentences
- To rewrite two simple sentences as a compound sentence
- To solve a crossword puzzle and to use two of the words in an original compound sentence

Options for Organizing and Differentiating Instruction

See pages T11 and T12.

Scaffolding for English Language Learners

Write the word sea horse on the board. Based on its name, invite students to speculate about what a sea horse looks like. (See picture on page 41.)

Read aloud **Part 1**. If necessary, clarify the words *armor, predators,* and *pouch.* Call on volunteers to tell whether each sentence is simple or compound. To reinforce understanding, have students reread the compound sentences as two simple sentences. Point out that the word *but* signals a contrast—it links two things or ideas that are different from each other.

Read aloud the sentences in **Part 2** and have students discuss whether to use *and, but,* or a semicolon to join each pair. (Use *but* in 16, 18, and 20; use a semicolon or a comma and *and* in 17; use a semicolon in 19.) Explain that a semicolon can be used when two clauses are closely related. (Male sea horses bear young; so do male sea dragons.)

Students can complete **Part 3** in pairs. Model using two words from the puzzle in an original compound sentence. (Example: *Predators* hide in the *sea grass,* and they look for prey.)

Speaking and Listening

Call on a volunteer to say aloud two simple sentences about the ocean. Call on a second volunteer to restate the sentences as a compound sentence. (Example: The ocean is beautiful. It can be dangerous becomes The ocean is beautiful, but it can be dangerous.)

Reinforcement and Reteaching

Review **Read and Discover** and the rule statement, refer students to the **G.U.M. Handbook**, or use the **Extra Practice** activity on page 256.

Dependent Clauses and Independent Clauses

Objectives

- To learn that a dependent clause is a group of words with a subject and a predicate that does not make sense by itself, and that a dependent clause needs to be joined with an independent clause in order to tell a complete thought
- To understand that a dependent clause often begins with a subordinating conjunction such as *although, because, if, as,* or *when*
- To identify dependent clauses, independent clauses, and subordinating conjunctions in sentences
- To match dependent and independent clauses and to work cooperatively to write humorous complex sentences

Options for Organizing and Differentiating Instruction

See pages T11 and T12.

Scaffolding for English Language Learners

Display the picture of the sea otter on page 43, and ask if any students have seen this playful creature. Discuss its food (clams, sea urchins) and its home (kelp beds near shore).

Have students read **Part 1** silently. If necessary, clarify the words *insulating* and *blubber* and the phrase *put an end to the slaughter* (stopped the killing). Then reread each sentence aloud, one at a time. First have students identify the dependent clause. To help them test their answers, have them read the dependent clause by itself and confirm that it does not make sense.

Read aloud each dependent clause in **Part 2** one at a time and help students determine which independent clause matches it. Then read the entire complex sentence aloud, emphasizing the pause where the comma belongs, before having students write the sentence.

For **Part 3**, generate several dependent clauses as a group before having students complete the activity.

Speaking and Listening

Write these dependent clauses on the board: because it rained, although I was tired, when I got home, as I was sleeping. Call on several volunteers to join the phrases with independent clauses to form sentences that tell a complete thought. (Example: Because it rained, the game was canceled.)

Reinforcement and Reteaching

Review **Read and Discover** and the rule statement, refer students to the **G.U.M. Handbook**, or use the **Extra Practice** activity on page 257.

Objectives

- To learn that a complex sentence is made up of an independent clause and a dependent clause
- To distinguish between complex and compound sentences
- To create complex sentences by joining two simple sentences with a subordinating conjunction
- To identify a compound-complex sentence, an independent clause, and a dependent clause in a literary passage

Options for Organizing and Differentiating Instruction

See pages T11 and T12.

Scaffolding for English Language Learners

Point out the picture of the octopus on page 45 and invite students to share what they know about octopuses.

Read aloud the sentences in **Part 1,** and have students summarize the information. Then ask volunteers to tell whether each sentence is compound or complex. Remind them that subordinating conjunctions (*although, because, if, as, when*) often begin dependent clauses. Help students confirm their responses by reading each clause separately. If both make sense, the sentence is compound; if one clause cannot stand alone, the sentence is complex.

Model completing **Part 2** by rewriting item 16 on the board with the conjunction in place. Have students complete Part 2 in pairs.

For **Part 3,** read aloud the passage and clarify the meaning of *stern, crest, surveyed, tumultuous,* and *wind-riven.* Have students work with an English-proficient partner to choose a story or chapter from which to identify compound-complex sentences. Have volunteers read the sentences they find to the class.

Speaking and Listening

Write several coordinating and subordinating conjunctions on separate index cards. Give a card to each student. Then ask students to compose a compound or a complex sentence using the word on their card.

Reinforcement and Reteaching

Review **Read and Discover** and the rule statement, refer students to the **G.U.M. Handbook,** or use the **Extra Practice** activity on page 257.

Objectives

- To learn that an adjective clause is a dependent clause that describes a noun and that adjective clauses always follow the nouns they describe
- To learn that an adjective clause begins with a relative pronoun such as *who, whom, whose, which,* or *that*
- To identify adjective clauses, the nouns they describe, and the relative pronoun that begins the clause
- To rewrite pairs of sentences as a single complex sentence containing an adjective clause
- To find words in a word search and use them in a sentence that includes an adjective clause

Options for Organizing and Differentiating Instruction

See pages T11 and T12.

Scaffolding for English Language Learners

Encourage students to describe some unusual creatures that might live in the darkest depths of the sea. Tell students that describing words are called *adjectives.*

Read aloud the sentences in **Part 1.** Then call on volunteers to describe the deep-sea angler, the gulper eel, and the oarfish. (See pictures on page 47.) Ask students to identify the adjective clause in each sentence. To verify their responses, have students read each sentence aloud without the adjective clause and discuss how the adjective clause adds to the sentence. (Example: item 1: Explorers returned with tales of bizarre, unknown creatures; the adjective clause *who first descended to the sea's deep regions* tells which explorers.)

Use item 16 to model completing **Part 2.** Point out that the words that rename the subject of the second sentence (*The scientists* in item 16) should be replaced with a relative pronoun (who). Students may work individually or in pairs to complete the section.

Students can complete **Part 3** with the help of an English-proficient partner.

Speaking and Listening

List several nouns on the board, such as fish, plume, diver, scientist, eel, clam, and ocean. Also write these indefinite pronouns on separate index cards: who, whom, whose, that, which. Have students take turns drawing a pronoun card and using it in a sentence that has an adjective clause describing one of the nouns on the board. (Example: The diver who saw the eel was not frightened.)

Reinforcement and Reteaching

Review **Read and Discover** and the rule statement, refer students to the **G.U.M. Handbook,** or use the **Extra Practice** activity on page 258.

Objectives

- To learn that an adverb clause is a dependent clause that tells more about a verb, an adjective, or an adverb
- To learn that an adverb clause can begin with a subordinating conjunction (*than, although, because, if, before, after, where, wherever*)
- To identify adverb clauses in sentences and to rewrite pairs of sentences as a single complex sentence containing an adverb clause
- To identify the differences among an adverb, an adverb phrase, and an adverb clause

Options for Organizing and Differentiating Instruction

See pages T11 and T12.

Scaffolding for English Language Learners

Ask students to describe the appearance and habits of seals. Point out that this lesson is about different kinds of seals.

Explain that some of the words listed in the rule statement can also serve other functions, such as prepositions or conjunctions. Have students read **Part 1** silently, and then call on volunteers to summarize the information. Read each sentence aloud, one at a time, and have students identify the adverb clause. To help them, suggest that they first find the part of the sentence that can stand alone (the independent clause). Explain that the adverb clause is the rest of the sentence.

Model completing **Part 2** by writing the answer to item 16 on the board. (Because seals' eyes look much like human eyes, the Scottish have made up legends about seal-people, or selkies.) Have students complete items 17–21 independently and then read the completed sentences aloud.

Students can complete **Part 3** in pairs.

Speaking and Listening

Write short, simple sentences on the board, such as: The seal dove; A selkie danced; The sea lion slept. Then write these words on separate index cards: because, although, when, before, after, where. Have students select a word card and use it in a complex sentence that incorporates one of the simple sentences on the board. (Example: The seal dove when the polar bear appeared.)

Reinforcement and Reteaching

Review **Read and Discover** and the rule statement, refer students to the **G.U.M. Handbook**, or use the **Extra Practice** activity on page 258.

Objectives

- To learn that infinitives are formed by placing the word *to* before the present form of a verb
- To learn that an infinitive phrase is made up of an infinitive and other words that complete its meaning
- To identify infinitive phrases in sentences
- To complete sentences by adding an infinitive
- To create an aphorism using infinitives

Options for Organizing and Differentiating Instruction

See pages T11 and T12.

Scaffolding for English Language Learners

Point out the illustration and read aloud the caption on page 51. Ask students to suggest several simple sentences describing crabs.

Have students read **Part 1** silently. Clarify any words or phrases that are unfamiliar. Then work with students to identify the infinitive phrase in each sentence.

For **Part 2**, have students work with English-proficient partners. Clarify the meaning of each infinitive in the word bank before having students use it to complete a sentence.

Read aloud **Part 3**. Explain the meaning of each aphorism to students. Have pairs work together to discuss something they think will be important for others to know. Invite volunteers to write their aphorism on the board and to explain what it means.

Speaking and Listening

Ask students to use infinitive phrases to describe the behavior of animals, birds, or fish they have observed. (Example: The kitten used its tongue to groom itself; The lion sat behind a bush to watch its prey.)

Reinforcement and Reteaching

Review **Read and Discover** and the rule statement, refer students to the **G.U.M. Handbook**, or use the **Extra Practice** activity on page 259.

Objectives
- To discover that participles are verbals (words formed from verbs) that act as adjectives
- To learn that a present participle is formed by adding -*ing* to the present form of a verb, that a past participle is formed by adding -*ed* to a regular verb, and that irregular verbs change their spelling in the past participle
- To learn that a participial phrase is made up of a participle and other words that complete its meaning
- To identify participial phrases in sentences
- To rewrite confusing sentences by placing the participial phrase in the correct place in a sentence
- To identify absolute phrases in sentences

Options for Organizing and Differentiating Instruction
See pages T11 and T12.

Scaffolding for English Language Learners
Write the compound words turkeyfish, scorpionfish, lionfish, and stonefish on the board and invite students to guess what each is like, based on its name.

Read the sentences in **Part 1** aloud, and have students describe ways fish use their distinctive markings and ways they defend themselves. Then help students identify the participial phrase in each sentence. Suggest that they refer to the rule box to decide which words act as verbs and which act as adjectives.

Read aloud the sentences in **Part 2** and discuss why each one is confusing. (Example: item 19: The sentence seems to state that the instructor did not know how to scuba dive.) Then have students work with partners to rewrite each sentence with the participial phrase in the correct place.

Read aloud the explanation of absolute phrases in **Part 3**. Then have students work with English-proficient partners to identify the absolute phrases.

Speaking and Listening
Write these participial phrases on the board.
- walking through the classroom
- studying for my exams
- visiting my relatives

Ask students to create oral sentences using these participial phrases or others of their own.

Reinforcement and Reteaching
Review **Read and Discover** and the rule statement, refer students to the **G.U.M. Handbook**, or use the **Extra Practice** activity on page 259.

Objectives
- To discover that gerunds are verbals ending in -*ing* that act as nouns
- To learn that a gerund phrase is made up of a gerund and the other words that complete its meaning
- To identify gerunds and gerund phrases in sentences
- To use gerunds to complete sentences
- To find and list written works or movies that have gerunds in their titles

Options for Organizing and Differentiating Instruction
See pages T11 and T12.

Scaffolding for English Language Learners
Direct students' attention to the illustration of the starfish on page 55, and read the caption aloud. Encourage students to share information they know about coral reefs and the plants and animals commonly found there.

Read aloud the sentences in **Part 1** and clarify any unfamiliar vocabulary, such as *coral, anemone, parasites,* and *souvenirs.* Then reread each sentence aloud, and call on students to identify the gerund and gerund phrase.

For **Part 2**, have students work with partners to discuss what they would like to do on their imaginary vacations. Then have students complete the sentences using gerund phrases.

Have students read the directions for **Part 3** silently. Then have pairs work together to find five titles of books, poems, movies, or songs. Invite students to share the titles with the class.

Speaking and Listening
Invite students to use gerunds and gerund phrases to talk about things that are important to them. (Example: Spending time with my grandmother is important. Going to a movie is our favorite Saturday activity.)

Reinforcement and Reteaching
Review **Read and Discover** and the rule statement, refer students to the **G.U.M. Handbook**, or use the **Extra Practice** activity on page 260.

Objectives

- To learn that
  - a sentence fragment does not tell a complete thought
  - a run-on sentence is a compound sentence without a comma and a conjunction
  - a comma splice is a run-on sentence with a comma but no conjunction
  - a ramble-on sentence contains unnecessary words or phrases
- To identify and correctly rewrite sentence fragments, run-ons, comma splices, and ramble-ons
- To rewrite a ramble-on sentence

Options for Organizing and Differentiating Instruction

See pages T11 and T12.

Scaffolding for English Language Learners

Point out the picture of the electric ray on page 57 and explain that this lesson is about different kinds of animals called rays.

Have students read the sentences in **Part 1** with partners and decide which kind of error each sentence contains. Then reread each sentence aloud, and call on students to give their answers and to explain why each sentence is incorrectly written.

For **Part 2**, model revising the incorrect sentences. Explain that there is more than one way to revise each one. For instance, item 3 could be revised in these ways: Their eyes are on the tops of their heads. or Although their eyes are on the tops of their heads, their mouths are on the undersides.

Have students complete the monster ramble-on in **Part 3** in pairs. To help them find the important information in the sentence, ask: What are most rays covered with?

Speaking and Listening

Have small groups of students work cooperatively to compose an example of a fragment, a run-on, a comma splice, and a ramble-on sentence. Have groups alternate reading aloud one of their examples. Listeners should identify the error and suggest ways to correct it.

Reinforcement and Reteaching

Review **Read and Discover** and the rule statement, refer students to the **G.U.M. Handbook**, or use the **Extra Practice** activity on page 260.

Objectives

- To place sentences containing compound subjects and compound predicates in sentence diagrams
- To learn how to diagram a compound sentence

Recall with students that a sentence diagram helps to show how different parts of a sentence fit together. Review diagraming a sentence containing a simple subject, a simple predicate, an adjective, an article, and a direct object, such as: A hungry shark chased a seal.

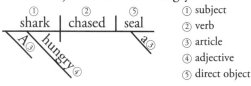

① subject
② verb
③ article
④ adjective
⑤ direct object

Diagraming Compound Subjects

Ask students to find out how to diagram a sentence containing a compound subject by looking at the example. Then have students diagram the three sentences containing compound subjects, using the lines provided. If necessary, begin by having students identify the subjects, predicates, articles, adjectives, and direct objects in the sentences.

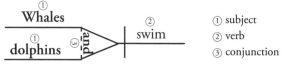

① subject
② verb
③ conjunction

Diagraming Compound Predicates

Have students look at the example to find out how to diagram a sentence with a compound predicate. Then have them diagram the three sentences containing compound predicates using the lines provided.

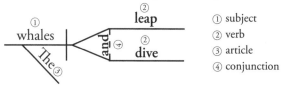

① subject
② verb
③ article
④ conjunction

Diagraming Compound Sentences

Before having students diagram compound sentences, have them identify the two simple sentences and the conjunction in each sentence to be diagrammed.

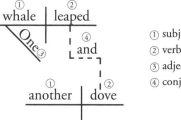

① subject
② verb
③ adjective
④ conjunction

Writing Sentences   (student page 61)

Point out to students that on this page they will practice rewriting some sentences that have been poorly written. Direct students to read the directions at the top of page 61 and then read the two sentences. Call on volunteers to suggest ways the first sentence might be rewritten. Explain that there is more than one way to revise it.

After students have rewritten the sentences, call on different volunteers to read aloud their revisions. Encourage students to discuss the revisions they feel work best and to explain why.

Remind students that they have learned about the four kinds of sentences. Ask them to identify the different kinds of sentences in the model paragraph at the bottom of the page. Then ask how including a variety of sentence types can improve a paragraph. (A variety can make a paragraph more interesting to read; questions and exclamations can grab a reader's attention.)

Writing a Paragraph   (student page 62)

Direct students to read the directions at the top of the page. Explain that they will use the sentences they rewrote on page 61 to write a paragraph. Students might work cooperatively to decide on a sequence for the sentences and revise them to include questions, commands, and explanations. To help students come up with a topic sentence, have them think about what all the revised sentences on page 61 are about. (how and what otters eat)

Students can work independently to write their original paragraphs. Suggest that they look back at the information about ocean life in Unit 2 to help them with the content of their paragraphs. Also remind them to use the checklist at the bottom of page 62 to evaluate their paragraphs for substance, style, and mechanics.

Proofreading   (student pages 63–64)

Scaffolding for English Language Learners

Have students work with a partner who is fluent in English for the proofreading activities.

Proofreading Practice

Ask students to identify the topic of the report on page 63. (sperm whales) Explain that the report contains several mistakes and that as they read, they should look for these mistakes.

Review the **Proofreading Marks** chart and the examples. Remind students that these marks are used by professional writers to check their work before publication. Read the first sentence aloud. Discuss the error (*Whales* should be in lowercase.) and how it should be marked. Ask students (in pairs or independently) to mark how the errors should be corrected with proofreading marks. You may wish to have students correct the spelling errors.

After they have completed the activity, ask volunteers to read each sentence aloud and to identify errors. Ask students to mark overlooked errors in another color. **Note:** Some errors can be corrected in more than one way.

Proofreading Checklist

Ask students to select a recent piece of their own writing and to write the title of that piece at the top of the chart. Have them put a check mark next to each item in the checklist after they have checked it in their work. Students might first work independently and then trade papers with a partner to double-check each other's work. You might model, or ask a student to model, using the **G.U.M. Handbook** (beginning on student page 303) to clarify a concept or rule.

Also Remember…

Remind students that capitalization and punctuation are important for clear writing. If necessary, help students use the **G.U.M. Handbook** to clarify when commas should be used and to review the use of capital letters.

Your Own List

Suggest that students look at the errors they did not find in the proofreading activity and add them to the checklist. Ask students to think about other kinds of errors they make and to add these to the checklist.

Ask students to place this page in their writing portfolios. These pages may be used to assess students' progress over the course of the year.

Assessment Options

See page T11 for ways to use *G.U.M.* assessments to differentiate instruction.

Unit Review

The **Unit Review** (pp. 65–66) allows you to check students' progress and determine when reteaching is necessary. The review pages may be completed in class or as homework. If a student responds incorrectly to two or more items involving the same skill, you may want to work directly with the student to review the relevant lesson. The lesson number to which each review item relates appears in parentheses on the review pages in the Teacher Edition.

Assign the **Extra Practice** activities (pp. 256–260) to reteach targeted skills in a more focused way.

Unit Assessment

The **Unit Assessment** (pp. 225–228) is intended to (1) familiarize students with standardized testing procedures, (2) check students' ability to apply key unit concepts in a different format, and (3) serve as an indicator of student progress.

- When used as a **pretest,** the Unit Assessment helps you determine, prior to instruction, your students' strengths, weaknesses, knowledge, and skills.
- When used as a **posttest,** the Unit Assessment provides feedback that you can use to guide further instruction.

Follow this procedure for administering the Unit Assessment.

1. Read aloud the Test Tip and the test instructions. (**Note:** For additional scaffolding, you may wish to read the test questions and answer choices aloud.)
2. Tell students that they will have 20 minutes to read and answer the questions independently.
3. When time is up, collect and correct the tests. Use the results to measure student progress and guide reteaching.

Assign the **Extra Practice** activities (pp. 256–260) to reteach targeted skills in a more focused way.

Note: The **Unit Review** may be reused after reteaching to check students' understanding of lesson concepts.

Unit Test

The **Unit Test** (pp. 289–290) helps you judge students' achievement while providing them with valuable practice for high-stakes tests. When you are ready to administer the test, ask students to carefully tear it out of their books. (**Note:** If the test has already been removed, distribute it to students.) Read aloud the directions for each section and make sure students understand how to answer the questions. Ask students to work independently to complete the test.

Students who miss two questions focusing on the same grammar element may need additional help understanding the concept. Reteach the concept, following this procedure:

1. Review **Read and Discover.**
2. Review the rule statement for the concept.
3. Guide students through items a second time. Ask the students to explain why each correct answer belongs in each sentence.
4. Refer students to the **G.U.M. Handbook** for further reinforcement.

Community Connection (student pages 67–68)

These two pages provide interesting activities that reinforce the skills and concepts students learned in Lessons 11 to 20. These activities provide opportunities for students to extend what they have read about in the unit by finding out more about marine life, occupations related to the sea, and laws governing fair use of the world's oceans. You might utilize the **Community Connection** pages in one of the following ways:

- Ask students to take the pages home, select one activity to do, and then share the results of that activity with the class.
- Have pairs of students select one activity to complete together.
- Preview the activities as a class, and then assign the activities to small groups of students to complete cooperatively. Set aside a time for groups to share the results.

When you are ready to have students select activities, direct them to pages 67–68. Explain that the activities on page 67 will give them an opportunity to explore other topics related to the ocean, such as maritime careers. Explain that one activity gives them an opportunity to interview an adult who has an ocean-related job. Point out that page 68 is a planning guide that will help them take notes as they conduct the interview. Then ask students to carefully tear the pages out of the book, and explain how you wish students to use them.

Unforgettable Folks

Unit 3 Parts of Speech

Pretest Option

You may use the **Unit Assessment** as a pretest. See pages T10 and T11.

Building Grammar Awareness

Write this sentence on the board:

Individuals throughout history have shown great courage by overcoming obstacles.

Explain to students that different words have different jobs in sentences. Ask volunteers to look at the sentence and find a word that names people (Individuals), words that name actions (shown and overcoming), and words that name things (history, courage, and obstacles). Inform students that in Unit 3 they will learn about the parts of speech that make up a sentence. Point out that learning about different kinds of words and using them correctly in sentences helps other people understand what they say and write.

Introducing "Unforgettable Folks"

People Who Overcame Challenges

Inform students that the title of Unit 3 is "Unforgettable Folks." Explain that each lesson tells about a person who has overcome great obstacles to achieve his or her dreams. Invite volunteers to share personal stories of people they know or have read about who have shown tremendous courage when faced with a challenge. Record students' responses in a chart using the words CHALLENGE and HOW IT WAS OVERCOME as headings. Record students' stories on the chart.

CHALLENGE	HOW IT WAS OVERCOME

Objectives

- To learn that a common noun names any person, place, thing, or idea
- To discover that a proper noun names a particular person, place, thing, or idea
- To identify common and proper nouns in sentences
- To rewrite sentences, replacing common nouns with proper nouns
- To complete a crossword puzzle using common and proper nouns

Options for Organizing and Differentiating Instruction

See pages T11 and T12.

Scaffolding for English Language Learners

Discuss the events that led Roger Williams to flee Massachusetts. Read aloud the sentences in **Part 1**. If necessary, clarify the phrase *he never went back on his convictions*. Ask volunteers to point out the common and proper noun(s) in each sentence. Remind them that the words that name a particular person, place, thing, or idea and begin with a capital letter are **proper nouns** and words that name any person, place, thing, or idea are **common nouns**. Note that *1631* in item 1 and *October 1635* in item 9 are proper nouns because they name particular times. If necessary, point out that in item 8, *Williams's* is a possessive proper noun telling *whose* ideas.

For **Part 2** have students work with partners to decide which proper noun can replace each common noun. Explain that *Algonquian* is a group of languages spoken by several Native American peoples.

Have students work in pairs to complete the puzzle in **Part 3**. If necessary, review the sentences from Parts 1 and 2 that contain the answer to each clue.

Speaking and Listening

Distribute index cards that list either a proper noun or a common noun. Call on volunteers to read the word on a card, tell which type of noun it is, and compose an oral sentence using the noun.

Reinforcement and Reteaching

Review **Read and Discover** and the rule statement, refer students to the **G.U.M. Handbook**, or use the **Extra Practice** activity on page 261.

Objectives
- To learn that a singular noun names one person, place, thing, or idea and a plural noun names more than one
- To identify singular and plural nouns in sentences
- To write the plural form of singular nouns
- To learn that a collective noun names a group of people or things that act as one unit

Options for Organizing and Differentiating Instruction

See pages T11 and T12.

Scaffolding for English Language Learners

Invite volunteers to share what they know about track and field. Guide students to understand that this sport includes races on a *track* (e.g., sprints, hurdles, long-distance runs, relay races) and contests on an athletic *field* (e.g., high jump, shot put, long jump). Then explain that the *heptathlon* is a track-and-field event for women which combines seven individual events—three track events and four field events.

Read aloud the sentences in **Part 1**. Call on volunteers to identify the singular and plural nouns in the sentences. To verify their responses, ask them if the word they have chosen names one or more than one person, place, thing, or idea.

For **Part 2** have volunteers first name the singular common nouns in Part 1. Discuss which ending should be added to create each plural form.

For **Part 3** discuss the meaning of the words in the box. Have volunteers tell which words name a group of people or things. Help them understand that the other words are plural nouns.

Speaking and Listening

Have students imagine that they are participating in a track-and-field competition. Ask volunteers to take turns describing an event in which they are competing. Encourage students to use singular, plural, and collective nouns. (Example: Our relay team has four fast runners.)

Reinforcement and Reteaching

Review **Read and Discover** and the rule statement, refer students to the **G.U.M. Handbook**, or use the **Extra Practice** activity on page 261.

Objectives
- To learn that a possessive noun shows ownership
- To identify singular possessive nouns and plural possessive nouns in sentences
- To rewrite sentences using possessive nouns
- To find hidden nouns in a word search and to identify the possessive nouns

Options for Organizing and Differentiating Instruction

See pages T11 and T12.

Scaffolding for English Language Learners

Ask students to suggest qualities they think every Olympic athlete should have.

Have volunteers read **Part 1** aloud. Clarify the terms *scarlet fever, contracted polio,* and *brace.* Then ask volunteers to identify the singular possessive and plural possessive noun(s) in each sentence. Remind students that in most cases the position of the apostrophe, before or after the *s,* can help them figure out whether the word is a singular possessive or a plural possessive noun.

For **Part 2** have students work with an English-proficient partner. Explain that they will have to cross out some of the underlined words and rearrange others to create a new sentence that contains a possessive noun.

Have students work in pairs to complete **Part 3**. Explain that the hidden words go both down and across, and point out an example of each.

Speaking and Listening

Write several short phrases on the board, such as these.

> the shoes of the runner
> the voices of the men
> the flexibility of the gymnasts

Have volunteers shorten each phrase to include a possessive noun and use it in an oral sentence. (Examples: The runner's shoes were full of mud. The men's voices sounded beautiful. The gymnasts' flexibility was astonishing.)

Reinforcement and Reteaching

Review **Read and Discover** and the rule statement, refer students to the **G.U.M. Handbook**, or use the **Extra Practice** activity on page 262.

Objectives

- To learn that the personal pronouns *I, me, we,* and *us* can be used to refer to oneself and the personal pronouns *she, her, he, him, you, they, them,* and *it* can be used to refer to others
- To identify personal pronouns in sentence context
- To write sentences using personal pronouns
- To rewrite sentences replacing the universal pronoun *he*

Options for Organizing and Differentiating Instruction

See pages T11 and T12.

Scaffolding for English Language Learners

Point out the picture of Nelson Mandela on page 75, and invite volunteers to share what they know about him and the system of apartheid.

Read aloud the sentences in **Part 1**. Call on volunteers to identify the personal pronoun in each sentence. Students can verify their responses by telling to whom the pronoun refers.

For **Part 2**, have students work with an English-proficient partner. They can begin by reviewing an example of each type of pronoun from the rule statement. Invite students to read their completed sentences aloud.

Read aloud the explanation and solutions for **Part 3**. Have students work in pairs to complete the sentences.

Speaking and Listening

Invite students to describe any experiences they have had as part of a team. Ask listeners to raise their hand each time they hear a pronoun and tell to whom or to what the pronoun refers.

Reinforcement and Reteaching

Review **Read and Discover** and the rule statement, refer students to the **G.U.M. Handbook,** or use the **Extra Practice** activity on page 262.

Objectives

- To learn that the compound personal pronouns *myself* and *ourselves* can be used to refer to oneself, the compound personal pronouns *herself, himself, yourself, yourselves,* and *themselves* can be used to refer to others, and *itself* can refer to animals or things
- To identify compound personal pronouns in written text
- To rewrite sentences using compound personal pronouns
- To use compound personal pronouns when writing an account of an experience

Options for Organizing and Differentiating Instruction

See pages T11 and T12.

Scaffolding for English Language Learners

Display the picture of the *Gossamer Condor,* on page 77, and ask students how they think this machine was able to fly without the help of an engine.

Have students read **Part 1** silently. Clarify any unfamiliar words and phrases, such as *held aloft only through frantic pedaling*. Call on volunteers to identify the compound personal pronouns as you reread each sentence aloud. Have other volunteers name the noun each pronoun refers to.

Pair students with English-proficient partners to complete **Part 2**.

Have students dictate their paragraphs for **Part 3** to an English-proficient partner. Invite students to read their completed accounts to the class.

Speaking and Listening

Invite students to pretend that they were part of the team that guided the *Gossamer Condor* across the English Channel for the first time. Have them imagine what happened along the way and share their stories with the class. Remind them to use compound personal pronouns. (**Example:** I found *myself* exhausted by the end of the journey. We towed the plane *ourselves* when Allen couldn't pedal.)

Reinforcement and Reteaching

Review **Read and Discover** and the rule statement, refer students to the **G.U.M. Handbook,** or use the **Extra Practice** activity on page 263.

Objectives

- To learn that possessive pronouns such as *her, his, its, their, my, our,* and *your* show possession and that possessive pronouns such as *hers, his, theirs, mine, ours,* and *yours* can replace both a possessive noun and the noun that is a possession
- To identify possessive pronouns in sentences
- To rewrite sentences using possessive pronouns
- To find the possessive pronouns in four riddles, solve the riddles, and then write new riddles using possessive pronouns

Options for Organizing and Differentiating Instruction

See pages T11 and T12.

Scaffolding for English Language Learners

Ask students to name a famous author from their native country or the United States and tell about one book that author has written.

Read aloud the sentences in **Part 1**. Discuss the job of an *investigative journalist,* and have students give reasons why having this job might have forced Allende to flee when the government was overthrown. Have volunteers identify the possessive pronoun(s) in each sentence. Remind them to take care not to circle the personal pronouns such as *she* that also appear in the sentences.

Model completing **Part 2** using item 17. Have students say the revised sentences aloud before writing them.

Students can complete **Part 3** with the help of an English-proficient partner. You may wish to work with students to compose original riddles (items 26 and 27).

Speaking and Listening

Invite students to name their favorite author and to share any information they may know about the author's life. Encourage them to use as many possessive pronouns as they can.

Reinforcement and Reteaching

Review **Read and Discover** and the rule statement, refer students to the **G.U.M. Handbook,** or use the **Extra Practice** activity on page 263.

Objectives

- To learn that when the pronouns *who, whom, whose, which,* and *that* are used to introduce an adjective clause, they are called relative pronouns
- To learn that when the pronouns *who, whom, whose, which,* and *what* are used to begin a question, they are called interrogative pronouns
- To identify relative pronouns and interrogative pronouns in sentences
- To complete sentences using a relative pronoun or an interrogative pronoun
- To rewrite sentences using appropriate relative pronouns

Options for Organizing and Differentiating Instruction

See pages T11 and T12.

Scaffolding for English Language Learners

Tell students that this lesson is about a scientist who developed a theory about black holes. If necessary, read aloud a definition of black holes from the encyclopedia to help students understand what they are.

Read aloud the sentences from **Part 1**. Call on students to paraphrase the information. Then have volunteers identify the relative pronouns and the adjective clauses they introduce. Have students verify their responses by reading aloud each sentence without the relative pronoun and the adjective clause. (Example: item 6: Dying stars may collapse in on themselves.) Call on other students to identify the interrogative pronouns. Remind them that an interrogative pronoun begins a question.

Have students work with an English-proficient partner to complete **Part 2**.

Read aloud the tips at the beginning of **Part 3**. Have students work in pairs to rewrite the sentences. Then call on volunteers to tell why the pronoun in the original sentence was wrong and which pronoun they used to correct it. Note in item 23 that *which* should be *that* because the clause is restrictive and is not set off by a comma in this sentence.

Speaking and Listening

List all the pronouns from the rule statement under two headings on the board: Relative Pronouns and Interrogative Pronouns. Challenge pairs of students to brainstorm questions that include both a relative and an interrogative pronoun. (Example: *What* is the name of the scientist *who* developed a theory about black holes?)

Reinforcement and Reteaching

Review **Read and Discover** and the rule statement, refer students to the **G.U.M. Handbook,** or use the **Extra Practice** activity on page 264.

Objectives
- To learn that indefinite pronouns refer to persons or things that are not identified as individuals
- To identify indefinite pronouns in sentences
- To complete sentences using indefinite pronouns
- To identify the indefinite pronouns in riddles, to answer the riddles, and to use the answers to solve a puzzle

Options for Organizing and Differentiating Instruction
See pages T11 and T12.

Scaffolding for English Language Learners
Ask students what they know about the South Pole, its climate and landscape, and the creatures that live there. (You may wish to show the Pole's location on a world map.)

Read aloud the sentences in **Part 1**. Clarify any unfamiliar words or terms. Have volunteers reread each sentence aloud and then identify the indefinite pronoun.

Students can work in pairs to complete **Part 2**. Suggest they complete the sentences orally before writing their responses.

Partners can work cooperatively to complete **Part 3**. Invite a volunteer to read aloud the answer to the final question.

Speaking and Listening
Have students imagine that they are part of a pioneering journey to a place that no one has ever been. Ask them to describe what happens during the journey. Encourage them to use as many indefinite pronouns as they can. (Example: *Everyone* was excited about the journey. We didn't see *anybody* for days.)

Reinforcement and Reteaching
Review **Read and Discover** and the rule statement, refer students to the **G.U.M. Handbook**, or use the **Extra Practice** activity on page 264.

Objectives
- To learn that adjectives describe nouns and pronouns and that there are different kinds of adjectives
- To identify different kinds of adjectives in sentences
- To complete sentences using adjectives from a word bank
- To identify adjectives and nouns in a word search puzzle
- To write an original sentence including nouns and adjectives

Options for Organizing and Differentiating Instruction
See pages T11 and T12.

Scaffolding for English Language Learners
Ask students to describe a work of art they have seen (mural, painting, public sculpture) and to tell why they like it. Explain that the describing words they used are called adjectives.

Read the sentences in **Part 1** aloud. Clarify the terms *contracted polio* and *muralist*. Have volunteers reread the sentences, identify the adjectives, and tell whether each adjective tells *what kind* or *how many*.

Students can complete **Part 2** independently. They can choose adjectives from the word bank or other words they think will complete the sentences. Invite volunteers to read their sentences aloud.

Students can work with partners to complete the word search in **Part 3** and write their sentences.

Speaking and Listening
Invite several volunteers to use adjectives to describe an object in the classroom without naming it. Others should try to guess what that object is. (Example: It has four legs and is hard and flat on top. Answer: A table.)

Reinforcement and Reteaching
Review **Read and Discover** and the rule statement, refer students to the **G.U.M. Handbook**, or use the **Extra Practice** activity on page 265.

Demonstrative Pronouns and Demonstrative Adjectives

Objectives
- To learn that *this, these, that,* and *those* are demonstratives
- To learn that a demonstrative pronoun takes the place of a noun and that a demonstrative adjective describes a noun by indicating which one it is
- To identify demonstrative adjectives and demonstrative pronouns in sentences
- To rewrite sentences using demonstrative pronouns or demonstrative adjectives
- To identify the demonstrative pronouns in famous quotations and to research these quotations

Options for Organizing and Differentiating Instruction
See pages T11 and T12.

Scaffolding for English Language Learners
Display a world map to help students visualize the voyage described in **Part 1**. (The map on page 87 will also help.) Read aloud the sentences and have students summarize the events. Clarify unfamiliar terms such as *clipper ship, perilous,* and *treacherous*. Ask students to identify the demonstrative adjectives and demonstrative pronouns. Remind them that a demonstrative adjective comes before the noun, while a demonstrative pronoun takes the place of the noun. Note in item 9 that *those* refers to the understood antecedent *the people*.

Have students work on **Part 2** in pairs. Suggest that they say each revised sentence aloud before writing it.

Students can complete **Part 3** with the help of an English-proficient partner. You may wish to guide students in their research. Encourage volunteers to share their findings with the class.

Speaking and Listening
Invite students to bring in photographs of a family vacation or magazine pictures of a family outing. Have them describe the people and objects in the pictures, using demonstrative pronouns and demonstrative adjectives. (Examples: *This* is the van Dad drove. *These* people are my cousins. *That* is an all-terrain vehicle.)

Reinforcement and Reteaching
Review **Read and Discover** and the rule statement, refer students to the **G.U.M. Handbook**, or use the **Extra Practice** activity on page 265.

(you) | Diagram | sentences

Objectives
- To learn how to diagram sentences containing the understood *you*
- To learn how to diagram sentences containing different kinds of pronouns

Recall with students how to diagram sentences that contain simple subjects and simple predicates as well as those that contain compound subjects and compound predicates. You may wish to use a sentence such as: Julio and Sara admire Martin Luther King, Jr.

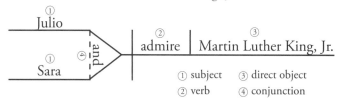

① subject   ③ direct object
② verb   ④ conjunction

Diagraming Understood *You*
Have students read about where the understood *you* goes in an imperative sentence. Ask them where the pronoun *you* would go in each of the three target sentences. Then have them diagram the sentences on the lines provided.

Diagraming Possessive Pronouns
Have students look at the example to find out where possessive pronouns belong in a sentence diagram. Before students complete their sentence diagrams for this section, have them identify the possessive pronoun and the noun to which it refers in each sentence. Point out that item 6 has a compound subject and that they should use what they learned in Unit 2 (pages 59 and 60) to diagram the sentence.

Diagraming Demonstrative Pronouns
Invite students to read about where demonstrative pronouns belong in a sentence diagram and to look at the examples before they answer the question.

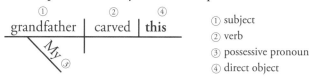

① subject
② verb
③ possessive pronoun
④ direct object

If necessary, point out that a pronoun in the subject position goes where the subject of a sentence belongs in a diagram and a pronoun that is a direct object goes where a direct object would go. Then have them identify the demonstrative pronoun as they diagram each of the three sentences. Call on a volunteer to diagram the compound predicate in the last sentence on the board.

Diagraming Indefinite Pronouns
Have students identify the indefinite pronoun in each sentence and diagram the three sentences.

Writing Sentences (student page 91)

Explain to students that on this page they will rewrite some sentences to give more information. Ask students to read the directions at the top of page 91 and the five sentences below. Then have students rewrite each sentence so it gives clear, detailed, colorful information.

After students have rewritten the sentences, call on several volunteers to reread items 1 and 2. Encourage the others to identify the elements that were added, such as adjectives, adverbs, and prepositions, and to tell which revised sentences they like best.

Review the parts of a paragraph with students. (topic sentence, supporting sentences, concluding sentence) Then have students read the model paragraph at the bottom of the page and identify these elements.

Writing a Paragraph (student page 92)

Have students read the directions at the top of the page. Explain that they can adapt one of the sentences as the topic sentence, or they may wish to compose a new topic sentence and a new concluding sentence. Encourage students to share their completed paragraphs.

Students can work independently to compose their original paragraphs. Remind them to use the checklist at the bottom of the page to evaluate their writing. Encourage them to make any necessary revisions.

Proofreading (student pages 93–94)

Scaffolding for English Language Learners

Have students work with a partner who is fluent in English for the proofreading activities.

Proofreading Practice

Ask students to identify the topic of the report on page 93. (sea turtles and their eggs) Explain that the report contains several mistakes and that as they read, they should look for these mistakes.

Review the **Proofreading Marks** chart and the examples. Remind students that these marks are used by professional writers to check their work before publication. Read the first sentence aloud. Discuss the errors (*Georgias'* should be *Georgia's; united states* should be *United States; there* should be *their*) and how each error should be marked for correction.

After they have completed the proofreading activity, ask volunteers to read each sentence aloud and to identify errors. Ask students to mark overlooked errors in another color. **Note:** Some errors can be corrected in more than one way.

Proofreading Checklist

Ask students to select a recent piece of their own writing and to write the title of that piece at the top of the chart. Ask students to put a check mark next to each item in the checklist after they have checked it in their work. Students might first work independently and then trade papers with a partner to double-check each other's work. You might model, or ask a student to model, using the **G.U.M. Handbook** (beginning on student page 303) to clarify a concept or rule.

Also Remember...

Remind students that capitalization and punctuation are important for clear writing. If necessary, help students use the **G.U.M. Handbook** to clarify when commas should be used and to review the use of capital letters.

Your Own List

Suggest that students look at the errors they did not find in the proofreading activity and add them to the checklist. Ask students to think about other kinds of errors they make and to add these to the checklist.

Ask students to place this page in their writing portfolios. These pages may be used to assess students' progress over the course of the year.

Assessment Options

See page T11 for ways to use *G.U.M.* assessments to differentiate instruction.

Unit Review

The **Unit Review** (pp. 95–96) allows you to check students' progress and determine when reteaching is necessary. The review pages may be completed in class or as homework. If a student responds incorrectly to two or more items involving the same skill, you may want to work directly with the student to review the relevant lesson. The lesson number to which each review item relates appears in parentheses on the review pages in the Teacher Edition.

Assign the **Extra Practice** activities (pp. 261–265) to reteach targeted skills in a more focused way.

Unit Assessment

The **Unit Assessment** (pp. 229–232) is intended to (1) familiarize students with standardized testing procedures, (2) check students' ability to apply key unit concepts in a different format, and (3) serve as an indicator of student progress.

- When used as a **pretest,** the Unit Assessment helps you determine, prior to instruction, your students' strengths, weaknesses, knowledge, and skills.
- When used as a **posttest,** the Unit Assessment provides feedback that you can use to guide further instruction.

Follow this procedure for administering the Unit Assessment.

1. Read aloud the Test Tip and the test instructions. (**Note:** For additional scaffolding, you may wish to read the test questions and answer choices aloud.)
2. Tell students that they will have 20 minutes to read and answer the questions independently.
3. When time is up, collect and correct the tests. Use the results to measure student progress and guide reteaching.

Assign the **Extra Practice** activities (pp. 261–265) to reteach targeted skills in a more focused way.

Note: The **Unit Review** may be reused after reteaching to check students' understanding of the lesson concepts.

Unit Test

The **Unit Test** (pp. 291–292) helps you judge students' achievement while providing them with valuable practice for high-stakes tests. When you are ready to administer the test, ask students to carefully tear it out of their books. (**Note:** If the test has already been removed, distribute it to students.) Read aloud the directions for each section and make sure students understand how to answer the questions. Ask students to work independently to complete the test.

Students who miss two questions focusing on the same grammar element may need additional help understanding the concept. Reteach the concept, following this procedure:

1. Review **Read and Discover**.
2. Review the rule statement for the concept.
3. Guide students through items a second time. Ask the students to explain why each correct answer belongs in each sentence.
4. Refer students to the **G.U.M. Handbook** for further reinforcement.

Community Connection (student pages 97–98)

These two pages provide interesting and fun activities that reinforce the skills and concepts students learned in Lessons 21–30. These activities give students the opportunity to expand what they have read in the unit by finding out more about people in your community who have faced and overcome challenges. You might utilize the **Community Connection** pages in one of the following ways:

- Ask students to take the pages home, select one activity to do, and then share the results of that activity with the class.
- Have pairs of students select one activity to complete together.
- Preview the activities as a class, and then assign the activities to small groups of students to complete cooperatively. Set aside a time for groups to share the results.

When you are ready to have students select activities, direct them to pages 97–98. Explain that the activities on page 97 will give them an opportunity to find out about organizations that help people facing challenges and to explore ways *they* can help others overcome challenges. Explain that one activity gives them an opportunity to conduct interviews to help them find out about jobs that are available to people who want to help others overcome challenges. They can learn about the skills and training required for such a job. Point out that page 98 includes a planning guide that will help them take notes as they conduct the interview. Then ask students to carefully tear the pages out of the book, and explain how you wish students to use them.

The World Outside

Unit 4 Parts of Speech

Pretest Option

You may use the **Unit Assessment** as a pretest. See pages T10 and T11.

Building Grammar Awareness

Write this sentence on the board:

All living creatures depend greatly on their environment for survival.

Ask students to find a word that names an action (depend), a word that tells to what extent (greatly), and words that name things (creatures, environment, survival). Inform students that in Unit 4 they will learn more about parts of speech and verb tenses. Remind students that knowing the parts of speech and how to use them correctly will help others understand what they say and write.

Introducing "The World Outside"

Cycles in Nature

Tell students that the title of Unit 4 is "The World Outside." Explain that the lessons in Unit 4 describe some of the natural relationships and cycles of life on Earth. Have volunteers describe some life cycles they know about, such as that of a tadpole turning into a frog. Record their responses in an idea web on the board.

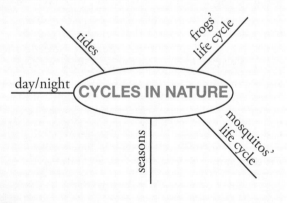

Lesson 31 (student pages 99–100)
Action Verbs and Linking Verbs

Objectives
- To learn that an action verb shows action
- To learn that a linking verb connects the subject of a sentence to a word or phrase that describes or renames the subject
- To identify action verbs and linking verbs in sentences
- To complete sentences using action verbs and linking verbs

Options for Organizing and Differentiating Instruction
See pages T11 and T12.

Scaffolding for English Language Learners
Read aloud the sentences in **Part 1.** Call on volunteers to identify the verb in each sentence, tell whether or not it shows action, and then indicate whether it is an action verb or a linking verb.

For **Part 2,** have students each work with an English-proficient partner. Instruct students to choose and fill in a verb to complete the sentence, and then identify the verb as an action verb or a linking verb.

For **Part 3,** students should work with partners to figure out whether the verb in each sentence is an action verb or a linking verb. Use item 26 to model the substitution strategy. (*They* were *ready to pick.*) Tell students that since the sentence makes sense when you replace *looked* with a form of the verb *be,* then *looked* is a linking verb in this sentence.

Speaking and Listening
List nouns such as cactus, rain, scorpion, and sun on the board. Invite students to use these words with action verbs and linking verbs to create original sentences.

Reinforcement and Reteaching
Review **Read and Discover** and the rule statement, refer students to the **G.U.M. Handbook,** or use the **Extra Practice** activity on page 266.

Objectives
- To learn that a transitive verb is an action verb that transfers its action to a direct object
- To learn that an intransitive verb does not have a direct object and shows action that the subject does alone
- To identify transitive verbs and their direct objects and intransitive verbs in sentences
- To complete sentences using transitive and intransitive verbs correctly
- To write sentences using the same verb in a transitive and an intransitive form

Options for Organizing and Differentiating Instruction
See pages T11 and T12.

Scaffolding for English Language Learners
Point out the illustration of an ant's life cycle on page 101 and read aloud the name for each stage.

Read aloud the sentences in **Part 1**. Clarify any difficult words or phrases. Ask students to identify the transitive verbs, their direct objects, and the intransitive verbs. To help students identify direct objects, suggest that they say the verb and then ask *what?* or *whom?* The answer is the direct object. (For example, in item 2, they can ask "Begin what?" The answer is *begin lives*. *Lives* is the direct object of the verb *begin*.) If there is no answer, there is no direct object and the verb is intransitive.

For **Part 2**, have students determine which verbs take a direct object. Then have partners name the transitive verbs and the intransitive verbs and write the correct letter in the blank after the sentence.

Have students work with an English-proficient partner to complete **Part 3**. Invite volunteers to read their sentence pairs to the class.

Speaking and Listening
Invite students to discuss insects they may have observed. Ask them to use as many transitive and intransitive verbs as they can. (Examples: A red ant *stung* the dog. The bee *flew* from flower to flower.)

Reinforcement and Reteaching
Review **Read and Discover** and the rule statement, refer students to the **G.U.M. Handbook**, or use the **Extra Practice** activity on page 266.

Objectives
- To learn that if the subject performs an action, the verb is in the active voice
- To learn that if the subject is acted upon by something else, the verb is in the passive voice
- To discover that in many sentences written in the passive voice, the preposition *by* follows the verb
- To identify the active voice and the passive voice in sentences
- To rewrite sentences so the verb is changed from the passive voice to the active voice
- To identify verbs in the active voice in a literary excerpt
- To review students' own writing and revise a sentence, changing the verb in it from the passive voice to the active voice

Options for Organizing and Differentiating Instruction
See pages T11 and T12.

Scaffolding for English Language Learners
Point out the illustration and read the caption on page 103. Explain that some pine trees produce very large pinecones.

Read the sentences in **Part 1** aloud. Help students understand why small fires may be good for the life of the forest, and why huge fires disrupt the ecology of the forest. Clarify the meanings of *vegetation, flammable, incinerate,* and *inferno.* Call on volunteers to tell whether the verb in each sentence is in the active voice or the passive voice. Help them then identify verbs in the passive voice that are followed by a prepositional phrase beginning with *by*.

Students can work in pairs to complete **Part 2**. Model revising item 2 in Part 1, and tell students to write the revised sentence on the lines for item 19. (*Many animals are killed by the raging flames* becomes *The raging flames kill many animals.*)

Read aloud the passage in **Part 3**. Then have students work with partners to find the verbs in the active voice. You may need to work with students to revise sentences from their own writing.

Speaking and Listening
Invite students to talk about a fire they have read about, seen in real life, or watched on television. Have them use the active voice to describe the fire.

Reinforcement and Reteaching
Review **Read and Discover** and the rule statement, refer students to the **G.U.M. Handbook**, or use the **Extra Practice** activity on page 267.

Lesson 34 (student pages 105–106)
The Simple Tenses: Present, Past, and Future

Objectives
- To discover that the present tense indicates that something happens regularly or is true now
- To learn that past tense verbs tell about something that has already happened
- To learn that future tense verbs tell about something that is going to happen
- To identify verbs in past, present, and future tenses in sentences
- To complete sentences using the past, present, and future tense forms of verbs
- To write a journal entry using past, present, and future tense verbs

Options for Organizing and Differentiating Instruction
See pages T11 and T12.

Scaffolding for English Language Learners
Ask students if they have ever seen a flock of migrating birds. Then ask a volunteer to explain why birds migrate.

Have volunteers read the sentences in **Part 1** aloud. Clarify the meaning of unfamiliar terms and phrases, such as *banded, travel invisible routes,* and *field guide.* Call on volunteers to identify the verb in each sentence and to tell whether it is in the past, present, or future tense. Remind students that some of the verbs are irregular verbs, so their past tense form will not end in *-ed.* Point out that *found* in sentence 8 and *bought* in sentence 14 are past tense forms of irregular verbs.

For **Part 2,** students can work in pairs to decide which verb belongs in the blank and to use its past, present, or future form to complete the sentence.

For **Part 3,** model creating sentences from each bulleted item. Construct the journal entry orally as a group before having students write it.

Speaking and Listening
Invite volunteers to discuss different migrating birds, fish, or animals they have read about or seen in real life or on television. Direct them to use present, past, and future tense verbs in their discussion. (Example: Canada geese *fly* over my house every year. I *saw* some yesterday. They *will travel* many miles before they reach their destination.)

Reinforcement and Reteaching
Review **Read and Discover** and the rule statement, refer students to the **G.U.M. Handbook,** or use the **Extra Practice** activity on page 267.

Lesson 35 (student pages 107–108)
The Perfect Tenses: Present, Past, and Future

Objectives
- To learn that the present perfect tense indicates action that began in the past and was recently completed or is still happening
- To learn that the past perfect tense indicates action that was completed by a certain time in the past
- To learn that the future perfect tense indicates action that will be completed by a certain time in the future
- To learn how to form the perfect tenses by using a form of *have* with the past participle of a verb
- To identify perfect tense verbs in sentences and to complete sentences using them
- To identify verbs in the past and past perfect tenses in a passage of literature

Options for Organizing and Differentiating Instruction
See pages T11 and T12.

Scaffolding for English Language Learners
Point out the picture of the bromeliad (broh MEE lee uhd) on page 107 and read the caption aloud.

Read **Part 1** aloud. Clarify unfamiliar terms, such as *ecosystems, one-celled creatures,* and *food-web interactions.* Tell students that one way of determining the present, past, or future form of a perfect tense verb is by looking at the tense of the helping verb *have.* If the tense is *present* (*have*), then the verb phrase is *present perfect tense;* if it is *past* (*had*), then the verb is *past perfect;* and if it is *future* (*will have*), then the verb is in the *future perfect tense.* Students can work in small groups to identify the perfect tense form of each of the boldfaced verbs.

For **Part 2,** have students work in pairs to determine when the action takes place in each sentence. Suggest that they look for clues in the prepositional phrases or in other verb tenses in the sentence.

Invite a volunteer to read aloud **Part 3.** Have students work with English-proficient partners to identify and categorize the verbs in the passage.

Speaking and Listening
Ask students to imagine that they are one of the tiny creatures that live in the bromeliad. Have them talk about what life is like inside the plant. Encourage them to use perfect tense verbs in their accounts. (Example: I *have lived* in the bromeliad for many days. It's wet in here because rain *has fallen* every day for a week.)

Reinforcement and Reteaching
Review **Read and Discover** and the rule statement, refer students to the **G.U.M. Handbook,** or use the **Extra Practice** activity on page 268.

Lesson 36 (student pages 109–110)
Progressive Verb Forms: Present, Past, and Future

Objectives
- To discover that progressive forms of verbs show continuing action
- To learn how to form progressive forms of verbs
- To distinguish verbs in progressive forms from other verb forms in sentences
- To complete sentences by writing the correct progressive form of the verb
- To identify the progressive form of verbs in crossword puzzle clues and then complete the puzzle

Options for Organizing and Differentiating Instruction
See pages T11 and T12.

Scaffolding for English Language Learners
Ask students how much sleep they normally get and what happens if they don't get enough.

Read aloud the sentences in **Part 1.** Ask volunteers to paraphrase the information. Point out that progressive forms of verbs use a form of the helping verb *be* and end in *-ing.* Have students reread the first sentence, decide which form the verb is in, and tell how they know. (progressive form; ends in *-ing,* uses helping verb *are*) Have student pairs complete the remaining items.

For **Part 2,** call on volunteers to tell which helping verb from the word bank is appropriate for each item. Have student pairs complete the sentences.

For **Part 3,** have volunteers identify the progressive verb form in each clue. Call on others to answer the clues, and then have students write the answers to the puzzle.

Speaking and Listening
Ask students to talk about a time when they had trouble falling asleep. Have them use progressive forms of verbs to tell what they did before they finally fell asleep. (Example: I *was tossing* in bed last night worrying about the game.)

Reinforcement and Reteaching
Review **Read and Discover** and the rule statement, refer students to the **G.U.M. Handbook,** or use the **Extra Practice** activity on page 268.

Lesson 37 (student pages 111–112)
Adverbs

Objectives
- To learn that adverbs describe verbs, adjectives, or other adverbs by explaining *how, when, where,* or *to what extent*
- To identify adverbs in sentences
- To identify adverbs and decide what kind of information they add in sentences
- To identify adverbs in a passage of literature

Options for Organizing and Differentiating Instruction
See pages T11 and T12.

Scaffolding for English Language Learners
Have students look at the picture on page 111 and read the caption. Invite volunteers to tell what they know about salmon.

Read aloud the sentences in **Part 1.** Ask a volunteer to identify the adverbs in the first sentence and to tell which verb, adjective, or adverb each describes. (*Almost* modifies the adverb *always,* which modifies the verb *bear.*) Call on others to identify the adverbs in the remaining sentences.

Have student pairs work on **Part 2** together. Invite volunteers to tell what each adverb explains. (Example: item 20: The adverb *once* explains *when.*)

Read aloud **Part 3** as students follow along. Have students complete the activity with the help of an English-proficient partner.

Speaking and Listening
Ask students to describe an outing they have taken. Encourage them to use as many adverbs as they can. (Example: We got to the park *early* in the morning. We watched some squirrels *first. Then* we took pictures of birds.)

Reinforcement and Reteaching
Review **Read and Discover** and the rule statement, refer students to the **G.U.M. Handbook,** or use the **Extra Practice** activity on page 269.

Objectives
- To learn what a preposition, an object of a preposition, and a prepositional phrase are
- To identify prepositions, objects of prepositions, and prepositional phrases in sentences
- To complete sentences using the appropriate prepositions
- To complete a crossword puzzle using prepositions and to write an original sentence using prepositions

Options for Organizing and Differentiating Instruction
See pages T11 and T12.

Scaffolding for English Language Learners
Explain what soil erosion is, using pantomime or quick sketches on the board. Brainstorm with students the causes of soil erosion and some of its possible consequences. You may wish to use the illustration on page 113 and point out that the waves are wearing down the land.

Read aloud the sentences in **Part 1** and clarify unfamiliar words and phrases, such as *mound, creeks,* and *low-lying farmlands.* Have students paraphrase the information. Then model naming a preposition, an object of the preposition, and a prepositional phrase, using item 5. (through, landscape, through a rocky landscape)

Demonstrate the meaning of each preposition in the word bank in **Part 2** by using objects in the classroom. (The eraser is *between* two pencils; the ruler is *on/under* the desk.) Have students work with English-proficient partners to complete Part 2.

Student pairs can complete the puzzle in **Part 3** and write their sentences.

Speaking and Listening
Write several prepositions on the board, such as *to, from, through,* and *in.* Ask students to create original sentences about a powerful storm, using the prepositions. Call on volunteers to name the prepositional phrase of each sentence said aloud. (Example: The wind blew large branches *to* the ground. Heavy rain poured *from* the sky.)

Reinforcement and Reteaching
Review **Read and Discover** and the rule statement, refer students to the **G.U.M. Handbook,** or use the **Extra Practice** activity on page 269.

Objectives
- To discover that the coordinating conjunctions *and, or,* and *but* connect words or groups of words (including independent clauses) that are similar
- To learn that subordinating conjunctions such as *although, since,* and *before* show how a dependent clause is related to an independent clause in a sentence
- To identify coordinating and subordinating conjunctions in sentences
- To complete sentences using the appropriate coordinating or subordinating conjunctions
- To identify subordinating conjunctions in wise sayings and to write an original saying that includes a subordinating conjunction

Options for Organizing and Differentiating Instruction
See pages T11 and T12.

Scaffolding for English Language Learners
Invite students to share what they know about the moon's monthly cycle and to describe its appearance at different times in the month.

Read aloud the sentences in **Part 1**. Clarify unfamiliar terms such as *crescent, gibbous,* and *lunar probes.* Call on volunteers to identify the separate independent or dependent clauses in each sentence and to tell whether they are connected by a coordinating or a subordinating conjunction. Have them name the conjunction.

Have student pairs complete **Part 2** orally before they write their answers.

Read aloud the statements in **Part 3**. Clarify the meaning of each saying. Then have partners find the subordinating conjunction and the subordinate clause in each sentence. Encourage partners to write original sayings that include a subordinating conjunction.

Speaking and Listening
Write the words *and, or, but, although, because, since,* and *if* on the board. Invite students to describe the night sky using these conjunctions. Model, using these examples: Although the moon was full, the stars seemed dim. The moon rose, and the stars appeared.

Reinforcement and Reteaching
Review **Read and Discover** and the rule statement, refer students to the **G.U.M. Handbook,** or use the **Extra Practice** activity on page 270.

Objectives

- To learn that correlative conjunctions always appear in pairs and that they connect words or groups of words
- To identify correlative conjunctions in sentences
- To rewrite pairs of sentences as a single sentence with correlative conjunctions
- To select the correct correlative conjunctions to complete sentences and then use the sentences to solve riddles

Options for Organizing and Differentiating Instruction

See pages T11 and T12.

Scaffolding for English Language Learners

Inform students that they are going to read about pairs of animals that depend on each other for their survival.

Read aloud the sentences in **Part 1**. Clarify the meanings of *symbiotic, parasites, commensal,* and *mutual* and of unfamiliar phrases, such as *to build up immunity to.* Call on volunteers to name the words that make up each correlative conjunction they identify. Ask others to identify the coordinating conjunctions in the remaining sentences.

Have students work with an English-proficient partner to complete **Part 2**. Point out that they may have to delete some words and add others when they rewrite each sentence pair as one sentence. Model, using item 17.

Have partners orally identify the correct correlative conjunctions for **Part 3**. Then have them answer each clue.

Speaking and Listening

Write several correlative conjunctions on index cards. Have student pairs pick a card and use the correlative conjunctions in sentences about favorite pets or about animals they have seen. (Example: I have *both* a dog *and* a cat.)

Reinforcement and Reteaching

Review **Read and Discover** and the rule statement, refer students to the **G.U.M. Handbook,** or use the **Extra Practice** activity on page 270.

Objectives

- To learn that sentence diagrams with linking verbs look different from those with action verbs
- To learn where to place predicate adjectives, predicate nouns, and adverbs in a sentence diagram

Diagraming Linking Verbs

Ask students what difference they see between the two model sentence diagrams. Elicit that in the sentence diagram with the action verb, the direct object is separated from the verb by a vertical line, and in the sentence diagram with the linking verb, the predicate noun is separated from the verb by a slanting line. Have students diagram the three sentences.

Hawks | eat | rodents

① subject
② verb
③ direct object

Diagraming Predicate Nouns and Predicate Adjectives

Have students examine the examples. (Students should note that predicate nouns and predicate adjectives go after the linking verb, separated from the verb with a slanting line.) Then have students diagram the four sentences.

Ospreys | are \ powerful

① subject
② verb
③ predicate adjective

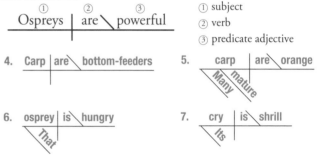

4. Carp | are \ bottom-feeders

5. carp | are \ orange
   Many \ mature

6. osprey | is \ hungry
   That

7. cry | is \ shrill
   Its

Diagraming Adverbs

Recall with students that in sentence diagrams containing adjectives, the adjective is connected to the noun it modifies by a slanted line below the noun. Have students look at the example; point out that an adverb is connected to the verb it modifies by a slanted line below the verb. Have students diagram the three sentences.

osprey | circled | river
The ④   slowly ⑤   the ④

① subject
② verb
③ direct object
④ article
⑤ adverb

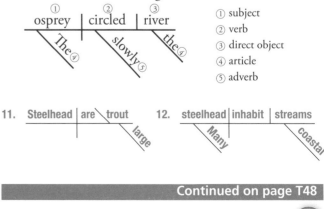

11. Steelhead | are \ trout
    large

12. steelhead | inhabit | streams
    Many \ coastal

Continued on page T48

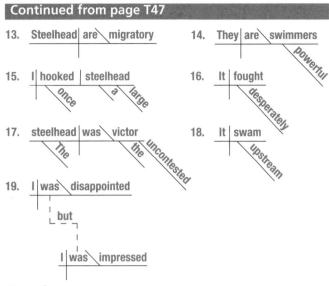

13. Steelhead are migratory
14. They are swimmers / powerful
15. I hooked steelhead / once / a / large
16. It fought / desperately
17. steelhead was victor / The / the / uncontested
18. It swam / upstream
19. I was disappointed / but / I was impressed

Practice

Have student pairs diagram the practice sentences.

Writing Sentences   (student page 121)

Tell students that the sentences in the top part of page 121 need to be revised so that they make sense. Read the first sentence aloud and call on a volunteer to tell why the sentence does not make sense. (The phrase that follows the subordinating conjunction *although* is misplaced.) Call on another volunteer to correct the sentence. (Although days grow longer after the winter solstice, springtime is still months away.) Then have students work independently or in pairs to correct the remaining sentences. Point out that there may be more than one way to revise each one. When the students have finished, encourage them to compare their revisions.

Ask students to name the parts of a paragraph. (topic sentence, supporting sentences, concluding sentence) Then ask them to read the model paragraph at the bottom of the page and to identify the time-order words and the transition sentence (the fourth sentence). Point out that writers often use a transition sentence to go smoothly from one topic to the next; in the model paragraph, the transition sentence ties the topic of the first sentences (camping) to the topic of the last part of the paragraph (fishing).

Writing a Paragraph   (student page 122)

Ask students to read aloud the instructions at the top of the page and then to write a paragraph using the sentences they revised on page 121. Tell students that they may need to add a transition sentence to make the sentences flow better. Encourage students to read aloud their completed paragraphs.

Have students work independently to write their personal narratives in the space provided or on another sheet of paper. Remind them to check their work using the checklist at the bottom of the page.

Proofreading   (student pages 123–124)

Scaffolding for English Language Learners

Have students work with a partner who is fluent in English for the proofreading activities.

Proofreading Practice

Ask students to identify the topic of the report on page 123. (the miniature ecosystem within an acorn) Explain that the report contains several mistakes and that as they read, they should look for these mistakes.

Review the **Proofreading Marks** chart and the examples. Remind students that these marks are used by professional writers to check their work before publication. Read the first sentence aloud. Discuss the error (*believe* is spelled incorrectly) and how it should be marked for correction. You may wish to have students correct the spelling errors.

After they have completed the proofreading activity, ask volunteers to read each sentence aloud and to identify errors. Ask students to mark overlooked errors in another color. **Note:** Some errors can be corrected in more than one way.

Proofreading Checklist

Ask students to select a recent piece of their own writing and to write the title of that piece at the top of the chart. Ask students to put a check mark next to each item in the checklist after they have checked it in their work. Students might first work independently and then trade papers with a partner to double-check each other's work. You might model, or ask a student to model, using the **G.U.M. Handbook** (beginning on student page 303) to clarify a concept or rule.

Also Remember…

Remind students that capitalization and punctuation are important for clear writing. If necessary, help students use the **G.U.M. Handbook** to clarify when commas should be used and to review the use of capital letters.

Your Own List

Suggest that students look at the errors they did not find in the proofreading activity and add them to the checklist. Ask students to think about other kinds of errors they make and to add these to the checklist.

Ask students to place this page in their writing portfolios. These pages may be used to assess students' progress over the course of the year.

Assessment Options

See page T11 for ways to use *G.U.M.* assessments to differentiate instruction.

Unit Review

The **Unit Review** (pp. 125–126) allows you to check students' progress and determine when reteaching is necessary. The review pages may be completed in class or as homework. If a student responds incorrectly to two or more items involving the same skill, you may want to work directly with the student to review the relevant lesson. The lesson number to which each review item relates appears in parentheses on the review pages in the Teacher Edition.

Assign the **Extra Practice** activities (pp. 266–270) to reteach targeted skills in a more focused way.

Unit Assessment

The **Unit Assessment** (pp. 233–236) is intended to (1) familiarize students with standardized testing procedures, (2) check students' ability to apply key unit concepts in a different format, and (3) serve as an indicator of student progress.

- When used as a **pretest,** the Unit Assessment helps you determine, prior to instruction, your students' strengths, weaknesses, knowledge, and skills.
- When used as a **posttest,** the Unit Assessment provides feedback that you can use to guide further instruction.

Follow this procedure for administering the Unit Assessment.

1. Read aloud the Test Tip and the test instructions. (**Note:** For additional scaffolding, you may wish to read the test questions and answer choices aloud.)
2. Tell students that they will have 20 minutes to read and answer the questions independently.
3. When time is up, collect and correct the tests. Use the results to measure student progress and guide reteaching.

Assign the **Extra Practice** activities (pp. 266–270) to reteach targeted skills in a more focused way.

Note: The **Unit Review** may be reused after reteaching to check students' understanding of the lesson concepts.

Unit Test

The **Unit Test** (pp. 293–294) helps you judge students' achievement while providing them with valuable practice for high-stakes tests. When you are ready to administer the test, ask students to carefully tear it out of their books. (**Note:** If the test has already been removed, distribute it to students.) Read aloud the directions for each section and make sure students understand how to answer the questions. Ask students to work independently to complete the test.

Students who miss two questions focusing on the same grammar element may need additional help understanding the concept. Reteach the concept, following this procedure:

1. Review **Read and Discover**.
2. Review the rule statement for the concept.
3. Guide students through items a second time. Ask the students to explain why each correct answer belongs in each sentence.
4. Refer students to the **G.U.M. Handbook** for further reinforcement.

Community Connection (student pages 127–128)

These two pages provide interesting and fun activities that reinforce the skills and concepts students learned in Lessons 31 to 40. These activities give students the opportunity to extend what they have read about in the unit by finding out more about natural and human-made cyclical patterns in your community. You might utilize the **Community Connection** pages in one of the following ways:

- Ask students to take the pages home, select one activity to do, and then share the results of that activity with the class.
- Have pairs of students complete one activity.
- Preview the activities as a class, and then assign the activities to small groups of students to complete cooperatively. Allow time for groups to share the results.

When you are ready to have students select activities, direct them to pages 127–128. Explain that the activities on page 127 will give them an opportunity to observe and find out more about natural and human-made cyclical patterns in the world around them. Explain that one activity gives them an opportunity to conduct an interview to learn more about these cycles and possible careers. Point out that page 128 is a planning guide that will help them take notes as they conduct their interview. Then ask students to carefully tear the pages out of the book, and explain how you wish students to use them.

Grab Bag

Unit 5 Usage

Pretest Option

You may use the **Unit Assessment** as a pretest. See pages T10 and T11.

Building Usage Awareness

Write the following sentences on the board:
If your in my town in July, their is a festival you might want too come two.

Its called the Gilroy Garlic Festival. They're isn't no bigger garlic festival in the world.

Invite a volunteer to read aloud the sentences. Ask students if the words sound correct. Then ask them if all the words look correct. Ask volunteers to correct the words that are used incorrectly in each sentence. (Sentence 1: *your, their, too,* and *two;* Sentence 2: *Its;* Sentence 3: *They're*) Ask students what else is wrong with the third sentence. (It has a double negative—*isn't* and *no.*) Help students rewrite the sentences correctly. Tell them that in Unit 5 they will learn how to correctly use words that sound alike but have different meanings and spellings. Explain that they will also learn about other words that are often used incorrectly in speaking and writing. Remind students that using words and word forms correctly will help others understand them when they speak and write.

Introducing "Grab Bag"
Cultural Snapshots

Inform students that the title of Unit 5 is "Grab Bag" and that each lesson is about a people or nation with a distinctive culture. Review with students what elements comprise a people's culture: language, food, clothing, religion, customs, celebrations, and so on. Encourage students to describe cultures they have encountered or read about. Record their responses in a chart.

Language	Food	Clothing	Religion	

Lesson 41 (student pages 129–130)
Your and *You're*

Objectives

- To discover that *your* and *you're* sound the same but have different spellings and meanings
- To learn that the word *your* is a possessive pronoun that shows ownership and *you're* is a contraction of the words *you* and *are*
- To select the correct use of *your* and *you're* in sentences
- To answer questions using the words *your* and *you're* correctly
- To learn that *your* and *you're* are homophones and to identify other homophones in sentences

Options for Organizing
and Differentiating Instruction

See pages T11 and T12.

Scaffolding for English Language Learners

Tell students that they are going to read about cultural traditions of the Hawaiian people, the original residents of the islands that are now the state of Hawaii. Invite students to share what they know about Hawaiian culture and traditions.

Read aloud **Part 1.** Have a volunteer reread the sentences one at a time. Ask students if the possessive pronoun *your* or the words *you are* make sense in the sentence. Tell students that if the words *you are* make sense, then they should use the contraction *you're.*

Before students complete **Part 2,** read aloud the questions. Ask pairs to say each answer orally before writing it and then to determine whether *your* or *you're* belongs in the sentence.

Read aloud the sentences in **Part 3.** Then explain the meaning of the incorrectly written words in each sentence. Have partners work together to replace each incorrect homophone with the correct word.

Speaking and Listening

Divide the class into two groups: the pronoun *your* group and the contraction *you're* group. Then have a volunteer give oral instructions to the class about an activity or game he or she enjoys doing. Each time the word *your* or *you're* is used in a sentence, the appropriate members of the group should raise their hands. (Example: In the game of tag, if someone touches *your* arm, *you're* IT!)

Reinforcement and Reteaching

Review **Read and Discover** and the rule statement, refer students to the **G.U.M. Handbook,** or use the **Extra Practice** activity on page 271.

Objectives
- To discover that *their, they're,* and *there* sound the same but have different spellings and meanings
- To learn that *their* is a possessive pronoun, *they're* is a contraction of the words *they* and *are,* and *there* is an adverb usually meaning "in that place" and is also used as an introductory word
- To select the correct use of *their, they're,* and *there* in sentences
- To replace short phrases in a sentence with *their, they're,* and *there*
- To correct the incorrect use of *their, they're,* and *there* in a cartoon

Options for Organizing and Differentiating Instruction
See pages T11 and T12.

Scaffolding for English Language Learners
Locate Norway, Sweden, Finland, and Denmark on a world map. Explain that this region is known as Scandinavia. Then point to the lands of Scandinavia that lie to the north of the Arctic Circle. Tell students that a people known as the Lapps, or Sami, have lived in this region for a very long time.

Read aloud **Part 1**. Discuss the terms which may be unfamiliar, such as *reindeer, flourish, abundant, lichen, seafarers,* and *parliament.* Ask volunteers to read each sentence aloud, tell which word correctly completes that sentence, and explain why. Point out that if the words *they are* make sense, then the contraction *they're* belongs in that sentence.

Have students work with English-proficient partners to complete **Part 2**. Suggest that they read each sentence aloud before they write.

Have student pairs take turns reading aloud the speech bubbles from the cartoon before they correct the written mistakes in **Part 3**.

Speaking and Listening
Invite students to talk about an annual celebration they participate in with their family and friends. Encourage students to use the words *their, they're,* and *there* as they speak. Call on listeners to tell which spelling of the homophone should be used in each case.

Reinforcement and Reteaching
Review **Read and Discover** and the rule statement, refer students to the **G.U.M. Handbook,** or use the **Extra Practice** activity on page 271.

Objectives
- To discover that *its* and *it's* sound the same but have different spellings and meanings
- To learn that *its* is a possessive pronoun and *it's* is a contraction of the words *it* and *is* or *it* and *has*
- To select the correct use of *its* or *it's* in sentences
- To complete sentences using *its* or *it's*
- To add missing apostrophes to literary excerpts

Options for Organizing and Differentiating Instruction
See pages T11 and T12.

Scaffolding for English Language Learners
Ask students to share what they know about Russia. Have a volunteer point out this nation on a world map. Explain to students that the art, music, architecture, literature, plays, and dances created by a nation are part of its culture. Tell students that Russians have created some of the world's greatest works of art, music, literature, and dance in recent centuries.

Read aloud the passage in **Part 1** and clarify unfamiliar words such as *czar, architects, classical music, ballet, choreographers,* and *ballet companies.* Help students with the first sentence by rereading it aloud and asking whether the possessive pronoun *its* or the words *it is* make sense in the sentence. (it's) Follow a similar procedure with the remaining sentences before having students circle their answers. Remind them that if the words *it is* make sense in a sentence then they should circle the contraction *it's.*

Have students work with English-proficient partners to complete **Part 2**. Partners should discuss their answers before they write them.

Read aloud the passages for **Part 3**. Help students understand the meaning and humor in each passage. Then have students work with an English-proficient partner to add apostrophes in each contraction.

Speaking and Listening
Tell students that many people have difficulty remembering when to write *it's* and when to write *its.* Challenge partners to devise a clever way to help people remember which of these words is spelled with an apostrophe. Have them present their method to the class. After all the ideas have been presented, have students vote for the one they think would be most effective.

Reinforcement and Reteaching
Review **Read and Discover** and the rule statement, refer students to the **G.U.M. Handbook,** or use the **Extra Practice** activity on page 272.

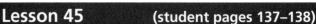

Lesson 44 (student pages 135–136)
Who's and Whose

Lesson 45 (student pages 137–138)
To, Too, Two

Objectives

- To discover that *who's* and *whose* sound the same but have different spellings and meanings
- To learn that *who's* is a contraction of *who is* or *who has* and that *whose* shows ownership or possession
- To select the correct use of *whose* and *who's* in sentences
- To compose questions using *who's* and *whose*

Options for Organizing and Differentiating Instruction
See pages T11 and T12.

Scaffolding for English Language Learners

Point out Tanzania and the region of East Africa on a world map. Explain that much of this region is covered with grassland. Explain to students that for the past few centuries people known as the Maasai have herded cattle in this region, moving from place to place when new grazing grounds are needed. Tell students that they will learn more about the Maasai in this lesson.

Read aloud the sentences for **Part 1**. Explain that community-run cultural programs are programs for visitors that are organized by people of a particular culture. Visitors get to see how local people really live today, and local people benefit from the fees that visitors pay. Have volunteers summarize the information. Then reread the first sentence aloud and ask students which word makes sense in the sentence. Remind students that if the words *who is* or *who has* make sense, then they should use the contraction *who's*.

Read aloud the first answer in **Part 2** and model composing a question, using item 13 as an example. (*Who's downloading photos of Maasai villagers?*) Have students complete the remaining items in pairs.

For **Part 3,** make sure students have access to the Internet or to geographic magazines. Have students work in pairs to choose a culture to focus on, find pictures, and write questions. Then have pairs trade pictures and questions and write answers on another sheet of paper.

Speaking and Listening

Distribute index cards to students and have them write down a question with *who's* or *whose*. Then shuffle the cards and give one to each student. Call on volunteers to read aloud the question on the card, tell if *who's* or *whose* is spelled correctly and why, and then answer the question.

Reinforcement and Reteaching

Review **Read and Discover** and the rule statement, refer students to the **G.U.M. Handbook**, or use the **Extra Practice** activity on page 272.

Objectives

- To discover that *to, too,* and *two* sound the same but have different spellings and meanings
- To learn that *to* can be a preposition that means "in the direction of" and can also be used with a verb to form an infinitive
- To learn that *too* is an adverb and means "also" or "excessively"
- To learn that *two* names a number
- To distinguish among *to, too,* and *two* in sentences
- To choose *to, too,* or *two* to complete sentences
- To write original riddles based on homophones

Options for Organizing and Differentiating Instruction
See pages T11 and T12.

Scaffolding for English Language Learners

Have students locate Brazil on a world map and share what they know about this country and its culture. If necessary, explain that Brazil is famous throughout the world for, among other things, its great soccer teams, colorful parades, and its unique music.

Read aloud the sentences for **Part 1**. Clarify unfamiliar terms such as *indigenous, panpipes, tambourine, accordion, bossa nova* (a style of music and a dance), and *colorfully clad*. Then ask volunteers to read aloud each sentence, identify the word in parentheses that correctly completes that sentence, and explain the reason for their choice.

For **Part 2,** have students work in pairs to fill in the blanks. Invite volunteers to read aloud their completed sentences, spelling the word they have written in each blank. Pairs of students might enjoy reading the completed sentences as dialogue.

Have volunteers read aloud the sample riddles in **Part 3**. Clarify the meanings of the homophones *course/coarse* and *scent/cent/sent*. You may wish to work with students to write three group riddles.

Speaking and Listening

Write the words *to, too,* and *two* on index cards and place the cards in a hat or bowl. Have students take turns drawing a card and using that word in a sentence. Listeners should tell how the word should be spelled and why. Cards should be returned to the hat after each turn.

Reinforcement and Reteaching

Review **Read and Discover** and the rule statement, refer students to the **G.U.M. Handbook**, or use the **Extra Practice** activity on page 273.

Objectives
- To discover that *than* and *then* sound similar but are different words with different spellings and meanings
- To learn that *than* is a subordinating conjunction that is used to make comparisons and *then* can be an adverb that tells about time and can also mean "therefore"
- To choose *than* or *then* to complete sentences
- To write sentences using *than* or *then*
- To replace incorrectly used words with correct, similar-sounding words

Options for Organizing and Differentiating Instruction

See pages T11 and T12.

Scaffolding for English Language Learners

Point out Scotland on a world map. Discuss with students distinctive elements of Scottish culture, including kilts, plaid patterns, and bagpipes.

Read aloud the sentences for **Part 1**. If necessary, explain to students that the *shot put* is an event in track and field in which competitors attempt to throw a heavy iron ball as far as they can, using a pushing motion. For each sentence, ask students to pick the word they think belongs in the sentence and to explain why. To help students decide, have them think about whether a comparison is being made. If there is, the word *than* is correct in that sentence.

Students can work with partners to complete **Part 2**. Have them respond to each writing prompt orally before writing their responses.

For **Part 3**, read each sentence aloud and help students choose the word from the box that should replace the boldfaced word. Explain the difference in meaning between the two words if necessary.

Speaking and Listening

Have students work cooperatively to use the words *than* and *then* in sentences about a parade they have seen. Invite volunteers to say their sentences aloud. (**Example:** I thought the float with dragons was bigger *than* any float I had ever seen. *Then* I saw the float with dinosaurs!)

Reinforcement and Reteaching

Review **Read and Discover** and the rule statement, refer students to the **G.U.M. Handbook**, or use the **Extra Practice** activity on page 273.

Objectives
- To learn that a negative word means "no" or "not" and that double negatives should be avoided
- To learn that *doesn't* is used with a singular subject and that *don't* is used with a plural subject
- To discover that *I* and *you* are used with *don't*
- To identify the correct use of negatives in sentences
- To rewrite sentences, replacing double negatives with correct usage of negatives
- To answer questions using negatives correctly

Options for Organizing and Differentiating Instruction

See pages T11 and T12.

Scaffolding for English Language Learners

Ask students if they have heard of an Asian nation called Thailand; then ask if any of them have ever eaten Thai food. Show Thailand's location on a map. Then tell students that in this lesson they will learn about the cultural values of the Thai people.

Read aloud each sentence in **Part 1**, saying both answers in parentheses. Ask students to tell which word or words belong in the sentence and why.

Have students work with an English-proficient partner to read and correct the sentences in **Part 2**. Ask them to discuss why each sentence is wrong and how to reword the sentence correctly. If your class includes Spanish speakers, explain that, unlike Spanish, double negatives are not used in English.

For **Part 3**, students can work with a partner to write a positive answer and a negative answer to each question.

Speaking and Listening

Have groups of students brainstorm lists of rules of behavior when visiting another country. Encourage groups to share their lists with the class. (Examples: *Never* wander away from the adults you are with. *Don't* get too rowdy!)

Reinforcement and Reteaching

Review **Read and Discover** and the rule statement, refer students to the **G.U.M. Handbook**, or use the **Extra Practice** activity on page 274.

Lesson 48 (student pages 143–144)
Words Often Misused: Go, Went, Like, All

Objectives

- To learn that *go* and *went* mean "move(d) from place to place," that *is like* means "resembles something," and that *all* means "the total of something"
- To discover that these words cannot be used to indicate that someone is speaking
- To cross out the incorrect use of these words in sentences
- To correctly rewrite sentences that use *go*, *went*, and *like* incorrectly
- To use a variety of descriptive verbs that can take the place of *said*

Options for Organizing and Differentiating Instruction

See pages T11 and T12.

Scaffolding for English Language Learners

Have volunteers read aloud **Part 1**. Point out the location of Hong Kong. Call on volunteers to summarize the narrative and the information about dragon boats. Then have volunteers identify the incorrect uses of *go*, *went*, *like*, and *all* in the sentences. Call on others to tell which verbs could be used instead.

Have students work with partners to complete **Part 2**. Suggest that pairs first read the sentences as written and then discuss how the sentences should be corrected before rewriting them.

Read aloud **Part 3**. Have students work with partners to write a different verb for each sentence. Then invite volunteers to read aloud their sentences, using the tone indicated by the verbs. Model the process if necessary. Discuss the different meanings of these verbs.

Speaking and Listening

Write *go, went, like,* and *all* on the board. Have students take turns selecting a word and using it in two oral sentences—one using the word correctly and one using it incorrectly. Have listeners identify the correct usage.

Reinforcement and Reteaching

Review **Read and Discover** and the rule statement, refer students to the **G.U.M. Handbook**, or use the **Extra Practice** activity on page 274.

Lesson 49 (student pages 145–146)
Lie and Lay, Set and Sit

Objectives

- To learn that *lie* and *lay* are different verbs that sound similar; *lay* takes a direct object, but *lie* does not
- To learn that *set* and *sit* are different verbs that sound similar; *set* takes a direct object, but *sit* does not
- To distinguish among *lie* and *lay* and *sit* and *set* in sentences
- To rewrite sentences using the correct form of *lie, lay, set,* or *sit*
- To correct the incorrect use of *lay* and *lie* in examples from published works

Options for Organizing and Differentiating Instruction

See pages T11 and T12.

Scaffolding for English Language Learners

Have a volunteer point out Japan on a world map. Ask students to share what they know about Japanese culture. Tell students that in this lesson they will learn about one of Japan's most distinctive ceremonies, the Tea Ceremony.

Read aloud the sentences in **Part 1**. Clarify the meaning of unfamiliar terms such as *etiquette* and *ladle*. Have a volunteer reread the first sentence, tell which word is correct, and explain why. Have students complete the remaining sentences in pairs. Suggest they refer to the rule statement at the top of the page if they need help.

For **Part 2**, have students circle the word or words they must replace in each sentence before writing the new sentence. Model revising the first sentence.

Students can work with English-proficient partners to complete **Part 3**.

Speaking and Listening

Ask students to compose oral sentences telling what they do during warm weather. Have them use one of the words *lie, lay, sit,* or *set* in each sentence. (Examples: Mom *sets* out a picnic lunch in our front yard. We *lie* in the sun and drink lemonade.)

Reinforcement and Reteaching

Review **Read and Discover** and the rule statement, refer students to the **G.U.M. Handbook**, or use the **Extra Practice** activity on page 275.

Objectives
- To learn that irregular verbs do not add *-ed* in the past tense
- To identify the correct past tense forms of irregular verbs in sentences
- To complete sentences using the correct form of the verb
- To complete a crossword puzzle using the past tense forms of irregular verbs

Options for Organizing and Differentiating Instruction
See pages T11 and T12.

Scaffolding for English Language Learners
Read each sentence in **Part 1** aloud twice, saying a different answer choice each time. Have students take turns picking the correct word and rereading the completed sentence aloud. Make sure students understand the meaning of *abundance, tortillas, tamales,* and *porridge.*

For **Part 2**, have students complete the sentences orally before writing the correct past tense form of the verb.

Students can work cooperatively to complete the puzzle in **Part 3.** They may wish to make a chart showing all the tenses of the verbs in the word bank before completing the activity. Invite them to substitute verbs orally before writing in their books.

Speaking and Listening
Invite students to discuss and compare different cultures' cuisines (dishes and styles of food) with which they are familiar. Encourage students to identify past forms of irregular verbs used correctly in the discussion.

Reinforcement and Reteaching
Review **Read and Discover** and the rule statement, refer students to the **G.U.M. Handbook,** or use the **Extra Practice** activity on page 275.

Objectives
- To learn that in sentence diagrams, adjectival prepositional phrases modify a noun and adverbial prepositional phrases can modify a verb
- To discover how to diagram indirect objects
- To learn how to diagram sentences with *There*

Diagraming Prepositions and Prepositional Phrases
Ask students what difference they see between the two diagrams at the top of the page. Elicit that in the first diagram, the adverbial prepositional phrase is connected to the verb *celebrate* and in the second, the adjectival prepositional phrase is connected to the noun *foods.* Have student pairs determine whether the prepositional phrase modifies the noun or the verb in each of the four sentences and then diagram the sentences.

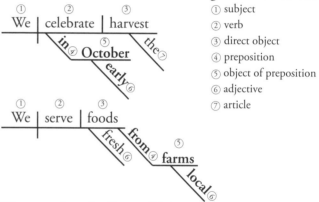

① subject
② verb
③ direct object
④ preposition
⑤ object of preposition
⑥ adjective
⑦ article

Diagraming Indirect Objects
Recall with students that in a sentence diagram, the direct object is placed on the horizontal line after the verb and is separated by a short vertical line. Ask students where the indirect object is placed in the example. (It is below the verb, connected by a slanted line.) Students can work independently or in pairs to diagram the sentences.

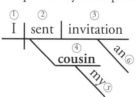

① subject
② verb
③ direct object
④ indirect object
⑤ possessive pronoun
⑥ article

Diagraming Sentences with *There*
Have students note where the word *There* appears when it begins a sentence. Then have them work in pairs to diagram the sentences in this section.

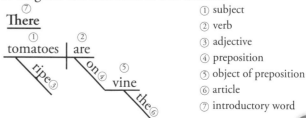

① subject
② verb
③ adjective
④ preposition
⑤ object of preposition
⑥ article
⑦ introductory word

Writing Sentences (student page 151)

Inform students that sentences 1 through 6 on page 151 need to be revised so they are correct. Have a volunteer read aloud the first sentence, tell what is wrong with it, and then tell how it should be corrected. (*Its* should be spelled *It's*) Then have students work independently or in pairs to correct the remaining sentences. Have students compare their revisions.

Read aloud the informative paragraph at the bottom of the page. Draw students' attention to the introductory sentence, the sentences that give more information, and the concluding sentence. Call on volunteers to name the topic of the paragraph. (winter traditions in different cultures)

Writing a Paragraph (student page 152)

Have students look back at their revised sentences on page 151. Explain that the sentences are out of order, but when ordered correctly they can form a complete paragraph of information. Ask a volunteer to name the introductory sentence. (item 1) Call on others to name the supporting sentences in order (items 6, 2, 4, and 3) and the concluding sentence (item 5). Tell students that they can use verb tenses as clues to the order of the sentences.

Have students read the directions to the second activity and then write about a festival featured in Unit 5 or another celebration of their choice. Remind them to use the correct homophones and the correct forms of irregular verbs in their writing. Remind them to check their work using the checklist at the bottom of the page. Invite volunteers to read their completed paragraphs aloud.

Proofreading (student pages 153–154)

Scaffolding for English Language Learners

Have students work with a partner who is fluent in English for the proofreading activities.

Proofreading Practice

Ask students to identify the topic of the report on page 153. (Mongolia) Explain that the report contains several mistakes and that as they read, they should look for these mistakes.

Review the **Proofreading Marks** chart and the examples. Remind students that these marks are used by professional writers to check their work before publication. Read the first sentence aloud. Discuss the errors (*lays* should be *lies*; *china* should be *China*) and how each error should be marked for correction. You may wish to have students correct the spelling errors.

After they have completed the proofreading activity, ask volunteers to read each sentence aloud and to identify errors. Ask students to mark overlooked errors in another color. **Note:** Some errors can be corrected in more than one way.

Proofreading Checklist

Ask students to select a recent piece of their own writing and to write its title at the top of the chart. Ask students to put a check mark next to each item in the checklist after they have checked it in their work. Students might first work independently and then trade papers with a partner to double-check each other's work. You might model, or ask a student to model, using the **G.U.M. Handbook** (beginning on student page 303) to clarify a concept or rule.

Also Remember...

Remind students that correct capitalization and punctuation are important for clear writing. If necessary, help students use the **G.U.M. Handbook** to clarify when commas should be used and to review the use of capital letters.

Your Own List

Suggest that students look at the errors they did not find in the proofreading activity and add them to the checklist. Ask students to think about other kinds of errors they make and to add these to the checklist.

Ask students to place this page in their writing portfolios. These pages may be used to assess students' progress over the course of the year.

Assessment Options

See page T11 for ways to use *G.U.M.* assessments to differentiate instruction.

Unit Review

The **Unit Review** (pp. 155–156) allows you to check students' progress and determine when reteaching is necessary. The review pages may be completed in class or as homework. If a student responds incorrectly to two or more items involving the same skill, you may want to work directly with the student to review the relevant lesson. The lesson number to which each review item relates appears in parentheses on the review pages in the Teacher Edition.

Assign the **Extra Practice** activities (pp. 271–275) to reteach targeted skills in a more focused way.

Unit Assessment

The **Unit Assessment** (pp. 237–240) is intended to (1) familiarize students with standardized testing procedures, (2) check students' ability to apply key unit concepts in a different format, and (3) serve as an indicator of student progress.

- When used as a **pretest,** the Unit Assessment helps you determine, prior to instruction, your students' strengths, weaknesses, knowledge, and skills.
- When used as a **posttest,** the Unit Assessment provides feedback that you can use to guide further instruction.

Follow this procedure for administering the Unit Assessment.

1. Read aloud the Test Tip and the test instructions. (**Note:** For additional scaffolding, you may wish to read the test questions and answer choices aloud.)
2. Tell students that they will have 20 minutes to read and answer the questions independently.
3. When time is up, collect and correct the tests. Use the results to measure student progress and guide reteaching.

Assign the **Extra Practice** activities (pp. 271–275) to reteach targeted skills in a more focused way.

Note: The **Unit Review** may be reused after reteaching to check students' understanding of the lesson concepts.

Unit Test

The **Unit Test** (pp. 295–296) helps you judge students' achievement while providing them with valuable practice for high-stakes tests. When you are ready to administer the test, ask students to carefully tear it out of their books. (**Note:** If the test has already been removed, distribute it to students.) Read aloud the directions for each section and make sure students understand how to answer the questions. Ask students to work independently to complete the test.

Students who miss two questions focusing on the same grammar element may need additional help understanding the concept. Reteach the concept, following this procedure:

1. Review **Read and Discover**.
2. Review the rule statement for the concept.
3. Guide students through items a second time. Ask the students to explain why each correct answer belongs in each sentence.
4. Refer students to the **G.U.M. Handbook** for further reinforcement.

Community Connection (student pages 157–158)

These two pages provide interesting and fun activities that reinforce the skills and concepts students learned in Lessons 41 to 50. These activities give students the opportunity to extend what they have read about in the unit by finding out more about festivals and celebrations in your community. You might utilize the **Community Connection** pages in one of the following ways:

- Ask students to take the pages home, select one activity to do, and then share the results of that activity with the class.
- Have pairs of students select one activity to complete together.
- Review the activities as a class, and then assign the activities to small groups of students to complete cooperatively. Set aside a time for groups to share the results.

When you are ready to have students select activities, direct them to pages 157–158. Explain that the activities on page 157 will give them an opportunity to find out more about celebrations in your community. Explain that one activity gives them an opportunity to learn how to plan a cultural celebration. Point out that page 158 is a planning guide that will help them take notes as they conduct their research. Then ask students to carefully tear the pages out of the book, and explain how you wish students to use them.

Timeless Tales

Unit 6 Grammar

Pretest Option

You may use the **Unit Assessment** as a pretest. See pages T10 and T11.

Building Grammar Awareness

Write the following sentence on the board:
Me and Sarah thinks Mom has the more beautiful voice in the world.

Read the sentence aloud and ask students if it sounds correct. (no) Invite volunteers to tell what is wrong with it. (The subject pronoun *I* should be used instead of *me* and it should come after *Sarah;* the verb *thinks* should be *think,* to agree with the plural subject; *most* should be used instead of *more* because the sentence compares more than two things.) Tell students that in Unit 6 they will learn how to use pronouns correctly, to make verbs agree with their subjects, and how to use helping verbs correctly. Remind them that using words and word forms correctly will help others understand them when they speak and write.

Introducing "Timeless Tales"
Folktale Characters

Inform students that the title of Unit 6 is "Timeless Tales" and that each lesson tells about a folktale or a folktale character from a different part of the world. Invite students to name their favorite folktale or folktale character. You may wish to make a chart on the board noting students' responses.

Folktale	Folktale Character

Lesson 51   (student pages 159–160)
Subject Pronouns and Object Pronouns

Objectives

- To learn that subject pronouns (*I, he, she, we, they*) can take the place of a subject in a sentence
- To learn that object pronouns (*me, him, her, us, them*) can be used after an action verb or a preposition
- To learn that the pronouns *it* and *you* can be either subject or object pronouns
- To identify subject and object pronouns in sentences and to rewrite sentences using subject or object pronouns
- To replace archaic pronouns with modern pronouns in a literary passage

Options for Organizing and Differentiating Instruction

See pages T11 and T12.

Scaffolding for English Language Learners

Read aloud the caption on page 159, and have students point out the location of Ghana on a world map. Explain the meaning of *trickster tales* and encourage students to share any trickster tales they know.

Read **Part 1** aloud. Clarify the meaning of *swindle*. Call on a volunteer to reread the first sentence, name the correct pronoun (me), and tell whether it is a subject or an object pronoun and why. (It is an object pronoun; it follows the action verb *tell.*) Have students complete the remaining sentences in pairs.

Have students work cooperatively to complete **Part 2**. Model using item 15 as an example.

Read aloud the dialogue in **Part 3**. You may wish to briefly explain the background of the play to help students understand the context of this passage. Clarify the passage's language and then help students identify the archaic pronouns and suggest replacements.

Speaking and Listening

Have students take turns describing a joke they played on someone or someone played on them. Encourage them to use subject pronouns and object pronouns as they speak. (Example: *I* tried to play a trick on my little brother but *he* ended up tricking *me* instead!)

Reinforcement and Reteaching

Review **Read and Discover** and the rule statement, refer students to the **G.U.M. Handbook**, or use the **Extra Practice** activity on page 276.

Objectives

- To learn that a subject pronoun should be used in a compound subject
- To learn that an object pronoun should be used in a compound direct or indirect object or in a compound object of a preposition
- To choose appropriate subject or object pronouns to complete sentences
- To rewrite sentences using subject or object pronouns
- To learn that *I* and *me* always come last in a pair with a noun or another pronoun

Options for Organizing and Differentiating Instruction

See pages T11 and T12.

Scaffolding for English Language Learners

Read aloud **Part 1**. Ask students to identify which pronoun choice in parentheses is correct in each sentence. To help students determine the correct pronoun, suggest that they say the sentence without the name of the other person. (Example: item 4: Take away *and Bobby* and read the sentence as "*Her* explained that enslaved African Americans developed the Brer Rabbit stories." and then try "*She* explained that enslaved African Americans developed the Brer Rabbit stories.")

Have pairs of students complete **Part 2**. Suggest that they make a list of several subject and object pronouns and then work together to determine which pronoun should replace each boldfaced noun.

Partners can continue to work together to complete **Part 3**.

Speaking and Listening

Have students compose oral sentences about a time they worked with a friend or sibling to do something together, such as working on household or classroom chores or completing a class project. (Example: Ms. March asked Henry and *me* to work together. *He* wrote the story and *I* drew the pictures.) Listeners can identify the pronouns being used and tell whether they are subject or object pronouns.

Reinforcement and Reteaching

Review **Read and Discover** and the rule statement, refer students to the **G.U.M. Handbook**, or use the **Extra Practice** activity on page 276.

Objectives

- To discover that an antecedent is the word or phrase that a pronoun refers to and that pronouns and antecedents must agree in number and gender
- To identify pronoun antecedents in sentences
- To complete sentences using appropriate pronouns
- To rewrite a passage using nouns to replace pronouns that have no antecedents

Options for Organizing and Differentiating Instruction

See pages T11 and T12.

Scaffolding for English Language Learners

Ask students if they are familiar with the stories "Aladdin," "Sinbad the Sailor," and "Ali Baba and the Forty Thieves." Tell them that in Lesson 53 they will learn where these stories came from.

Read the sentences in **Part 1** aloud. Call on a volunteer to identify the word or group of words the boldfaced pronoun in each sentence refers to. Students can verify their responses by replacing the pronoun with its antecedent and rereading the sentence. Model using item 3. (The first story tells of a cruel king. The *king* does not trust women.)

For **Part 2**, read aloud the first item. Help students decide which pronoun belongs in the blank. (the object pronoun *them*) Have students complete the remaining sentences with partners.

For **Part 3**, write Ali Baba, Scheherazade, the king, the thieves, the treasure cave, the treasure, and "Ali Baba and the Forty Thieves" on the board. Then work with students to choose the correct nouns that take the place of the pronouns without antecedents in the paragraph.

Speaking and Listening

Write several nouns on the board, such as teacher, students, pencil, book, desk, and chalkboard. Have students work in pairs to compose two oral sentences telling about something that happens in class every day. The first sentence should use nouns, and the second should replace the nouns with pronouns. (Example: *The teacher* read *the story* aloud to *the students*. *She* read *it* aloud to *them*.)

Reinforcement and Reteaching

Review **Read and Discover** and the rule statement, refer students to the **G.U.M. Handbook**, or use the **Extra Practice** activity on page 277.

Objectives

- To use *who* as the subject of a sentence or clause
- To use *whom* as the object of a verb or preposition
- To choose *who* or *whom* in sentences
- To write questions with *who* and *whom*
- To choose *who* or *whom* to complete famous quotations and then write an original saying

Options for Organizing and Differentiating Instruction

See pages T11 and T12.

Scaffolding for English Language Learners

Read aloud the caption on page 165 and invite volunteers to share anything they might know about John Henry.

Read aloud **Part 1**. Clarify the meanings of unfamiliar words such as *legendary, sledgehammers,* and *dynamite.* Then call on volunteers to reread each sentence and tell whether *who* or *whom* belongs in each sentence. Remind students that *whom* follows a preposition, such as *with* (item 5) and *to* (item 9). *Whom* is also needed when the word is a direct object (item 2: *whom* a railroad company had hired; item 14: *whom* they buried).

Have students work in pairs to complete **Part 2**. Model using item 16 as an example.

Read aloud the quotations in **Part 3**. Explain the meaning of each quotation, and then help students identify whether *who* or *whom* is correct in each one. Have students work with an English-proficient partner or an aide to discuss and then write their saying. Invite volunteers to read aloud their sayings.

Speaking and Listening

Invite students to take part in a guessing game. Have volunteers give clues, in the form of questions using *Who* and *Whom,* about a story character the class has read about together. The rest of the class should try to guess the name of the character. (Example: *Who* tried to trick Brer Rabbit? To *whom* did Scheherazade tell stories for a thousand and one nights?)

Reinforcement and Reteaching

Review **Read and Discover** and the rule statement, refer students to the **G.U.M. Handbook**, or use the **Extra Practice** activity on page 277.

Objectives

- To learn that the subject and the verb in a sentence must agree
- To learn how to make present tense verbs agree with singular and plural subjects
- To choose the verb form that agrees with the subject in sentences
- To complete sentences using the correct present tense form of verbs
- To identify the correct verb form in three sayings

Options for Organizing and Differentiating Instruction

See pages T11 and T12.

Scaffolding for English Language Learners

Point to the picture and read aloud the caption on page 167. Ask students who are familiar with the figure of a golem to share what they know about it.

Read aloud **Part 1**. Clarify the meaning of *persecuted, rabbi,* and *false accusations.* Call on volunteers first to identify the simple subject in each sentence and then to determine whether it is singular or plural. To decide which verb form belongs in the sentences, model reading item 1 without the intervening words between the simple subject and the verb answer choices. (Stories… *is/are* still told and read today.) Have student pairs complete the remaining sentences.

Students can work cooperatively with an English-proficient partner to complete **Part 2**.

Read aloud **Part 3**. Help students identify the correct verb form in each aphorism. Help students understand the meaning of each aphorism, and ask them if they agree with the message.

Speaking and Listening

Have each student write the singular and plural forms of a noun from Lesson 55 on an index card. (person/people; story/stories; street/streets) Put the cards in a hat and have students take turns drawing an index card and using the nouns on it as the subjects of two oral sentences, making sure that each subject and verb agree.

Reinforcement and Reteaching

Review **Read and Discover** and the rule statement, refer students to the **G.U.M. Handbook**, or use the **Extra Practice** activity on page 278.

Lesson 56 (student pages 169–170)
Agreement with Compound Subjects

Objectives
- To learn that a compound subject and its verb must agree
- To understand that a compound subject is plural when it is joined by *and* and that the verb must agree with the last item in the subject if the compound subject is joined by *or* or *nor*
- To choose the verb form that agrees with the compound subject in sentences
- To complete sentences using the correct verb forms
- To complete sentence clues for a crossword puzzle, and then identify the correct verb in compound sentences

Options for Organizing and Differentiating Instruction
See pages T11 and T12.

Scaffolding for English Language Learners
Ask volunteers to describe stories they have read in which a dog, wolf, fox, or coyote is a main character. Point out the illustration on page 169, and explain that Coyote is a main character in the stories of many Native American groups.

For **Part 1**, ask students to identify the compound subject in each sentence and tell which word joins the different parts of the subject. Call on volunteers to identify the verb that completes each item.

Have students work with partners to complete **Part 2**.

Read aloud the clues for **Part 3**. Pair students with English-proficient partners to review the previous lessons and name the correct answer that completes each clue. If necessary, direct students to the topic index at the back of the book to review the names of folktale characters.

Speaking and Listening
Invite students to compare two or more characters from the lessons they have read so far or from other stories they have read. (Example: Neither Anansi *nor* the wicked wolf *is* very likable. Both John Henry *and* Scheherazade *show* great courage.) Call on listeners to tell whether the subject and verb agree in each sentence.

Reinforcement and Reteaching
Review **Read and Discover** and the rule statement, refer students to the **G.U.M. Handbook**, or use the **Extra Practice** activity on page 278.

Lesson 57 (student pages 171–172)
Making Subject and Verb Agree: Special Cases

Objectives
- To discover that there are special cases for the subject and verb agreement rule
- To learn that titles of books, movies, stories, or songs are always considered singular
- To learn that collective nouns are almost always considered singular
- To learn that most indefinite pronouns are considered singular
- To complete sentences by selecting the correct verb forms
- To match collective nouns with the groups of animals they name

Options for Organizing and Differentiating Instruction
See pages T11 and T12.

Scaffolding for English Language Learners
Briefly retell the familiar version of the story of Cinderella. Then inform students that many countries have their own version of this story. Have students read the caption and notice the illustration on page 171.

Read aloud **Part 1**. Help students identify the simple subject in each sentence and tell whether it is a title, a collective noun, or an indefinite pronoun. Then call on volunteers to tell which verb belongs in the sentence.

Have students work with partners to complete **Part 2**, following a similar procedure as in Part 1.

Help students match each collective noun to the group of animals it names in **Part 3**. Suggest that students consult a dictionary if necessary. Invite volunteers to read their sentences aloud.

Speaking and Listening
Have students compose oral sentences about one or more groups of animals listed in Part 3. Remind them to be sure that the verb agrees with the collective noun in each sentence they say. (Example: A swarm of bees lives in a tree near my house.) Ask students why they think each collective noun was coined for each group of animals.

Reinforcement and Reteaching
Review **Read and Discover** and the rule statement, refer students to the **G.U.M. Handbook**, or use the **Extra Practice** activity on page 279.

T61

Objectives

- To learn that a verbal phrase always refers to, or modifies, a noun or pronoun in the main part of a sentence
- To learn that a dangling modifier is a phrase that does not refer to any particular word
- To identify dangling modifiers in sentences
- To revise sentences containing dangling modifiers
- To find examples in literature of long introductory verbal phrases

Options for Organizing and Differentiating Instruction

See pages T11 and T12.

Scaffolding for English Language Learners

Invite students who are familiar with Juan Bobo stories to share what they know about them.

Read aloud **Part 1**. Clarify the unfamiliar phrase *even easy tasks spell disaster.* Tell students that when they want to correct a dangling modifier, they should first ask themselves if the question *Who?* or *What?* is answered by the verbal phrase. Model item 2 by asking: *Who* needs his help? (Mama) Help students complete the remaining sentences in the same way.

Pair students with English-proficient partners to read **Part 2**. Model using item 17. (Warning him to be polite, Mama takes Juan Bobo to Señora Soto's house for lunch.) Have pairs rewrite the sentences cooperatively. Invite students to read their revised sentences to the class.

Read aloud **Part 3**. Tell students that the line *Like Birnam Wood to Dunsinane* refers to the play *Macbeth,* by William Shakespeare, in which three witches predict that King Macbeth will be defeated only after Birnam Wood comes to Dunsinane Hill, where Macbeth lives. Explain the meaning of the passage to students and then help them find long introductory verbal phrases in books they are reading.

Speaking and Listening

Invite students to talk about something humorous they have seen or experienced. Ask them to use at least one verbal phrase as they speak. (Example: Running for the school bus, I realized I still had my slippers on!)

Reinforcement and Reteaching

Review **Read and Discover** and the rule statement, refer students to the **G.U.M. Handbook,** or use the **Extra Practice** activity on page 279.

Objectives

- To learn that comparative forms of adjectives or adverbs compare two people, places, things, or actions and that the superlative forms compare three or more
- To learn how to create the comparative and superlative forms of adjectives and adverbs
- To discover that the words *better* and *less* compare two things and that *best* and *least* compare three or more things
- To identify the correct use of comparative adjectives and adverbs in sentences
- To complete sentences using the correct form of adjectives or adverbs
- To learn that some adjectives are absolute
- To write sentences using absolute adjectives

Options for Organizing and Differentiating Instruction

See pages T11 and T12.

Scaffolding for English Language Learners

Read **Part 1** aloud. Clarify unfamiliar words such as *lumberjack* and *frontier,* and then locate North Dakota, South Dakota, and the Great Lakes on a map of the United States. Ask students to identify how many people or things are being compared in each sentence. Have students complete the section in pairs.

For **Part 2**, help students identify what is being compared in each sentence. Help them determine whether they can create the comparative form by adding *-er* or *-est* or the words *more* or *most.* Ask students which word changes completely in its superlative form (item 20: *good* becomes *best*).

Have students work on **Part 3** with English-proficient partners.

Speaking and Listening

Have students orally compare their favorite folktale with their least favorite folktale. Remind them to use comparative adjectives and adverbs correctly as they make their comparisons. (Example: I like Beauty from "Beauty and the Beast" *best* because she is *braver* than the other characters. The two stepsisters in "Cinderella" are the *meanest* characters I have ever read about.)

Reinforcement and Reteaching

Review **Read and Discover** and the rule statement, refer students to the **G.U.M. Handbook,** or use the **Extra Practice** activity on page 280.

Objectives

- To learn that an auxiliary verb, or helping verb, works with a main verb
- To learn that auxiliary verbs such as *could* and *may* show how likely it is that something will happen and that others such as *did, is,* and *will* indicate the tense of the main verb
- To identify the correct forms of auxiliary verbs in sentences and to complete sentences using these forms
- To find auxiliary verbs in a word search puzzle and to write sentences using helping verbs

Options for Organizing and Differentiating Instruction

See pages T11 and T12.

Scaffolding for English Language Learners

Point out the picture and read the caption on page 177. Ask students if they have ever heard of Mother Goose. Explain that the name *Mother Goose* appears on the cover of many collections of nursery rhymes.

Read aloud **Part 1**. Clarify the meanings of unfamiliar words and phrases such as *scholars, colonial Boston,* and *fictitious.* For each sentence, have a volunteer identify the auxiliary verb orally before students underline it. Have students also identify the main verb in each sentence.

Help students complete **Part 2** by writing the auxiliary verbs from the rule box and the word *was* on the board. Have volunteers choose an auxiliary verb from the board to complete the first item. Have pairs complete the remaining items.

To help students complete **Part 3,** add *have* and *does* to the list of auxiliary verbs you wrote on the board for Part 2. Help students find the eight auxiliary verbs in the puzzle. Then work with students to write original sentences.

Speaking and Listening

Invite students to talk about some of their plans for the next holiday or school vacation. Ask them to use auxiliary verbs as they speak. (Example: I *would* like to learn how to swim this summer. I *will* be visiting the Grand Canyon during spring break.)

Reinforcement and Reteaching

Review **Read and Discover** and the rule statement, refer students to the **G.U.M. Handbook,** or use the **Extra Practice** activity on page 280.

Objectives

- To learn how to diagram sentences containing subject and object pronouns
- To learn how to diagram sentences containing adjective clauses and adverb clauses

Diagraming Subject and Object Pronouns

Have students read the explanation and sample sentences in the first section. Point out that the two diagrams are similar because the pronouns in the second diagram are put in the same place as the nouns they replaced from the first diagram.

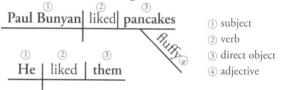

① subject
② verb
③ direct object
④ adjective

As students diagram items 1–3, remind them to think about what noun each pronoun replaces.

Diagraming Adjective Clauses

Draw students' attention to the first sentence diagram and help them notice that the adjective clause is connected to the subject. Point out that in the second sentence diagram, the relative pronoun *that* is the subject of the adjective clause.

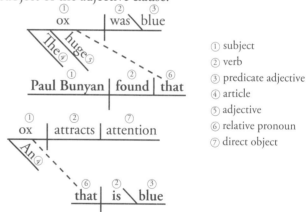

① subject
② verb
③ predicate adjective
④ article
⑤ adjective
⑥ relative pronoun
⑦ direct object

Help students answer the question. (c) Then help them diagram items 5 and 6. If necessary, help them understand that in the first sentence, the relative pronoun is the subject of the adjective clause and in the second sentence it is the direct object of the verb *possessed.*

Diagraming Adverb Clauses

Have students look at how a sentence with an adverb clause is diagramed. Explain that although the dependent clause comes before the independent clause in the sentence, it goes below the independent clause in the sentence diagram. Help students answer the question. (b)

Continued on page T64

Continued from page T63

As partners diagram the two sentences, remind them to think about how each subordinating conjunction connects the verb in the independent clause to the word it modifies in the dependent clause.

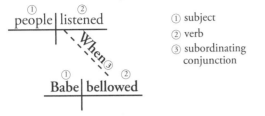

① subject
② verb
③ subordinating conjunction

Writing Sentences   (student page 181)

Inform students that sentences 1 through 7 on page 181 need to be revised so that the subject and verb agree. Have a volunteer read the first sentence aloud, tell what is wrong with it, and show how it should be corrected. Then have students work independently or in pairs to correct the remaining sentences. Have students compare their revisions.

Writing a Paragraph   (student page 182)

Read aloud the paragraphs on page 181. Draw students' attention to each paragraph's topic sentence and to the sentences that give supporting details. Call on volunteers to name the topic of each paragraph. (The first states that Sleeping Beauty and Beauty are similar in some ways. The second states that they are different in some ways.)

Have students look back at their revised sentences on page 181. Explain that the sentences are out of order but when ordered correctly they form a complete paragraph. Ask a volunteer to name the topic sentence. (item 2) Call on others to name in order the sentences that give supporting details. (items 5, 4, 1, 7, 6, and 3)

Have students read the directions to the second activity and then write two paragraphs comparing and contrasting two folktale characters. Remind them that as they write they should be sure that the verbs always agree with their subjects. Remind them to check their work using the checklist at the bottom of the page.

Proofreading   (student pages 183–184)

Scaffolding for English Language Learners

Have students work with a partner who is fluent in English for the proofreading activities.

Proofreading Practice

Ask students to identify the topic of the report on page 183. (Hans Christian Andersen) Explain that the report contains several mistakes and that as they read, they should look for these mistakes.

Review the **Proofreading Marks** chart and the examples. Remind students that these marks are used by professional writers to check their work before publication. Read the first sentence aloud. Discuss the errors (*invention* is spelled incorrectly, the first period should be a comma, *Folklore* should be lowercase, and *were* should be *was*) and how they should be marked for correction. You may wish to have students correct the spelling errors.

After they have completed the proofreading activity, ask volunteers to read each sentence aloud and to identify errors. Ask students to mark overlooked errors in another color. **Note:** Some errors can be corrected in more than one way.

Proofreading Checklist

Ask students to select a recent piece of their own writing and to write the title of that piece at the top of the chart. Ask students to put a check mark next to each item in the checklist after they have checked it in their work. Students might first work independently and then trade papers with a partner to double-check each other's work. You might model, or ask a student to model, using the **G.U.M. Handbook** (beginning on student page 303) to clarify a concept or rule.

Also Remember...

Remind students that capitalization and punctuation are important for clear writing. If necessary, help students use the **G.U.M. Handbook** to clarify when commas should be used and to review the use of capital letters.

Your Own List

Suggest that students look at the errors they did not find in the proofreading activity and add them to the checklist. Ask students to think about other kinds of errors they make and to add these to the checklist.

Ask students to place this page in their writing portfolios. These pages may be used to assess students' progress over the course of the year.

Assessment Options

See page T11 for ways to use *G.U.M.* assessments to differentiate instruction.

Unit Review

The **Unit Review** (pp. 185–186) allows you to check students' progress and determine when reteaching is necessary. The review pages may be completed in class or as homework. If a student responds incorrectly to two or more items involving the same skill, you may want to work directly with the student to review the relevant lesson. The lesson number to which each review item relates appears in parentheses on the review pages in the Teacher Edition.

Assign the **Extra Practice** activities (pp. 276–280) to reteach targeted skills in a more focused way.

Unit Assessment

The **Unit Assessment** (pp. 241–244) is intended to (1) familiarize students with standardized testing procedures, (2) check students' ability to apply key unit concepts in a different format, and (3) serve as an indicator of student progress.

- When used as a **pretest,** the Unit Assessment helps you determine, prior to instruction, your students' strengths, weaknesses, knowledge, and skills.
- When used as a **posttest,** the Unit Assessment provides feedback that you can use to guide further instruction.

Follow this procedure for administering the Unit Assessment.

1. Read aloud the Test Tip and the test instructions. (**Note:** For additional scaffolding, you may wish to read the test questions and answer choices aloud.)
2. Tell students that they will have 20 minutes to read and answer the questions independently.
3. When time is up, collect and correct the tests. Use the results to measure student progress and guide reteaching.

Assign the **Extra Practice** activities (pp. 276–280) to reteach targeted skills in a more focused way.

Note: The **Unit Review** may be reused after reteaching to check students' understanding of the lesson concepts.

Unit Test

The **Unit Test** (pp. 297–298) helps you judge students' achievement while providing them with valuable practice for high-stakes tests. When you are ready to administer the test, ask students to carefully tear it out of their books. (**Note:** If the test has already been removed, distribute it to students.) Read aloud the directions for each section and make sure students understand how to answer the questions. Ask students to work independently to complete the test.

Students who miss two questions focusing on the same grammar element may need additional help understanding the concept. Reteach the concept, following this procedure:

1. Review **Read and Discover**.
2. Review the rule statement for the concept.
3. Guide students through items a second time. Ask the students to explain why each correct answer belongs in each sentence.
4. Refer students to the **G.U.M. Handbook** for further reinforcement.

Community Connection (student pages 187–188)

These two pages provide interesting and fun activities that reinforce the skills and concepts students learned in Lessons 51 to 60. These activities give students the opportunity to extend what they have read about in the theme by finding out more about storytellers and storytelling in your community. You might utilize the **Community Connection** pages in one of the following ways:

- Ask students to take the pages home, select one activity to do, and then share the results of that activity with the class.
- Have pairs of students select one activity to complete together.
- Preview the activities as a class, and then assign the activities to small groups of students to complete cooperatively. Set aside a time for groups to share the results.

When you are ready to have students select activities, direct them to pages 187–188. Explain that the activities on page 187 will give them an opportunity to find out more about storytelling opportunities in your community. Explain that one activity gives them an opportunity to learn how to plan a storytelling festival. Point out that page 188 is a planning guide that will help them take notes as they conduct their research. Then ask students to carefully tear the pages out of the book, and explain how you wish students to use them.

Great **Getaways**

Unit 7 Mechanics

Pretest Option

You may use the **Unit Assessment** as a pretest. See pages T10 and T11.

Building Mechanics Awareness

Write this sentence on the board and read it aloud:
I'd love to visit india china and kenya when im older said David.

Then write the sentence with the correct punctuation and capitalization, and ask a volunteer to read it aloud again. ("I'd love to visit India, China, and Kenya when I'm older," said David.)

Ask students which sentence is easier to read and why. (the second one, because it has the proper punctuation) Call on volunteers to name the different kinds of punctuation they see. (quotation marks, commas, apostrophes)

Inform students that in Unit 7 they will learn how to use these and other punctuation marks. Explain that they will also learn some rules for capitalizing words, as well as how to write initials, abbreviations, titles, quotations, letters, and e-mails correctly. Point out to students that using correct punctuation and capitalization in sentences helps others understand what they write.

Introducing "Great Getaways"

Islands and Near-Islands

Inform students that the title of Unit 7 is "Great Getaways" and the lessons are about different islands and peninsulas. Invite students to name some of the islands they know and to tell their location. Create a four-column list on the board and label the columns *Northern Hemisphere, Southern Hemisphere, Eastern Hemisphere,* and *Western Hemisphere.* As students name the islands they are familiar with, write them in the appropriate columns. (You may wish to use a globe and locate the islands to help students identify each hemisphere.)

Lesson 61 (student pages 189–190)
Capitalization

Objectives

- To learn that a proper noun names a specific person, place, thing, or idea and that important words in proper nouns are capitalized
- To learn that proper adjectives are descriptive words formed from proper nouns and that they are capitalized
- To learn that titles of respect, such as *Mr.* or *Judge,* are used before a person's name and are capitalized
- To correct capitalization errors in sentences and to identify proper nouns and adjectives
- To add capitalization and punctuation to a passage written in lowercase letters

Options for Organizing and Differentiating Instruction

See pages T11 and T12.

Scaffolding for English Language Learners

Locate the Caribbean Sea and its island countries on a world map. Ask students what they know about this region. If some students from your class have lived in this area, invite them to talk about what it is like.

Read aloud **Part 1.** Clarify the meaning of *perished, waged against,* and *forced into labor.* Have students work in pairs to identify the words that should be capitalized. Remind them to look for words that begin a sentence and those that name specific people, countries, nationalities, or months.

Have students complete **Part 2** in pairs. Explain that in these paragraphs, *Carnival* is used as a proper noun because it names a certain celebration.

Read aloud **Part 3.** Explain the meaning of the passage and ask students if they agree with what archy says. Help them find and punctuate the two sentences in the passage. Remind them that the subject pronoun *I* should also be capitalized.

Speaking and Listening

Invite students to name some different cities, states, and countries they have visited and to describe some of the foods they sampled there. Ask listeners to identify proper nouns that should be capitalized.

Reinforcement and Reteaching

Review **Read and Discover** and the rule statement, refer students to the **G.U.M. Handbook,** or use the **Extra Practice** activity on page 281.

Objectives

- To learn that an abbreviation is a shortened form of a word
- To discover that titles of respect, addresses, the names of days and some months, and certain words in the names of businesses can be abbreviated in informal writing
- To learn that an initial can replace a person's name and the name of a place, and that an initial is written as a capital letter followed by a period
- To identify and correct abbreviations and initials in sentences
- To rewrite names using abbreviations and initials
- To complete a crossword puzzle

Options for Organizing and Differentiating Instruction

See pages T11 and T12.

Scaffolding for English Language Learners

Read aloud the caption on page 191 and, if possible, display some pictures of Hawaii. Ask students to share what they know about these islands' climate, landscape, vegetation, and people.

Read aloud **Part 1**. Explain the following abbreviations: *Inc./Incorporated; St./Street;* and *Mt./Mount* (mountain). Have students correct the errors in pairs.

Have the same partners complete **Part 2**. If necessary, tell them how to abbreviate some less familiar items such as *Mistress* (*Mrs.* or *Miss*), *March* (*Mar.*), and *Corporation* (*Corp*). Model completing the activity using item 21 as an example. (Dr. H.M. Kealoha)

Before students complete **Part 3,** point out that the answers to the puzzle can be found in Part 1. Have students complete the puzzle independently.

Speaking and Listening

Have students, in turn, tell the class their address (street, city, state) and the full name of a person they know, using a title of respect. Listeners should tell how each address and name could be abbreviated.

Reinforcement and Reteaching

Review **Read and Discover** and the rule statement, refer students to the **G.U.M. Handbook,** or use the **Extra Practice** activity on page 281.

Objectives

- To discover that titles of books, movies, magazines, and newspapers should be underlined and titles of songs, stories, and poems should be in quotation marks
- To learn that titles written with an underline should be written in italics in printed text
- To learn which words in a title should be capitalized
- To identify and add correct capitalization and punctuation to titles in sentences
- To rewrite titles of books and movies using correct capitalization and punctuation
- To write a convincing argument using correct capitalization and punctuation

Options for Organizing and Differentiating Instruction

See pages T11 and T12.

Scaffolding for English Language Learners

Refer students to the illustration on page 193, and read the caption aloud. Ask if any of the students have ever seen a nene, and encourage them to describe the bird.

Read aloud the sentences in **Part 1**. Have students correct the titles independently.

For **Part 2,** have volunteers read aloud the titles on the bookshelf. Then read the first question aloud and ask students which title best answers the question. (Hawaii's Tropical Splendor) Then have students work cooperatively to write the book title with correct capitalization and punctuation. Complete the remaining items the same way.

Have students work on **Part 3** with an English-proficient partner.

Speaking and Listening

Begin a discussion with students about books, stories, and poems they have read, songs they have heard, or movies they have seen. Then call on volunteers to name their favorite, tell whether it is a book, story, poem, song, or movie, and to write the title on the board. Have the class verify the capitalization and punctuation.

Reinforcement and Reteaching

Review **Read and Discover** and the rule statement, refer students to the **G.U.M. Handbook,** or use the **Extra Practice** activity on page 282.

Objectives

- To learn how to form singular and plural possessive nouns and contractions using apostrophes
- To identify possessive nouns and contractions in sentences
- To rewrite sentences using possessives or contractions
- To analyze how apostrophes are used in dialect

Options for Organizing and Differentiating Instruction

See pages T11 and T12.

Scaffolding for English Language Learners

Ask students to share what they know about Ellis Island.

Read aloud the sentences in **Part 1**. Clarify unfamiliar words and phrases, such as *dietary preferences, contracted diseases, quarters,* and *dormitories.* To help students choose the correct words, rephrase each sentence without the possessive noun or the contraction. (Examples: item 1, …Samuel Ellis was *the owner of the island;* item 4, …but pleasing that many *was not* easy.)

For **Part 2** have students work with English-proficient partners to rewrite the sentences using possessive pronouns or contractions. Model using item 16. Point out that phrases containing *of* should be rewritten as possessives.

Read aloud the background information and the directions in **Part 3**. Then tell students you are going to read a poem that is written exactly as it was spoken many years ago. Read the poem aloud slowly, pausing at words written in dialect to be sure students understand what is being said. Reread the poem if necessary. Then help students identify each word in which the spelling has been altered in any way, either by substituting an apostrophe for letters or by changing letters. Ask students to name the word the respelling stands for.

Speaking and Listening

Invite students to describe monuments they have seen, using possessives and contractions when possible. (Example: There's a statue of a horseman in the park. The rider's hat is made of copper.) Ask listeners to identify words that contain apostrophes.

Reinforcement and Reteaching

Review **Read and Discover** and the rule statement, refer students to the **G.U.M. Handbook,** or use the **Extra Practice** activity on page 282.

Objectives

- To discover that a series is a sequence of three or more words, phrases, or clauses and that commas separate items in a series
- To learn that a comma is used to separate some pairs of adjectives
- To learn that commas are used to set off an appositive
- To add missing commas in sentences
- To rewrite two or more sentences as one sentence using commas
- To examine the way commas in a series can be used to add drama and emphasis to writing by evaluating famous speeches

Options for Organizing and Differentiating Instruction

See pages T11 and T12.

Scaffolding for English Language Learners

Point to the picture and read aloud the caption on page 197. Ask students to share what they know about New York City and its famous attractions, such as the Empire State Building and the Statue of Liberty. As you read the sentences in "Read and Discover," tell students that the commas in item **a.** are used to set off the phrase *the legend goes,* which interrupts an otherwise complete sentence.

Read aloud **Part 1**. Clarify unfamiliar words and phrases such as *boroughs; ferries; commute; suave, cosmopolitan bandleader;* and *elusive dreams.* Then reread each sentence, pausing where a comma should be placed. Ask students whether the sentence lists a series of items, a pair of adjectives, or an appositive, and then to tell where the commas should be placed.

For each item in **Part 2,** have partners decide which words from the second or third sentence repeat information from the previous sentence and which tell more about the subject. Model using item 18. (New York's Greenwich Village is home to poets, artists, and dancers.)

Read aloud the speech excerpts in **Part 3,** emphasizing the pauses where the commas appear. Help students understand the meaning of each quotation. Then help them identify each series of phrases.

Speaking and Listening

Write several nouns on index cards and place them facedown. Invite each student to pick three cards and to compose oral sentences using the words on the cards in a series. Then have each student write his or her sentence on the board as the class verifies the use of the commas.

Reinforcement and Reteaching

Review **Read and Discover** and the rule statement, refer students to the **G.U.M. Handbook,** or use the **Extra Practice** activity on page 283.

Objectives

- To learn that a comma is used to separate introductory words, independent clauses, and nouns of direct address
- To add the missing commas to sentences and to identify why commas are needed
- To rewrite sentences adding introductory words, independent clauses, and nouns of direct address
- To learn that an interjection expresses strong or sudden feeling and to use interjections correctly as introductory words in sentences

Options for Organizing and Differentiating Instruction

See pages T11 and T12.

Scaffolding for English Language Learners

Locate Japan on a world map and invite students to share what they know about Japanese culture.

Read aloud each sentence in **Part 1,** pausing where a comma should be placed. Then call on volunteers to say where the comma should be added and to tell whether it comes after an introductory word or a noun of direct address or whether it separates independent clauses in a compound sentence.

Before students complete **Part 2,** ask them where each word or independent clause in parentheses should be placed. Have students say the revised sentence aloud before writing it and adding the comma.

Have students work with English-proficient partners to complete **Part 3.** Encourage students to read their completed sentences aloud, using appropriate inflection.

Speaking and Listening

Have students take turns asking another student a question that includes an introductory word. The second student should respond with a sentence that uses an introductory word or with a compound sentence. (Example: Student 1: Fred, what is your favorite movie? Student 2: Well, it would have to be Ratatouille. or I like Ratatouille, but I also like Willy Wonka and the Chocolate Factory.)

Reinforcement and Reteaching

Review **Read and Discover** and the rule statement, refer students to the **G.U.M. Handbook,** or use the **Extra Practice** activity on page 283.

Objectives

- To learn that a semicolon can be used instead of a comma and a conjunction to separate related independent clauses in a compound sentence
- To learn that a colon can be used to separate two independent clauses when the second clause explains the first
- To add semicolons or colons to separate clauses in sentences and to combine sentences using semicolons or colons
- To understand that the colon has many additional uses in writing and to use examples to identify those uses

Options for Organizing and Differentiating Instruction

See pages T11 and T12.

Scaffolding for English Language Learners

Locate the Galápagos Islands on a world map. Tell students that these islands are famous for their wildlife, especially the giant Galápagos tortoise.

Read aloud **Part 1.** Clarify unfamiliar words and phrases such as *barren, rough surf, predation,* and *captive-breeding station.* Be sure students understand that an independent clause is a complete sentence. Then help students identify where the colons or semicolons should be added.

Read aloud **Part 2** and help students match the sentences from each column. As you match each pair of sentences, ask volunteers to tell how they know the two sentences go together.

Read aloud each rule in **Part 3** as students work with partners to identify and call out the sentence that matches the rule. You might compose additional original sentences as a group activity.

Speaking and Listening

Have students look through literary works or textbooks and find other examples of sentences containing colons or semicolons. Ask students to share their findings and to explain why the semicolons or colons have been used.

Reinforcement and Reteaching

Review **Read and Discover** and the rule statement, refer students to the **G.U.M. Handbook,** or use the **Extra Practice** activity on page 284.

Lesson 68   (student pages 203–204)
Using Hyphens and Parentheses

Objectives
- To learn that hyphens have many uses: to separate syllables at the end of a line, to link some compound words, to link pairs or groups of words that act as adjectives, to link the parts of some numbers
- To learn that parentheses set off an explanation or example
- To identify correct and incorrect use of hyphens and parentheses in sentences
- To add hyphens or parentheses to sentences
- To match rules about dashes with their examples and to write examples for stated rules

Options for Organizing and Differentiating Instruction
See pages T11 and T12.

Scaffolding for English Language Learners
Help volunteers locate Gibraltar on a world map or on a map of Europe. Ask if they have heard of Gibraltar before. Some may recall the saying that refers to something steady or dependable as being "as solid as the rock of Gibraltar." Then explain that some very important fossils were discovered about 160 years ago in a cave on Gibraltar. Tell students that the fossils were bones of Neanderthals, humanlike creatures who existed from about 200,000 years ago until about 30,000 years ago.

Read the sentences in **Part 1** aloud. Clarify the meanings of *visually arresting, outcropping,* and *sieges.* Help students determine which sentences use parentheses or hyphens correctly and which use them incorrectly. Have them explain their reasons. Review the rule box, if necessary.

Read each sentence in **Part 2** aloud. Then help students add hyphens or parentheses where they belong.

For **Part 3,** read aloud the rules for using a dash. Then help students match each rule to its example. Have students work with an English-proficient partner to write a new example for each rule.

Speaking and Listening
Ask each student to find one example of parentheses, hyphens, or dashes in a book. Then have students present the examples they found and tell why that punctuation was used.

Reinforcement and Reteaching
Review **Read and Discover** and the rule statement, refer students to the **G.U.M. Handbook,** or use the **Extra Practice** activity on page 284.

Lesson 69   (student pages 205–206)
Direct and Indirect Quotations

Objectives
- To discover that a direct quotation is a speaker's exact words and that quotation marks are used at the beginning and the end of a direct quotation
- To learn that an indirect quotation is a retelling of a speaker's words and that quotation marks are not used when the words *that* or *whether* come before a speaker's words
- To identify direct and indirect quotations and to supply appropriate punctuation and capitalization
- To rewrite indirect quotations as direct quotations and direct quotations as indirect quotations
- To complete a crossword puzzle

Options for Organizing and Differentiating Instruction
See pages T11 and T12.

Scaffolding for English Language Learners
Point out the illustration on page 205, and have a volunteer read the caption aloud. Help students locate Australia on a world map, and tell them that it is a continent, an island, and a country. Ask students to share what they know about Australia.

Read aloud **Part 1.** If possible, display pictures of wallabies, wombats, and bandicoots. Clarify the meanings of *marsupial* and *mammal.* Have students work with partners to find sentences that have direct quotations and to add the missing punctuation. Suggest that they look for key words such as *said, asked,* and *replied.* Remind students that the word *that* or *whether* often comes before the speaker's words in an indirect quotation. Point out that item 16 is an example of an interrupted quotation.

Read aloud the sentences in **Part 2.** Clarify the meaning of *penal colony* and *Australian outback.* Help students complete items 17 and 18, and have partners complete the remaining items together.

For **Part 3,** have students work with an English-proficient partner to complete the puzzle.

Speaking and Listening
Invite students to retell a brief conversation they had with a friend. As each student tells what was said, ask the class to decide whether a direct or an indirect quotation was used. (Example: Joni asked, "What's wrong, Sarah?" I told her that I wasn't feeling well.)

Reinforcement and Reteaching
Review **Read and Discover** and the rule statement, refer students to the **G.U.M. Handbook,** or use the **Extra Practice** activity on page 285.

Objectives
- To learn that a friendly letter has a heading, a greeting, a body, a closing, and a signature
- To learn that a business letter has the same parts as a friendly letter but also includes the complete address of the recipient and substitutes a colon for a comma after the greeting
- To label the five parts of a friendly letter
- To rewrite a business letter correctly
- To write an e-mail requesting information

Options for Organizing and Differentiating Instruction
See pages T11 and T12.

Scaffolding for English Language Learners
Ask students if they enjoy writing letters and whom they like writing to the most. Ask them how a letter written to a friend might look and sound different from a letter written to a business.

Read aloud the letter in **Part 1**. Have students orally identify each part of the letter before writing the label.

Have a volunteer read **Part 2** aloud. Pairs of students can first discuss what goes on each line before writing the letter.

For **Part 3,** have partners decide where they would like to visit. Help students look for information in the phone book, at the library, or on the Internet. Have students work with an English-proficient partner to write their e-mail. Encourage them to review correct e-mail form by looking in Handbook section 35. Suggest that they jot down what they would like to ask before composing their e-mails.

Speaking and Listening
Ask students to bring to class copies of friendly letters, business letters, and business e-mails they or members of their family have received. Have students display the letters, compare them, and point out the parts.

Reinforcement and Reteaching
Review **Read and Discover** and the rule statement, refer students to the **G.U.M. Handbook,** or use the **Extra Practice** activity on page 285.

Diagraming Subjects, Verbs, Adjectives, Articles, and Direct Objects
Tell students that on these pages they will review what they have learned about diagraming sentences. Review the model diagram in this section. Then have student pairs diagram items 1–3.

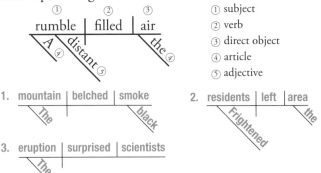

Diagraming Compound Subjects, Compound Predicates, and Compound Sentences
Ask a volunteer to describe the diagram in this section. (The compound subject is placed on parallel lines to the left of the bisecting vertical line, and the compound predicate is placed to the right.) Have students diagram items 4–6.

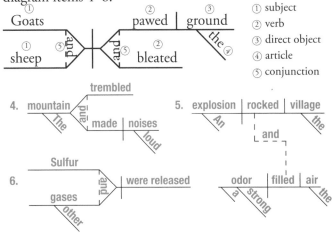

Diagraming Understood *You*, Possessive Pronouns, Demonstrative Pronouns, and Indefinite Pronouns
Recall with students that possessive pronouns are placed on a slanted line below the nouns they modify, while demonstrative and indefinite pronouns are placed on the horizontal line where the nouns they replace would go. Have pairs diagram items 7–10.

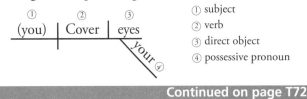

Continued on page T72

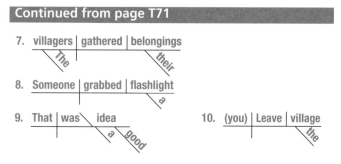

7. villagers | gathered | belongings — The, their

8. Someone | grabbed | flashlight — a

9. That | was \ idea — a, good

10. (you) | Leave | village — the

14. boy | put | camera — The, the, in pocket, his

15. There family | was — a, in truck, a small

16. They | offered | ride — neighbors, their, a

17. driver | drove — The, quickly, toward highway, the

Diagraming Linking Verbs, Predicate Nouns, Predicate Adjectives, and Adverbs

Remind students that a slanted line separates a linking verb and a predicate adjective or a predicate noun. Ask where an adverb is placed in a diagram. (on a slanted line below the word it modifies) Have student pairs diagram items 11–13.

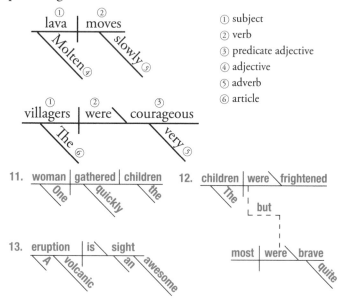

① lava ② moves — Molten ④, slowly ⑤

① subject
② verb
③ predicate adjective
④ adjective
⑤ adverb
⑥ article

① villagers ② were \ ③ courageous — The ⑥, very ⑤

11. woman | gathered | children — One, quickly, the

12. children | were \ frightened — The, but, most | were \ brave, quite

13. eruption | is \ sight — A volcanic, an awesome

Diagraming Prepositional Phrases, Indirect Objects, and *There*

Review the examples in this section and then help students diagram items 14–17.

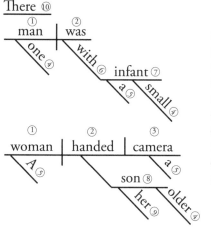

There ⑩

① man ② was — one ④, with ⑥ infant ⑦, a ⑤, small ④

① subject
② verb
③ direct object
④ adjective
⑤ article
⑥ preposition
⑦ object of preposition
⑧ indirect object
⑨ possessive pronoun
⑩ introductory word

① woman ② handed ③ camera — A ⑤, son ⑧, her ⑨, a ⑤, older ④

Diagraming Subject and Object Pronouns, Adjective Clauses, and Adverb Clauses

Help students analyze the model diagrams in this section. Then have them diagram items 18–20.

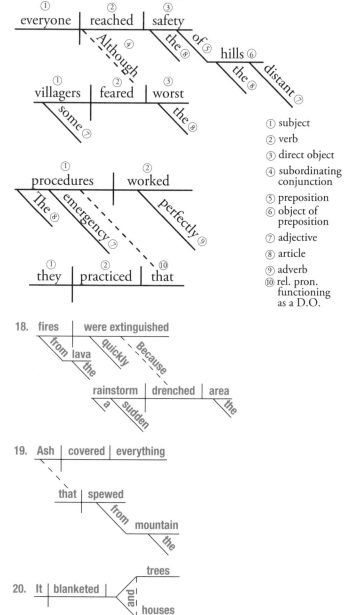

① everyone ② reached ③ safety — Although ④, the ⑧, of ⑤ hills ⑥, the ⑧, distant ⑦

① villagers ② feared ③ worst — some ⑦, the ⑧

① procedures ② worked — The ⑧, emergency ⑦, perfectly ⑨

① they ② practiced ⑩ that

① subject
② verb
③ direct object
④ subordinating conjunction
⑤ preposition
⑥ object of preposition
⑦ adjective
⑧ article
⑨ adverb
⑩ rel. pron. functioning as a D.O.

18. fires | were extinguished — from lava, the, quickly, Because, rainstorm | drenched | area, a sudden, the

19. Ash | covered | everything — that | spewed — from mountain, the

20. It | blanketed — trees, and, houses

Writing Sentences (student page 211)

Inform students that sentences 1 through 5 on page 211 need to be revised so that they make sense. Have a volunteer read the first sentence aloud, identify what is wrong with it, and tell how it should be corrected. (The colon should be deleted, and the phrase *with an area of fifty-seven square miles* should be placed in parentheses; *fifty seven* should have a hyphen.) Then have students work independently or in pairs to correct the remaining sentences. Have students compare their revisions.

Writing a Paragraph (student page 212)

Read the friendly letter on page 211 aloud. Draw students' attention to the different parts of the letter. Call on volunteers to take turns identifying and then reading aloud the heading, greeting, body, closing, and signature. Ask students what the body of the letter tells about. (a summer vacation)

Have students look back at their revised sentences on page 211. Explain that the sentences are out of order, but when ordered correctly they could form the body of a letter. Ask a volunteer to name the introductory sentence. (item 4) Call on others to name, in order, the sentences that give more information. (items 1, 5, 2, and 3) Then ask students to write the revised, corrected letter in the space provided on page 212.

Have students read the directions to the second activity and then write their e-mails. Remind them that as they write, they should be sure they have punctuated their sentences and used capitalization correctly. Remind them to check their work using the checklist at the bottom of the page. Invite volunteers to read their completed e-mails aloud.

Proofreading (student pages 213–214)

Scaffolding for English Language Learners

Have students work with a partner who is fluent in English for the proofreading activities.

Proofreading Practice

Ask students to identify the topic of the report on page 213. (the island of Tahiti) Explain that the report contains several mistakes and that as they read, they should look for these mistakes.

Review the **Proofreading Marks** chart and the examples. Remind students that these marks are used by professional writers to check their work before publication. Read the first sentence aloud. Discuss the errors (there should be a comma after *lush* and no comma after *tropical*) and how they should be marked for correction. You may wish to have students correct the spelling errors.

After they have completed the proofreading activity, ask volunteers to read each sentence aloud and to identify errors. Ask students to mark overlooked errors in another color. **Note:** Some errors can be corrected in more than one way.

Proofreading Checklist

Ask students to select a recent piece of their own writing and to write the title of that piece at the top of the chart. Ask students to put a check mark next to each item in the checklist after they have checked it in their work. Students might first work independently and then trade papers with a partner to double-check each other's work. You might model, or ask a student to model, using the **G.U.M. Handbook** (beginning on student page 303) to clarify a concept or rule.

Also Remember…

Remind students that correct capitalization and punctuation are important for clear writing. If necessary, help students use the **G.U.M. Handbook** to clarify when commas should be used and to review the use of capital letters.

Your Own List

Suggest that students look at the errors they did not find in the proofreading activity and add them to the checklist. Ask students to think about other kinds of errors they make and to add these to the checklist.

Ask students to place this page in their writing portfolios. These pages may be used to assess students' progress over the course of the year.

Assessment Options

See page T11 for ways to use *G.U.M.* assessments to differentiate instruction.

Unit Review

The **Unit Review** (pp. 215–216) allows you to check students' progress and determine when reteaching is necessary. The review pages may be completed in class or as homework. If a student responds incorrectly to two or more items involving the same skill, you may want to work directly with the student to review the relevant lesson. The lesson number to which each review item relates appears in parentheses on the review pages in the Teacher Edition.

Assign the **Extra Practice** activities (pp. 281–285) to reteach targeted skills in a more focused way.

Unit Assessment

The **Unit Assessment** (pp. 245–248) is intended to (1) familiarize students with standardized testing procedures, (2) check students' ability to apply key unit concepts in a different format, and (3) serve as an indicator of student progress.

- When used as a **pretest,** the Unit Assessment helps you determine, prior to instruction, your students' strengths, weaknesses, knowledge, and skills.
- When used as a **posttest,** the Unit Assessment provides feedback that you can use to guide further instruction.

Follow this procedure for administering the Unit Assessment.

1. Read aloud the Test Tip and the test instructions. (**Note:** For additional scaffolding, you may wish to read the test questions and answer choices aloud.)
2. Tell students that they will have 20 minutes to read and answer the questions independently.
3. When time is up, collect and correct the tests. Use the results to measure student progress and guide reteaching.

Assign the **Extra Practice** activities (pp. 281–285) to reteach targeted skills in a more focused way.

Note: The **Unit Review** may be reused after reteaching to check students' understanding of the lesson concepts.

Unit Test

The **Unit Test** (pp. 299–300) helps you judge students' achievement while providing them with valuable practice for high-stakes tests. When you are ready to administer the test, ask students to carefully tear it out of their books. (**Note:** If the test has already been removed, distribute it to students.) Read aloud the directions for each section and make sure students understand how to answer the questions. Ask students to work independently to complete the test.

Students who miss two questions focusing on the same grammar element may need additional help understanding the concept. Reteach the concept, following this procedure:

1. Review **Read and Discover**.
2. Review the rule statement for the concept.
3. Guide students through items a second time. Ask the students to explain why each correct answer belongs in each sentence.
4. Refer students to the **G.U.M. Handbook** for further reinforcement.

Community Connection (student pages 217–218)

These two pages provide interesting and fun activities that reinforce the skills and concepts students learned in Lessons 61 to 70. These activities give students the opportunity to extend what they have read about in the unit by finding out more about resources in your community that are connected to travel and tourism. You might utilize the **Community Connection** pages in one of the following ways:

- Ask students to take the pages home, select one activity to do, and then share the results of that activity with the class.
- Have pairs of students select one activity to complete together.
- Preview the activities as a class, and then assign the activities to small groups of students to complete cooperatively. Set aside a time for groups to share the results.

When you are ready to have students select activities, direct them to pages 217–218. Explain that the activities will give them an opportunity to find out more about resources in your community that enable travel. Explain that one activity gives them an opportunity to learn how to create a travel itinerary. Point out that page 218 is a planning guide that will help them take notes as they conduct their research. Then ask students to carefully tear the pages out of the book, and explain how you wish students to use them.

Notes

Notes

Notes

Notes

Notes

Notes

G.U.M.

Grammar, Usage, and Mechanics

ZB Zaner-Bloser
The Language Arts and Reading Company

Grade Level Consultants

S. Elaine Boysworth
Lincolnton, North Carolina

Linda Crawford
Calhoun, Georgia

Martha Swan Novy
Florissant, Missouri

Heather Stanton
Colorado Springs, Colorado

Jaqueline Xavier
Cleveland, Ohio

Developed by Straight Line Editorial Development, Inc., and Zaner-Bloser, Inc.

Cover photo: Rycus Associates Photography

Book Design: Dominion Design

Illustration: Tom Kennedy, Tracy Greenwalt

ISBN: 978-0-7367-5741-6

Zaner-Bloser, Inc., P.O. Box 16764, Columbus, Ohio 43216-6764 (1-800-421-3018)

Printed in the United States of America   08 09 10 11 12 997 5 4 3 2 1

Table of Contents

Unit 1 Sentence Structure

Looking Back Innovations That Changed History

Unit 2 Sentence Structure

Beasts & Critters Sea Creatures

Unit 5 Usage

Grab Bag Cultural Snapshots

Unit 6 Grammar

Timeless Tales Folktale Characters

Unit 7 Mechanics

Great Getaways **Islands and Near-Islands**

Unit Tests

G.U.M. Handbook

G.U.M. Indexes

Read and Discover

The development of agriculture / changed human society forever.
       a.   **b.**

Which part (a. or b.) of this sentence tells whom or what the sentence is about? **a.**

Which part (a. or b.) tells what happened? **b.**

Every sentence has a subject and a predicate. The **complete subject** is made up of a noun or pronoun and words that tell about it. The subject tells whom or what the sentence is about. The **complete predicate** is made up of a verb and words that tell what the subject is, has, or does.

See Handbook Sections 11, 12

Part 1

Underline the complete subject in each sentence once. Underline each complete predicate twice.

1. Prehistoric humans were hunter-gatherers for millions of years.

2. Small groups of people traveled around to the areas with the most plentiful plants and animals.

3. Earth's climate changed suddenly about eleven thousand years ago.

4. The familiar foods were often not available.

5. Some people experimented with agriculture in the Middle East, Asia, and Mexico.

6. People in these areas grew plants from wild seeds.

7. Nutritious grains were grown by these farmers.

8. They kept animals for their milk, wool, and meat.

9. The new farmers built permanent dwellings near their fields.

10. Some of these farmers lived in an area called the Fertile Crescent.

11. Humans considered land their property for the first time.

12. Some of the arid regions in Egypt and Sumeria had fertile soil.

13. Farmers developed complex irrigation, or watering, systems there.

14. Irrigation required the labor and cooperation of many people.

15. Extra food was produced as a result of irrigation.

16. Food production no longer required every person's effort.

17. Some people became craftspeople, soldiers, or merchants instead of farmers.

18. The abundant food supply enabled more people to live in villages.

19. These developments led to the establishment of the first civilizations.

Croplands in ancient Egypt were irrigated with water from the Nile River.

Looking Back

Part 2   Answers will vary.

Add a subject or a predicate to each phrase to make a sentence. Underline the complete subject in each sentence you write. Circle the complete predicate in each sentence.

20. hunted bison and mammoth _____

_____

21. agriculture _____

_____

22. grew barley and wheat _____

_____

23. the world's earliest civilizations _____

_____

24. flocks of sheep _____

_____

Part 3

Complete subjects and predicates may be very short (*Dogs / bark.*) or very long. Short sentences can make a passage seem spare and direct. They tend to focus the reader's attention on actions and events. Long sentences can create a smooth flow that carries the reader along from idea to idea while providing clear descriptive or explanatory information.

Notice the differences between these two passages by famous authors. Draw a slash (/) between the complete subject and the complete predicate in each sentence.

His face/was sweaty and dirty. The sun/shone on his face. The day/was very hot.

—Ernest Hemingway, from *In Our Time*

The curious things about her/were her hands, strange terminations to the flabby white arms splattered with pale tan spots—long, quivering hands with deep and convex nails.

—Dorothy Parker, from "Big Blonde"

Write a paragraph of your own about meeting an unusual or interesting person. Try making the subjects and predicates in your sentences very short. Then rewrite your paragraph, adding words and phrases to make the subjects and predicates long. Now compare the two paragraphs. Which version do you prefer?

Answers will vary. _____

_____

_____

_____

_____

Name _____

Looking Back

a. **Oral (stories) of gods and heroes** carried the beliefs of a culture from one generation to the next.

b. Tell us the story of Gilgamesh.

The complete subject of sentence a. is in boldfaced type. Circle the most important word in the complete subject. Underline the verb that tells what the subject did.

Can you find a subject at the beginning of sentence b.? _____**no**_____

Circle the word below that fits as the subject of sentence b.

Gilgamesh   (you)   tell   story

The **simple subject** is the most important word or words in the complete subject. It is a noun or pronoun and tells whom or what the sentence is about. The subject of a request or command (an imperative sentence) is usually not named. The person being spoken to, *you,* is the **understood subject**. The **simple predicate** is the most important word or words in the predicate. It is a verb. The simple predicate tells what the subject did or what was done to the subject. The simple predicate may also be a form of the verb *be.*

See Handbook Sections 11, 12

Part 1

Circle the simple subject in each sentence. If the understood subject is *you,* write *you* on the line. Underline the simple predicate.

1. The (people) of Sumeria developed a writing system more than 5,000 years ago. _____

2. Find the Euphrates River on a map. __**you**__

3. Ancient (Sumeria) included the fertile lands near this river. _____

4. Some (Sumerians) owned large quantities of goods. _____

5. A (record) of these goods was often necessary for business purposes. _____

6. (Sumerians) drew marks or symbols on wet clay tablets for their records. _____

7. Some (people) became experts at the use of symbols. _____

8. These (scribes) could draw symbols for objects easily. _____

9. (Ideas) presented the scribes with a much greater challenge. _____

10. Draw a symbol for "life" or "freedom." __**you**__

11. Your (drawing) must be understandable to other people. _____

12. Guess the Sumerian scribes' solution to this problem. __**you**__

13. (Ti) meant both "arrow" and "life" in the Sumerian spoken language. _____

14. Clever (scribes) used a picture of an arrow as the symbol for both words. _____

15. (Symbols) eventually represented sounds such as *ti* instead of objects such as *arrow.* _____

16. (People) could then write any word in the Sumerian language. _____

3000 B.C.

2000 B.C.

700 B.C.

500 B.C.

The early symbol for *fish* changed over time.

Part 2

Write five sentences about the invention of writing. You may use nouns and verbs from the word bank as simple subjects or simple predicates. Use the understood subject *you* in one of your sentences.

symbols recorded	scribe imagine	invention represented	draw Sumerians	wrote picture	arrow ideas

17. Answers will vary.
_____

18. _____
_____

19. _____
_____

20. _____
_____

21. _____
_____

Part 3

A symbol that stands for a sound in a puzzle is called a *rebus*. For instance, a picture of an eye 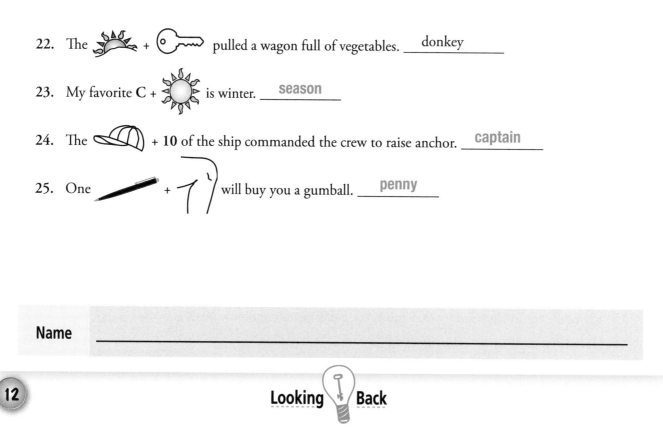 can stand for "I" in a rebus. Solve the rebus puzzles below to find the simple subject of each sentence. The first one has been done for you.

22. The [sun] + [key] pulled a wagon full of vegetables. ____donkey____

23. My favorite C + [sun] is winter. ____season____

24. The [cap] + **10** of the ship commanded the crew to raise anchor. ____captain____

25. One [pen] + [knee] will buy you a gumball. ____penny____

Name _____

Looking Back

Read and Discover

S Clocks and calendars are very important in modern life.
P They wake us up, measure our working hours, and inform us of holidays.

Write *S* next to the sentence with two or more simple subjects. Write *P* next to the sentence with two or more simple predicates.

A **compound subject** is two or more subjects joined by a conjunction (*and*, *or*).
A **compound predicate** is two or more verbs joined by a conjunction.

See Handbook Sections 11, 12

Part 1

Each sentence below has either a compound subject or a compound predicate. If a sentence has a compound subject, circle the two or more nouns that are the simple subjects. If a sentence has a compound predicate, underline the two or more verbs that are the simple predicates.

1. The concept of time <u>fascinates</u> and <u>perplexes</u> humans.

2. Prehistoric (men) and (women) probably saw time as a circle.

3. These early people <u>observed</u> and <u>noted</u> regular changes in the sky.

4. The sun <u>rose</u> and <u>set</u> every day.

5. (Spring), (summer), (fall), and (winter) occurred in the same sequence over and over.

6. People in several regions <u>studied</u> and <u>recorded</u> these yearly cycles.

7. The (Sumerians), (Mayas), and (Chinese) invented calendars independently.

8. Calendar-makers <u>carved</u> marks in stone or <u>tied</u> knots in string.

9. These early calendars <u>predicted</u> the times for harvests and <u>indicated</u> the days for festivals.

10. The (sun) and (stars) seem to change their position in the sky over the course of a year.

11. The moon <u>moves</u> across the sky and <u>seems</u> to change shape.

12. Ancient peoples <u>observed</u> and <u>celebrated</u> these celestial events.

13. Many ancient (temples) and (monuments) face the dawn or the North Star.

14. The sun's yearly (cycle) and the (cycle) of the moon are out of step with each other.

15. This <u>confused</u> most ancient astronomers and <u>caused</u> inaccuracies in some calendars.

16. Modern (astronomers) and (physicists) occasionally add leap seconds to a year for greater accuracy.

This calendar stone shows the days of the Aztec month.

Looking Back

Part 2   Possible answers appear below. Accept all reasonable responses.

Combine each pair of sentences to form one sentence that has either a compound subject or a compound predicate.

17. The world's first mechanical clock was made in China. The world's first mechanical clock showed changes in the phases of the moon. __The world's first mechanical clock was made in China and showed changes in the phases of the moon.__

18. The Buddhist monk I-Hsing designed a mechanical clock. Then he built this clock. __The Buddhist monk I-Hsing designed and built a mechanical clock.__

19. Gears controlled the clock's movements. Shafts controlled the clock's movements, too. __Gears and shafts controlled the clock's movements.__

20. Water in a stream turned a water wheel. This water made the clock function. __Water in a stream turned a water wheel and made the clock function.__

21. A bell announced the time. A drum announced the time. __A bell and a drum announced the time.__

Part 3

It is possible to have both a compound subject and a compound predicate in the same sentence. (*The boys* and *girls splashed* and *swam together*.) However, both parts of the compound subject must be performing both actions of the compound predicate. Avoid sentences like this one: *The wolves and frogs howled and croaked*. This sentence might make the reader think that the frogs howled and the wolves croaked.

On the lines below, rewrite the incorrect sentence as two separate sentences. Write *C* beside the sentence that uses compound subjects and predicates correctly.

22. The sun and moon light up the day and shine at night. ____
    __The sun lights up the day. The moon shines at night.__

23. Ice and snow come in winter and make travel difficult. __C__

Name _____

a. Early peoples made crude (tools) and (weapons) out of stone, wood, and bone.

b. The invention of bronze brought great (changes) to the ancient world.

Circle the nouns in sentence a. that tell what early peoples made. Circle the noun in sentence b. that tells what the invention of bronze brought.

The **direct object** is the noun or pronoun that receives the action of the verb. Only action verbs can take a direct object. A **compound direct object** occurs when more than one noun or pronoun receives the action of the verb. To find the direct object, say the verb and then ask "What?" or "Whom?" For example, to find the direct object of sentence b., ask "The invention of bronze brought what? Answer: It brought *changes*."

See Handbook Section 21

Part 1

Circle the direct object in each sentence. If there is a compound direct object, circle each noun or pronoun that is a direct object.

1. Craftspeople first produced (bronze) in about 3800 B.C., in Sumeria.

2. These craftspeople melted (copper) in a kind of furnace.

3. They accidentally mixed (arsenic) and other (minerals) with the copper.

4. This combination produced a stronger (metal.)

5. Eventually, metalworkers combined (copper) and (tin) into bronze.

6. Sumerian metalworkers could form this new (metal) into almost any shape.

7. Craftspeople in Egypt and other nearby areas soon learned the (secret) of bronze production.

8. People made durable (tools), (weapons), and (statues) out of bronze.

9. Farmers tilled (fields) with bronze-tipped plows.

10. They could cultivate larger (areas) with these efficient plows.

11. Soon Middle Eastern civilizations needed new (sources) of tin.

12. This stimulated (trade) with distant regions.

13. People from widespread cultures exchanged (ideas) as well as (goods.)

14. The expansion of trade also encouraged the (expansion) of empires.

15. Nations conquered other (nations) for their tin.

16. Over time, however, the Iron Age overcame the (Bronze Age.)

17. Iron replaced (tin) as the main metal.

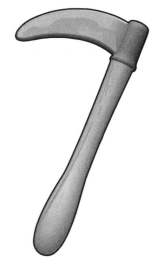

Tools like this bronze-tipped sickle made life a little easier for ancient farmers.

Looking Back

Part 2

Write a direct object from the word bank to complete each sentence. Draw an arrow from the verb to the direct object.

model	horse	trick	bronze	civilization	stories	Trojans

18. The Mycenaeans used _____ **bronze** _____ for weapons and sculptures during the Bronze Age in Greece.

19. In about 1200 B.C., some disastrous event destroyed their _____ **civilization** _____.

20. Greeks in later times told _____ **stories** _____ about the heroic deeds and amazing palaces of their Bronze Age ancestors.

21. In one of these legends, the Greeks played a clever _____ **trick** _____ on their enemies, the Trojans.

22. They built a huge wooden _____ **model** _____ of a horse, and some soldiers hid inside.

23. The Trojans brought the _____ **horse** _____ inside their walled city.

24. In the middle of the night, the Greek soldiers climbed out of their hiding place and defeated the _____ **Trojans** _____.

Part 3

An action verb that takes a direct object is a *transitive* verb. An action verb without a direct object is an *intransitive* verb. Many action verbs may be either transitive (*Mr. Garcia __runs__ the store.*) or intransitive (*Mark __runs__ fast.*), depending on whether they are used with a direct object. You will learn more about transitive and intransitive verbs in Lesson 32.

In the following sentences, write *transitive verb* on the line if there is a direct object. Write *intransitive verb* if there is no direct object.

25. Sculptors work very hard. _____ **intransitive verb** _____

26. Sculptors work soft clay into figures. _____ **transitive verb** _____

27. They make molds from the clay figures. _____ **transitive verb** _____

28. Molten bronze pours easily. _____ **intransitive verb** _____

29. The sculptor pours molten bronze into the mold. _____ **transitive verb** _____

30. This material hardens to make a permanent model of the sculpture. _____ **intransitive verb** _____

Name _____

Looking Back

Read and Discover

In today's society, people give **clerks money** in exchange for food and other necessities.

Which boldfaced noun tells what people give? ___money___

Which boldfaced noun tells *to whom* they give it? ___clerks___

An **indirect object** is a person or thing to whom something is given, told, or taught. The indirect object is a noun or pronoun, and it comes before the direct object. To test whether a word is an indirect object, move it after the direct object and put the word *to* or *for* in front of it. Example: *People give money to clerks.*

See Handbook Section 21

Part 1

First underline the direct object in each sentence. Then circle the indirect object.

1. In ancient times, farmers traded others their crops in exchange for different foods or useful things.

2. For example, a farmer might have offered a neighbor some beans.

3. The neighbor might have offered the farmer some plums from her garden in exchange.

4. But what if a plum gave the farmer a stomachache?

5. The farmer might have traded a cousin the other plums for some cucumbers.

6. Then the farmer might have traded a friend some cucumbers in exchange for a chicken.

7. This complicated system caused people problems.

8. China probably brought the world the first monetary system.

9. Money provided people a convenient method of exchange.

10. People give money its value.

11. Merchants will trade you goods for money.

12. Paper money gives the public a lightweight medium of exchange.

13. Enough money will buy you almost any product.

14. History teaches us lessons about how the value of money can change.

15. In times of economic disaster, people have given merchants wheelbarrows full of paper money in exchange for a few days' food.

16. Many people today give cashiers a plastic card to complete a purchase.

The earliest coins were shaped like small tools.

Looking Back

Part 2

Rewrite each sentence, changing the underlined phrase into an indirect object.

17. Mary's grandfather showed his collection of old and rare money <u>to us</u>. **Mary's grandfather showed us his collection of old and rare money.**

18. He told a story about the use of rice as money in seventeenth-century Japan <u>to Mary</u>. **He told Mary a story about the use of rice as money in seventeenth-century Japan.**

19. He showed a playing card that was used as money in colonial Canada <u>to me</u>. **He showed me a playing card that was used as money in colonial Canada.**

20. I made a thank-you card with drawings of coins on it <u>for him</u>. **I made him a thank-you card with drawings of coins on it.**

Part 3

Write a word from the word bank to give each sentence an indirect object. Then use the numbered letters to form the mystery word.

coins	Mary	us	her	me	him

21. Mary's grandfather gave ___m___ ___e___ the idea of starting my own coin collection.
$$\qquad\qquad 4$$

22. I traded ___h___ ___i___ ___m___ a summer of yard work for some old coins.
$$\qquad\qquad 1$$

23. Mary's grandfather taught ___u___ ___s___ his methods for coin collecting.

24. He never gives the ___c___ ___o___ ___i___ ___n___ ___s___ a scrub or a polish.
$$\qquad\qquad 2 \qquad 3$$

25. One year later I showed ___M___ ___a___ ___r___ ___y___ the coin collection her grandfather had inspired.
$$\qquad\qquad\qquad 5$$

Mystery word: ___m___ ___o___ ___n___ ___e___ ___y___
$$\qquad\qquad\quad 1 \quad 2 \quad 3 \quad 4 \quad 5$$

Name _____

Looking Back

Movable type is a (method) of printing with letter stamps.
Each letter is **separate**.

Circle the boldfaced noun that tells more about who or what the subject is.
Underline the boldfaced adjective that tells what the subject is like.

A **predicate noun** follows a linking verb and tells more about who or what the subject is. A **predicate adjective** follows a linking verb and describes the subject.

See Handbook Section 12

Part 1

Draw a box around the linking verb in each sentence. Circle each boldfaced word that is a predicate noun. Underline each boldfaced word that is a predicate adjective.

1. First developed in 1045, movable type was a Chinese (invention).

2. The inventor was (Bi Sheng).

3. This type of printing was not **practical** in China at the time, however.

4. Chinese characters were too **numerous**.

5. Movable type was more **useful** in Europe.

6. Before the development of movable type, most European books were handmade (copies) of manuscripts.

7. Scribes were the experienced (writers) of these books.

8. Handwritten books were unique (works) of art.

9. The pages were **beautiful**, with elaborate decorations in the margins.

10. Unfortunately, these books were **expensive** and **scarce**.

11. The first European printer was (Johannes Gutenberg).

12. 1456 was the (year) of his innovation.

13. The Roman alphabet is a (set) of 26 characters.

14. The model for Gutenberg's printing press was a (press) for grapes or cheese.

15. Its output was 300 (copies) per day.

16. Soon books and pamphlets were **available** to many more people.

17. New ideas became the (property) of everyone, not just the rich.

Paper bed

Paper press

Type bed

Ink

The printing press helped spread new ideas across the world.

Looking Back

Part 2   Answers will vary.
Write a predicate noun or a predicate adjective to complete each sentence.

18. My favorite book is _____.

19. The main character in the book is _____.

20. This character's personality seems _____

   _____.

21. The setting for that mystery book is _____

   _____.

22. The mood of the story seems _____

   _____.

23. Even the illustrations appear _____.

24. The villain changes in the story and becomes _____.

25. Whenever I read this book, I feel _____.

26. The author of this new adventure story has become _____

   _____.

27. The most important problem in the novel's plot is _____

   _____.

28. When I saw the cover of the book, I thought it looked _____

   _____.

29. Of all the books I've read, this one remains _____.

Part 3
In the modern world, word processors help spread the written word. But sometimes words are mistyped. Circle the predicate noun in each sentence below. Unscramble that word to find a word that makes sense.

30. His best feature was his (slime). s m i l e

31. Manuela's tasty pies prove that she is a fine (brake). b a k e r

32. My favorite flowers are (sores). r o s e s

33. The distance 5,280 feet is a (lime). m i l e

34. Of all our field trips, my favorite place was the (diary). d a i r y

35. He ran as hard as he could, and his last jump was his greatest (peal). l e a p

Name _____

Looking Back

Read and Discover

Carracks once sailed throughout the world.

Where did these ships sail? _____ **throughout the world**

A **prepositional phrase** can tell *how, what kind, when, how much,* or *where.* A prepositional phrase begins with a **preposition,** such as *in, over, of, to,* or *by.* It ends with a noun or pronoun that is the **object of the preposition.** The words between the preposition and its object are part of the prepositional phrase. A prepositional phrase can appear at the beginning, middle, or end of a sentence.

See Handbook Section 20

Part 1

Underline each prepositional phrase. Circle the preposition that begins each phrase. Draw a box around the object of the preposition. There may be more than one prepositional phrase in each sentence.

1. In the fifteenth century, European shipbuilders built three-masted carracks with triangular sails.

2. The new design of these ships made long voyages easier.

3. The rudder and the compass, two inventions from China, helped sailors navigate and steer.

4. Europeans wanted silk and spices from Asia, and sailors began searching for better trade routes.

5. Seeking a new western route to Asia, Christopher Columbus landed on unfamiliar land.

6. Columbus thought the land was part of Asia, but others soon realized that this land to the west was an uncharted continent.

7. Soon sailors from many European countries were voyaging across the Atlantic.

8. In a few years, the invasion of the Americas had begun.

9. Corn, potatoes, and other nutritious crops from America were brought to Europe, and many European farm animals were brought to America.

10. People from different cultures exchanged ideas and customs.

11. The highly effective constitution of the Iroquois League would impress Benjamin Franklin and George Washington in later years.

12. This league comprised five Native American groups in the New York region.

13. The establishment of European colonies had terrible results for many Native Americans, however.

14. Thousands of Native Americans died in battle, and even more died from European diseases.

15. Africans were enslaved and brought in chains to the American colonies.

16. Many cultures and ways of life were lost to the world forever.

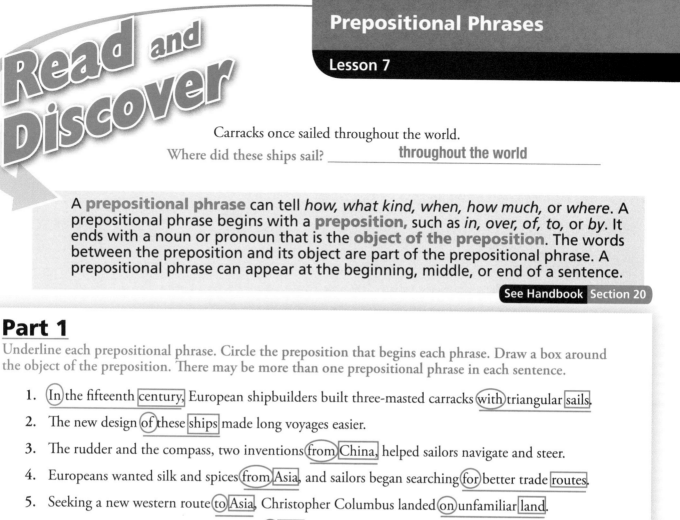

Improved ships and navigational methods brought widely separated cultures together.

Looking Back

Part 2 Possible answers appear below. Accept all reasonable responses.

Rewrite each sentence. Add at least one prepositional phrase to make the sentence give more information. Use phrases from the word bank, or think of your own.

for the U.S. Constitution	from Native Americans	in their fields
of Native American nations	about new agricultural methods	of a democratic government
from European crops	in many regions	such as corn and potatoes

17. Native American groups developed innovative agricultural methods. **Native American groups in**
many regions developed innovative agricultural methods.

_____

18. Their crops were different. **Their crops were different from European crops.**

_____

19. Europeans learned. **Europeans learned from Native Americans.**

_____

20. The Iroquois League provided an example. **The Iroquois League of Native American nations**
provided an example of a democratic government.

Part 3

What animal introduced to America by the Spanish became important to Native Americans? Underline each prepositional phrase. Then follow the directions through the maze to trace out the answer. **(21–36)**

Start at the square. Go to the star. Go through the fish to the heart. Go from the heart to the letter A. Loop around the flower. Stop at the tree. Go to the number 1. Follow a curved route to the triangle. Draw a line to the sun. Follow the path through the letter B and through the circle. Stop at the diamond. Loop to the number 2. Follow a curved route to the moon.

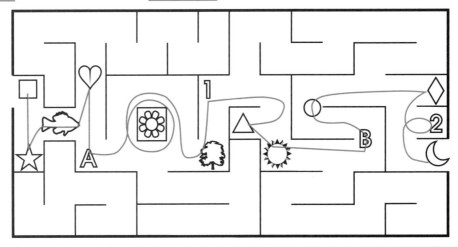

Name _____

Looking Back

Read and Discover

Modern photography began **in the 1830s**.
Photographs gave people a new view **of the world**.

Which of the boldfaced prepositional phrases gives more information about a noun? **of the world**

A prepositional phrase can modify, or tell more about, a noun or pronoun. Prepositional phrases that modify nouns or pronouns are called **adjectival prepositional phrases**. An adjectival prepositional phrase usually comes after the noun or pronoun it modifies.

See Handbook Section 20

Part 1

Underline each adjectival prepositional phrase. Circle the noun it tells about. A sentence may have more than one adjectival prepositional phrase. Be careful! Not all the prepositional phrases in these sentences modify nouns or pronouns.

1. The (man) in the cloak holds a small box.

2. One (side) of the box has a hole in it.

3. He chooses an interesting (scene) near him and points the hole there.

4. Light rays enter the tiny (hole) in the dark box.

5. Inside the box the rays create a perfect miniature (image) of the scene.

6. This special dark box, a camera obscura, was an (invention) of the 1500s.

7. However, (scientists) in that era lacked (knowledge) of chemical processes.

8. Without that knowledge, (film) for the camera obscura could not be invented.

9. In the 1720s, Johann Schulze, a (scientist) from Germany, made an important discovery.

10. (Exposure) to light turns some chemicals dark.

11. Schulze's discovery made the (invention) of photographic film possible.

12. The (images) inside the camera obscura could be captured and preserved.

13. Louis Daguerre, often called the (inventor) of photography, publicized his photographic process widely.

14. But William Henry Talbot's process became the (model) for modern photography.

15. Using Talbot's process, a photographer could create many (copies) of a single photograph.

16. By 1888, a Kodak (camera) from George Eastman made photography accessible to anyone.

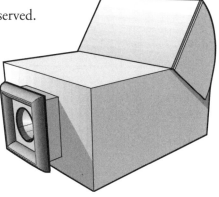

Artists often used images in a camera obscura to help them make sketches of large objects.

Looking Back

23

Part 2   Possible answers appear below. Accept all reasonable responses.

Choose an adjectival prepositional phrase to complete each sentence. Write the phrase in the blank.

for close-up photography	with a telephoto lens	of José's photographs
of light	from his camera	near his home
as a photographer	of a baseball game	of his best picture
of a robin's nest		

17. José dreams of a career _____ **as a photographer** _____.

18. Last winter he bought a digital camera _____ **with a telephoto lens** _____.

19. He borrowed a lens _____ **for close-up photography** _____ from his uncle.

20. José experimented with different levels _____ **of light** _____.

21. He took photographs _____ **of a baseball game** _____ with the telephoto lens.

22. He climbed up a tree and took pictures _____ **of a robin's nest** _____ with the close-up lens.

23. José uploaded the digital files _____ **from his camera** _____ to a photo processing Web site.

24. Most _____ **of José's photographs** _____ turned out sharp and clear.

25. José ordered enlargements _____ **of his best picture** _____ and gave them to his mother and his uncle.

26. José plans to take a photography course at the community college _____ **near his home** _____.

Part 3

Note: Some students may point out that the adjectival prepositional phrase on line 29 could be read as part of the phrase on line 28.

Read this short letter written by Abraham Lincoln during the Civil War. Note how he used prepositional phrases to convey his sympathy. List the eleven adjectival prepositional phrases in this letter.

Dear Madam, I have been shown in the files of the War Department a statement of the Adjutant-General of Massachusetts that you are the mother of five sons who have died gloriously on the field of battle. I feel how weak and fruitless must be any words of mine which should attempt to beguile you from the grief of a loss so overwhelming. But I cannot refrain from tendering to you the consolation that may be found in the thanks of the Republic they died to save. I pray that our heavenly Father may assuage the anguish of your bereavement, and leave you only the cherished memory of the loved and lost, and the solemn pride that must be yours to have laid so costly a sacrifice upon the altar of freedom.

—Abraham Lincoln, *Letter to Mrs. Bixby*

27. _____ of the War Department _____

28. _____ of the Adjutant-General _____

29. _____ of Massachusetts _____

30. _____ of five sons _____

31. _____ of battle _____

32. _____ of mine _____

33. _____ of a loss _____

34. _____ of the Republic _____

35. _____ of your bereavement _____

36. _____ of the loved and lost _____

37. _____ of freedom _____

Name _____

Looking Back

Read and Discover

In the 1940s, computer programmers could not create new programs efficiently. Each new program required a complete set **of machine instructions.** Grace Murray Hopper, a U.S. Navy computer expert, changed computer programming forever **with one brilliant invention.**

Which of the boldfaced prepositional phrases tells *when* about a verb?

<u>In the 1940s</u>

Which tells *how* about a verb? <u>**with one brilliant invention**</u>

Which does not modify a verb? <u>**of machine instructions**</u>

A prepositional phrase can modify, or tell more about, a verb, an adverb, or an adjective. These prepositional phrases are called **adverbial prepositional phrases**. Many adverbial prepositional phrases tell *when, where, how,* or *how long* something was done.

See Handbook Section 20

Part 1

Underline each adverbial prepositional phrase. Circle the verb or verb phrase it modifies. A sentence may have more than one adverbial prepositional phrase.

1. Rear Admiral Grace Hopper (developed) the first computer compiler <u>in 1952</u>.

2. Machine instructions (were gathered) <u>within the compiler</u>.

3. Programmers (could) now (use) the same routine <u>in many different programs</u>.

4. Hopper's bosses (had) not (encouraged) her <u>in her efforts</u>.

5. Automatic programming (seemed) impossible <u>to them</u>.

6. Hopper (was irritated) <u>by such old-fashioned thinking</u>.

7. <u>In the computer industry</u>, changes (come) fast.

8. Hopper (contributed) a great deal <u>to computer science</u>.

9. <u>In the 1950s</u>, she (developed) COBOL, (described) <u>as the first</u> <u>user-friendly computer programming language</u>.

Grace Murray Hopper

10. Businesses (used) COBOL <u>for data processing</u>.

11. <u>In 1964</u> Hopper (received) the Society of Women Engineers Achievement Award.

12. She (was given) the award <u>because of her original computer programming systems</u>.

13. Hopper first (joined) the United States Naval Reserve <u>during World War II</u>.

14. She (retired) <u>in 1966</u>, but she accepted a new assignment one year later.

15. <u>In 1986</u> Hopper, then eighty years old, (retired) again.

16. <u>Throughout her long and brilliant career</u>, Grace Hopper (made) important contributions <u>to computer science, business, and national security</u>.

Looking Back

Part 2   Answers will vary.

Write an adverbial prepositional phrase to complete each sentence. Use your imagination. Be sure the phrase you write answers the question in parentheses.

17. My new laptop will be delivered _____.

   (When?)

18. I will carry my new laptop _____. (Where?)

19. A laptop user controls the cursor on the screen _____.

   (With what?)

20. I have been studying computer science _____.

   (For how long?)

Part 3

Poets commonly use adverbial prepositional phrases in descriptions. Underline the adverbial prepositional phrases in the excerpt below. Be careful not to mark phrases that begin with *to* and end with a verb. **(21–26)**

> She dwelt <u>among the untrodden ways</u>
>
> > <u>Beside the springs</u> of Dove;
>
> A maid whom there were none to praise,
>
> > And very few to love.
>
> A violet by a mossy stone
>
> > Half hidden <u>from the eye</u>!
>
> Fair <u>as a star</u>, when only one
>
> > Is shining <u>in the sky</u>.
>
> > > —William Wordsworth, from "Lucy"

Now write a short poem of your own that includes at least two adverbial prepositional phrases. Circle these prepositional phrases.

Answers will vary.

_____

_____

_____

_____

_____

_____

Name _____

Looking Back

Read and Discover

a. The spinning jenny was a thread-making machine.
b. The spinning jenny, <u>a thread-making machine</u>, helped bring about the Industrial Revolution.

Underline the phrase in sentence b. that tells who or what the spinning jenny was. What punctuation marks separate this phrase from the rest of the sentence?
commas

An **appositive** is a phrase that identifies a noun. An appositive follows the noun it identifies and is usually separated from the rest of the sentence by commas.

See Handbook Section 24

Part 1

Underline the appositive in each sentence. Circle the noun it identifies.

1. The (Industrial Revolution), <u>a vast change in working methods</u>, began in England in the 1750s.

2. Before 1750 most people lived in rural areas where they farmed or participated in (domestic industry), <u>work done in the home</u>.

3. Clothing and other goods were either made at home or made by (craftspeople), <u>trained workers who crafted each item by hand</u>.

4. The Industrial Revolution began in towns where (textiles), <u>woven cloths</u>, were produced.

5. English colonies in America began producing large quantities of (cotton), <u>a cheap and useful alternative to wool</u>.

6. Inventors created complex (machines), <u>the spinning jenny and others</u>, which enabled spinners to make thread faster.

7. To keep up with the growing supply of cotton thread, inventors created (power looms), <u>machines for weaving thread into cloth quickly</u>.

8. These new machines were housed in (textile mills), <u>cloth factories whose machines were powered by water or steam</u>.

9. People moved from the (hinterlands), <u>the distant rural regions</u>, into cities to work in factories.

10. Many (people), <u>children as well as adults</u>, endured dangerous conditions in the factories.

11. Some people resisted these large changes; the (Luddites), <u>gangs of unhappy workers</u>, smashed machines in the new factories.

12. New working (methods), <u>methods opposed by the Luddites</u>, brought changes in politics and education.

13. Young unmarried (women), <u>the bulk of the workers in many textile factories</u>, were able to have some financial independence for the first time.

14. The (middle class), <u>mainly merchants and professional people</u>, grew and gained political power.

15. (Education), <u>once the privilege of the rich</u>, became available to many more young people.

New machines changed the way people worked and lived in industrialized countries.

Looking Back

Part 2   Possible answers appear below. Accept all reasonable responses.

Rewrite each pair of sentences as one sentence. Change the underlined sentence into an appositive.

16. <u>The steam engine was a very important invention.</u> The steam engine was first used mainly in factories.   __The steam engine, a very important invention, was first used mainly in factories.__

17. <u>John Fitch was a silversmith and clockmaker.</u> John Fitch built a boat powered by steam in 1787.
   __John Fitch, a silversmith and clockmaker, built a boat powered by steam in 1787.__

18. <u>Fitch's creation was a small, uncomfortable boat.</u> Fitch's creation was never popular.   _____
   __Fitch's creation, a small, uncomfortable boat, was never popular.__

19. Two other inventors later built more successful steamboats. <u>Robert Fulton and Nicholas Roosevelt each built steamboats that were successful.</u>   __Two other inventors, Robert Fulton and Nicholas Roosevelt, later built more successful steamboats.__

20. Peter Cooper built the *Tom Thumb* in 1830. <u>The *Tom Thumb* was the earliest steam-powered railroad train.</u>   __Peter Cooper built the <u>Tom Thumb</u>, the earliest steam-powered railroad train, in 1830.__

Part 3

> All of the appositives covered so far have been separated from the rest of a sentence by commas. These appositives just give more information about the nouns they describe. But some appositives should **not** be set off by commas. If an appositive is vital to the meaning of the sentence, it should not be set off by commas.

Example

Sarah Joseph, <u>my friend from camp</u>, sent me a letter.
(The appositive *my friend from camp* is not essential to the sentence; it tells more about Sarah Joseph and should be set off by commas.)

My friend <u>Sarah Joseph</u> went to camp with me.
(The appositive *Sarah Joseph* is necessary to explain which friend is meant.)

Add commas if they are needed around the appositives in the following sentences. Write *C* for correct if no commas are necessary.

21. My cousin Li is the oldest of all my cousins.   __C__

22. Li, the oldest of all my cousins, graduated from high school yesterday.   ____

Name   _____

A **sentence diagram** is a picture of a sentence that shows how the parts of a sentence fit together. Diagraming sentences can help you understand how the words in a sentence are related.

Diagraming Subjects and Verbs

A short sentence consisting of a simple subject and a simple predicate is diagramed this way:

Gold melts.   Gold | melts

Look at the structure of the diagram. Based on its structure, complete these sentences:

1. The simple subject and simple predicate go on a _____**horizontal**_____ line.
   horizontal/vertical

2. A _____**vertical**_____ line divides the subject and predicate.
   horizontal/vertical

3. The subject goes to the _____**left**_____ of the vertical line, and the predicate goes on the
   left/right
   _____**right**_____ side.
   left/right

Use what you have learned to diagram these sentences. Include only the simple subject and the simple predicate. Ignore all the other words in the sentences.

4. The miners rested.   miners | rested

5. A storm approached.   storm | approached

6. Rain fell.   Rain | fell

Diagraming Adjectives and Articles

An adjective (describing word) or an article (*a, an, the*) goes on a slanted line below the word it modifies. Look at the way this sentence has been diagramed.

The weary miners rested.   miners | rested
                                 The weary

Now diagram these sentences.

7. A violent storm approached.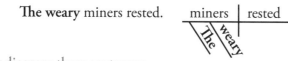

8. Torrential rains fell.

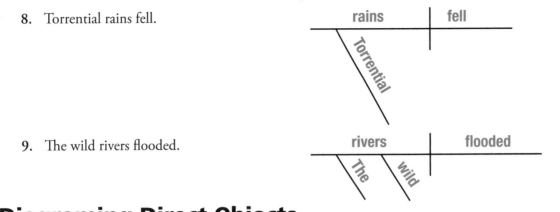

9. The wild rivers flooded.

Diagraming Direct Objects

A direct object (a noun that receives the action of the verb) is placed on a horizontal line to the right of the verb. Notice how the diagram changes when a direct object is added.

Few miners discovered **gold.**   miners | discovered | **gold**
                                           Few

How is the vertical line that separates the direct object and the verb different from the vertical line that separates the subject and predicate?

The line that separates the direct object from the verb does not cross the horizontal line.

Use what you have learned to diagram the simple subjects, simple predicates, adjectives, articles, and direct objects in these sentences.

10. One miner found a huge nugget.   miner | found | nugget
                                        One   a huge

11. Warm rains melted the snow.   rains | melted | snow
                                    Warm   the

12. Icy water filled the reservoir.   water | filled | reservoir
                                        Icy   the

Now diagram these sentences on another sheet of paper.

13. Heavy rains eroded the hillsides.

14. The floods uncovered more gold.

15. Surprised miners staked new claims.

16. The eager men led difficult lives.

17. Some miners left their families.

18. Many miners lost their lives.

19. A few miners found immense wealth.

20. The majority met great disappointment.

The diagrams for sentences 13–20 appear on pages T23–T24.

Name _____

Looking Back

Writing Sentences

Possible answers appear below. Accept all reasonable responses.

These sentences need your help. Rewrite each one so it is clearer and makes better sense.

1. With triangular sails and three masts, European shipbuilders built large ocean-going ships. _____ **European shipbuilders built large ocean-going ships that had triangular sails and three masts.**

2. Growing demand fueled an explosive growth of exploration and trade, in Europe, for treasures from distant lands. **Growing demand in Europe for treasures from distant lands fueled an explosive growth of exploration and trade.**

3. Silk dresses and spices were comfortable to wear and made food taste better. **Silk dresses were comfortable to wear, and spices made food taste better.**

4. Soon, more people in Europe that only the extremely wealthy could previously afford began to acquire goods. **Soon, more people in Europe began to acquire goods that only the extremely wealthy could previously afford.**

5. Brave captains sailed the tall ships to distant lands, and then these captains traded European goods for silks and spices. **Brave captains sailed the tall ships to distant lands, where they traded European goods for silks and spices.**

All the sentences in a paragraph relate to a single topic. A paragraph should have a topic sentence, at least two supporting sentences, and a concluding sentence. Notice these kinds of sentences in this model paragraph.

topic sentence
(states the main idea you are making)

supporting sentences
(give details to support your main idea)

concluding sentence
(summarizes the paragraph or restates the topic sentence)

Electric roller skates would be a useful invention, and they would be fun to use, too. Electric skates, or "electroblades," would give people a cheaper, safer way to travel. Running on rechargeable batteries, electroblades would save energy and reduce air pollution. People using electroblades would save money because electroblades would cost a lot less than cars. Since fewer people would be driving cars, there would also be fewer auto accidents. **Because skating is fun, people would actually enjoy traveling to work or school!**

Writing a Paragraph

The sentences you repaired on page 31 can be reordered to make a paragraph. Decide which sentence is the topic sentence, which are the supporting sentences, and which is the concluding sentence. Reorder the sentences, and write the paragraph on the lines below.

The rewritten sentences should appear in the following order: 2, 1, 5, 3, 4. Students may wish to

make additional revisions in their sentences as they write the paragraph.

_____

_____

_____

_____

_____

_____

_____

Think of a new invention that would make your life easier, safer, or more comfortable. Write a paragraph explaining why you think this invention would be useful. Be sure to include a topic sentence, two or more supporting sentences, and a concluding sentence.

Answers will vary.

_____

_____

_____

_____

_____

_____

_____

_____

Read your paragraph again. Use this checklist to make sure it is complete and correct.

- ❏ My paragraph has a topic sentence.
- ❏ My paragraph has at least two supporting sentences.
- ❏ All my sentences are clear and make sense.

- ❏ I have used prepositional phrases correctly.
- ❏ My paragraph has a concluding sentence.

Name _____

Looking Back

Proofreading Practice

Read this passage about patents and find the mistakes. Use the proofreading marks to show how the mistakes should be fixed.

Suggested answers appear below.
Accept all reasonable responses.

Proofreading Marks

Mark	Means	Example
ℒ	delete	This machine is is broken, too.
∧	add	This machine **is** broken, too.
≡	make into a capital letter	this machine is broken, too.
/	make into a lowercase letter	This Machine is broken, too.
⊙	add a period	This machine is broken, too⊙
sp	fix spelling	This macheen is broken, too.

My Idea for a Great Invention

You have just put the finnishing touches on your marvelous new invention, electric in-line skates. Before you send your skates to the assembly line, however, consider this question: What's to prevent other people from stealing your design and copying your invention. The answer is that you can obtain leagle protection for you idea from the united states Patent and Trademark Office.

In simplest terms, a patent is an agreament between the inventor and the rest of the nation. When the government issues a patent, it grants an inventor all rights to manufacture and profit from his or her invention. Once you have a patent for your electric in-line skates, No one can copy your idea exactly. Obtaining a patent isn't complicated, but it does take time, usually more than two years.

the Patenet and Trademark Office or PTO recieves about 100,000 patent applications every year. Each application is carfully evaluated by the staff at the PTO. First, officials must make sure that the invention hasn't already been patented by someone else. They must also decide weather the invention deserves a patent. It has to be entirely new, Not a variation of something that already exists. The invention must also be useful.

You don't need to put off production, While you are awaiting a response, however. Your skates can make their Debut in malls everywhere even if you haven't received your patent. Just make sure to put the notation *patent pending* somewhere on the product. These words aren't a legal guarantee, but they our usually enough to discouradge other people from producing exact copies of your invention.

Proofreading
Checklist

You can use the checklist below to help you find and fix mistakes in your own writing. Write the titles of your own stories or reports in the blanks at the top of the chart. Then use the questions to check your work. Make a check mark (✔) in each box after you have checked that item.

Answers will vary.

Proofreading Checklist for Unit 1

	Titles			
Does each sentence have a subject and a predicate?				
Have I used appositives correctly?				
Have I used prepositional phrases to make my writing more precise?				
Have I varied the length and type of sentences to add variety to my writing?				
Do all my sentences state complete thoughts?				

Also Remember . . .

Does each sentence begin with a capital letter?				
Does each sentence end with the right end mark?				
Have I spelled each word correctly?				
Have I used commas correctly?				

Your Own List

Use this space to write your own list of things to check in your writing.

Name _____

Looking Back

Review

(Numbers in parentheses identify related lessons.)

Subjects and Predicates

Underline the complete subject in each sentence. Circle the simple subject. If the understood subject is *you*, write *you* on the line.

1. Some (inventions) change almost everyone's life. _____ **(1, 2)**

2. Imagine a world without cell phones! __you__ **(2)**

3. The (hours) after school would be long and quiet. _____ **(1, 2)**

Underline the complete predicate in each sentence. Circle the simple predicate.

4. The United States (needed) a cheap replacement for rubber during World War II. **(1, 2)**

5. Engineer James Wright (experimented) with a substitute for rubber. **(1, 2)**

6. This substitute (would be used) in the production of jeep tires and military gear. **(1, 2)**

7. His strange substance (was) not useful. **(1, 2)**

8. The stretchy stuff (bounced) well. **(1, 2)**

9. Some stores (sell) his compound as "Silly Putty." **(1, 2)**

Draw one line under each compound subject in these sentences. Draw two lines under each compound predicate.

10. Levi Strauss invented blue jeans and became world-famous. **(3)**

11. Miners and cowboys needed durable clothes in the old West. **(3)**

12. Strauss designed and made overalls out of denim, a heavy cloth. **(3)**

13. Blue jeans were useful for work and became a fashion item by 1935. **(3)**

Objects, Predicate Nouns, and Predicate Adjectives

Circle the term in parentheses that correctly describes the boldfaced word in each sentence.

14. The ice cream cone is an American **invention**. (predicate noun/direct object) **(6)**

15. Two vendors at the 1904 St. Louis World's Fair created **it**. (predicate adjective/direct object) **(4)**

16. People at the fair were **hungry** for snacks. (predicate noun/predicate adjective) **(6)**

17. An ice cream vendor needed more **dishes**. (direct object/indirect object) **(4)**

18. He was becoming **desperate**. (predicate adjective/direct object) **(6)**

19. A nearby waffle vendor gave **him** some rolled waffles. (direct object/indirect object) **(5)**

20. The ice cream vendor put **ice cream** on the waffle cones. (predicate noun/direct object) **(4)**

21. He offered **customers** this portable treat. (direct object/indirect object) **(5)**

22. The ice cream cone was an instant **hit**. (predicate noun/predicate adjective) **(6)**

23. Ice cream cones are a common **sight** on warm summer evenings. (direct object/predicate noun) **(6)**

Prepositional Phrases

Underline the prepositional phrase or phrases in each sentence. Circle the preposition. Draw a box around its object.

24. (For) many years, zippers and buttons were the main fasteners (in) the garment industry. **(7)**

25. A mountain climber (in) Switzerland invented Velcro. **(7)**

26. Prickly burrs clinging (to) his clothing gave him an idea. **(7)**

27. Pairs (of) prickly cloth strips could substitute (for) zippers! **(7)**

28. Some shoes, especially (for) children, are fastened (with) Velcro. **(7)**

29. (By) the late 1950s, textile looms produced sixty million yards (of) Velcro. **(7)**

Circle each adjectival prepositional phrase. Underline each adverbial prepositional phrase. Draw a box around the word each phrase modifies.

30. The invention (of the Frisbee) was a happy accident. **(8)**

31. The creator (of this toy) was the Frisbie Pie Company. **(8)**

32. The Frisbie Pie Company was located in Bridgeport, Connecticut. **(9)**

33. Their pies were sold in round metal pans. **(9)**

34. The family name was etched across the bottom (of these pans). **(8, 9)**

35. Students (at Yale University) saved the pie pans. **(8)**

36. They flipped these metal pans to one another. **(9)**

37. The pans sailed gracefully through the air. **(9)**

38. The students' name (for this new game) was "Frisbie." **(8)**

39. Plastic Frisbees were soon sold throughout the country. **(9)**

40. This game is still a popular activity among children and adults. **(9)**

Appositives

Underline the appositive in each sentence.

41. H. Cecil Booth, an inventor of the late 1890s, lay on the floor and inhaled dust through a cloth
as an experiment. **(10)**

42. The secret, finding the right kind of filtering bag, would be his path to success. **(10)**

43. His messy experiment resulted in a suction cleaning machine, the vacuum cleaner. **(10)**

44. Regina and Hoover, early commercial vacuum cleaners, were known for their fine quality
and reliability. **(10)**

45. Some people today use a new type of cleaning device, a vacuum cleaner without a dust bag. **(10)**

Name _____

Looking Back

Community Connection

In Unit 1 of *G.U.M.* students learned about **different types of sentences** and **sentence structures** and used what they learned to improve their own writing. The content of these lessons focuses on the theme **Innovations That Changed History**. As students completed the exercises, they learned the stories behind some of the most influential creations in history—and some of the strangest. These pages offer a variety of activities that reinforce skills and concepts presented in the unit. They also provide opportunities for the student to make connections between the historical material in the lessons and innovative, productive activities going on today in the community.

Innovation Next Door

Identify a factory or manufacturing company in or near your community that produces something interesting or especially useful. Then arrange to visit it during working hours to see for yourself how the products are made. You might begin by contacting your Chamber of Commerce and asking for the names of some local factories or plants. Here are some questions you might try to answer about the place you select:

- What is the most interesting or important product manufactured here? What is innovative about it? What is its function?
- What raw materials are needed to produce the product? Where do these come from?
- What sequence of steps is involved in making the product? What is innovative about this process?
- Where is the finished product sold?
- Who are potential buyers of the product?
- How is the product transported?

Write answers to these questions in complete sentences. Check to make sure that each sentence has a subject and a predicate. Then use the questions and answers to prepare an oral or written report.

All-Star Inventors

Learn more about great inventors of the past and present by writing a business letter to the Inventors Hall of Fame. The Inventors Hall of Fame is housed at The Inventure Place in Akron, Ohio. It contains exhibits and displays about George Washington Carver, Thomas Edison, Alexander Graham Bell, and many other inventors. Here's the address:

> Inventure Place
> 221 South Broadway
> Akron, Ohio 44308-1505
> (330) 762-4463

Ask for information about one of these topics:

- inventors from your city or state
- the origins of one of your favorite products or devices
- the life and work of an inventor you admire

HINT: To review the format of a business letter, see **G.U.M. Handbook** Section 34.

Bright Ideas

Close your eyes and imagine an invention that would make life in your community easier, safer, or more fun. Draw a sketch of your invention. Then write a description of what it would do and how it would work. Use prepositional phrases to help readers understand where and when your invention would be used. Use appositives to give more information about your invention.

Example	My invention is a magnetic repulsion system, a device for preventing auto accidents. This system uses electromagnetism to deflect oncoming vehicles. It can be installed in any auto or truck. A car equipped with this system can sense when another vehicle is on a collision course with it. When the system senses that a collision may occur, it activates an extremely powerful electromagnet in the part of the car that may be hit. The magnetic force produced is so great that it deflects the other car and prevents a direct collision.

Patent Pending   Answers will vary.

Learn more about the process of obtaining a patent for an invention. Use this form to help you gather information and organize notes.

United States Patent and Trademark Office

Address: _____

Telephone Number: _____

Web site: _____

Questions I Want to Ask: _____

_____

_____

My Findings
Types of Patents:

1. _____

2. _____

3. _____

Cost of Obtaining a Patent: _____

Process of Obtaining a Patent:

1. _____

2. _____

3. _____

4. _____

5. _____

Name _____

Looking Back

Read and Discover

Read these four kinds of sentences.

Wow, that creature must be 40 feet long! Is it a whale?
No, it's a whale shark, the world's largest fish.
Tell me more.

Write the end mark that follows the command. __.__

Write the end mark that follows the sentence that shows excitement. __!__

Write the end mark that follows the question. __?__

Write the end mark that follows the statement. __.__

A **declarative sentence** makes a statement and ends with a period. An **interrogative sentence** asks a question and ends with a question mark. An **imperative sentence** gives a command and ends with a period or an exclamation point. An **exclamatory sentence** shows excitement and ends with an exclamation point. Begin every sentence with a capital letter.

See Handbook Section 10

Part 1

Add the correct punctuation mark to each sentence. Then label it *declarative, interrogative, imperative,* or *exclamatory.*

1. Listen to this. (or)! _imperative or exclamatory_

2. The mouth of a whale shark is big enough to swallow two people whole. _declarative_

3. What a big mouth! _exclamatory_

4. Are these fish dangerous to humans? _interrogative_

5. No, whale sharks eat only very small fish and plankton. _declarative_

6. If a whale shark accidentally swallows something large, it turns its stomach inside out to get rid of it. _declarative_

7. Imagine getting swallowed and spat out again. (or)! _imperative or exclamatory_

8. How can such a huge creature live on tiny animals? _interrogative_

9. Look at this picture of plankton. _imperative_

10. Wow, it looks like a big cloud in the water! _exclamatory_

11. Whale sharks vacuum in large gulps of plankton-filled water, filtering out millions of creatures. _declarative_

12. Do some whales eat that way, too? _interrogative_

13. Yes, baleen whales use the bony plates in their mouths as strainers to separate tiny creatures from seawater and eat them. _declarative_

14. May I borrow that book about whale sharks? _interrogative_

15. Remember to return it to the library. _imperative_

A whale shark weighs as much as an elephant.

Part 2   Possible answers appear below. Accept all reasonable responses.

Rewrite each sentence so it is the type of sentence indicated in parentheses.

16. You should tell me about the differences between whale sharks and other sharks. (imperative)
Tell me the differences between whale sharks and other sharks.

17. Most sharks bear live young. (interrogative) **Do most sharks bear live young?**

18. Whale sharks give birth to live young! (declarative) **Whale sharks give birth to live young.**

19. Whale sharks are amazing animals. (exclamatory) **Whale sharks are amazing animals!**

20. I don't understand why whale sharks aren't classified as whales. (interrogative) **Why aren't whale sharks classified as whales?**

21. Aren't whales mammals and whale sharks fish? (declarative) **Whales are mammals and whale sharks are fish.**

22. Will you read this book to learn more about whale sharks? (imperative) **Read this book to learn more about whale sharks.**

Part 3

Authors often use a variety of sentence types to make their writing more interesting. Herman Melville's novel *Moby-Dick* begins with the famous imperative sentence, "Call me Ishmael." Notice the declarative, interrogative, imperative, and exclamatory sentences the author uses in this passage.

Go from Corlears Hook to Coenties Slip, and from thence, by Whitehall, northward. What do you see?—Posted like silent sentinels all around the town, stand thousands upon thousands of mortal men fixed in ocean reveries....Are the green fields gone? What do they here?

But look! Here come more crowds, pacing straight for the water, and seemingly bound for a dive. Strange! Nothing will content them but the extremest limit of the land...

—Herman Melville, from *Moby-Dick*

Imagine you are a diver seeing a whale shark for the first time. Write three short sentences of different types giving your impressions.

23. **Answers will vary.**

24. _____

25. _____

Name _____

a. The sea horse has a horselike head **and** a curly tail.
b. The sea horse resembles a horse, **but** it is a true fish.

Cross out the boldfaced conjunction in each sentence.
Which sentence could be punctuated as two separate sentences? __b.__

A **simple sentence** is made up of a subject and a predicate and expresses only one complete thought. It is an *independent clause*. A **compound sentence** is made of two closely related independent clauses. The two clauses can be joined by a comma and a coordinating conjunction (*and, but,* or *or*) or by a semicolon (;).

See Handbook Sections 8, 13, 22

Part 1

Write *S* next to each simple sentence. Write *CD* next to each compound sentence. Circle the comma and conjunction or the semicolon in each compound sentence.

1. Most sea horses are less than six inches long, but the Eastern Pacific sea horse can be fourteen inches long. __CD__

2. Sea horses are covered with knobby, bony armor; few predators will eat them. __CD__

3. Sea horses are not strong swimmers. __S__

4. They live in warm, shallow water in the shelter of sea grass beds. __S__

5. Like a monkey's tail, a sea horse's tail can grasp things; scientists call this kind of tail prehensile. __CD__

6. Sea horses must grasp stems of sea grass with their tails, or currents might sweep them away. __CD__

7. A sea horse sucks plankton through its tube-shaped mouth. __S__

8. A sea horse's eyes swivel independently; it can spot prey in any direction. __CD__

9. Sea horses change color in response to their surroundings. __S__

10. The sea horse looks strange, but its appearance is not its most unusual feature. __CD__

11. Virtually unique in the animal kingdom, the male sea horse can become pregnant. __S__

12. At the full moon, the female sea horse lays eggs in the male sea horse's brood pouch. __S__

13. The brood pouch is like a kangaroo's pouch, and the male sea horse nurtures the eggs inside it. __CD__

14. Sea horses are monogamous; they remain with the same mate throughout the breeding season. __CD__

15. After about two weeks, tiny sea horses emerge from the pouch. __S__

Some sea horses can have as many as 300 babies at a time!

Part 2   Possible answers appear below. Accept all reasonable responses.

Rewrite each pair of simple sentences as one compound sentence.

16.   Sea dragons are related to sea horses. They look even stranger. __Sea dragons are related to sea__ __horses, but they look even stranger.__

17.   They live among leafy seaweed. Their bodies have developed leaflike appendages. __They live among__ __leafy seaweed, and their bodies have developed leaflike appendages.__

18.   Sea dragons are perfectly camouflaged. Most predators wouldn't eat this bony creature anyway. __Sea dragons are perfectly camouflaged, but most predators wouldn't eat this bony creature__ __anyway.__

19.   Male sea horses bear young. So do male sea dragons. __Male sea horses bear young; so do male__ __sea dragons.__

20.   Male sea dragons have no brood pouch. They are still able to nurture eggs. __Male sea dragons have__ __no brood pouch, but they are still able to nurture eggs.__

Part 3

Use clues from Parts 1 and 2 to complete the puzzle.

Across
2.   Ocean vegetation
4.   Remaining with one mate
5.   A tail capable of grasping
6.   Any animal that hunts other animals for food

Down
1.   Tiny ocean life
2.   A fish that resembles a horse
3.   Water that moves in a pattern

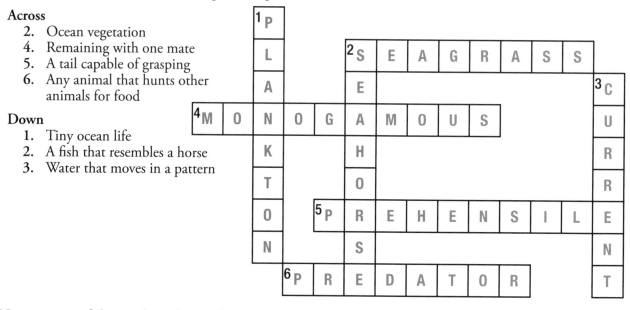

Now use two of the words in the puzzle to write a compound sentence.

21.   __Answers will vary.__

Name _____

Beasts & Critters

Read and Discover

Although California sea otters are mammals, <u>they usually spend their entire lives in the water.</u>

Look at the two parts of this sentence. Which part makes sense by itself? **b.**

a. the boldfaced part **b.** the underlined part

An **independent clause** is a group of words with a subject and a predicate that makes sense by itself. A **dependent clause** has a subject and a predicate, but it does not express a complete thought by itself. It needs—or is dependent on—an independent clause. Often a dependent clause begins with a subordinating conjunction such as *although, because, if, as,* or *when.* When a dependent clause begins a sentence, it is separated from the independent clause with a comma.

See Handbook Sections 8, 13, 22

Part 1

Draw one line under each independent clause. Draw two lines under each dependent clause. Circle the subordinating conjunction that begins each dependent clause.

1. (When) sea otters sleep, they roll themselves in a floating blanket of kelp.

2. A sea otter usually dives to the bottom (if) it becomes hungry.

3. (When) it has found a clam or a sea urchin and a flat rock, it brings them back to the surface.

4. The otter floats on its back (while) it prepares its lunch.

5. (As) the otter holds the rock on its chest, it bangs the clam or sea urchin against the rock.

6. (After) the shell breaks open, the otter has a tasty meal.

7. Otters smile (as) they eat.

8. (Because) shells often have sharp edges, an otter carefully holds its lips away from its teeth in a grin.

9. Whales, walruses, sea lions, and dolphins can thrive in icy ocean water (because) they have a thick layer of insulating blubber under their skin.

Sea otters use rocks as tools to break open shells.

10. (Although) sea otters have no blubber, their dense, luxurious fur keeps them warm.

11. (As) an otter grooms its fur, tiny insulating air bubbles are trapped among the hairs.

12. An otter would freeze to death (if) it did not groom itself regularly.

13. People once hunted sea otters (because) their fur is so warm and soft.

14. (When) a 1911 treaty finally put an end to the slaughter, sea otters had almost become extinct.

15. (Although) they have been an endangered species for many years, sea otters are making a comeback.

Beasts & Critters

Part 2   Possible answers appear below. Accept all reasonable responses.

Draw a line to match each dependent clause with an independent clause. Then write the new sentences you have created on the lines. Be sure to add punctuation.

Dependent Clauses

although otters are no longer threatened by hunting

if there was a major oil spill

since otters eat fish

when storms hit the California coast

when human volunteers teach orphaned pups how to live in the ocean

Independent Clauses

orphaned baby sea otters are sometimes washed ashore

more otters survive in the wild

they face other threats

hundreds of California sea otters might die in the muck

fisheries see them as competitors

16. Although otters are no longer threatened by hunting, they face other threats.

17. If there was a major oil spill, hundreds of California sea otters might die in the muck.

18. Since otters eat fish, fisheries see them as competitors.

19. Orphaned baby sea otters are sometimes washed ashore when storms hit the California coast.

20. When human volunteers teach orphaned pups how to live in the ocean, more otters survive in the wild.

Part 3

On the lines below, write three funny or unusual dependent clauses. (Example: "After the octopus waved goodbye,") Trade papers with a partner. Complete your partner's sentences by writing an independent clause to go with each dependent clause. Take your own paper back and read the independent clauses your partner wrote.

21. Answers will vary.

22.

23.

Name

Beasts & Critters

Read and Discover

a. Although octopuses once had a reputation as horrible monsters͵ most of these shy animals are not dangerous to humans.

b. Octopuses are the smartest invertebrates; they are as intelligent as house cats.

Cross out the comma in sentence a. and the semicolon in sentence b. Which sentence begins with a clause that would *not* be a sentence if a period were added to it? __a.__
Which sentence could become two separate sentences? __b.__

A dependent clause must be joined with an independent clause to make sense. A sentence made up of an independent clause and a dependent clause is a **complex sentence**. A dependent clause often begins with a subordinating conjunction such as *although, because, if, as,* or *when*.

See Handbook Sections 8, 13, 22

Part 1

Write *CX* next to each complex sentence. Write *CD* next to each compound sentence. Then circle each dependent clause and draw a box around each independent clause.

1. Because octopuses have no backbone, scientists call them invertebrates. __CX__

2. Octopuses are good hunters; they have a hard, beaklike mouth and eight legs with suckers. __CD__

3. Although octopuses have eight legs, they do not use them for swimming. __CX__

4. Octopuses take in water and squirt streams of it from their saclike bodies, and this propels them through the ocean. __CD__

5. If an octopus loses a leg, it can grow another. __CX__

6. An octopus might grab its prey with its legs, or it might drop down on top of its prey like a net. __CD__

Because octopuses are flexible, they can squeeze through crevices.

7. Though the octopus is a hunter, it is hunted by other creatures as well. __CX__

8. Seals, dolphins, and humans hunt octopuses; some people eat octopus meat raw in sushi. __CD__

9. Although octopuses are not related to sea horses, both animals change color for camouflage. __CX__

10. When an octopus is threatened, it squirts out a spray of black ink. __CX__

11. Because the cloud of ink is shaped like the octopus itself, it confuses the attacker. __CX__

12. Female octopuses lay as many as 80,000 eggs, and they tend them in underwater nests for six months or more. __CD__

13. The female octopus usually starves to death while she watches over her eggs. __CX__

14. Scientists call octopuses, squid, and nautiluses cephalopods; this word means "head-footed." __CD__

15. Scientists chose this name because the legs of these animals seem to grow from their heads. __CX__

Beasts & Critters

Part 2 Possible answers appear below. Accept all reasonable responses.

Combine each pair of simple sentences to create a complex sentence. Include the subordinating conjunction given in parentheses.

16. (because) The nautilus has two hundred tentacles and a spiral shell. It is not easily recognized as a relative of the octopus. _Because the nautilus has two hundred tentacles and a spiral shell, it is not easily recognized as a relative of the octopus._

17. (when) Dinosaurs roamed the earth. Thousands of species of shelled creatures like the nautilus filled the seas. _When dinosaurs roamed the earth, thousands of species of shelled creatures like the nautilus filled the seas._

18. (because) Its hard shell protects it from water pressure. The nautilus can survive at extreme depths. _The nautilus can survive at extreme depths because its hard shell protects it from water pressure._

19. (although) There are many chambers in a nautilus shell. The animal lives only in the outermost one. _Although there are many chambers in a nautilus shell, the animal lives only in the outermost one._

20. (as) The nautilus pumps gas in or out of the inner chambers of its shell. It lowers or raises itself in the water. _As the nautilus pumps gas in or out of the inner chambers of its shell, it lowers or raises itself in the water._

Part 3

> A complex sentence is made up of two clauses and shows the relationship between the clauses. It can make a narrative flow more smoothly. A *compound-complex* sentence goes even further. It joins three or more clauses together with subordinating and coordinating conjunctions. A compound-complex sentence includes both dependent and independent clauses. Authors can pack a huge amount of information into one compound-complex sentence.

Read the passage below and underline the compound-complex sentence. How many independent clauses does this sentence contain? __2__ How many dependent clauses does it contain? __2__

    As the boat bounced from the top of each wave, the wind tore through the hair of the hatless men, and as the craft plopped her stern down again the spray slashed past them. The crest of each of these waves was a hill, from the top of which the men surveyed for a moment a broad tumultuous expanse, shining and wind-riven.

—Stephen Crane, from "The Open Boat"

Now find your own examples of compound-complex sentences in a story or textbook chapter you are currently reading. List at least three on another sheet of paper. Circle each independent clause and underline each dependent clause in these sentences.

Name _____

Read and Discover

Scientists have developed submarines that can explore the deepest reaches of the ocean.

Underline the dependent clause that tells what kind of submarines have been developed. Could this part stand alone as a sentence? __no__

An **adjective clause** is a dependent clause that describes a noun or a pronoun. An adjective clause always follows the word it describes and begins with a relative pronoun such as *who, whom, whose, which,* or *that.*

See Handbook Sections 8, 13, 17g

Part 1

Underline the adjective clause in each sentence. Circle the noun the clause describes. Draw a box around the relative pronoun.

1. Explorers who first descended to the sea's deep regions returned with tales of bizarre, unknown creatures.

2. These creatures, which have adapted to conditions in the dark water below 1,000 feet, are unlike any others.

3. Many have huge eyes and mouths as well as organs that glow in the inky darkness.

4. Some deep-sea creatures glow for reasons that are sinister.

5. The deep-sea angler has a glowing plume that dangles over its mouth.

6. The plume, which resembles a tiny organism, attracts would-be predators.

7. The angler eats any fish that comes close enough.

8. The umbrella mouth gulper eel has a mouth that expands for huge bites.

9. This two-foot-long creature can eat fish that are larger than itself.

10. It couldn't eat an oarfish, whose narrow body can grow up to thirty-five feet long.

11. Sailors whom oarfish frightened on occasional trips to the surface probably started the old legends of "sea serpents."

12. Imaginary animals could never be as strange as the real animals that inhabit the deep sea.

13. The giant squid, which lives in the depths, can grow to sixty feet or more in length.

14. Divers who have seen these rare creatures consider themselves fortunate.

15. Clear photographs of strange creatures that live deep in the ocean are quite valuable.

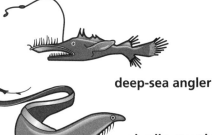

deep-sea angler

umbrella mouth gulper eel

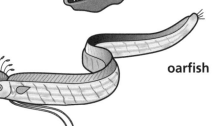

oarfish

Part 2 Possible answers appear below. Accept all reasonable responses.

Rewrite each pair of sentences as one complex sentence; change the underlined sentence into an adjective clause beginning with *who, which,* or *that.*

16. Bizarre undersea "gardens" were discovered by scientists. <u>The scientists studied thermal springs on the ocean floor.</u> **Bizarre undersea "gardens" were discovered by scientists who studied thermal springs on the ocean floor.**

17. The scientists found ten-foot-long bright red worms. <u>These worms bloomed from the tops of white tubes.</u> **The scientists found ten-foot-long bright red worms that bloomed from the tops of white tubes.**

18. Huge clumps of the worms grew around warm water. <u>The water streamed from volcanic rifts.</u> **Huge clumps of the worms grew around warm water, which streamed from volcanic rifts.**

19. The scientists also found foot-long clams with bright red meat. <u>The meat was colored by hemoglobin.</u> **The scientists also found foot-long clams with bright red meat that was colored by hemoglobin.**

Part 3

Find six words in the puzzle. Write them where they fit in the blanks.

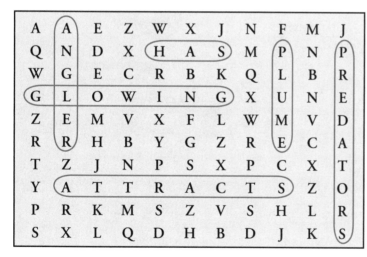

Across

H A S

G L O W I N G

A T T R A C T S

Down

A N G L E R

P L U M E

P R E D A T O R S

Use the words you found to make a complex sentence. Include an adjective clause that begins with *that.*

20. **Answers will vary.**

Name _____

Beasts & Critters

Read and Discover

An 8,000-pound elephant seal sleeps <u>wherever it wants</u>.

Underline the dependent clause that tells where an elephant seal sleeps. Does this part of the sentence make sense by itself? __no__

An **adverb clause** is a dependent clause that tells about a verb, an adjective, or an adverb. Adverb clauses tell *where, when, why,* or *how much*. They often begin with a subordinating conjunction such as *than, although, because, if, as, as if, while, when,* or *whenever*.

See Handbook Sections 8, 13, 22

Part 1

Underline the adverb clause in each sentence.

1. <u>Before they adapted to life in the sea</u>, seals were land animals similar to otters and bears.

2. <u>When seals' ancestors moved to the water</u>, changes to their bodies occurred from generation to generation.

3. Now flippers paddle <u>where paws once stepped</u>.

4. <u>Although seals still have all the bones for four legs</u>, only the ankle and foot bones protrude from their barrel-shaped bodies.

5. A seal's shape improves its speed in the water <u>because currents flow smoothly past its streamlined body</u>.

6. <u>As seals developed their swimming ability</u>, they gave up most of their agility on land.

7. However, eared seals, or sea lions, move more quickly on land <u>than true seals do</u>.

8. <u>While eared seals can walk on their flippers</u>, true seals must wriggle on land with a caterpillarlike motion.

9. <u>If they must find food or evade a predator</u>, some seals can dive down to 2,900 feet below the surface.

10. Seals need sharp vision <u>because there is little light in the ocean's depths</u>.

11. <u>Although they spend most of their time in the water</u>, true seals come to beaches for the breeding season.

12. Seals often breed <u>where they were born</u>.

13. Mother seals nurse their pups <u>while males compete for beach territory</u>.

14. Male elephant seals on breeding beaches look <u>as if they are immense slugs</u>.

15. <u>After the new pups have been weaned</u>, the seals return to the sea.

Fur seals were hunted for their coats, but now they are protected.

Part 2   Possible answers appear below. Accept all reasonable responses.

Rewrite each pair of simple sentences as one complex sentence. Use the word in parentheses to change the underlined sentence into an adverb clause.

16.   (because) <u>Seals' eyes look much like human eyes.</u> The Scottish have made up legends about seal-people, or selkies.   __Because seals' eyes look much like human eyes, the Scottish have__ __made up legends about seal-people, or selkies.__

17.   (although) <u>Selkies wear seal skins.</u> They look like humans underneath.   __Although selkies wear seal__ __skins, they look like humans underneath.__

18.   (since) <u>Selkies can't swim in their natural form.</u> They must wear a fish or seal skin.   __Since selkies__ __can't swim in their natural form, they must wear a fish or seal skin.__

19.   (whenever) <u>The moon is full.</u> Selkies shed their skins and dance on the beach in human form.   __Selkies shed their skins and dance on the beach in human form whenever the moon is full.__

20.   (If) <u>A human steals a selkie's skin.</u> The selkie will be in that human's power.   __If a human steals a__ __selkie's skin, the selkie will be in that human's power.__

21.   (When) <u>The selkie gets its skin back.</u> It will return to the sea.   __When the selkie gets its skin back,__ __it will return to the sea.__

Part 3

In this activity, you will distinguish among adverbs, adverb phrases, and adverb clauses. Draw a line from each sentence to the correct description of the boldfaced word or words.

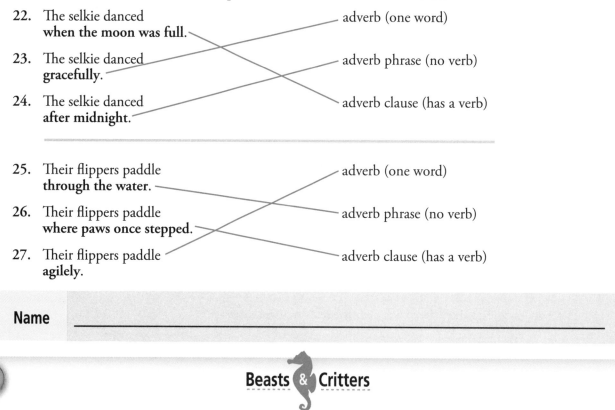

22.   The selkie danced **when the moon was full**.   adverb (one word)

23.   The selkie danced **gracefully**.   adverb phrase (no verb)

24.   The selkie danced **after midnight**.   adverb clause (has a verb)

25.   Their flippers paddle **through the water**.   adverb (one word)

26.   Their flippers paddle **where paws once stepped**.   adverb phrase (no verb)

27.   Their flippers paddle **agilely**.   adverb clause (has a verb)

Name _____

Beasts & Critters

Read and Discover

a. Crabs use their claws **to defend themselves**.
b. Crabs belong **to the crustacean family**.

Look at each boldfaced phrase. In which phrase is *to* followed by a verb? __a.__

In which phrase is *to* followed by an article, an adjective, and a noun? __b.__

An **infinitive** is a phrase made up of the word *to* followed by the present form of a verb (*to defend*). Infinitives may act as adjectives, adverbs, or nouns. An **infinitive phrase** is made up of an infinitive and any other words that complete its meaning. In sentence a. above, *to defend themselves* is an infinitive phrase.

See Handbook Section 25

Part 1

Underline each infinitive phrase.

1. Scientists use the term *exoskeleton* to talk about a crab's shell.

2. Most crabs molt, or shed their rigid shells, in order to grow larger.

3. Just after molting, without a hard shell to protect them, crabs are very vulnerable.

4. The hermit crab finds an abandoned spiral shell to make its home.

5. When a hermit crab grows too large for its shell, it searches for another shell to occupy.

6. If a crab loses a leg, it is able to regenerate, or grow another.

7. Eyes perched high on stalks allow a ghost crab to watch for prey while the rest of its body is buried in sand.

8. The pea crab is tiny enough to live inside the shell of a live oyster.

9. On the other hand, you might need a twelve-foot-long ruler to measure an adult giant spider crab.

10. Because the giant spider crab normally lives at depths of around 1,200 feet, divers are rarely able to observe this amazing creature.

11. You might be surprised to find that some "crabs" are not crabs at all.

12. Many people assume horseshoe crabs to be crustaceans, but they are actually relatives of spiders and scorpions.

13. These creatures appear to have changed little since prehistoric times.

14. They were already ancient animals when dinosaurs began to prowl the earth.

15. Scientists hope the horseshoe crab will be able to survive for another 360 million years.

The giant spider crab is the world's largest crustacean.

Beasts & Critters

Part 2

Write an infinitive from the word bank to complete each sentence.

to lay	to grasp	to describe	to molt	to wait

16. Observers use the phrase "shaking hands" _____ to describe _____ the mating ritual of the Alaskan king crab.

17. A male king crab looks for a female who is preparing _____ to molt _____, or shed her skin.

18. He uses his powerful claws _____ to grasp _____ her front legs tightly until molting occurs.

19. Only after molting is the female crab able _____ to lay _____ eggs.

20. The male crab may have as long as two weeks _____ to wait _____, but he hangs on nonetheless.

Part 3

Many *aphorisms,* or sayings, use infinitives to name actions. Underline the infinitive phrases in the following well-known aphorisms. Note that the last aphorism contains an understood infinitive, indicated in brackets.

"It is better to give than to receive."
—Anonymous

"'Tis better to have loved and lost than never to have loved at all."
—Alfred, Lord Tennyson

"To err is human, to forgive divine."
—Alexander Pope

"It is better to know some of the questions than [to know] all of the answers."
—James Thurber

Write an aphorism of your own, using an infinitive, to give your reader advice.

21. __Answers will vary.__
_____
_____
_____

Name _____

Beasts & Critters

Read and Discover

Armed with a deadly weapon, the scorpionfish swims calmly through tropical waters.

Circle the two verbs in the sentence above. Which verb has a subject just before it? _____ **swims** _____

Which verb is part of a phrase with no subject? _____ **armed** _____

Sometimes a verb does not act as the simple predicate of a sentence. A **verbal** is a word formed from a verb that plays another role in the sentence. One type of verbal is a **participle**. A participle may be a present participle (usually the present form + *-ing: eating*) or a past participle. Regular verbs form the past participle by adding *-ed* (*armed*). Irregular verbs change their spelling in the past participle (*eaten, brought*). A **participial phrase** is made of a participle and other words that complete its meaning. A participial phrase can act as an adjective. In the sentence above, *Armed with a deadly weapon* is a participial phrase describing the scorpionfish.

See Handbook Sections 18d, 25

Part 1

Underline each participial phrase. Then circle the participle.

1. Even a very hungry predator will avoid a fish (covered) with venomous spines.

2. (Fearing) the effects of the poison, divers stay well away from this colorful fish.

3. The fish (displaying) colorful, feathery fins with stripes is a turkeyfish, one variety of scorpionfish.

4. Children (visiting) aquariums often watch this beautiful fish for many minutes.

5. The type of scorpionfish (known) as the lionfish is also admired for its beauty.

6. A scorpionfish (displaying) its stripes and colors is giving a warning to other creatures.

7. Not all scorpionfish have colors or stripes (decorating) their bodies.

8. A type of scorpionfish (called) the stonefish has no distinctive markings.

9. (Resembling) a rock, the stonefish attracts no attention.

10. (Lying) motionless on the ocean floor, it waits for a slow-moving fish.

11. (Seeing) only a gray lump, other fish swim into this creature's reach.

12. Divers (exploring) the ocean floor may mistake a stonefish for a rock.

13. Needle-sharp spines (hidden) beneath the stonefish's skin deliver a painful, dangerous sting.

14. Venom (injected) by the stonefish quickly circulates through the diver's body.

15. Fortunately, an antidote to stonefish venom is available in a number of cities near parts of the ocean (inhabited) by stonefish.

16. A sting victim (taken) quickly to a hospital has a good chance for survival.

A scorpionfish can be extremely dangerous.

Beasts & Critters

Part 2 Possible answers appear below. Accept all reasonable responses.

A participial phrase must be placed near the noun or pronoun it modifies, or it can create confusion for the reader. The participial phrase in each sentence below is misplaced. Rewrite each sentence so that it makes sense.

17. Known throughout the world for its teeming sea life, Alex and Shanna couldn't wait to dive at the Great Barrier Reef. _Alex and Shanna couldn't wait to dive at the Great Barrier Reef, known throughout the world for its teeming sea life._

18. Hardened skeletons of dead water animals make up the coral in this reef called polyps. _Hardened skeletons of dead water animals called polyps make up the coral in this reef._

19. Alex and Shanna hired an instructor not knowing how to scuba dive. _Not knowing how to scuba dive, Alex and Shanna hired an instructor._

20. They gazed through their face masks at the astonishing creatures around them enjoying their new experience. _Enjoying their new experience, they gazed through their face masks at the astonishing creatures around them._

21. Covered with waving tentacles, Alex stared at a flowerlike sea anemone. _Alex stared at the flower-like sea anemone covered with waving tentacles._

Part 3

An absolute phrase consists of a noun or noun phrase followed by a descriptive word or phrase. Like a participial phrase, an absolute phrase may contain a verbal form ending in *-ing* or *-ed*. It may also contain an adjective, a noun, or a prepositional phrase.

Example

noun phrase + verbal phrase
The fish displayed its fins, <u>the stripes warning other creatures of the danger</u>.
noun phrase + adjective
The stonefish attracted no attention, <u>its body motionless</u>.

Underline the absolute phrase in each sentence below. Then discuss with a partner how that description makes the sentence interesting to read.

22. <u>Its fins feathery and bright</u>, the scorpionfish is gorgeous to look at.

23. Lila sat in the back of the boat, <u>her scuba gear on the deck beside her</u>.

24. We slowly toured the aquarium, <u>our teacher stopping at important exhibits</u>.

Name _____

Beasts & Critters

Read and Discover

Gerund Phrases

Lesson 19

a. **Building** a coral reef ⟨takes⟩ many centuries.
b. Tiny animals ⟨create⟩ the reef by **depositing** calcium carbonate.

Circle the simple predicate in each sentence. Draw a box around each verb form ending in *-ing*. Is either *-ing* form part of a simple predicate? __no__

Is the boldfaced phrase in sentence a. the subject of the sentence, the direct object, or an object of a preposition? __the subject of the sentence__

Is the boldfaced phrase in sentence b. the subject of the sentence, the direct object, or the object of a preposition? __the object of a preposition__

A **gerund** is a verbal that acts as a noun. All gerunds are verb forms that end with *-ing*. A **gerund phrase** is made up of a gerund and the other words that complete its meaning. In the sentences above, *Building a coral reef* and *depositing calcium carbonate* are gerund phrases.

See Handbook Section 25

Part 1

Underline each gerund phrase. Draw a box around the gerund itself.

1. Swimming near coral reefs will acquaint you with many colorful fish.

2. The long blue teeth of the harlequin tusk fish are ideal for crushing the hard shells of clams.

3. Living among an anemone's poisonous tentacles might seem impossible.

4. The striped clownfish can do this because it is not harmed by the stinging of the anemone.

5. The beaklike mouth of the parrotfish is effective in grinding coral into sand.

6. This fine sand seems perfect for building sandcastles.

7. Spindly little spider crabs protect themselves by establishing homes inside hollow tube sponges.

8. A tiny cleaner shrimp attracts a reef fish by waving its long antennae.

9. Cleaner shrimp help reef fish by eating parasites off their skin.

10. Seeing the bright blue fringe on the four-foot-wide mouth of a giant clam is an unforgettable experience.

11. Diving around reefs is made dangerous by scorpionfish and other fish with venomous spines.

12. Swimming in the ocean with an open wound may be a dangerous thing to do.

13. Sharks sometimes find prey by following the smell of blood.

14. Protecting live coral is a difficult task.

15. People harm coral by taking pieces as souvenirs.

16. Crown-of-thorns starfish have destroyed entire colonies of coral by devouring those tiny creatures.

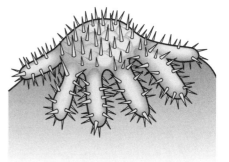

The crown-of-thorns starfish preys on living coral.

Part 2   Answers will vary.

Imagine you and your family are taking a vacation to an island in the South Pacific. Describe what you will do on this vacation by writing a gerund phrase to complete each sentence. The gerunds in the word bank may give you some ideas.

visiting	swimming	diving	photographing	eating	watching
catching	painting	protecting	helping	avoiding	seeing

17. I would enjoy _____.

18. _____ would be a new experience for me.

19. I would start each day by _____.

20. After breakfast I might try _____.

21. _____ would be fun for everyone in the family.

22. I would learn about coral reefs by _____.

23. Since I saw a documentary film on the tidewater pools, I think _____

_____ would be fun.

24. _____ is something that swimmers and

divers should try to do.

25. _____ would be a great activity toward

the end of the day.

Part 3

Authors, poets, and filmmakers frequently use gerund phrases as titles of works. "Crossing the Bar" is one of Alfred, Lord Tennyson's best-known poems, and "Stopping by Woods on a Snowy Evening" is one of Robert Frost's most famous works. *Living Free* was a popular movie about African lions.

Look in a library and in the entertainment section of a newspaper to find five other works that have gerund phrases as titles. List these titles on the lines below.

26. **Answers will vary.** _____

27. _____

28. _____

29. _____

30. _____

Name _____

Beasts & Critters

Read and Discover

Rays are related to sharks, both have skeletons made of cartilage. Although rays look very different, Differences in appearance or the way animals look to the observer are not always significantly important to the classification of those animals that may seem so different from each other.

Circle the dependent clause that is missing an independent clause. Underline the sentence that is written incorrectly because it is made up of two independent clauses without a conjunction. Write *X* at the beginning of the sentence that uses a lot of words to say very little.

A **fragment** does not tell a complete thought. A **run-on sentence** is a compound sentence that is missing a comma and a conjunction. A **comma splice** is a run-on sentence that has a comma but is missing a conjunction. A **ramble-on** sentence is correct grammatically but contains extra words and phrases that don't add to its meaning. Avoid fragments, run-ons, comma splices, and ramble-ons in the final versions of your written work.

See Handbook Sections 8, 14, 22

Part 1

Write *F* after each fragment. Write *RO* after each run-on. Write *CS* after each comma splice. Write *RA* after each ramble-on sentence.

1. Rays have wide, flat bodies and narrow tails, they are shaped almost like kites. __CS__

2. Rays flap their fins like a bird's wings they fly through the water. __RO__

3. Although their eyes are on the tops of their heads. __F__

4. Mouths on the underside. __F__

5. Rays cannot see their food, they must sense it with smell, touch, and electrosensors. __CS__

6. The low placement of the ray's mouth on the underside or bottom of its head makes the ray very well-suited for bottom feeding, or eating food off the sea floor, because its mouth is on the bottom near its food which is also there as well. __RA__

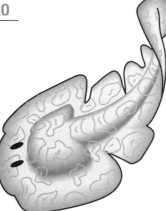

Electric rays can attack with electric shocks of up to 200 volts.

7. If a ray senses prey on the ocean floor. __F__

8. The ray's flat body drapes over the prey its mouth sucks the animal up. __RO__

9. Poisonous spines along a stingray's tail. __F__

10. Huge manta rays grow up to 20 feet across, these harmless animals eat only plankton. __CS__

11. A manta can jump six feet above the surface of the water it glides on its immense winglike fins. __RO__

12. Another fish in the ray family is the guitarfish, which was probably named in this way because it resembles that popular musical instrument known as the guitar, which has a shape somewhat similar to the shape of this fish. __RA__

Part 2 Answers will vary.

Rewrite the sentences from Part 1 that are listed below. Correct any fragments, run-ons, and comma splices. Shorten the ramble-ons. There is more than one way to correct each sentence. **(13–19)**

Sentence #2 _____

_____

Sentence #3 _____

_____

Sentence #5 _____

_____

Sentence #8 _____

_____

Sentence #9 _____

_____

Sentence #10 _____

_____

Sentence #12 _____

_____

_____

Part 3

This monster ramble-on sentence contains more than 50 words. Cross out unnecessary words, phrases, and clauses to make the sentence as short as possible. Write your revised sentence below.

~~Like sharks,~~ most fish of the ray variety, ~~including the manta ray, the stingray, and most other rays,~~ are covered ~~all over their bodies~~ with toothlike scales, ~~that resemble tiny teeth but are really scales, and which make the skin of these sharklike fish feel rough if you touch it with your hand.~~

20. **Suggested answer: Most fish of the ray variety are covered with toothlike scales.** _____

_____

Now try writing a monster sentence of your own. Start with a simple sentence, such as *The ray was swimming*. Add words, phrases, and clauses that add too much information for one good sentence. Then trade papers with a partner and trim each other's monster sentence.

21. **Answers will vary.** _____

_____

_____

Name _____

Beasts & Critters

Diagraming Compound Subjects

A sentence with a compound subject is diagramed this way:

Whales and dolphins swim.

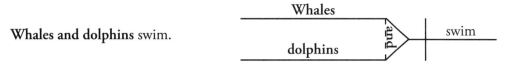

Diagram these sentences on the lines provided. (Refer to page 29 if you need help.)

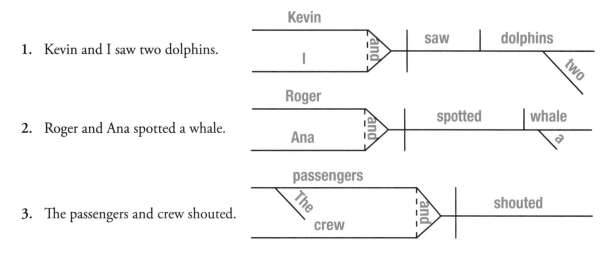

1. Kevin and I saw two dolphins.

2. Roger and Ana spotted a whale.

3. The passengers and crew shouted.

Diagraming Compound Predicates

A sentence with a compound predicate is diagramed this way:

The whales **leap and dive**.

Try diagraming these sentences.

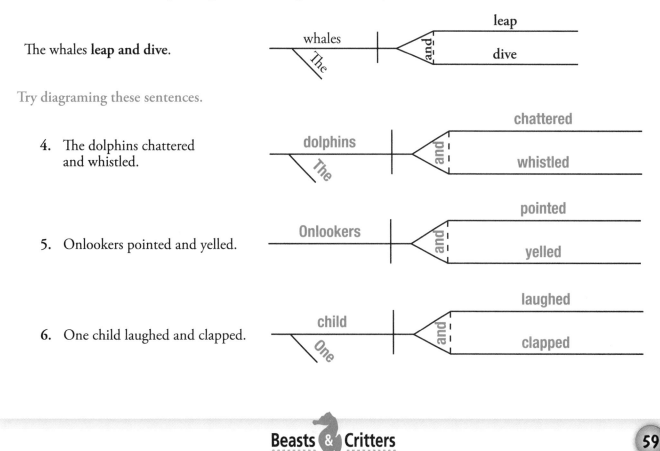

4. The dolphins chattered and whistled.

5. Onlookers pointed and yelled.

6. One child laughed and clapped.

Diagraming Compound Sentences

A compound sentence is diagramed this way:

One whale leaped, and another dove.

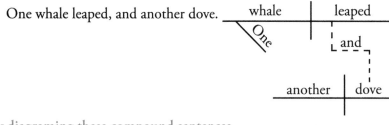

Try diagraming these compound sentences.

7. I carried binoculars, but they broke.

8. Ana had an extra pair, and I borrowed them.

9. The ship lurched, and some passengers stumbled.

10. The stormy clouds parted, and the sun shone.

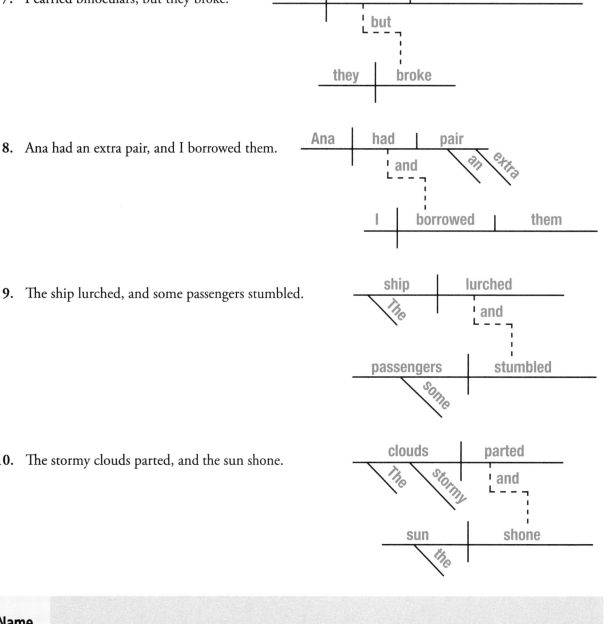

Name _____

Writing Sentences

Possible answers appear below. Accept all reasonable revisions.
The writer of these sentences has tried to include too many ideas. Rewrite each sentence as two or three shorter, clearer sentences. Make sure each sentence you write is complete.

1. Due to the great energy they expend, otters eat tremendous amounts of food, so they spend most of their day diving for shellfish such as abalone and sea urchins, which they crack with the help of a rock which they lay on their stomachs and use as an anvil.

   Because they expend a lot of energy, otters eat tremendous amounts of food. They spend most

   of their day diving for shellfish such as abalone and sea urchins. They crack the shellfish with

   the help of a rock that they place on their stomachs and use as an anvil.

   _____

   _____

   _____

   _____

   _____

2. Otters seem to smile as they eat the meat from the shellfish they have broken when they hold their lips away from their teeth because the broken shells often have sharp edges.

   Otters seem to smile as they eat the meat from the shellfish. This smile comes from holding

   their lips away from the sharp edges of the broken shells.

   _____

   _____

   _____

   _____

   _____

There are four kinds of sentences—a statement, a question, a command, and an exclamation. Any of these sentences may be simple, compound, or complex. Notice the different types of sentences in this model paragraph.

question ——————

statements ——————

complex sentence ——————

command ——————

exclamation ——————

Have you ever wondered what life is like at the bottom of the ocean? Last month I had a chance to find out by studying it with my own eyes. I rode in a submersible to explore an oceanic trench off the Pacific Coast. *Because the bottom of the trench is so deep, no sunlight reaches the creatures there.* Several fish that I saw glow through a process called bioluminescence. **Imagine seeing an anglerfish use its glowing lure to attract prey.** *Wow, that was impressive!*

Writing a Paragraph

The sentences you repaired on page 61 can be used to make a paragraph. Decide what order the sentences should be in. Then revise at least two of the sentences so your paragraph has a variety of sentence types. Use the model on page 61 as a reference. Write the paragraph on the lines below.

A possible answer appears below. Accept all reasonable responses.

     Because they expend a lot of energy, otters eat tremendous amounts of food. They spend most of their day diving for such shellfish as abalone and sea urchins. To crack the shellfish, they place a rock on their stomachs and use it as an anvil. Otters seem to smile as they eat the meat from the shellfish, but is it a real smile? No. They are just holding their lips away from the sharp edges of the broken shells.

Imagine that you are an ocean diver. You have just returned from a dive during which you saw many unusual creatures. Write a paragraph about your experience. Vary the types of sentences you use, and include different types of phrases to add variety and interest to your paragraph.

Answers will vary.

Read your paragraph again. Use this checklist to evaluate your writing.

- ❏ Does my paragraph have a topic sentence?
- ❏ Have I used at least two of the four kinds of sentences?
- ❏ Have I included at least one compound or one complex sentence?
- ❏ Do my sentences have correct punctuation?
- ❏ Does my paragraph have a concluding sentence?

Name _____

Beasts & Critters

Proofreading Practice

Read this passage about sperm whales and find the mistakes. Use the proofreading marks below to show how each mistake should be fixed.

Proofreading Marks

Suggested answers appear below.
Accept all reasonable responses.

Mark	Means	Example
℘	delete	Sperm whales eats squid, sharks, and other fish.
∧	add	Sperm whales eat squid, sharks, ^and other fish.
≡	make into a capital letter	sperm whales eat squid, sharks, and other fish.
⊙	add a period	Sperm whales eat squid, sharks, and other fish⊙
⋏	add a comma	Sperm whales eat squid⋏ sharks, and other fish.
(sp)	fix spelling	Sperm whales eat sqid, sharks, and other fish.
/	make into a lowercase letter	Sperm Whales eat squid, sharks, and other fish.

Sperm Whales

Sperm whales are the largest toothed Whales in the world. a fully grown sperm whale Can meshure anywhere from 38 to 60 feet in lenth and can be identified by its massive head.

groups of whales consisting primarily of females and there young travel through warm tropical waters. These groups are called pods. The young whales are raised not only by their mothers but by the other adults in the pod as well⊙

Young males leave the group by the time they are six they migrate to colder waters. They travel alone or with samll groups of other males. It is thought that the males leave their family units so that there is less competition for food⊙ they eat enormous quantities of food to satisfy their huge appetites. Adult males, called bulls, can be nearly one-third biger than the females.

After many years, when they are ready to mate, Bulls return to the warmer waters in which they were raised. They usually swim with many groups of female whales⊙ Before they find an appropriate mate.

People of various societies have created storys⋏ legends⋏ and works of art featuring whales. Perhaps the most famous whale in literature is the male sperm whale that is the focus of the action in Herman melville's novel *Moby-Dick*⊙

Proofreading
Checklist

You can use the list below to help you find and fix mistakes in your own writing. Write the titles of your own stories or reports in the blanks at the top of the chart. Then use the questions to check your work. Make a check mark (✓) in each box after you have checked that item.

Answers will vary.

Proofreading Checklist for Unit 2

	Titles			
Have I used the correct punctuation at the end of each kind of sentence?				
Have I used a comma and coordinating conjunction or a semicolon to separate compound sentences?				
Have I avoided run-on sentences, comma splices, and sentence fragments?				
Is each sentence an independent clause or an independent clause and a dependent clause?				

Also Remember . . .

Does each sentence begin with a capital letter?				
Have I spelled each word correctly?				
Have I used commas correctly?				

Your Own List

Use this space to write your own list of things to check in your writing.

Name _____

Beasts & Critters

Review

(Numbers in parentheses identify related lessons.)

Kinds of Sentences

Draw three lines (≡) under each letter that should be capitalized. Add correct punctuation. Label each sentence *declarative, interrogative, imperative,* or *exclamatory.*

1. tell me about prehistoric sea creatures. _____imperative_____ (11)

2. giant sea scorpions once grew eight feet long. _____declarative_____ (11)

3. wow, that's unbelievable! _____exclamatory_____ (11)

4. what else lived in ancient seas? _____interrogative_____ (11)

Simple Sentences, Compound Sentences, Complex Sentences

Write *S* next to each simple sentence. Write *CD* next to each compound sentence. Write *CX* next to each complex sentence.

5. Before anything lived on land, the seas were filled with creatures. __CX__ (13, 14)

6. Trilobites were once the most numerous species on the earth, but they died out about 300 million years ago. __CD__ (12)

7. These small bottom-dwellers had armored shells and many simple legs. __S__ (12)

8. Because huge fish dominated the world about 400 million years ago, scientists call that period the Age of Fishes. __CX__ (13, 14)

9. Armor of heavy, bony plates protected these fish. __S__ (12)

10. Although they did not have real teeth, these monsters bit with the sharp, exposed edges of their armor. __CX__ (13, 14)

11. Sharks developed in this period, and modern sharks are very similar to those prehistoric sharks. __CD__ (12)

Dependent Clauses and Independent Clauses

Draw one line under the independent clause in each sentence. Draw two lines under the dependent clause.

12. When some fish with lungs emerged on land, they became the first amphibians. (13, 14)

13. Although most types of fishes with lungs died out millions of years ago, the modern lungfish still survives. (13, 14)

Adjective Clauses

Underline the adjective clause in each sentence. Then circle the noun it modifies.

14. Plesiosaurs, which grew up to 46 feet long, were whalelike dinosaurs. (15)

15. Some had necks that were double the length of their bodies. (15)

16. According to scientists who study plesiosaurs, these dinosaurs flapped their flippers like wings. (15)

Beasts & Critters

Adverb Clauses

Underline the adverb clause in each sentence.

17. When the dinosaurs dominated Earth, some took to the sea. **(16)**

18. Many of these animals developed fins or flippers where they once had legs. **(16)**

19. Although ichthyosaurus resembled a modern porpoise, it was not a mammal but a reptile. **(16)**

20. Scientists chose the name *ichthyosaurus* because it means "fishlike lizard." **(16)**

Infinitive Phrases and Participial Phrases

Underline each infinitive phrase. Circle each participial phrase.

21. The large dinosaur (swimming gracefully in this picture) is a plesiosaur. **(18)**

22. The plesiosaur's long neck helped it to hunt food. **(17)**

23. (Stretching its long neck), the plesiosaur looked for prey. **(18)**

24. (Using its tail as a rudder), the mosasaur swam effectively. **(18)**

25. Miners in Holland in 1780 were the first people to find a mosasaur fossil. **(17)**

26. Scientists hope to find more fossils of this ancient aquatic creature. **(17)**

Gerund Phrases

Underline each gerund phrase.

27. Meeting a sea scorpion must have been an unpleasant experience for ancient sea creatures. **(19)**

28. The sea scorpion's huge claws were ideal for grabbing prey. **(19)**

29. The sea scorpion ended the struggles of its victims by stinging them with its venomous tail. **(19)**

Avoiding Fragments, Run-ons, Comma Splices, and Ramble-ons

Identify each item as a fragment, a run-on, a comma splice, or a ramble-on by writing *F, RO, CS,* or *RA* next to each.

30. Ammonites were tentacled animals they lived in spiral shells. __RO__ **(20)**

31. Similar to the modern nautilus. __F__ **(20)**

32. Ammonites changed through the ages, scientists use ammonite fossils to date rock layers. __CS__ **(20)**

33. Because the shells of the ammonites that lived in one period look very different from the shells of ammonites that lived in another period, scientists can look at the fossils of ammonites from each of these periods and notice the variations between them. __RA__ **(20)**

34. Another fish thought to be extinct is the coelacanth, one was caught near South Africa in the 1930s. __CS__ **(20)**

35. The coelacanth, related to the lungfish. __F__ **(20)**

Name _____

Beasts & Critters

Community Connection

In Unit 2 of *G.U.M.* students learned more about **different types of sentences and sentence structures** and used what they learned to improve their own writing. The content of these lessons focuses on the theme **Sea Creatures**. As students completed the exercises, they learned about some of the most impressive and unusual inhabitants of the world's oceans. These pages offer a variety of activities that reinforce skills and concepts presented in the unit. They also provide opportunities for the student to make connections between the material in the lessons and the community at large.

Local Fishes

Find out where the nearest saltwater aquarium is located. If possible, arrange to visit the aquarium. You might consider taking a younger family member with you and sharing with that person some of the things you have learned about the ocean in Unit 2.

Laws of the Sea

Because of its limited supply of fish and the presence of valuable minerals on and under the ocean floor, the question of who owns the world's oceans has become increasingly important. Learn about laws that govern the ocean. You might begin by finding out what the Law of the Sea Treaty, drafted in 1982 by the United Nations, suggests as fair use of the world's oceans. Find out which nations signed the treaty, which did not, and why. Summarize the information in a report.

Saving Water

Although some places have plenty of water for people to use however they want, many other places face a shortage of usable water. People there follow conservation rules so everyone will have the water they need for daily living. Organize a campaign to raise public awareness of the importance of water conservation in your school or neighborhood. Call your local water department and ask for water-saving tips. Make posters showing some of these suggestions, and display them at school or in other places so people will be motivated to take part in your campaign.

Sea Dreams

Learn about job opportunities for people who love the ocean and the creatures that inhabit it. Such opportunities include careers in marine biology, marine geology, and underwater archaeology. Organizations that offer maritime careers include the Merchant Marines and the United States Coast Guard. Choose one occupation that interests you and learn more about it. Try to answer these questions:

- What skills are required to do this job?
- What preparation and training would I need for this job?
- Where is this training available?
- How long does it take to become proficient at this work?
- What is a typical working day like in this profession?

If possible, interview an adult you know who has a maritime job you might be interested in. Take notes during the interview, and share the results of the interview with your class. Use the planning guide on the next page to help you plan the interview and organize your notes.

Interview Planner   Answers will vary.

Person I am interviewing:

Name _____

Age _____

Occupation _____

Number of years employed in that field _____

Date of interview: _____

Questions to ask:

1. _____
   _____

2. _____
   _____

3. _____
   _____

4. _____
   _____

5. _____
   _____

6. _____
   _____

7. _____
   _____

8. _____
   _____

Notes:

_____

_____

_____

_____

_____

Name _____

Beasts & Critters

Read and Discover

Roger Williams overcame difficult **challenges** to found the colony of Rhode Island.

Circle the boldfaced words that name particular persons, places, things, or ideas.

A **common noun** names any person, place, thing, or idea. A **proper noun** names a particular person, place, thing, or idea. Proper nouns must be capitalized. A proper noun made of several words (*Harriet Tubman* or *East Greenwood School*) is considered one proper noun.

See Handbook **Section 15**

Part 1

Circle the proper nouns in the sentences below. Underline the common nouns.

1. Roger Williams was a minister who came to Boston with the Puritans in 1631.

2. The Puritans had come to America so they could worship freely.

3. They did not give that privilege to others in their colony, however.

4. They felt that their ideas were best, and they wrote laws saying everyone must hold the same beliefs they did.

5. Roger Williams disagreed.

6. He felt that all people should be allowed to worship as they wanted.

7. He also believed that the Native Americans owned the land and that the colonists had no claim to it unless they bought it fairly.

8. Williams's radical ideas about religious freedom and fairness to Native Americans got him into trouble, but he never went back on his convictions.

9. In October 1635, the government of Massachusetts banished Williams from the colony.

10. The government tried to send him back to England, but Williams fled through the woods to stay with the Narragansett.

11. The Narragansett welcomed Williams and helped him learn their language, Algonquian.

12. After a few months, Williams purchased land from these Native Americans.

13. The land was located at the head of the bay now known as Narragansett Bay.

14. On this site he founded a settlement he called Providence.

15. The settlement grew into the colony of Rhode Island, where religious freedom was the right of all people.

Roger Williams founded Rhode Island on the principle of religious freedom.

Unforgettable Folks

Part 2 Possible answers appear below. Accept all reasonable responses.

Proper nouns specify whom and what you are talking about. Rewrite each sentence, and replace each common noun with a proper noun from the word bank. You may also need to change other words in your sentences.

England	Narragansett	Roger Williams	Algonquian	*A Key into the Language of America*

16. The minister became friendly with the local residents. <u>Roger Williams became friendly with the Narragansett.</u>

17. He stayed with them and learned to speak their language. <u>He stayed with them and learned to speak Algonquian.</u>

18. He later wrote a book. <u>He later wrote A Key into the Language of America.</u>

19. It was published in another country. <u>It was published in England.</u>

Part 3

Use information from Parts 1 and 2 to complete the puzzle. Then circle the proper nouns you wrote.

Across
6. Native American group
7. Roger Williams's occupation
8. Settlers

Down
1. Strong beliefs
2. Group that went to Boston in search of freedom
3. A European island country
4. A special right
5. Another word for *liberty*

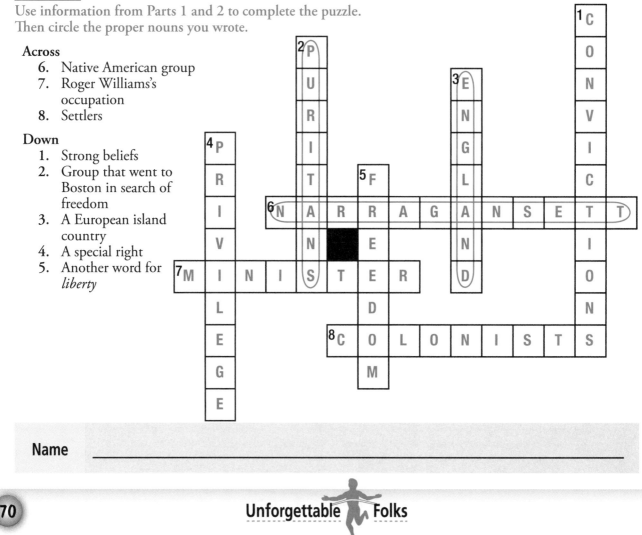

Name _____

Unforgettable Folks

Read and Discover

The **heptathlon** is one of the most demanding (contests) in (athletics.)
Circle the boldfaced nouns that name more than one person, place, or thing.

A **singular noun** names one person, place, thing, or idea. A **plural noun** names more than one. Most nouns add *s* or *es* to form the plural. The spelling of some nouns changes when *es* is added to form the plural (*sky / skies; wolf / wolves*). A few nouns do not add *s* or *es* to form the plural; instead, they change spelling (*woman / women*). A few other nouns have the same form in the singular and plural (*deer / deer*).

See Handbook Sections 18f, 29

Part 1

Circle each singular noun. Underline each plural noun.

1. Seven different events compose the (heptathlon,) an Olympic (competition) for women.

2. Among all athletes who competed in this (event) in the last (century,) Jackie Joyner-Kersee demonstrated the greatest (speed,) (strength,) and leaping (ability.)

3. (Joyner-Kersee) set a world (record) in the (heptathlon) at the 1988 Summer Olympic Games.

4. She has recorded the six best scores in the (history) of this (competition.)

5. She won medals in the (heptathlon) in three consecutive Olympics, from (1984) to (1992.)

6. (Joyner-Kersee) also won Olympic medals in another (event,) the (long jump.)

7. She set marks in the hurdles, too.

8. An all-around (athlete,) she even played professional (basketball) briefly.

9. A popular (magazine) named (Joyner-Kersee) the greatest female (athlete) of the (century.)

10. (Joyner-Kersee) achieved all these triumphs even though she has a (form) of (asthma.)

11. This (disease) affects the lungs; (Joyner-Kersee) sometimes had to be hospitalized after events.

12. For many athletes, (retirement) is the greatest (challenge.)

13. (Joyner-Kersee) has achieved (success) with her (charity) as well as in (business.)

14. (The Jackie Joyner-Kersee Foundation) has built athletic facilities for youths in her (hometown) of (East St. Louis, Illinois.)

15. This nonprofit (organization) also helps older adults in that (community.)

Jackie Joyner-Kersee became one of history's greatest athletes.

Part 2

Write the plural form of each singular common noun you identified in Part 1. If a singular noun appears more than once, just write its plural once.

16.	heptathlons	28.	magazines
17.	competitions	29.	forms
18.	events	30.	asthmas
19.	centuries	31.	diseases
20.	speeds	32.	retirements
21.	strengths	33.	challenges
22.	abilities	34.	successes
23.	records	35.	charities
24.	histories	36.	businesses
25.	long jumps	37.	hometowns
26.	athletes	38.	organizations
27.	basketballs	39.	communities

Part 3

A collective noun names a group of people or things that act as one unit. *Class, flock,* and *orchestra* are collective nouns. Circle the words below that are collective nouns. Then use three of them in sentences.

(family)   (fleet)   women   (team)   children
(jury)   events   (committee)   facilities   (audience)

40.   Answers will vary.

41.

42.

Name

Unforgettable Folks

Wilma **Rudolph's** triumph over a childhood disease made her a truly remarkable champion.

Circle the part of the boldfaced word that shows ownership.

A **possessive noun** shows ownership. **Singular** nouns add an apostrophe and *s* to form the possessive (*worker / worker's*). Most **plural** nouns add an apostrophe after the *s* to form the possessive (*workers / workers'*). Plurals that don't end in *s* (*men / mice*) add an apostrophe and *s* (*men's / mice's*) to show possession.

See Handbook Sections 7, 30

Part 1

Underline each singular possessive noun. Circle each plural possessive noun. There may be more than one possessive noun in each sentence.

1. Wilma Rudolph's early childhood was made painful by a series of illnesses.

2. She got pneumonia and scarlet fever, and soon afterward she contracted polio, that era's most dreaded childhood disease.

3. That illness's effects left her with one leg paralyzed.

4. Wilma's mother had 19 children then, but she found time to get expert treatment for her young daughter's condition.

5. Every week she and Wilma traveled 50 miles by bus from Clarksville, Tennessee, to a hospital in Nashville to obtain doctors' help.

6. The Rudolphs, an African American family, had to sit in the back of the bus; Wilma Rudolph never forgot segregation's injustice.

In 1961 Rudolph received the Sullivan Award, given each year to the top U.S. amateur athlete.

7. Thanks to the treatments and to her mother's encouragement, Wilma began to improve.

8. In time she was able to walk with a brace's support, but she was determined to walk without it.

9. By junior high, Wilma no longer needed the brace, and she joined the girls' basketball team.

10. Her legs' muscles were now strong, and she starred in basketball.

11. This brilliant athlete's greatest triumphs would come in the sport of track and field; she first qualified for the United States Olympic Team in 1956, at the age of 16.

12. At the 1960 Olympics, Rudolph became the first American woman to win three gold medals, gaining recognition as the world's greatest woman sprinter.

13. The champion's homecoming parade in Clarksville was the first integrated event in the town's history.

14. Rudolph set world records in the women's 100- and 200-meter races and the 4 x 100-meter relay.

15. Working with young people after her Olympic triumphs, Rudolph became many youths' inspiration.

Unforgettable Folks

Part 2   Possible answers appear below. Accept all reasonable responses.

Rewrite each sentence, shortening the underlined section by using a possessive noun.

16. The biographies of many athletes include stories of their triumphs over physical problems.   **Many athletes' biographies include stories of their triumphs over physical problems.**

17. The strong swimming of Tom Dolan earned him gold medals in the 1996 and 2000 Olympics. **Tom Dolan's strong swimming earned him gold medals in the 1996 and 2000 Olympics.**

18. An abnormally narrow windpipe provides Dolan with air at only 20 percent of the capacity of a normal windpipe. **An abnormally narrow windpipe provides Dolan with air at only 20 percent of a normal windpipe's capacity.**

19. The condition which Dolan has only made him train harder. **Dolan's condition only made him train harder.**

20. The persistence of this swimmer brought him a world record and a gold medal in the men's 400-meter medley. **This swimmer's persistence brought him a world record and a gold medal in the men's 400-meter medley.**

Part 3

Circle six nouns hidden in the puzzle. Write each one in the column where it belongs. Then write the possessive form of each noun.

F	A	M	I	L	Y	C	D
Q	T	H	B	S	D	H	I
W	H	J	N	P	F	I	S
R	L	K	M	O	G	L	E
T	E	L	Q	R	H	D	A
Y	T	Z	W	T	J	R	S
P	E	X	R	S	K	E	E
S	S	C	T	S	L	N	B
D	M	V	W	O	M	E	N

Singular Nouns   **Possessive Forms**

21. _____ family _____   family's

22. _____ disease _____   disease's

Plural Nouns   **Possessive Forms**

23. _____ athletes _____   athletes'

24. _____ sports _____   sports'

25. _____ children _____   children's

26. _____ women _____   women's

Use one of the possessive forms you wrote in a sentence about Wilma Rudolph.

27. **Answers will vary.**

Name _____

Unforgettable Folks

Read and Discover

(I) have always admired Nelson Mandela.

Circle the word in the sentence that shows who is speaking.

A **pronoun** can take the place of a noun. **Personal pronouns** can be used to stand for the person speaking, the person spoken to, or the person spoken about. **First person** pronouns refer to the speaker (*I, me*) or include the speaker (*we, us*). **Second person** pronouns refer to the person being spoken to (*you*). **Third person** pronouns refer to the person, place, or thing being spoken about (*he, him, she, her, it, they, them*). **Remember to use this information when you speak, too.**

See Handbook Section 17a

Part 1

Circle each personal pronoun. Write *1* if it is a first person pronoun, *2* if it is second person, or *3* if it is third person.

1. Do (you) know who Nelson Mandela is? __2__

2. In 1994 (he) became the first Black president of South Africa. __3__

3. (I) am amazed by the obstacles Mandela overcame to reach the presidency. __1__

4. From the 1940s through the 1980s, South Africa's laws took away most of Black South Africans' lands and prohibited (them) from voting. __3__

5. (We) learned in history class that this system was known as apartheid. __1__

6. Nelson Mandela joined the African National Congress, a group that denounced apartheid and acted to try to end (it). __3__

7. The South African government imprisoned (him) for taking action against apartheid. __3__

8. Although Mandela was a prisoner for 27 years, (he) never lost hope. __3__

9. Mandela secretly wrote a book and helped other prisoners as (they) waged a struggle for better prison conditions. __3__

10. (You) will be glad to know that international outrage finally led to Mandela's release. __2__

11. Mandela negotiated the end of apartheid with South African President F.W. De Klerk, and together (they) were awarded the Nobel Peace Prize. __3__

12. Nelson Mandela is a hero to (me). __1__

13. This great leader's courage is an example for all of (us). __1__

14. (He) proved to the world that oppression can be ended without widespread bloodshed. __3__

Nelson Mandela helped end apartheid in South Africa.

Unforgettable Folks

Part 2 Answers will vary.

Write four sentences about a hero of yours, using the types of personal pronouns indicated.

15. first person: _____

_____

16. second person: _____

_____

17. third person singular: _____

_____

18. third person plural: _____

_____

Part 3 Possible answers appear below. Accept all reasonable responses.

The word *he* once was accepted as a universal pronoun that could refer to anyone, male or female, if a generalization about people was being made.

| Example | Early childhood experiences affect a person for **his** entire life. |

Now most writers try to avoid the use of universal *he*. Here are two ways the sentence above might be revised.

Solution #1:
Make the noun and the word it refers to plural.   Early childhood experiences affect people for their entire lives.

Solution #2:
Replace *his* with *his or her*.   Early childhood experiences affect a person for his or her entire life.

Try both of these solutions for replacing the universal *he* in these sentences.

The food a person eats affects his health.

19. The food people eat affects their health. _____

_____

20. The food a person eats affects his or her health. _____

_____

Each student scheduled his choice of activity during gym class.

21. Students scheduled their choices of activity during gym class. _____

22. Each student scheduled his or her choice of activity during gym class. __

_____

Name _____

Unforgettable Folks

Read and Discover

a. Keiran bought a book about the history of human flight.
b. Keiran bought (himself) a book about the history of human flight.

Circle the word in sentence b. that tells for whom the book was bought.

A **compound personal pronoun** ends in *-self* or *-selves*. It usually shows that the subject of a sentence is doing something to itself. (*I dressed myself in blue.*) Sometimes it gives emphasis. (*He cooked the chicken himself. Carolyn herself made the arrangements.*) A compound personal pronoun refers back to the subject of the sentence. The noun or pronoun that a pronoun replaces is its **antecedent**. **Remember to use this information when you speak, too.**

See Handbook Sections 17c, 17e

Part 1

Circle each compound personal pronoun in the paragraphs below. Draw a box around the antecedent of each pronoun you circle. (1–11)

Since ancient times, we humans have imagined ourselves flying. Until recently, however, airplane pilots have not been able to lift themselves off the ground without the help of an engine.

In the 1970s engineer Paul MacCready dedicated himself to the dream of achieving human-powered flight. MacCready's first successful plane, the *Gossamer Condor,* had a wingspan of almost 100 feet but was made of extremely light materials. By itself the plane weighed only 70 pounds. Bicyclist Bryan Allen pedaled hard in the cockpit to spin the plane's propeller and lift himself and the *Condor* into the air for a flight of over one mile.

Paul MacCready and his team achieved the previously impossible goal of human-powered flight.

After the success of the *Gossamer Condor,* MacCready and his team set themselves another challenge. Their new plane, the *Gossamer Albatross,* was designed to carry a pilot across the 22.5-mile-wide English Channel. Bryan Allen volunteered himself again to be both pilot and power source. Can you imagine yourself fluttering a few feet above the waves, being held aloft only through frantic pedaling? Because air turbulence would almost certainly slow the plane to a standstill at some points, MacCready and his team resigned themselves to having to tow the plane now and then. But, in an amazing feat of endurance, Bryan Allen managed the crossing by himself and made history a second time.

The *Gossamer Condor* is on display at the National Air and Space Museum in Washington, D.C. I hope to see that historic plane myself someday.

Unforgettable Folks

Part 2

Rewrite each sentence, replacing the underlined word or words with a compound personal pronoun.

12. Jasmine bought <u>Jasmine</u> a model of the *Gossamer Condor*. **Jasmine bought herself a model of the Gossamer Condor.**

13. We put it together <u>without help</u>. **We put it together ourselves.**

14. I gave <u>me</u> three tries to get the plane to fly. **I gave myself three tries to get the plane to fly.**

15. After a successful flight, the model plane settled <u>the plane</u> on a patch of soft grass. **After a successful flight, the model plane settled itself on a patch of soft grass.**

Part 3

Imagine that you piloted the *Gossamer Condor* on a short flight. Write an account of your experience. Use a compound personal pronoun in each sentence.

Answers will vary.

Name

Unforgettable Folks

Isabel Allende **wrote** a **book** about (her) daughter, Paula.

Circle the boldfaced word that shows ownership or indicates a relationship. To whom does it refer? _____**Isabel Allende**_____

Possessive pronouns show ownership. The possessive pronouns *her, his, its, their, my, our,* and *your* can replace possessive nouns. (*Nancy's house is blue.—Her house is blue.*) The possessive pronouns *hers, his, theirs, mine, ours,* and *yours* can replace both a possessive noun and the noun that is a possession. (*Nancy's house is the blue house.—Hers is the blue house.*)

See Handbook Section 17d

Part 1

Circle the possessive pronouns. There may be more than one in a sentence.

1. (My) favorite author is Isabel Allende.

2. Who is (yours)?

3. Allende was an investigative journalist in (her) native country, Chile.

4. (Its) government was overthrown in the 1970s.

5. At that time (her) uncle, Salvador Allende, was the president of that country.

6. Many people lost (their) lives, and Isabel Allende was forced to flee.

7. In exile in Venezuela, Allende heard that (her) grandfather was very ill in Chile.

8. She began writing him a long letter about the Allende family in which she recalled all (their) sad, happy, and wonderful stories.

9. This long letter grew into (her) first great novel, *The House of the Spirits.*

10. (My) favorite of Allende's books, *Paula,* also had (its) beginning as a letter.

11. Allende was taking care of (her) daughter, Paula, who lay in a coma for a year as the result of an illness.

12. She wrote Paula a letter, relating in great detail the story of Paula's life and (hers).

13. Allende hoped Paula would read the letter when she recovered from (her) coma, but Paula never regained consciousness.

14. Greatly saddened by Paula's death, Allende almost gave up writing (her) marvelous stories.

15. But instead she decided to create for (her) daughter the best memorial she could.

16. People all over the world have read Allende's book *Paula* and as a result keep (her) memory alive.

Isabel Allende has lived in places on three continents.

Part 2

Rewrite each sentence, replacing each group of underlined words with a possessive pronoun.

17. I really like <u>Cynthia Lord's</u> book *Rules*. **I really like her book <u>Rules</u>.**

18. <u>The book's</u> subject is a girl named Catherine, whose brother has a disability. **Its subject is a girl named Catherine, whose brother has a disability.**

19. Catherine learns that <u>people's</u> ideas of what is normal can vary. **Catherine learns that their ideas of what is normal can vary.**

20. That red book over there is <u>the one belonging to me</u>. **That red book over there is mine.**

21. <u>The one belonging to you</u> is on the table. **Yours is on the table.**

Part 3

Circle the possessive pronouns in the riddles below. Then try to solve the riddles. (Answers are given below.)

22. You can see (mine), (his), (hers), and (theirs), but you can never see (yours).

23. Nobody wanted it. First it was (hers), and then it was (mine), and now it's (yours).

24. The more you give (yours), the more others give you (theirs).

25. What is it, do you suppose? The more I take from (mine), the bigger it grows.

Now write two of your own riddles using possessive pronouns, and give them to a friend to solve.

26. **Answers will vary.**

27. _____

(answers: 22: your back; 23: a cold; 24: friendship; 25: a hole)

Name _____

Unforgettable Folks

Who is Stephen Hawking? He is a brilliant physicist who has developed new theories about black holes.

Draw a box around the boldfaced word that asks a question. Circle the boldfaced word that refers to the noun just before it.

When the pronouns *who, whom, whose, which,* and *that* are used to introduce an adjective clause, they are called **relative pronouns**. A relative pronoun always follows the noun the adjective clause is describing. When the pronouns *who, whom, whose, which,* and *what* are used to begin a question, they are called **interrogative pronouns**.

See Handbook Sections 17g, 17h

Part 1

Circle each relative pronoun. Underline the noun the adjective clause is describing. Draw a box around each interrogative pronoun.

1. Stephen Hawking has a disease that has left him almost completely paralyzed and unable to speak.

2. He taps out messages on a special computer, which communicates the messages with its synthesized voice.

3. What effects has this disability had on Hawking's work?

4. Stephen Hawking's brilliant mind is the only tool that he needs for the study of black holes.

5. Who knows the meaning of the term *black hole*?

6. Dying stars whose masses are great enough may collapse in on themselves.

7. They then form black holes, areas that may not allow the escape of any matter or energy, not even rays of light.

8. There are many theories that attempt to describe black holes.

9. Which did Hawking think up?

10. He developed the widely accepted theory that describes singularities.

11. What is a singularity?

12. It is the infinitely dense point that scientists believe lies at the heart of a black hole.

13. Hawking has also envisioned shrinking black holes, whose final explosions would release huge bursts of energy.

14. There are several physicists who disagree with this theory, however.

15. Who do you believe is correct, Hawking or his critics?

Stephen Hawking studied physics and mathematics at Oxford and Cambridge in England.

Part 2

Complete each sentence by writing a relative pronoun or an interrogative pronoun.

16. Hawking has proposed many theories _____ **that** _____ cannot be proven.

17. _____ **What** _____ could prove that other universes exist next to ours?

18. Hawking has a theory _____ **that** _____ proposes the existence of wormholes.

19. _____ **What** _____ is a wormhole?

20. A wormhole is a tiny spot _____ **that** _____ connects one universe to another.

21. *A Brief History of Time,* _____ **which** _____ Hawking published in 1988, explains his ideas in relatively simple terms.

22. People _____ **who** _____ read this book may not understand all of Hawking's ideas, but they are likely to learn a great deal about the universe.

Part 3

As you revise your writing, keep in mind these tips about the correct usage of relative pronouns:
1. *Who* is used only to refer to people.
2. *That* and *which* refer to things.
3. *Which* is generally used to introduce nonrestrictive clauses. These clauses are set off by commas and provide information about the noun they describe.
4. *That* is used to introduce restrictive clauses. These clauses are not set off by commas. They give information about a noun that is essential to the meaning of the sentence.

Circle the relative pronoun that is used incorrectly in each sentence. Then rewrite each sentence with the appropriate relative pronoun.

23. My favorite chapter of *A Brief History of Time* is the one (which) tells about black holes. **My favorite chapter of A Brief History of Time is the one that tells about black holes.**

24. In this section, Hawking describes what would happen to a person (which) flew a spaceship into a black hole. **In this section, Hawking describes what would happen to a person who flew a spaceship into a black hole.**

25. The black hole's gravity, (that) is immensely powerful, creates forces that would compress and pull the spaceship out of shape. **The black hole's gravity, which is immensely powerful, creates forces that would compress and pull the spaceship out of shape.**

26. People (that) watched the spaceship from a distance would see it fall more and more slowly into the hole. **People who watched the spaceship from a distance would see it fall more and more slowly into the hole.**

Name _____

Unforgettable Folks

Read and Discover

(Someone) is coming across the ice!

Circle the word that refers to an unknown person.

> **Indefinite pronouns** refer to persons or things that are not identified. Indefinite pronouns include *all, anybody, both, either, anything, nothing, everyone, few, most, one, no one, several, nobody,* and *someone.*

See Handbook Section 17f

Part 1

Circle each indefinite pronoun in these sentences.

1. Does (anybody) know about the explorations of Sir Ernest Shackleton?

2. This British captain was the first (one) to locate the South Magnetic Pole.

3. In 1914 he led an expedition to cross Antarctica, a challenge (no one) had ever attempted before.

4. He set out in the sailing ship *Endurance* with a crew of 27, but soon (everything) went wrong.

5. The *Endurance* became trapped in ice far from the Antarctic shore, and there was (nothing) the crew could do to free it.

6. (Everyone) loaded the ship's supplies into lifeboats and began walking across the frozen sea, dragging the boats.

7. Shackleton and his crew walked 250 miles before they saw (anything) besides water and ice.

8. Finally the men reached a tiny island, but they found (nothing) to eat there.

9. Winter was coming, and supplies were running out; Shackleton knew he had to do (something) to save his crew.

Siberian ponies pulled heavy loads on one Shackleton expedition.

10. (Someone) had to seek help, so Shackleton and five crew members sailed away in a small lifeboat.

11. (Everything) was against these brave sailors: they faced huge waves and violent storms, and they had little water to drink.

12. After almost two weeks of sailing, (somebody) saw land!

13. Shackleton landed on the treacherous coast of South Georgia Island and climbed over a mountain before he found (anyone) able to rescue the rest of the crew.

14. Because of Shackleton's courage, (everybody) was saved.

15. (Few) could have done what Ernest Shackleton and his crew did.

Part 2   Possible answers appear below. Accept all reasonable responses.

Complete each sentence by writing an indefinite pronoun.

16. It was more than forty years before _____ anyone _____ tried to cross Antarctica again.

17. A person who had been _____ one _____ of Shackleton's original team members backed a new expedition in 1957.

18. The new team traveled by dog sled and snowmobile; _____ both _____ were very useful.

19. _____ All _____ of the snowmobiles had to be connected together by cable.

20. That way, if _____ someone _____ fell into a crevasse in the ice, the cable could be used for a rescue.

21. _____ Everything _____ went well on this expedition.

22. The team had several close calls, but _____ nothing _____ stopped them from traveling the 2,158 miles.

Part 3

Circle the indefinite pronoun in each sentence. Then write the answer to each clue. Each answer appears in this lesson.

23. Thanks to his bravery, (everyone) on the expedition survived.

    $\underline{S}$ $\underline{H}$ $\underline{A}$ $\underline{C}$ $\underline{K}$ $\underline{L}$ $\underline{E}$ $\underline{T}$ $\underline{O}$ $\underline{N}$
    10   12   2   7

24. Before Shackleton found it in 1908, (no one) had determined its location.

    $\underline{S}$ $\underline{O}$ $\underline{U}$ $\underline{T}$ $\underline{H}$
             8 5

    $\underline{M}$ $\underline{A}$ $\underline{G}$ $\underline{N}$ $\underline{E}$ $\underline{T}$ $\underline{I}$ $\underline{C}$
    6   13   9

    $\underline{P}$ $\underline{O}$ $\underline{L}$ $\underline{E}$
    4   11

25. (All) should agree that this was a good name for Shackleton's ship.

    $\underline{E}$ $\underline{N}$ $\underline{D}$ $\underline{U}$ $\underline{R}$ $\underline{A}$ $\underline{N}$ $\underline{C}$ $\underline{E}$
    3   14   1

Use the numbered letters to answer this question:

What was the name of the tiny island where most of Shackleton's crew awaited rescue?

$\underline{E}$ $\underline{L}$ $\underline{E}$ $\underline{P}$ $\underline{H}$ $\underline{A}$ $\underline{N}$ $\underline{T}$ $\underline{I}$ $\underline{S}$ $\underline{L}$ $\underline{A}$ $\underline{N}$ $\underline{D}$
1 2 3 4 5 6 7 8   9 10 11 12 13 14

Name _____

Unforgettable Folks

The Two Fridas is a colorful, memorable painting.
Circle the two words that describe the painting. Draw a box around the short word that comes right before these words.

Adjectives describe nouns and pronouns. Some adjectives, like *colorful* and *memorable*, **describe** or tell **what kind**. Others, like *many* and *six*, tell **how many**. The **articles** *a*, *an*, and *the* are also adjectives.

See Handbook Section 16

Part 1

Circle each adjective that tells *what kind*. Underline each adjective that tells *how many*. Draw a box around each article. Finally, draw a star above the noun each adjective describes.

1. Frida Kahlo was an important modern painter.

2. As a young child in Mexico, much of her creative life was spent in bed; she had contracted polio, which left her with a weak right leg.

3. As a teenager, while a passenger on a bus, Kahlo was in a dreadful accident.

4. The terrible injuries left her in continuous pain.

5. Several months after the accident, Kahlo began painting.

6. Her vivid paintings, mostly self-portraits that dealt with feminist issues, expressed her pain as well as her joy in life.

7. In 1929 she married the famous muralist Diego Rivera.

8. Under his guidance she became a skillful painter.

9. Kahlo painted many portraits of herself over the years.

10. In one self-portrait, twisted roots grow from her body.

11. Another self-portrait shows her head on the body of a wounded deer.

12. In addition to her self-portraits, Kahlo created precise, detailed images of individual events on canvas.

13. Kahlo's paintings can evoke strong emotions.

14. Over the course of her short career, Kahlo made about two hundred paintings that told the story of her life.

15. As Kahlo gained importance as a leading Mexican artist, her paintings were classified as national treasures by the government of Mexico.

Frida Kahlo used images from traditional Mexican art in many of her paintings.

Unforgettable Folks

Part 2   Answers will vary.

Complete these sentences with adjectives from the word bank, or use your own words.

memorable	straight	happy	imaginative	zany
curly	strange	flowing	bright	blue
green	beautiful	pleasant	angry	a
brown	curious	frizzy	pale	an

16. If I were painting a self-portrait, it would be ____ _____ painting.

17. I would use _____ colors.

18. In the painting, I would have _____ hair.

19. My eyes would be _____.

20   I would have ____ _____ expression.

21. The background would be _____.

Part 3

Circle four adjectives and four nouns in the puzzle. Then write each word in the correct group.

```
A  R  T  M  X  Z  T  P
A  P  U  U  T  L  E  R
Z  A  C  R  H  X  R  U
X  I  Z  A  E  H  R  S
B  N  E  L  X  Z  I  Z
G  T  I  I  Q  O  B  P
N  E  R  S  X  Z  L  K
T  R  Q  T  V  E  E  X
F  A  M  O  U  S  Q  T
A  C  C  I  D  E  N  T
P  S  E  V  E  R  A  L
```

Adjectives

22. _____ the

23. _____ terrible

24. _____ famous

25. _____ several

Nouns

26. _____ art

27. _____ painter

28. _____ muralist

29. _____ accident

Now choose at least one noun and one or more adjectives from the puzzle and write a sentence about Frida Kahlo.

30. **Answers will vary.** _____

_____

_____

Name _____

Unforgettable Folks

This is a picture of Mary Patten.

That ship is a replica of the one she commanded.

Circle the word that modifies the noun *ship* and tells *which one*. Underline the word that stands for the noun *picture*.

This, these, that, and *those* are **demonstratives**. **Demonstrative adjectives** describe nouns and tell which one. **Demonstrative pronouns** take the place of nouns. *This* and *these* refer to a thing or things close by. *That* and *those* refer to a thing or things farther away. ◀ **Remember to use this information when you speak, too.**

See Handbook **Sections 16, 17i**

Part 1

Circle each demonstrative adjective. Underline each demonstrative pronoun. Draw a box around each noun the demonstrative modifies or replaces.

1. This is an old map of San Francisco Bay.

2. Fast-sailing clipper ships from New York once docked in that bay.

3. Those ships carried supplies to California during the Gold Rush, which began in 1849.

4. The sea route was 15,000 miles long, but clipper ships could cover that distance much faster than wagons could travel 3,000 miles overland to San Francisco.

5. In 1856 Captain Patten, of the clipper ship *Neptune's Car*, took his 18-year-old wife on this perilous journey.

6. That was not their first voyage together; she had traveled with him around the world and was an expert sailor.

7. Early in the trip, this brave young woman's husband became ill with tuberculosis.

8. That terrible disease was common in the nineteenth century.

9. The captain became too sick to command the ship, so a new commander had to be chosen from among those on board.

10. In that era, women were not expected to command ships, but no one on the ship besides Mary Patten knew how to navigate.

11. Soon after she took command, the ship entered the treacherous seas surrounding Cape Horn; this was the most dangerous part of the journey.

12. A series of terrible storms battered the ship; the crew had never seen gales like those before.

13. To avoid the storms, Mary Patten dared to sail into freezing Antarctic waters, and that risk paid off.

14. Patten guided the *Neptune's Car* to San Francisco, and the crew called her a hero for this achievement.

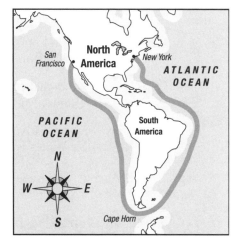

Mary Patten sailed a clipper ship around Cape Horn in the 1850s.

Part 2   Possible answers appear below. Accept all reasonable responses.

Rewrite each sentence, replacing the underlined words with a demonstrative pronoun or with a demonstrative adjective and any other needed words.

15. <u>The model I'm pointing to</u> is a replica of another clipper ship. __This is a replica of another__
    __clipper ship.__

16. <u>The three masts shown in the model</u> would have risen one hundred feet above the deck. __Those__
    __three masts would have risen one hundred feet above the deck.__

17. <u>The mast closest to the front of the ship</u> is called the foremast. __This mast in front is called the__
    __foremast.__

18. <u>The model across the room</u> is a replica of a five-masted ship from the late nineteenth century.
    __That model across the room is a replica of a five-masted ship from the late nineteenth__
    __century.__

Part 3   Possible answers appear below. Accept all reasonable responses.

Authors and speakers sometimes begin sentences with demonstrative pronouns for a dramatic or stirring effect. Circle the demonstrative pronouns in the famous quotations below.

(This) was their finest hour.
        —Sir Winston Churchill (England, 1940)

(These) are the times that try men's souls.
        —Thomas Paine (North America, 1776)

(This) is my own, my native land!
        —Sir Walter Scott (Scotland, 1805)

Now research what the demonstrative pronoun refers to in each quotation. The place and time the quotation was said or written may give you a hint. Write your answers on the lines below.

19. __Churchill was speaking about people's actions during the early years of World War II.__

20. __Paine is referring to the American Revolution.__

21. __Scott's native land was Scotland.__

Name _____

Unforgettable Folks

Diagraming Understood *You*

Imperative sentences (commands) usually contain the understood *you* as the subject. When the subject is understood, write *(you)* in the sentence diagram, like this:

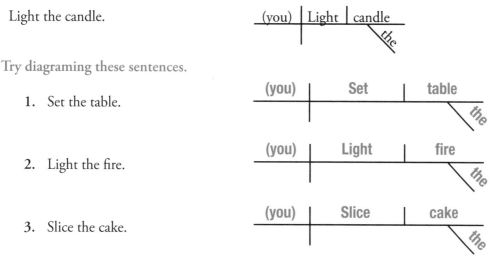

Light the candle.

Try diagraming these sentences.

1. Set the table.

2. Light the fire.

3. Slice the cake.

Diagraming Possessive Pronouns

Look at the way the possessive pronouns *my* and *their* are diagramed in these sentences.

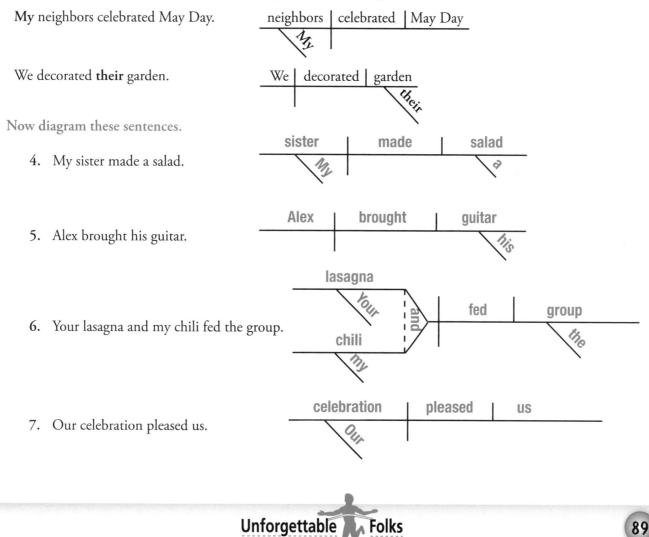

My neighbors celebrated May Day.

We decorated **their** garden.

Now diagram these sentences.

4. My sister made a salad.

5. Alex brought his guitar.

6. Your lasagna and my chili fed the group.

7. Our celebration pleased us.

Diagraming Demonstrative Pronouns

You have learned that the demonstrative pronouns *this, that, these,* and *those* take the place of nouns. Look at how the demonstrative pronouns in these sentences are diagramed.

My grandfather carved **this**.

grandfather | carved | **this**
My

That demands courage.

That | demands | courage

8. Based on these diagrams, which sentence below tells where to place a demonstrative pronoun in a sentence diagram? __**c.**__

   a. Always place it where the subject belongs.   b. Always place it where the direct object belongs.

   c. Put it wherever the noun it replaces would go.

Now diagram these sentences.

9. These need repair.

   These | need | repair

10. We ate those.

    We | ate | those

11. This works better and costs less.

    This | and works / better | costs / less

Diagraming Indefinite Pronouns

Indefinite pronouns include *anybody, somebody, both,* and *no one*.

12. Where do you think an indefinite pronoun belongs in a sentence diagram? __**c.**__

    a. where the subject goes   b. where the predicate goes

    c. wherever the noun it replaces would go

Try diagraming these sentences.

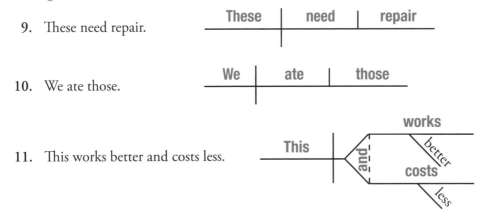

13. Everyone liked your song.

    Everyone | liked | song / your

14. The music bothered no one.

    music / The | bothered | no one

15. Somebody ate my sandwich and drank my juice.

    Somebody | and ate | sandwich / my ; drank | juice / my

Name _____

Unforgettable Folks

Writing Sentences

Answers will vary.

These sentences need help! Rewrite them so they give more information about Jackie Joyner-Kersee and her accomplishments. Refer to Lesson 22 if you need to.

1. Jackie Joyner-Kersee was a good athlete. _____
_____
_____

2. She was in the Olympics. _____
_____
_____

3. She won some medals and set some records. _____
_____
_____

4. She had an illness. _____
_____
_____

5. She did well after retiring. _____
_____
_____

When you write a paragraph, always include a topic sentence, two or more supporting sentences that add details about your topic, and a concluding sentence. Your reader will enjoy your paragraph more if you include colorful adjectives and use pronouns and possessives appropriately. Notice how this model paragraph is written.

topic sentence

supporting sentences

colorful adjectives

pronouns and possessives

concluding sentence

My father is a hero to me because he was willing to risk everything to gain freedom. After the Vietnam War ended in 1975, life became very difficult for many people in Vietnam. Late in 1976 *my* father decided to escape. Crowded together with twelve other people in a small wooden boat, *he* endured a dangerous journey across the stormy South China Sea. After being picked up by a fishing boat, *he* came to the United States to start a new life. Here *he* has built a successful business, publishing a newspaper in Vietnamese. *My* father says *he* is grateful for the freedom of speech allowed in the United States. *I* am also very glad to be living in the United States. *I will always be grateful to my father for having the courage to seek freedom.*

Writing a Paragraph

The sentences you revised on page 91 can be used to make a paragraph. Decide what order the sentences should be in. Write the paragraph on the lines below. Add other words, such as transition words, if necessary.

Answers will vary, including the choice of topic sentence.

_____

_____

_____

_____

_____

_____

_____

Write a paragraph about one of your personal heroes. You might write about someone you learned about in Unit 3 or about another person. Refer to the model paragraph on page 91 if you need help. Be sure to include a variety of interesting adjectives. Use pronouns and possessives when appropriate.

Answers will vary.

_____

_____

_____

_____

_____

_____

_____

Read your paragraph again. Use this checklist to evaluate your writing.

- ❏ Does my paragraph have a topic sentence?
- ❏ Have I included a variety of interesting descriptive words in my supporting sentences?
- ❏ Have I used pronouns and possessives appropriately?
- ❏ Do my sentences have correct punctuation?
- ❏ Does my paragraph have a concluding sentence?

Name _____

Unforgettable Folks

Proofreading Practice

Read this passage about sea turtle eggs and find the mistakes. Use the proofreading marks to show how the mistakes should be fixed.

Suggested answers appear below.
Accept all reasonable responses.

Proofreading Marks

Mark	Means	Example
ℒ	delete	Sea turtles hidde their eggs in sand.
∧	add	Sea turtles hide their egg in sand.
≡	make into a capital letter	sea turtles hide their eggs in sand.
⌒	close up	Sea tur tles hide their eggs in sand.
(sp)	fix spelling	Sea tirtels hide their eggs in sand.
⊙	add a period	Sea turtles hide their eggs in sand
/	make into a lowercase letter	Sea Turtles hide their eggs in sand.

Guardian of the Eggs

Georgias' Barrier Islands are among the few places in the united states where sea turtles can find open beach land to lay there eggs. these round eggs, about the size of table tennis balls, are wite and leathery. Its common on warm summer nights there to see a female turtle drag her self high onto the beach, dig a hole, deposit more than a 100 eggs, cover up the hole, and then slowly return to the ocean. These sea turtles that consistently brede along the southeastern koastline are called *loggerheads*.

By hiding her eggs, The mother turtle does all she can to protect her young. But without some extra help, many of the turtle eggs laid on them islandses wouldn't never hatch. Wild pigs and other animals dig up turtle eggs and eat them. Humans also dig up turtle nests It has taken speshel efforts by naturalists to protect the eggs.

Carol Ruckdeschel one of the turtle egg guardians on the Barrier Islands. each summer night for a number of years Ruckdeschel has patrolled the beachs, watching for turtles and driving off predators and human trespassers. Its not easy to stay awake ever nite for sevrel monthes, but Ruckdeschel believes that helping sea turtles excape extinction is worth missing sum sleep.

Proofreading
Checklist

You can use the checklist below to help you find and fix mistakes in your own writing. Write the titles of your own stories or reports in the blanks at the top of the chart. Then use the questions to check your work. Make a check mark (✓) in each box after you have checked that item.

Answers will vary.

Proofreading Checklist for Unit 3

	Titles			
Have I capitalized proper nouns?				
Have I written plural forms of nouns correctly?				
Have I written possessive forms of nouns correctly?				
Have I used correct forms of personal pronouns?				
Have I used possessive pronouns correctly?				
Have I used appropriate relative pronouns?				

Also Remember . . .

Does each sentence begin with a capital letter?				
Have I spelled each word correctly?				
Have I used commas correctly?				

Your Own List

Use this space to write your own list of things to check in your writing.

Name _____

Unforgettable Folks

Review

(Numbers in parentheses identify related lessons.)

Singular Nouns and Plural Nouns

Underline the correct plural form in parentheses.

1. Most people's (lifes/<u>lives</u>) involve some sort of challenge. **(22)**

2. Challenges make our (victorys/<u>victories</u>) sweeter. **(22)**

3. There are (<u>touches</u>/touchs) of greatness in all of us. **(22)**

Common Nouns and Proper Nouns

Write whether the boldfaced word is a *common* noun or a *proper* noun.

4. When **Raden Kartini** was young, few Indonesian girls received an education. _____proper_____ **(21)**

5. Kartini rebelled against this restrictive **system**. _____common_____ **(21)**

6. A **princess,** she insisted on going to school. _____common_____ **(21)**

7. Kartini spent her life working for girls' **education**. _____common_____ **(21)**

8. She founded a school for boys and girls in the town of **Japara**. _____proper_____ **(21)**

9. Many women of **Indonesia** consider Kartini a hero. _____proper_____ **(21)**

Singular Possessive Nouns and Plural Possessive Nouns

Write the possessive form of this noun from the sentences above.

10. girls _____girls'_____ **(23)**

Write the singular possessive nouns from the sentences above.

11. Raden Kartini _____Raden Kartini's_____ **(23)**   12. Indonesia _____Indonesia's_____ **(23)**

Personal Pronouns

Circle each personal pronoun. Write *1* if it is a first person pronoun, *2* if it is second person, or *3* if it is third person.

13. (I) admire Raden Kartini. __1__ **(24)**

14. Kartini wanted all women in Indonesia to have the same educational opportunities (she) had. __3__ **(24)**

15. What would (you) have done in a similar situation? __2__ **(24)**

Kinds of Pronouns

Circle the phrase that tells what kind of pronoun the boldfaced word is.

16. Mount Everest, **which** is more than 29,000 feet high, is the tallest mountain in the world. **(27)**

    (relative pronoun)   indefinite pronoun   interrogative pronoun

17. **What** are the climbing conditions on Mount Everest? **(27)**

    compound personal pronoun   (interrogative pronoun)   possessive pronoun

Unforgettable Folks

18. **Its** steepness and dangerous crevasses make this mountain extremely difficult to climb. **(26)**

    relative pronoun   compound personal pronoun   (possessive pronoun)

19. The air **itself** is so thin that climbers take oxygen to breathe. **(25)**

    indefinite pronoun   possessive pronoun   (compound personal pronoun)

20. **Who** were Sir Edmund Hillary and Tenzing Norgay? **(27)**

    possessive pronoun   (interrogative pronoun)   relative pronoun

21. They were the climbers **who** first scaled Mount Everest successfully. **(27)**

    compound personal pronoun   possessive pronoun   (relative pronoun)

22. **No one** else had reached the top and returned alive. **(28)**

    (indefinite pronoun)   interrogative pronoun   compound personal pronoun

23. A team set up camps on the lower slopes, but Hillary and Norgay continued on by **themselves**. **(25)**

    (compound personal pronoun)   relative pronoun   possessive pronoun

24. Hillary and Norgay made **their** final camp almost 28,000 feet up the mountainside. **(26)**

    relative pronoun   (possessive pronoun)   interrogative pronoun

25. **Both** then began the climb to the top. **(28)**

    interrogative pronoun   (indefinite pronoun)   compound personal pronoun

26. **Nothing** could have been more exciting than reaching Everest's peak. **(28)**

    compound personal pronoun   relative pronoun   (indefinite pronoun)

27. Hillary wrote about **his** experiences in *High Adventure*. **(26)**

    relative pronoun   indefinite pronoun   (possessive pronoun)

Adjectives

Circle each adjective that tells *what kind*. Underline each adjective that tells *how many*. Draw a box around each article (*a, an, the*). Draw a star above the word each adjective modifies.

28. Kate Shelley lived near a⃞ ⭐(remote) bridge in Iowa. **(29)**

29. During a⃞ (fierce) ⭐rainstorm a⃞ (violent) ⭐flood washed out the⃞ bridge. **(29)**

30. Shelley knew that a⃞ ⭐train with many passengers would soon reach the⃞ ⭐bridge. **(29)**

Demonstrative Adjectives and Demonstrative Pronouns

Circle each demonstrative adjective. Underline each demonstrative pronoun. Draw a box around the word each demonstrative modifies or replaces.

31. (This) teenager⃞ climbed across another bridge in the heavy rain to warn the train's engineer. **(30)**

32. Kate Shelley was just in time; she saved many lives on (that) night⃞. **(30)**

33. <u>This</u> is the lantern⃞ Kate Shelley carried through the dark. **(30)**

Name _____

Community Connection

In Unit 3 of *G.U.M.* students learned about **different kinds of nouns, pronouns, and adjectives** and used what they learned to improve their own writing. The content of these lessons focuses on the theme **People Who Overcame Challenges**. As students completed the exercises, they learned about people who have overcome different kinds of challenges. These pages offer activities that reinforce skills and concepts presented in the unit. They also provide opportunities for the students to make connections between the materials in the lessons and the community at large.

Community Services

Find out what services for people facing challenges are available in your community. Look for rehabilitation programs, food distribution centers, shelters, immigrant resource centers, help centers for people with disabilities, and so on. Contact the organizations to find out what services they offer and whom they serve. Then create a descriptive list of helpful organizations. Make sure you include the name of each organization, its phone number and address, and how it helps members of your community. When you have finished, decide whether you think your community has services for all who need them or if other services should also be offered. Add your suggestions for new services to your list.

Any Volunteers?

Choose one organization in your community that helps people overcome challenges, such as a home for the elderly or a help center for wounded veterans. Visit or call the organization to find out about ways you might get involved with the organization as a volunteer. If possible, spend some time volunteering for the organization. Then write an advertisement to convince others to become volunteers for the organization. Include what services the organization offers, what jobs the volunteers do, and why volunteers are important. You may also want to invite a representative from the organization to talk to your class about community needs and the value of volunteers.

Local Heroes

Research people in your community, region, or state who have overcome challenges of various kinds. Use what you find out to create a scrapbook of local heroes. In your scrapbook, include a brief biography of each of the people you found. Or, choose two or three of the people and write a short report about each one.

Fundraising

Join a fundraiser, such as a walk-a-thon that raises money for a good cause. Answer each of these questions:

- What type of fundraiser will you join?
- How does the fundraiser work?
- What organization or group will the money go to?
- What is the target amount for funds raised?
- How many people will participate?
- How does the sponsoring organization get people interested in participating?
- Do the participants get any rewards for their participation? If so, what?

Write the details of the fundraising event in a report.

Unforgettable Folks

A Special Person

Interview a family member, friend, or acquaintance about a challenge he or she had to overcome in order to achieve an important goal. Before holding the interview, write a list of questions that you will ask. Take notes during the interview to record the person's responses. After the interview, write a descriptive paragraph about the challenge the person faced and how he or she overcame it.

Work That Helps

Learn about and list some of the job opportunities available for people who want to help others overcome challenges. Look for jobs in education, medicine and science, and social work. Then learn more about one job that interests you. Find out what skills are required for the job, how to get the training required to do the job, and what the job responsibilities are. Use the planner that follows to help you find and organize the information.

Job Information   Answers will vary.

People/Organizations to call for information:

_____

_____

_____

_____

Information given:

_____

_____

_____

_____

Training needed:

_____

_____

_____

_____

Where to get the training/how long it takes:

_____

_____

_____

_____

Special skills needed/suggested:

_____

_____

_____

Job responsibilities:

_____

_____

_____

Other information:

_____

_____

Name _____

Unforgettable Folks

The Sonoran Desert (is) one of the largest deserts in North America. Its weather patterns <u>give</u> this vast area a fifth season.

In the first sentence, circle the verb that links the subject of the sentence to words in the predicate that rename and describe it. In the second sentence, underline the verb that shows action.

An **action verb** shows action. It usually tells what the subject of a clause is doing, will do, or did. An action verb may include one or more helping verbs in addition to the main verb. A **linking verb** does not show action. It connects the subject of a sentence to a word or words that describe or rename the subject. Linking verbs are usually forms of *be*. Some common linking verbs are *am, is, are, was, were, been,* and *will be*. The verbs *become, seem, appear,* and *look* can also be used as linking verbs. A linking verb may also include one or more helping verbs in addition to the main verb.

See Handbook Sections 18a, 18c

Part 1

Underline each action verb. Circle each linking verb. Be sure to include any helping verbs you find.

1. The Sonoran Desert (is) one of the hottest and driest areas in North America.

2. Seasons in the Sonoran Desert (are) different from the seasons in temperate climates.

3. The amount of rainfall <u>determines</u> the timing and nature of each season there.

4. Because the rainfall (is) so unpredictable, not everyone <u>agrees</u> on the number of seasons in the Sonoran Desert.

5. The Arizona-Sonora Desert Museum officially <u>recognizes</u> five seasons.

6. The annual cycle <u>begins</u> with the summer rainy season, from July through early September.

7. This period of heavy rainfall <u>relieves</u> the extreme heat of the previous two months.

8. It also <u>provides</u> much-needed water for desert plants and animals.

9. After the rainy season, temperatures (become) cooler and rainfall <u>diminishes</u>.

10. The fall season <u>has begun</u>; it typically <u>lasts</u> through November.

11. The winter months of December, January, and February (are) mostly sunny and mild, although they occasionally <u>bring</u> wind, rain, and cold temperatures.

12. Spring (mid-February through April) <u>features</u> mild temperatures and little rain.

13. This (is) the main flowering season for small plants, shrubs, and trees.

14. In a normal year, no rain <u>falls</u> during the foresummer drought months of May and June, and temperatures (are) high.

15. Plants and animals (remain) in survival mode during the drought months.

16. The return of the summer rains <u>starts</u> the cycle over; flora and fauna <u>thrive</u> in their desert home.

Part 2

Complete each sentence below with a verb from the word bank. On the line, write *A* if the verb you wrote is an action verb and *L* if the verb you wrote is a linking verb.

are	jump	captures	become
is	thrive	work	appears

17. The Sonoran Desert _____is_____ home to many species of wildlife. __L__

18. Many species of plants and animals _____thrive_____ despite the scarcity of water. __A__

19. On a hot, still day, the desert _____appears_____ to be empty, but in fact it is full of life. __A__

20. There _____are_____ more than 2,000 species of plants in the Sonoran Desert. __L__

21. Thousands of harvester ants _____work_____ in their underground tunnels. __A__

22. Ants above ground _become (or) are_ breakfast for a hungry horned lizard. __L__

23. The lizard _____captures_____ the hapless insects with its sticky tongue. __A__

24. Bighorn sheep _____jump_____ from ledge to ledge in the desert mountain range. __A__

Part 3

Some verbs, such as *appear, look, smell, feel, grow,* and *taste,* can be either action verbs or linking verbs, depending on how they are used in a sentence. You can test whether a verb is a linking verb by substituting a form of the verb *be* (*am, is, are, was, were,* or *been*) in its place. If the form of *be* makes sense, the verb probably is a linking verb.

In the sentences below, circle each boldfaced verb that is used as a linking verb. Underline each boldfaced verb that is used as an action verb.

25. I **grew** strawberries in my backyard.

26. They **looked** ready to pick.

27. I **smelled** one.

28. It **smelled** delicious.

29. I rinsed it off and **tasted** it.

30. It **tasted** better than the strawberries you buy at the store.

Name _____

Some wasps **lay** their eggs on other insects.
Caterpillars **change** in their cocoons.

Which boldfaced verb says an action the subject did by itself? _____ **change** _____

Which boldfaced verb tells about an action the subject did to something else?
_____ **lay** _____

A **transitive verb** is an action verb that transfers its action to a direct object. (*Wasps lay eggs.*) An **intransitive verb** does not have a direct object. An intransitive verb shows action that the subject does alone. (*Caterpillars change.*) Many verbs can be either transitive or intransitive, depending on whether there is a direct object.

See Handbook Section 18b

Part 1

Underline each transitive verb and draw a box around its direct object. Circle each intransitive verb.

1. Most insects (grow) in stages.
2. They begin their lives as eggs.
3. The number of eggs and their size, shape, and color (vary) from insect to insect.
4. Soon a juvenile insect, or larva, (hatches).
5. Most larvae scarcely resemble the adults of their species.
6. Many (live) in very different habitats.
7. Mosquito larvae (swim) in the water.
8. Cicada nymphs devour roots underground for as long as seventeen years.
9. Some wasp larvae (live) inside the bodies of other insects.
10. Ants feed their colonies' larvae with great care.
11. Some beetle larvae imitate ant larvae for a free meal.
12. Larvae (eat) constantly for maximum growth.
13. Some enter a pupal stage before adulthood.
14. Some of a pupa's tissues (dissolve) inside its cocoon or shell.
15. The insect (emerges) from its cocoon as an adult.
16. In time, the female adult lays many eggs.
17. For many insects the entire cycle (lasts) only a few days.
18. A few insects have a seventeen-year life cycle.

Egg

Adult

Larva

Pupa

Life Cycle of an Ant

Part 2

Write a verb from the word bank to complete each sentence. Then label each transitive verb *T* and each intransitive verb *I*. Circle the direct object of each transitive verb.

begins	lay	live	have	attract	fly

19. Unlike larvae, adult insects often _____**have**_____ beautiful (wings). __T__

20. After pumping blood through the new wings, they _____**fly**_____ for the first time. __I__

21. Some adults _____**attract**_____ a (mate) with a scent or a flashing signal. __T__

22. Most adult insects do not _____**live**_____ very long. __I__

23. They must _____**lay**_____ their own (eggs) quickly. __T__

24. Then the life cycle _____**begins**_____ again. __I__

Part 3

> Many verbs can be transitive or intransitive, depending on whether they are used with a direct object.
>
> D.O.
> The butterfly *grew* wings inside its cocoon. (transitive)
> The wings *grew* inside the cocoon. (intransitive)

Use the verbs *stopped* and *broke* in two sentences. In one sentence, use the verb as a transitive verb with a direct object. In the other, use it as an intransitive verb. Circle the direct object of each transitive verb.

25. stopped (transitive): **Answers will vary.** _____

_____

_____

26. stopped (intransitive): _____

_____

_____

27. broke (transitive): _____

_____

_____

28. broke (intransitive): _____

_____

_____

Name _____

The World Outside

Read and Discover

Hot (flames) scorched the underbrush. ___X___

The (underbrush) was scorched by the hot flames. ___O___

Circle the simple subject in each sentence. Write *X* by the sentence in which the subject does something. Write *O* by the sentence in which something is done to the subject.

If the subject performs an action, the verb is said to be in the **active voice**. (*Hot flames scorched.*) If the subject is acted upon by something else, the verb is said to be in the **passive voice**. (*The underbrush was scorched.*) Many sentences in the passive voice have a prepositional phrase that begins with the word *by* and follows the verb.

See Handbook Sections 18g, 20

Part 1

Circle the simple subject in each sentence. Draw a box around the simple predicate. Be sure to include helping verbs. Write *A* if the verb is in the active voice. Write *P* if it is in the passive voice.

1. Forest (fires) |consume| trees and other vegetation. ___A___

2. Many (animals) |are killed| by the raging flames. ___P___

3. But a fire's (destruction) |clears| the way for new life. ___A___

4. Small (trees) and sickly (trees) |have been incinerated| by the fire. ___P___

5. Strong, healthy (trees) |have been saved| from damage by their thick bark. ___P___

6. (Sunlight) |pours| through the open spaces between bare branches. ___A___

7. New (grasses), (wildflowers), and (seedlings) |sprout| in the ashes. ___A___

8. The (number) of plant and animal species in a forest |may| actually |increase| after a fire. ___A___

9. In a forest, small (fires) |are sparked| frequently by lightning. ___P___

10. Dead (material) on the forest floor |is eliminated| by these small fires. ___P___

11. Small (fires) rarely |cause| serious harm to a forest. ___A___

12. This natural (cycle) of destruction and rebirth |has been upset| by humans. ___P___

13. Until recently, (firefighters) |fought| all forest fires, large and small. ___A___

14. Flammable dead (materials) on the forest floor |were| not |eliminated|. ___P___

15. In a region with much dry brush and dead wood on the forest floor, a small (fire) |can| quickly |grow| into an inferno. ___A___

16. Soon the furious (flames) |incinerate| healthy adult trees. ___A___

17. Today, small natural (fires) generally |are ignored| by firefighters. ___P___

18. (They) |battle| only dangerous ones. ___A___

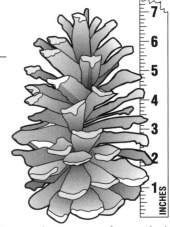

Some pinecones release their seeds only after a forest fire.

Part 2 Suggested answers appear below. Accept all reasonable responses.

Look again at each sentence in Part 1 that has a verb in the passive voice. Rewrite each sentence so the verb is in the active voice.

19. **The raging flames kill many animals.**

20. **The fire has incinerated small trees and sickly trees.**

21. **Their thick bark has saved strong, healthy trees from damage.**

22. **In a forest, lightning frequently sparks small fires.**

23. **These small fires eliminate dead material on the forest floor.**

24. **Humans have upset this natural cycle of destruction and rebirth.**

25. **Nothing has eliminated flammable dead materials on the forest floor.**

26. **Today, firefighters generally ignore small natural fires.**

Part 3

> The active voice communicates action briefly and powerfully. Some writers believe that the passive voice should be used only when an action is done by an unknown or unimportant agent—for example, *The clock had been dropped.*

Read the passage below. Notice that all of the sentences are in strong active voice. Then underline each verb in the active voice in the excerpt. (27–37)

> I kicked into the muscles of the horse. Once again it reared and snorted. Then it began to run. I didn't know what to do. Instead of running across the field to the irrigation ditch the horse ran down the road to the vineyard of Dikran Halabian where it began to leap over vines. The horse leaped over seven vines before I fell. Then it continued running.
> —William Saroyan, from "The Summer of the Beautiful White Horse"

Look over a story or a report you have written recently. Find a sentence with a verb in the passive voice. Rewrite the sentence so the verb is in the active voice.

38. **Answers will vary.**

Name _____

Every year, migrating geese [pass] over my community. In September I <u>watched</u> them on their southward journey. In spring the geese (will fly) north again.

Circle the verb phrase that tells about something that will happen in the future. Underline the verb that tells about something that happened in the past. Draw a box around the verb that tells about something that happens regularly or is true now.

A **present tense verb** indicates that something happens regularly or is true now. A **past tense verb** tells about something that happened in the past. Regular verbs form the past tense by adding *-ed* (*watch/watched*). The spelling of most irregular verbs changes in the past tense (*fly/flew*). A **future tense verb** tells what will happen in the future. Add the helping verb *will* to the present tense form of a verb to form the future tense (*pass/will pass*). 📢 **Remember to use this information when you speak, too.**

See Handbook Sections 18d, 18e

Part 1

Circle the verb in each sentence. (Don't forget to include helping verbs.) Write whether the verb is in the *present*, *past*, or *future* tense.

1. About sixty percent of all birds (migrate) to warmer places in the winter. _____ present

2. This fall you (will) probably (see) many migrating birds. _____ future

3. The arctic tern (holds) the world record for long-distance yearly migration. _____ present

4. This hardy bird (spends) the summer months near the North Pole. _____ present

5. Each fall it (travels) to the continent of Antarctica. _____ present

6. In July of 1951 scientists (banded) an arctic tern in Greenland. _____ past

7. The bird (traveled) 11,000 miles in three months. _____ past

8. In October the scientists (found) it in South Africa on its way to Antarctica. _____ past

9. On their migrations, birds (travel) invisible routes called flyways. _____ present

10. Billions of birds (fly) these routes each year. _____ present

11. I (live) under one of North America's major flyways. _____ present

12. Next fall I (will borrow) some binoculars from my grandmother. _____ future

13. I (will watch) the birds on their way south. _____ future

14. I (bought) a field guide to Western birds last year. _____ past

15. I (will record) my observations carefully. _____ future

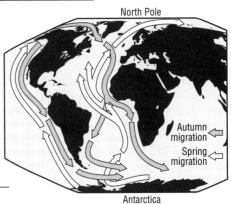

North Pole

Autumn migration

Spring migration

Antarctica

Twice a year, the arctic tern migrates from pole to pole.

Part 2 Suggested answers appear below. Accept all reasonable responses.

Write the past, present, or future tense form of a verb from the word bank to complete each sentence. Use a helping verb to form future tense verbs.

watch	take	have	go	photograph	swim

16. Many creatures besides birds _____ **have** _____ both a winter and a summer address.

17. Last year I _____ **watched** _____ gray whales on their southern migration.

18. A gray whale typically _____ **swims** _____ up to 16,000 miles on its way from the Arctic seas to Baja California.

19. Next year I _____ **will go** _____ on a whale-watching expedition.

20. On an expedition last year my uncle _____ **photographed** _____ some gray whales.

21. I _____ **will take** _____ my camera with me the next time I go whale watching.

Part 3

Use these notes about a group of monarch butterflies to write a journal entry about phases of the monarchs' migration. Play the role of a scientist who has observed the monarchs. Use past, present, and future tenses in your entry.

- Monarchs—amazing insects (beautiful orange butterflies, black spots)
- Fall—fly to mountains in Michoacán, Mexico
- Spring—fly to Canada
- Journey begins in September in Canada, ends in Mexico in November (3,000 miles)
- Spend winter in Mexico—cover trees with a blanket of color
- Reproduce in spring—begin northward journey again

22. **Answers will vary.**

_____

_____

_____

_____

_____

_____

_____

_____

_____

_____

_____

Name _____

The World Outside

Before I studied ecology, I **had** not **understood** the importance of each individual in a community of living things. Now I (**have gained**) a better understanding of how living things in an ecosystem affect one another. Before it dies, each organism will **have affected** other creatures, eating some or becoming food for others.

Circle the boldfaced verb phrase that tells about an action that began in the past and continues today. Draw a box around the boldfaced verb phrase that tells about actions that will be complete before a certain time in the future. Underline the boldfaced verb phrase that tells about actions that were completed by a certain time in the past.

The **present perfect** tense (*have gained*) shows action that started in the past and was recently completed or is still happening. The **past perfect** tense (*had understood*) shows action that was completed by a certain time in the past. The **future perfect** tense (*will have affected*) shows action that will be complete by a certain time in the future. To form perfect tenses, use a form of *have* with the past participle of a verb. **Remember to use this information when you speak, too.**

See Handbook Sections 18d, 18e

Part 1

Circle boldfaced verbs in the present perfect tense. Underline boldfaced verbs in the past perfect tense. Draw a box around boldfaced verbs in the future perfect tense. **(1–13)**

Scientists (**have discovered**) ecosystems in very small places. Looking into the center of a bromeliad (broh MEE lee uhd), they found that a diverse group of animals **had established** a community there. Bromeliads are pineapple-like plants that trap water that (**has fallen**) into their leaves. This protected, watery environment is rich in nutrients. By the time it dies, a typical bromeliad will **have supported** thousands of tiny animals in the pools among its leaves.

For example, a tadpole swims in the water that (**has collected**) in the center of a bromeliad. The tadpole hatched yesterday from an egg a frog **had laid** a few weeks before. By the time the tadpole grows into a frog, it will **have eaten** many mosquito larvae. These larvae (**have lived**) on one-celled creatures floating in the water, which (**have eaten**) waste from frogs and other creatures. The cycle of food-web interactions will **have repeated** itself many times before the bromeliad dies.

I (**have**) just (**completed**) a report on bromeliads. In the past I **had thought** ecology was boring. This report (**has changed**) my view.

A universe of creatures may live their entire lives in the tiny ecosystem in a bromeliad.

The World Outside

Part 2

Write the present perfect form (*has* or *have* + past participle), the past perfect form (*had* + past participle), or the future perfect form (*will have* + past participle) of the verb in parentheses to complete each sentence correctly.

14. For the last ten years I _____ **have studied** _____ bromeliad plants. (study)

15. Before I looked inside my first bromeliad, I _____ **had expected** _____ to find only a few bugs inside. (expect)

16. I was astonished by the number of creatures that _____ **had made** _____ their homes inside. (make)

17. Over the past decade I _____ **have examined** _____ hundreds of tiny creatures under my microscope. (examine)

18. By the time my research is finally complete, I _____ **will have counted** _____ thousands of animals. (count)

Part 3

Authors usually write fiction as if a story's events happened in the past. Actions happening in the "now" of the story are written in the simple past tense. The past perfect tense is often used to indicate events that came before the time in which the story is taking place.

Notice the verb tenses used in this passage.

> He felt that his luck was better than usual today. When he had reported for work that morning he had expected to be shut up in the relief office at a clerk's job, for he had been hired downtown as a clerk, and he was glad to have, instead, the freedom of the streets and welcomed, at least at first, the vigor of the cold and even the blowing of the hard wind.
>
> —Saul Bellow, from "Looking for Mr. Green"

Read the passage again, and write the verbs. Then write whether each verb is in the past tense or the past perfect tense.

19. _____ **felt** _____   _____ **past** _____

20. _____ **was** _____   _____ **past** _____

21. _____ **had reported** _____   _____ **past perfect** _____

22. _____ **had expected** _____   _____ **past perfect** _____

23. _____ **had been hired** _____   _____ **past perfect** _____

24. _____ **was** _____   _____ **past** _____

25. _____ **welcomed** _____   _____ **past** _____

Name _____

The World Outside

At midnight last night, Rick **was playing** a video game.
Now he **is snoring** loudly.
Soon his alarm clock **will be ringing**.

Circle the boldfaced verb phrase that tells about an action that is going on now. Underline the boldfaced verb that tells about an action that was happening for a while in the past. Draw a box around the verb phrase that tells about an action that will happen in the future.

Progressive forms of verbs show continuing action. The **present progressive** form of a verb consists of the helping verb *am, is,* or *are* and the present participle of that verb. (*I am watching.*) The **past progressive** form consists of the helping verb *was* or *were* and the present participle. (*They were listening.*) The **future progressive** form consists of the helping verbs *will be* and the present participle. (*You will be studying.*) ◀ **Remember to use this information when you speak, too.**

See Handbook Sections 18d, 18e

Part 1

Read each sentence. If the boldfaced verb in it is a progressive form, write *P* on the line. If the boldfaced verb is not a progressive form, write *X*.

1. Birds that fly south in the fall **are listening** to their biological clocks. __P__

2. Scientists **have shown** that many human activities are controlled by biological clocks. __X__

3. Changes in body temperature called circadian rhythms **are waking** us up every morning and putting us to sleep every night. __P__

4. These natural cycles can cause problems for people who **are trying** to work late at night. __P__

5. Scientists **have reset** people's biological clocks successfully by having those people sit under bright lights. __X__

6. Every night, biological cycles **are controlling** not only when we sleep but also how we sleep. __P__

7. Before 1951, most people **believed** that the brain shut down during sleep. __X__

8. That year, a scientist who **was studying** his son's sleep patterns made an important discovery. __P__

9. For short periods while the boy **was sleeping,** his eyes moved back and forth quickly. __P__

10. Scientists **have labeled** this phase of sleep REM (rapid eye movement) sleep. __X__

11. During the night, you normally **move** from deep sleep to REM sleep and back several times. __X__

12. Your eyes **are moving** constantly during REM sleep, and this is when most dreams occur. __P__

13. Some scientists believe that REM sleep **helps** the brain with learning and emotional adjustment. __X__

14. By age 70, most people **will have slept** for more than 200,000 hours. __X__

15. Tomorrow at 8 A.M. I **will be sleeping** soundly. __P__

16. By sleeping late, perhaps I **will be helping** my brain! __P__

Part 2

Use a helping verb from the word bank plus a form of the verb in parentheses to complete each sentence. Each verb you write should be a progressive form.

am	was	were	will be

17. Last night I dreamed that I _____**was walking**_____ through a huge swamp. (walk)

18. In the dream, a big mosquito _____**was buzzing**_____ around my head. (buzz)

19. Its transparent wings _____**were tickling**_____ me. (tickle)

20. When I woke up, I _____**was laughing**_____ out loud. (laugh)

21. Now I _____**am writing**_____ about my mosquito dream in a journal. (write)

22. If I have my way, tonight I _____**will be dreaming**_____ about something else! (dream)

Part 3

Circle the progressive verb form in each clue. Then write the answers in the puzzle.

Across
2. Scientists are studying this state of deep sleep.
4. When you grow sleepy tonight, this rhythm will be influencing your energy level.
5. You will be doing this tonight.
7. When you look at this, you are checking the time.

Down
1. When you think, you are using this.
3. Some scientists are using bright lights to reset people's ___ clocks.
6. One scientist observed that these were moving rapidly at certain times as his son slept.

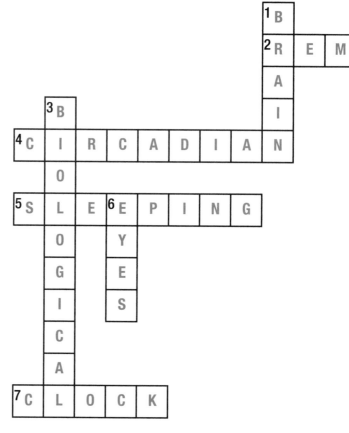

The World Outside

Read and Discover

The current flows **swiftly**. Salmon must be **very** strong to swim **upstream** against it.

Which boldfaced word tells how the current flows? _____ swiftly

Which tells where salmon swim? _____ upstream

Which modifies an adjective by telling how much? _____ very

Adverbs modify verbs, adjectives, or other adverbs. They tell **how, when, where,** or **to what extent** (*how much*). Many adverbs end in *-ly*. Other common adverbs are *fast, very, often, again, sometimes, soon, only, too, later, first, then, there, far,* and *now*.

See Handbook Section 19

Part 1

Circle each adverb. There is at least one adverb in each sentence.

1. Some animals (almost) (always) bear their young in their own place of birth.

2. Salmon hatch in streams, but they swim (steadily) to the ocean.

3. After several years at sea, salmon return (instinctively) to their native streams.

4. The journey upstream is (extremely) hard.

5. The water flows (powerfully) in the other direction.

6. The big fish swim (forcefully) against the current.

7. They leap (high) in the air over small waterfalls.

8. (Finally) they reach their birthplace.

9. (There,) females lay eggs, and males fertilize them.

10. (Then) the salmon collapse (wearily.)

11. Their lives (usually) end near their own birthplace.

12. Tiny salmon (soon) hatch and begin the cycle (again.)

13. (Sometimes) salmon cannot return to their birthplace.

14. Dams can block their journey (upstream.)

15. (Specially) built fish ladders in some streams can help salmon (safely) around obstacles such as dams and power plants.

16. Drought can (temporarily) turn a river into a dry, sandy path.

17. Salmon are (eagerly) sought by commercial fishing boats.

18. Bears (thoroughly) enjoy fishing in the salmon-rich streams.

19. (Fortunately,) hatcheries (sometimes) can restock streams that have been overfished.

Salmon battle upstream to lay eggs where they themselves once hatched.

The World Outside

Part 2

Circle the adverb in each sentence that tells about the underlined word. Then write *how, when, where, how often,* or *to what extent* to tell what the adverb explains.

20. The ability of salmon to find their birthplace (once) <u>seemed</u> magical. _____**when**_____

21. One scientist (wisely) <u>guessed</u> that smell might guide these fish. _____**how**_____

22. He plugged the noses of salmon, and the fish were (completely) <u>unable</u> to find their streams of birth. _____**to what extent**_____

23. He (next) <u>exposed</u> hatching salmon to a certain chemical smell and let them go free in the water. _____**when**_____

24. He spread the chemical smell in a stream, and all of his salmon <u>swam</u> (there) _____**where**_____

25. The sense of smell is (extremely) <u>important</u> to salmon. _____**to what extent**_____

Part 3

Often, adverbs concisely convey information that would otherwise need to be stated in a series of prepositional phrases. Read the sentence below, and circle the eleven adverbs it contains. Remember, adverbs can modify other adverbs. **(26–36)**

[The river] ran (seemingly) (straight) for a while, turned (abruptly) (then) ran (smoothly) (again), (then) met another obstacle, (again) was turned (sharply) and (again) ran (smoothly).

—Norman Maclean, from *A River Runs Through It*

Now rewrite the sentence, replacing as many adverbs as you can with phrases. Then work with a partner to decide which version—the original or your revision—seems clearer and easier to understand.

37. ____**Answers will vary.**_____

_____

_____

_____

_____

_____

_____

_____

_____

_____

_____

Name _____

The World Outside

During a storm, rainwater carries small particles **of soil** downhill **into** streams or storm drains.

Which boldfaced word begins a phrase that tells *when*? ___during___

Which begins a phrase that tells about a noun? ___of___

Which begins a phrase that tells *where*? ___into___

A **preposition** shows a relationship between the noun or pronoun that follows the preposition (the **object of the preposition**) and another word or group of words in the sentence. The preposition, its object, and the word(s) between them make a **prepositional phrase**.

See Handbook Section 20

Part 1

Underline each prepositional phrase. Circle the preposition and draw a box around its object.

1. The process of erosion changes the shape of the earth.

2. Water, wind, and ice break solid rock into small pieces.

3. These forces remove soil and rocks from hillsides.

4. After many centuries, a mountain may be reduced to a broad mound.

5. A swift stream can carve a path through a rocky landscape.

6. Creeks in the mountains carry eroded material downward to wide rivers.

7. During a flood, rivers deposit tiny grains of soil across low-lying farmlands.

8. Floods destroy homes, but they increase the fertility of the farmlands.

9. A river may spread soil near its mouth, across a triangle-shaped area.

10. The geographic term for such a region is a delta.

11. Some particles of eroded material eventually reach the ocean.

12. The sand grains on your favorite beach were probably transported to the sea by rivers.

13. They were possibly then carried along the shoreline by a current.

14. Finally some gentle waves carried the tiny grains onto the beach.

15. Rain in the mountains today may be moving grains of sand that someday will stick between your toes!

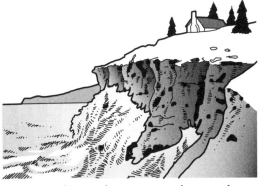

The force of water can change the shape of landforms.

Part 2   Suggested answers appear below. Accept all reasonable responses.

Fill each blank with an appropriate preposition from the word bank, or use one of your own. You may use a preposition more than once.

of	with	by	among	from	between	in	on	under	along

16. Trees and other plants hold down soil _____ **with** _____ their roots.

17. When people cut down trees and remove bushes _____ **from** _____ hillsides, rains may carry
    away large amounts _____ **of** _____ soil.

18. Farmers have developed several methods _____ **of** _____ soil conservation.

19. Strip-cropping involves planting two different crops _____ **in** _____ alternating strips.

20. A soil-holding crop is planted _____ **on** _____ a strip of land _____ **between** _____
    grain fields to reduce the amount of soil carried off _____ **by** _____ the wind.

Part 3

Use the clues to help you complete the crossword puzzle with prepositions. Then circle the object (in the clues) of each preposition you wrote.

Across
1. We looked __ the canyon to the other side.
3. It was thousands __ feet wide.
4. Carolyn rose an hour __ dawn and made hot oatmeal for our breakfast.
6. We decided to start hiking __ seven A.M., while it would still be cool.
7. A narrow trail led __ the edge down into the canyon.
8. We descended carefully __ the canyon.

Down
1. __ a long time, we reached the river at the bottom.
2. The canyon walls loomed __ our heads.
5. We drank from our water bottles and splashed some water __ our faces.
6. The sound of rushing water echoed all __ us.

Crossword solution:
1 ACROSS / 2 OVER / 3 OF / 4 BEFORE / 5 ON / 6 AT / 7 FROM / 8 INTO / AROUND

Now choose one or more prepositions from the puzzle and use them in a sentence about erosion.

21. **Answers will vary.** _____

_____

Name _____

The World Outside

Read and Discover

Kiesha **and** Reiko went outside **because** they wanted to paint a picture of the moon in the night sky. They stared at the sky for hours, **but** they never did see the moon.

Which boldfaced word links two nouns? _____ and _____

Which links two independent clauses? _____ but _____

Which begins a dependent clause? _____ because _____

Coordinating conjunctions (*and, but, or*) connect words or groups of words (including independent clauses) that are similar. **Subordinating conjunctions** such as *although, because, since, so, if,* and *before* show how one clause is related to another. Subordinating conjunctions are used at the beginning of adverb clauses.

See Handbook Section 22

Part 1

Underline each coordinating conjunction. Circle each subordinating conjunction.

1. The moon often lights up the sky, <u>but</u> sometimes it is not visible at all.

2. The moon's appearance changes nightly, <u>and</u> the times at which it is in the sky vary also.

3. The moon may look like a half circle one night, <u>and</u> a few nights later it may look like a crescent.

4. Over 29½ days, the moon changes from a thin sliver to a full round disc <u>and</u> back again.

5. These changes, <u>or</u> phases, are called new, crescent, quarter, gibbous, <u>and</u> full.

6. People once associated the moon with unreliability (because) they saw it changing constantly.

7. The moon may have a reputation for unreliability, <u>but</u> it is actually very consistent.

8. (Although) the moon's appearance varies, it never turns different sides toward Earth.

9. (As) the moon revolves around Earth, one side permanently faces us.

10. (Before) lunar probes visited the moon, humans had never seen its far side.

11. The moon's phases occur (because) the sun's light hits different parts of its face.

12. (If) you look at a crescent moon through a telescope, you can see the dark part dimly lit by Earth's reflected light.

13. (Because) that dim light has been reflected by Earth, it is called earthshine.

14. (When) Earth passes between the sun <u>and</u> the moon, a lunar eclipse occurs.

15. In a partial lunar eclipse, Earth blocks part of the sun's light for a short period of time, <u>and</u> a portion of the moon temporarily becomes dark.

The Moon's Phases

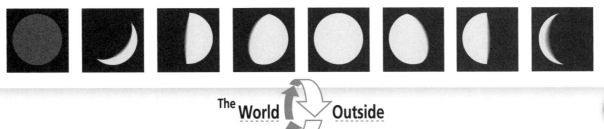

Part 2

Complete each sentence with a conjunction from the word bank. Write *C* if you used a coordinating conjunction or *S* if you used a subordinating conjunction.

because	but	although	as	and

16. _____**Because**_____ the earth rotates, the moon's gravity pulls on the water in the oceans. __**S**__

17. _____**Although**_____ the moon's gravity is too weak to pull water off the earth, it is strong enough to create bulges. __**S**__

18. _____**Because**_____ the earth is constantly rotating, these bulges move steadily across the face of the earth. __**S**__

19. The bulges of water create high tides _____**and**_____ low tides. __**C**__

20. Tides are highest during the new moon, when the sun _____**and**_____ the moon pull the waters in the same direction. __**C**__

21. There are also tides in the air, _____**but**_____ they can be detected only with sensitive machines. __**C**__

Part 3

> Subordinating conjunctions are commonly used in proverbs, aphorisms, and other wise sayings. In many of these, the subordinating conjunction introduces a clause that tells the conditions under which something is true.

Underline the subordinate clause in each wise saying below; circle each subordinating conjunction.

(When) the well's dry, we know the worth of water.

Don't throw stones at your neighbors', (if) your own windows are glass.

Three may keep a secret, (if) two of them are dead.
—Benjamin Franklin, from *Poor Richard's Almanac*

Now try your hand at writing a proverb, aphorism, or wise saying of your own that includes a subordinating conjunction.

22. **Answers will vary.** _____

_____

_____

_____

Name _____

Read and Discover

For your report on how one creature can benefit from a symbiotic relationship with another, focus on <u>either</u> the <u>cattle egret</u> <u>or</u> the <u>clownfish</u>.

Circle the word that joins the two underlined nouns. Underline another word that helps this word show how the nouns are linked.

Correlative conjunctions always appear in pairs. They connect words or groups of words and provide more emphasis than coordinating conjunctions. Some common correlative conjunctions are *both...and, either...or, neither...nor, not only...but (also),* and *whether...or.*

See Handbook | Section 22

Part 1

Circle the correlative conjunctions and coordinating conjunctions in these sentences. If a sentence contains correlative conjunctions, write *COR*. Write *X* if the sentence does not contain correlative conjunctions.

1. When two animal species (not only) live together (but also) have a very close relationship, we call them symbiotic. __COR__

2. Symbiotic relationships can be (either) parasitic, commensal, (or) mutual. __COR__

3. Parasites may hurt their hosts (or) even kill them. __X__

4. In a commensal relationship, the host is (neither) hurt (nor) helped by its neighbor. __COR__

5. Mutual symbiotic relationships involve a cycle of give (and) take. __X__

6. For example, (both) the cattle egret (and) the African buffalo benefit from their relationship. __COR__

7. A buffalo might be infested with skin parasites, (but) the egret cleans them off. __X__

8. In return, the egret gets a tasty meal of (both) the parasites (and) the insects the buffalo kicks up from the grass. __COR__

9. The sea anemone's sting is (not only) painful (but also) deadly to most fish. __COR__

10. Only the clownfish is able to build up immunity to the sting (and) live in harmony with this dangerous predator. __X__

11. The clownfish (both) lures prey for the anemone (and) chases away fish that might damage it. __COR__

12. In return, the anemone provides the clownfish with protection (and) scraps from its meals. __X__

13. If you study (either) biology (or) environmental science, you may learn about lichens. __COR__

14. Lichens, gray-green organisms that live on rocks (and) trees, appear to be plants (but) are actually a combination of an alga (and) a fungus. __X__

15. (Neither) the alga (nor) the fungus can survive alone. __COR__

16. The alga produces food for the fungus, (and) the fungus protects the alga from the drying effects of sun (and) wind. __X__

Part 2   Possible answers appear below. Accept all reasonable responses.

Rewrite each sentence pair as one new, shorter sentence using the correlative conjunctions in parentheses.

17. Swollen-thorn acacia trees provide food for acacia ants. The trees provide a home for the ants.

    (not only/but also) __Swollen-thorn acacia trees provide acacia ants not only with food but also__

    __with a home.__

18. The ants protect the tree from harmful insects. They clear other plants away from it. (both/and)

    __The ants both protect the tree from harmful insects and clear other plants away from it.__

19. Swollen-thorn acacia trees benefit from their mutual relationship with acacia ants. Acacia ants benefit

    from the mutual relationship, too. (both/and) __Both swollen-thorn acacia trees and acacia ants__

    __benefit from their mutual relationship.__

20. Acacia ants may be the subject of my oral report. Perhaps clownfish will be the subject of my oral

    report instead. (either/or) __Either acacia ants or clownfish will be the subject of my oral report.__

Part 3

Circle the correct correlative conjunction in each clue. Use information from the lesson to label each symbiotic relationship.

21. (Both/Neither) the host creature and its neighbor benefit in this kind of relationship.

    M   U   T   U   A   L

22. The host may be (either/neither) hurt or killed in this kind of relationship.

    P   A   R   A   S   I   T   I   C

23. The host is (either/neither) harmed nor helped in this kind of relationship.

    C   O   M   M   E   N   S   A   L

Name _____

The World Outside

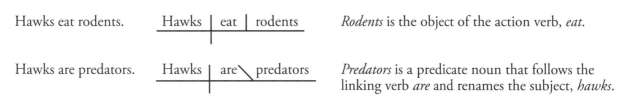

Diagraming Linking Verbs

Notice the difference between these two sentence diagrams.

Hawks eat rodents.   Hawks | eat | rodents   *Rodents* is the object of the action verb, *eat*.

Hawks are predators.   Hawks | are \ predators   *Predators* is a predicate noun that follows the linking verb *are* and renames the subject, *hawks*.

Diagram these sentences yourself. Make a slanting line after each linking verb and a vertical line after each action verb.

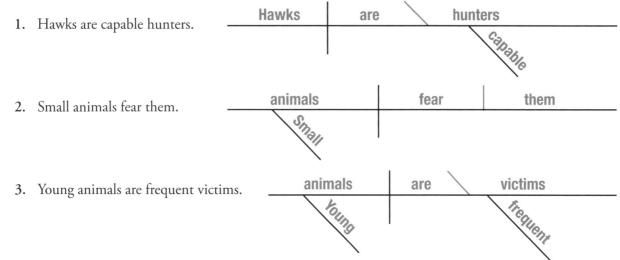

1. Hawks are capable hunters.

2. Small animals fear them.

3. Young animals are frequent victims.

Diagraming Predicate Nouns and Predicate Adjectives

You have learned that a predicate noun follows a linking verb and renames the subject of the sentence. Notice the way a predicate noun is diagramed.

The osprey is a **hawk**.   osprey | is \ **hawk**

You have learned that a predicate adjective follows a linking verb and describes the subject of the sentence. Here's how to diagram a predicate adjective.

Ospreys are **powerful**.   Ospreys | are \ **powerful**

Diagram these sentences on another sheet of paper.   **Answers appear on page T47.**

4. Carp are bottom-feeders.
5. Many mature carp are orange.
6. That osprey is hungry.
7. Its cry is shrill.

Diagraming Adverbs

You have learned how to diagram sentences containing adjectives (page 29). Like adjectives, adverbs are diagramed on slanted lines. An adverb is connected to the word it modifies. This model shows how to diagram an adverb.

The osprey circled the river **slowly**.

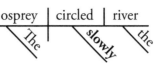

Diagram these sentences to show where the adverb belongs.

8. The big bird watched the water intently.

9. Suddenly it dove.

10. It deftly seized a glistening carp.

Some adverbs modify other adverbs. Notice how these adverbs are diagramed.

Ospreys dive **very** swiftly.

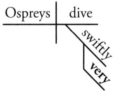

Use what you have learned to diagram these sentences on another piece of paper. Look back at this lesson to recall how to diagram action and linking verbs, adverbs, predicate nouns, and predicate adjectives.

11. Steelhead are large trout.
12. Many steelhead inhabit coastal streams.
13. Steelhead are migratory.
14. They are powerful swimmers.
15. I hooked a large steelhead once.
16. It fought desperately.
17. The steelhead was the uncontested victor.
18. It swam upstream.
19. I was disappointed, but I was impressed.

Answers appear on pages T47–T48.

Writing Sentences

Possible answers appear below. Accept all reasonable responses.
Revise each sentence written in the passive voice so that it is in the active voice. Revise each sentence in which the coordinating conjunction and the dependent clause are misplaced so that the sentence makes sense.

1. Although springtime is still months away, days grow longer after the winter solstice. **Although days grow longer after the winter solstice, springtime is still months away.**

2. Because animals shed their winter coats, the air temperature grows warmer. **As the air temperature grows warmer, animals shed their winter coats.**

3. The cycle of the seasons is demonstrated by longer days, warmer temperatures, and renewed plant life. **Longer days, warmer temperatures, and renewed plant life demonstrate the cycle of the seasons.**

4. The landscape looks alive again, so new buds form on the trees. **Because new buds form on the trees, the landscape looks alive again.**

5. Every year the winter solstice is celebrated by people in some cultures. **Every year people in some cultures celebrate the winter solstice.**

6. The longer, warmer days of spring are welcomed by most people. **Most people welcome the longer, warmer days of spring.**

A well-written paragraph has a topic sentence, at least two or three supporting sentences, and a concluding sentence. Your reader will understand your writing more easily if you use correct verb tenses, time-order words, and clear transitions. Notice how this model paragraph is written.

topic sentence	*Every year my family celebrates the coming of summer with a camping trip.* Last year we *went* to Yellowstone National Park in June.
time-order words	
verb tense	This year we *will go* to Crater Lake, Oregon. **Although sleeping out in the open is fun, what I like best about our camping trips is fishing.**
transition sentence	My sister and I *have caught* trout, steelhead, and salmon in some of America's most beautiful
concluding sentence	streams. *Nothing beats wide-open spaces, clean air, and the smell of fish sizzling over the fire.*

Writing a Paragraph

The sentences you revised on page 121 can be used to make a paragraph. Decide what order the sentences should be in. If necessary, add transition words to make the sentences flow more easily. Write the paragraph on the lines below.

Answers will vary.

_____

_____

_____

_____

_____

_____

_____

_____

Write a personal narrative about what you do at your favorite annual event. A personal narrative is a passage about a real experience you have had in which you refer to yourself as _I_. Make sure you use verb tenses correctly. Also, make sure you use clear transitions and time-order words to help your reader follow changes in place, time, or idea. Use the paragraph at the bottom of page 121 as a model.

Answers will vary.

_____

_____

_____

_____

_____

_____

_____

_____

Reread your paragraph. Use this checklist to make sure it follows the style of a personal narrative.

- ❏ Does my paragraph have a topic sentence?

- ❏ Have I written in the first-person voice?

- ❏ Have I included time-order words and clear transitions to make my personal narrative easy to follow?

- ❏ Have I used verb tenses correctly?

- ❏ Does my paragraph have a concluding sentence?

Name _____

The World Outside

Proofreading Practice

Read this passage about a mini-ecosystem that exists inside an acorn and find the mistakes. Use the proofreading marks below to show how each mistake should be fixed. **Suggested answers appear below. Accept all reasonable responses.**

Proofreading Marks

Mark	Means	Example
ℒ	delete	Many creatures maked their home inside an acorn.
∧	add	Many creatures make their home inside a acorn. (n)
≡	make into a capital letter	many creatures make their home inside an acorn.
(sp)	fix spelling	Many creetures make their home inside an acorn.
⊙	add a period	Many creatures make their home inside an acorn⊙
/	make into a lowercase letter	Many creatures make their home inside an Acorn.

More Than Just an Acorn

Would you beleive (sp) that the humble acorn is responsible for the survival of numerous creatures in the wild? If you don't. Just crack open an acorn. Inside you will find all kinds of creatures flourishing. Living off the *(They are)* *(not only)* acorn but also one another. Even before an acorn is full ripe, insects burrow or gnaw their way into its shell. *(y)* Acorn weevils dig holes with their tiny, sharp teeth. After dining on the nutmeat, The females lay their *feed* eggs inside the shell. The eggs hatch, and the larvae had fed on the soft flesh within the acorn. Once the acorn falls to the ground, the now fully grown larvae emerge, squeezing through a whole they gnaw in the shell! *(sp)*

A whole host of creatures, looking for sustenance, may find their way into a fallen acorn. These creatures, *(sp)* as well as the parasites that live off them, make they're home inside it. They enter the shell through holes and *(s)* cracks created by previous insect residents, Or by the fall from the tree. The nutmeat offer them nourishment, *and* and the shell offers shelter from the sun the wind.

even decaying acorns attract a variety of creatures. Scavengers look for remains left by other insects⊙ Carnivores had gone from acorn to acorn looking for prey inside the shells Empty acorn shells serve as houses for both small insects, such as the tiny fungus beetle, and larger ones, such as the slug⊙

Birds and animals hoard acorns for the winter by burying them in the soil. More than a few are *lucky* *are* forgotten. Some of these luckily survivors take root and grow into oak trees. in doing so they beginning a new cycle, and in time they will produce acorns that will sustain new generations of tiny creatures.

Proofreading
Checklist

You can use the list below to help you find and fix mistakes in your own writing. Write the titles of your own stories or reports in the blanks at the top of the chart. Then use the questions to check your work. Make a check mark (✓) in each box after you have checked that item.

Answers will vary.

Proofreading Checklist for Unit 4

	Titles			
Have I used colorful action verbs in sentences?				
Have I used the simple tense, the perfect tense, and the progressive tense correctly?				
Have I used adverbs and prepositions effectively?				
Have I used correlative conjunctions correctly?				

Also Remember . . .

Have I written complete sentences?				
Does each sentence begin with a capital letter?				
Have I included correct end punctuation?				
Have I spelled each word correctly?				

Your Own List

Use this space to write your own list of things to check in your writing.

Name _____

The World Outside

Review

(Numbers in parentheses identify related lessons.)

Verbs

Circle each linking verb. Underline each action verb. Then label each action verb as transitive (with *T*) or intransitive (with *I*).

1. Nature's most celebrated cycle (is) the yearly cycle of seasons. _____ **(31)**

2. Most temperate regions <u>experience</u> four seasons each year. __T__ **(32)**

3. The seasons (are) spring, summer, fall, and winter. _____ **(31)**

4. With each new season, weather and temperatures <u>change</u>. __I__ **(32)**

5. In autumn the days (become) shorter and cooler. _____ **(31)**

6. Winter <u>brings</u> early darkness and cold. __T__ **(32)**

7. The days <u>lengthen</u> again in spring. __I__ **(32)**

8. Summer (is) the hottest season in most areas. _____ **(31)**

9. Long summer days often <u>provide</u> hours of sunshine. __T__ **(32)**

10. I <u>like</u> the days of early summer best. __T__ **(32)**

Verb Tense

Circle the word or phrase in parentheses that identifies the tense of each boldfaced verb.

11. In the Southern Hemisphere, summer **begins** in late December. ((present)/present perfect) **(34)**

12. Many tourists **will visit** Australia next January. ((future)/future perfect) **(34)**

13. Some already **have reserved** hotel rooms. (present/(present perfect)) **(35)**

14. Here in the Northern Hemisphere, many of us **will be shoveling** snow in January. (present progressive/(future progressive)) **(36)**

15. Last year snow **fell** throughout the Northeast in mid-April. ((past)/present) **(34)**

16. During that snowstorm, we **were dreaming** of flying to South America for a long visit. (past perfect/(past progressive)) **(36)**

17. A shipment of delicious grapes from Chile **had arrived** in our markets just a few days earlier. ((past perfect)/past progressive) **(35)**

18. Chilean farmers **are growing** more fruits and vegetables each year for sale in the United States during our winter and spring months. (simple present/(present progressive)) **(36)**

19. By the middle of next March, those farmers **will have harvested** most of their crops. ((future perfect)/future progressive) **(35)**

The World Outside

Active and Passive Voice

Write *A* after each sentence with a verb in the active voice. Write *P* after each sentence with a verb in the passive voice.

20. In the mountains, snow is melted by the warm sunshine. __P__ **(33)**

21. At the beach, sunbathers lie on towels and mats. __A__ **(33)**

22. In the forest, deer browse on fresh green leaves. __A__ **(33)**

23. In the desert, most creatures are driven from open areas by the fierce heat. __P__ **(33)**

Adverbs and Prepositions

Draw a star above each boldfaced word that is an adverb. Circle each boldfaced word that is a preposition. Underline the prepositional phrase it begins and draw a box around its object.

24. Knowledge of the cycle of seasons was **very** important to many ancient peoples. **(37)**

25. In some cultures, astronomers understood the relationships between the length of days and the progression of seasons. **(38)**

26. These ancient scientists **also** learned to use the angle of the sun's rays to identify the longest and shortest days of the year. **(37)**

27. On winter's shortest day, people celebrated the approach of spring. **(38)**

28. In some regions people **joyfully** danced around bonfires. **(37)**

29. They knew that lengthening days would **eventually** bring spring. **(37)**

30. Some cultures **still** celebrate this day, which is called the winter solstice. **(37)**

Conjunctions

Circle each coordinating conjunction. Underline each subordinating conjunction. Draw boxes around the two parts of each correlative conjunction.

31. Plants sense the changing seasons; they sprout, bloom, and drop their leaves according to the seasonal cycle. **(39)**

32. Not only plants but also people can be affected by the seasons. **(40)**

33. If people continually feel sad in winter, they may have winter depression. **(39)**

34. A lack of sunlight can produce feelings of sadness, anger, or despair. **(39)**

35. Because the sun shines very little in the far north during winter, people there commonly experience winter depression. **(39)**

36. Since the condition is brought on by reduced amounts of sunlight, doctors renamed it light deprivation syndrome. **(39)**

37. Doctors use either medication or bright sunlamps to treat this condition. **(40)**

Name _____

The **World** **Outside**

Community Connection

In Unit 4 of *G.U.M.* students learned about **verbs**, **adverbs**, **prepositions**, and **conjunctions** and used what they learned to improve their own writing. The content of these lessons focuses on the theme **Cycles in Nature**. As students completed the exercises, they learned about things in the natural world that follow a cyclical pattern, from ocean tides to migration. These pages offer a variety of activities that reinforce skills and concepts presented in the unit. They also provide opportunities for students to make connections between the materials in the lessons and the community at large.

Animal Migration

Conduct research about animal migration in the United States to find out what animals, if any, pass through or near your community as they migrate. Follow these steps to aid your research:

- Find out if you live near any major paths of bird migration, especially one of the four main flyways (the Pacific, Central, Mississippi, or Atlantic flyway).
- Learn about the routes that are followed by other long-distance migrants, such as monarch butterflies or gray whales.
- Look for migratory patterns of animals indigenous to your region or state. Keep in mind that some animals migrate over relatively short distances. For instance, mule deer migrate between mountains in the summer and valleys in the winter.

If you discover that some animals come near your community during migration, find out when they are most likely to be nearby. If possible, try to see the animals as they pass through your area.

Unnatural Cycles

In imitation of nature, people have created cyclical systems to organize or regulate human activities. For example, the repeated green-yellow-red cycle of a traffic light is used to control the flow of traffic. List as many artificial cycles as you can; describe what purpose each one was invented to serve.

The Cycle of Life

Insects develop in one of three basic ways: through simple growth, incomplete metamorphosis, or complete metamorphosis. Research the life cycle of one insect from each of these three groups:

    Simple growth: silverfish, springtail

    Incomplete metamorphosis: grasshopper, roach, dragonfly, cicada

    Complete metamorphosis: butterfly, moth, beetle, bee, ant

Develop a chart that illustrates the life cycles of the three insects you have chosen.

Who Works with Cycles in Nature?

Many occupations are affected by cycles in nature. Some examples include farmers, park rangers, snowplow operators, astronomers, biologists, and lifeguards.

Work with a partner to add some other jobs to your list. Then think of someone in your community who does one of these jobs, and arrange to interview her or him. Prepare your questions in advance. Use the planning guide on page 128 to help you plan the interview. Take notes during the interview, and share the results of the interview with your class.

Interview Planner   Answers will vary.

Person I am interviewing:

Name _____

Age _____

Occupation _____

Number of years employed in that field _____

Date of interview: _____

Questions to ask:

1. _____
   _____

2. _____
   _____

3. _____
   _____

4. _____
   _____

5. _____
   _____

6. _____
   _____

7. _____
   _____

8. _____

Notes:

_____

_____

_____

_____

_____

Name _____

Read and Discover

You're going to have such fun in Hawaii. Don't forget **your** swimsuit!

Circle the boldfaced word that shows ownership. Underline the boldfaced word that means "you are."

The words **your** and **you're** sound alike but have different spellings and meanings. *Your* is a possessive pronoun and shows ownership. *You're* is a contraction made from the words *you* and *are*.

See Handbook Section 33

Part 1

Read the conversation below. Circle the word in parentheses that completes each sentence correctly. (1–17)

"It's so great that (your/you're) aunt invited you to Hawaii," said Rita. "(Your/You're) really going to enjoy it."

"What did you like best about (your/you're) visit?" asked May.

"My favorite part was the luau we attended. You should definitely ask (your/you're) aunt to take you to a luau."

"I'm sorry, but I don't know what (your/you're) talking about," said May.

"A luau is a modern version of a traditional Hawaiian feast. Be sure to take (your/you're) appetite when you go!"

"I'll take (your/you're) advice. But what does the word *luau* mean?"

"It refers to the young tops of the taro root. They're always part of the feast.

Many Hawaiian luaus feature hula dancing.

The centerpiece of a luau is kalua pig. It's roasted in an imu, a hot pit dug into the ground and layered with stones and banana stalks. These days, (your/you're) given other food, too, such as fish or chicken."

"(Your/You're) making me hungry!" May exclaimed.

"Another traditional food is poi," Rita added. "That's a dish made of fermented taro root. I'm not sure (your/you're) going to like it, but you should try it anyway."

"What was (your/you're) favorite part of the luau?" May asked.

"I really enjoyed the hula dancing. Traditionally, it was performed as a way of telling history or praising a great Hawaiian leader. (Your/You're) not going to believe this, but I even tried some hula dancing myself!"

"(Your/You're) kidding!" exclaimed May. "Was it hard?"

"(Your/You're) really self-conscious at first, but then (your/you're) shyness goes away. You follow the leader, pay attention to the chant, and move (your/you're) hands and feet."

"So show me (your/you're) hula photos!" demanded May, smiling.

Part 2   Answers will vary.

Imagine that you are at the beach in Hawaii and a friend asks you these questions. Answer each question with a complete sentence. Use *your* or *you're* in each answer.

18. Am I wearing my snorkel correctly? _____

_____

19. Do you want to borrow my flippers? _____

_____

20. Do you think I'm a strong enough swimmer to try surfing? _____

_____

21. Do you think I'm going to be able to stand on the surfboard? _____

_____

22. Would you like to use my board? _____

_____

23. Have you seen my bottle of sunscreen? _____

_____

24. Am I getting sunburned? _____

_____

Part 3

> Words like *your* and *you're* that sound alike but have different spellings and meanings are called homophones.

Each sentence below uses one or more homophones incorrectly. Circle the misused word(s) in each one. Then write the correct word(s) on the line.

25. The (son) (beet) down on the beach. _____ **sun, beat** _____

26. The sand was hot on our (bear) feet. _____ **bare** _____

27. The hula told a (tail) of the island long ago. _____ **tale** _____

28. The pig was roasted in a (whole) in the ground. _____ **hole** _____

29. We (eight) a lot of that tasty (meet). _____ **ate, meat** _____

30. (To) of us went to (here) Hawaiian music. _____ **Two, hear** _____

31. The ukulele player (inn) the band was (grate). _____ **in, great** _____

Name _____

Grab   Bag

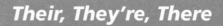
The Sami are proud of **their** heritage and cultural traditions. Their traditional homeland is in the northernmost region of Europe. They have lived **there** for many centuries. **They're** known to other peoples as Lapps, but they prefer their own name for themselves, Sami.

Which boldfaced word means "belonging to them"? ___**their**___

Which means "they are"? ___**they're**___

Which means "in that place"? ___**there**___

The words *their, they're,* and *there* sound the same but have different meanings and spellings. *Their* is a possessive pronoun that means "belonging to them." *They're* is a contraction that means "they are." *There* is an adverb and usually means "in that place." *There* may also be used as an introductory word.

See Handbook Section 33

Part 1

Circle the word in parentheses that correctly completes each sentence.

1. Today about half of the Sami people make (**their**/they're/there) homes in northern Norway.

2. (**Their**/They're/There) ancestors came to northern Scandinavia more than 8,000 years ago.

3. Sami people have herded, hunted, fished, and gathered berries (their/they're/**there**) for centuries.

4. (**Their**/They're/There) language is related to Finnish and Estonian.

5. The rugged, treeless lands of northern Norway may appear barren to outsiders, but (their/**they're**/there) home to abundant wildlife.

6. Reindeer flourish (their/they're/**there**); in winter they eat lichen, which is plentiful in Arctic regions.

7. The Sami have herded reindeer for a very long time; this animal has been (**their**/they're/there) most important single source of food and clothing.

8. The Sami divide (**their**/they're/there) year into eight seasons, all of which relate to reindeer activities.

9. Many Sami who do not herd reindeer make (**their**/they're/there) living from the sea.

10. (Their/**They're**/There) known as skillful seafarers, fishers, and hunters of seals.

11. (Their/They're/**There**) are also many Sami who are artists, farmers, writers, educators, and musicians.

12. Sami students can formally study (**their**/they're/there) traditional language in major Norwegian universities.

13. The Sami people of Norway now have (**their**/they're/there) own parliament.

Many Sami brides and grooms wear traditional Sami costumes.

Grab Bag

Part 2

Rewrite each sentence, replacing the boldfaced words with *their, they're,* or *there.*

14. If you visit the town of Kautokeino at Easter, you may see many people in bright blue and red clothing **in that place**. <u>If you visit the town of Kautokeino at Easter, you may see many people in bright blue and red clothing there.</u>

15. Long ago, the Sami wore these outfits as everyday clothing; today **these outfits are** worn only at festivals and special events. <u>Long ago, the Sami wore these outfits as everyday clothing; today they're worn only at festivals and special events.</u>

16. Sami people are famous for **the Sami people's** unusual form of song, called *joik*. <u>Sami people are famous for their unusual form of song, called *joik*.</u>

17. These songs are sung and hummed without instrumental accompaniment; **these songs are** composed for many occasions, including courtship. <u>These songs are sung and hummed without instrumental accompaniment; they're composed for many occasions, including courtship.</u>

Part 3

Find the mistakes in the dialogue in this cartoon. Then rewrite the dialogue, correcting the errors, on the lines below.

18. <u>Look at those giraffes. They're so odd looking! Why are their necks so long?</u>

19. <u>Their necks are so long because they have to reach all the way from their shoulders to their heads!</u>

Grab Bag

Read and Discover

Russia is known throughout the world for <u>its</u> great composers, ballet dancers, and especially writers. (It's) not unusual for the works of Tolstoy and Dostoevsky to be listed among the greatest novels ever written.

Circle the boldfaced word that means "it is." Underline the boldfaced word that shows ownership.

Its and *it's* sound the same but are spelled differently and have different meanings. *Its* is a possessive pronoun; it means "belonging to it." *It's* is a contraction that means "it is" or "it has." The apostrophe takes the place of the missing letter(s).

See Handbook **Section 33**

Part 1

Circle the words in parentheses to complete these sentences correctly. (1–16)

(It's/Its) an understatement to say that Russia is a big country. (It's/Its) land stretches across eleven time zones. (It's/Its) population includes many peoples with distinct cultural backgrounds. (It's/Its) history is dramatic and turbulent. For centuries (it's/its) people were dominated by the Mongols of eastern Asia. (It's/Its) rather surprising that the great music, art, and literature of Russia is so much a part of the European tradition.

The link between the arts in Russia and the rest of Europe began in 1682. In that year Peter the Great became the czar, or ruler, of Russia. He was determined to make (it's/its) way of life more modern. Peter admired the arts of Europe and brought several of (it's/its) most skillful architects to Russia to create great buildings.

In the middle of the eighteenth century, European music became popular in Russia. Russian classical music reached (it's/its) height more than 100 years later. (It's/Its) likely that you have heard Peter Ilyich Tchaikovsky's music for the ballet *Swan Lake*. (It's/Its) played and broadcast almost everywhere. So is his music for another popular ballet, *The Nutcracker*.

Tchaikovsky composed the music for several ballets, including *Swan Lake*.

Ballet did not begin in Russia, but many of (it's/its) greatest choreographers and dancers have come from there. The Bolshoi Ballet of Moscow, Russia's capital, tours the world; (it's/its) considered to be one of the greatest classical ballet companies of our time.

At the heart of Russia's culture are (it's/its) great poet, Alexander Pushkin, and (it's/its) most celebrated novelists, Leo Tolstoy and Fyodor Dostoevsky. Tolstoy's *War and Peace* and *Anna Karenina* are long, complex books, as is Dostoevsky's *Crime and Punishment*. (It's/Its) not easy for readers to finish these books, but those who do are richly rewarded, for these writers are matchless storytellers.

Grab Bag

Part 2

Write *its* or *it's* to complete each sentence correctly. Remember to capitalize a word that begins a sentence.

17. Russia is also known for __its__ superb playwrights.

18. __It's__ almost impossible to study theater without reading the plays of Anton Chekhov.

19. __It's__ rare for a great play to be considered both a comedy and a tragedy.

20. *The Cherry Orchard* has moments of comedy among __its__ tragic events.

Part 3

Charles Lutwidge Dodgson, who used the pen name Lewis Carroll, wrote two immensely popular fantasies, *Alice's Adventures in Wonderland* and *Through the Looking-Glass*. In these works Dodgson, who was a mathematician by profession, presented characters who argue whether particular statements are nonsensical.

The passages below have been printed without apostrophes. Read each passage and add apostrophes to the contractions. Then work with a partner to decide whether what each character is saying makes sense.

"Take some more tea," the March Hare said to Alice, very earnestly.

"I've had nothing yet," Alice replied in an offended tone: "so I can't take more."

"You mean you can't take *less*," said the Hatter: "it's very easy to take *more* than nothing."

—*Alice's Adventures in Wonderland*

"There's no use trying," she said: "one can't believe impossible things."

"I daresay you haven't had much practice," said the Queen. "When I was your age, I always did it for half-an-hour a day. Why, sometimes I've believed as many as six impossible things before breakfast."

—*Through the Looking-Glass*

"The rule is, jam tomorrow, and jam yesterday—but never jam today."

"It must come sometimes to 'jam today,'" Alice objected.

"No, it can't," said the Queen. "It's jam every other day: today isn't any other day, you know."

—*Through the Looking-Glass*

Name _____

Grab Bag

Read and Discover

"**Who's** familiar with the traditions of the Maasai people?" asked the speaker from Tanzania.

"Aren't the Maasai a people (whose) traditional way of life involves cattle herding?" responded Frank.

Underline the boldfaced word that means "who is." Circle the boldfaced word that shows ownership.

Who's and *whose* sound alike but are spelled differently and have different meanings. *Whose* shows ownership or possession. *Who's* is a contraction of "who is" or "who has."

See Handbook Section 33

Part 1

Circle the correct word in parentheses.

1. "The Maasai, (who's/**whose**) traditional homelands are in Kenya and Tanzania, are known for strength and bravery," said the speaker.

2. "(**Who's**/Whose) willing to face a lion with only a few simple weapons?" she then asked the students.

3. "Young Maasai (who's/**whose**) job it is to guard the village's cows and goats must be alert for predators of many kinds," the speaker continued.

4. "(**Who's**/Whose) interested in learning more about Maasai life today?" she asked next.

5. "Many cultural programs in Tanzania are run by Maasai (who's/**whose**) goal is to educate visitors about the lives of Maasai people today," she explained.

6. "Aren't the Maasai the people (who's/**whose**) traditional diet includes only meat and milk?" asked Isabel.

7. "Yes, but now many Maasai eat *ugali,* which is made of corn meal," replied the speaker. "(**Who's**/Whose) eaten foods made of corn meal?"

8. "Anyone (**who's**/whose) eaten tamales has eaten corn meal," said Dexter.

9. "So the Maasai are a people (who's/**whose**) culture is changing?" asked Debra.

10. "(**Who's**/Whose) surprised to hear that some Maasai live very modern lives, while others continue to live in traditional ways?" asked the speaker.

11. "My friend Gerald, (**who's**/whose) a true Maasai warrior, has two daughters studying computer science in India," she explained.

12. "I believe that a people (who's/**whose**) children are well-educated have a bright future," she concluded.

Grab Bag

Part 2 Possible answers appear below. Accept all reasonable responses.

Write a question to go with each answer below. Use *who's* or *whose* in each question you write.

13. My sister is downloading photos of Maasai villagers. __Who's downloading photos of Maasai villagers?__

14. The man in the red cloak is a Maasai warrior. __Is the man whose cloak is red a Maasai warrior?__

15. The tall woman's necklace has the most beads on it. __Whose necklace has the most beads on it?__

16. Our family hopes to visit East Africa someday. __Whose family hopes to visit East Africa someday?__

17. My sister is going to study Swahili. __Who's going to study Swahili?__

18. Residents of Kenya, Tanzania, and other East African countries speak Swahili. __Whose residents speak Swahili?__

Maasai children herd livestock and take care of younger brothers and sisters.

Part 3

See Handbook Section 37

Look on the Internet or in a geographic magazine to find pictures of a people whose traditional way of life interests you. Write four questions about what the pictures show; use *who's* or *whose* in each question. Then show the pictures to a classmate and have him or her answer the questions.

19. __Answers will vary.__

20. _____

21. _____

22. _____

Name _____

Grab Bag

Read and Discover

To, Too, Two

Lesson 45

Have you traveled **to** Brazil? You might hear samba music there. **Two** friends of mine can play samba drum beats. I'm learning a samba beat, **too**.

Which boldfaced word names a number? **two** Which means "in the direction of"? **to** Which means "also"? **too**

The words **to, too,** and **two** sound the same but have different meanings and spellings. *To* can be a preposition that means "in the direction of." *To* can also be used with a verb to form an infinitive, as in the sentence *We like to play the drums. Too* is an adverb and means "also" or "excessively." *Two* means the number 2.

See Handbook Section 33

Part 1

Circle the word in parentheses that correctly completes each sentence.

1. Have you listened (**to**/too/two) samba music?

2. If you travel (**to**/too/two) Brazil, you will surely hear this distinctive mix of three musical traditions.

3. For thousands of years Brazil's indigenous Indians had chanted (**to**/too/two) rhythmic sounds of rattles, panpipes, and flutes.

4. In the 1500s, (to/too/**two**) other groups arrived in Brazil: Portuguese and Africans.

5. Portuguese settlers brought captured Africans to Brazil (**to**/too/two) work on plantations there.

6. The captured Africans would play the music of their homeland (**to**/too/two) lighten their spirits.

7. In time, they began playing European instruments, (to/**too**/two).

8. (To/Too/**Two**) of the instruments they picked up were tambourine and guitar; accordion was another.

9. Over the years, (to/too/**two**) uniquely Brazilian kinds of music resulted from the blend of these three cultures: samba and the more modern bossa nova.

10. (To/Too/**Two**) popular types of samba are hill samba and theme samba.

11. Hill samba is very exciting (**to**/too/two) hear; it is performed by a large group on drums and other percussion instruments.

12. During Carnival parades, colorfully clad dancers march (**to**/too/two) theme samba; theme samba has a lead singer, a chorus, and a percussion section.

13. There are many other types of samba, (to/**too**/two).

14. Samba has given rise (**to**/too/two) other forms of music, most notably bossa nova in the 1950s and 1960s.

15. Bossa nova is less percussive than most types of samba; it's more harmonious, (to/**too**/two).

Drums and other percussion instruments are the backbone of samba music.

Grab Bag

Part 2

Write *too, to,* or *two* to complete each sentence correctly.

Brazil

Pacific Ocean

Atlantic Ocean

16. My family is going ____to____ Brazil next summer.

17. We're going to be there about ____two____ weeks.

18. I'm not ____too____ sure where we're going yet.

19. Hopefully, we'll visit São Paulo; I'd enjoy visiting
    Rio de Janeiro, ____too____.

20. I might try ____to____ take a samba drumming
    workshop while I'm there.

21. I've been drumming for ____two____ years now.

22. Samba beats are still ____too____ tricky for me to play in public.

23. I want ____to____ learn to speak Portuguese, the language of Brazil.

24. I like ____to____ listen to tapes and repeat what I hear.

25. I do lessons in a workbook, ____too____.

Part 3

To, too, and *two* are homophones; they sound the same but are spelled differently. These riddles are based on other homophones.

Question: How can you tell when food goes bad?
Answer: Your nose knows.

Question: Why was the race rough?
Answer: The course was coarse.

Choose three of the following sets of homophones to create your own riddles. Write them on the lines below. Use a dictionary to check the meaning of any word you don't know.

| to/too/two | course/coarse | bored/board | vain/vein | see/sea |
| scent/cent/sent | wail/whale | bolder/boulder | pair/pear | heel/heal |

26. Answers will vary. _____

_____

27. _____

_____

28. _____

_____

Name _____

Grab Bag

Read and Discover

The Braemar Gathering is more famous **than** any other Highland games event. It is said to date back to the eleventh century. King Malcolm III ruled Scotland **then**.

Which boldfaced word is used to make a comparison? __than__

Which is used to talk about time? __then__

Than and *then* sound similar but are different words with different spellings and meanings. *Than* is a subordinating conjunction used to make comparisons, as in the sentence *Malcolm is younger than Derrick*. *Then* can be an adverb that tells about time. It can also mean "therefore."

See Handbook Section 33

Part 1

Circle the correct word in parentheses to complete each sentence.

1. I've never had more fun (**than**/then) I did at the Braemar Gathering last year.

2. We flew into Aberdeen and (than/**then**) drove to Braemar, in the Scottish Highlands.

3. Highland games take place throughout the summer in Scotland; many tourists visit (than/**then**).

4. The Braemar games are more famous (**than**/then) Highland games held elsewhere.

5. They are much larger (**than**/then) Scottish games held here in the States.

6. People were wearing more patterns of plaid (**than**/then) I thought existed.

7. A boy presented Queen Elizabeth with a bouquet, and (than/**then**) the festivities began.

8. One band marched onto the field, and (than/**then**) another and another until the sound of bagpipes echoed through the hills.

9. (Than/**Then**) groups began performing traditional dances.

10. Each one was more impressive (**than**/then) the last.

11. There were many more competitions (**than**/then) I expected.

12. First we watched the Stone Put, and (than/**then**) we watched the Tossing the Caber event.

13. One of the stones in the men's Stone Put event is much heavier (**than**/then) the shot in men's shot put.

14. In Tossing the Caber, each competitor runs with a very long piece of wood on his shoulder and (than/**then**) tosses it.

15. In my opinion, the Braemar Gathering is more fun (**than**/then) the Summer Olympics.

16. If you find yourself in Scotland on the first Saturday of September, (than/**then**) you should definitely make your way to Braemar!

The length and weight of a caber varies.

Part 2   Answers will vary.

Write a sentence that follows each direction. Use *then* or *than* in each answer.

17. Compare two games you enjoy. _____

_____

18. Write simple instructions for beginning a game. _____

_____

19. Compare two kinds of music. _____

_____

20. Imagine you are watching a Highland games event. In order, tell about three things that you see.

_____

_____

21. Describe two things you would do to plan a trip to Scotland. _____

_____

22. Compare a kilt to traditional clothing from another culture. _____

_____

23. Name one event you attended last summer. _____

_____

Part 3

People often confuse words that sound similar. Decide which word from the word bank should be used in place of each boldfaced word. Then write the correct word on the line.

descent	formally	precede	accept	accent

24. I'm afraid I cannot **except** your invitation to the party. _____accept_____

25. An opening ceremony will **proceed** the first event. _____precede_____

26. His Scottish **ascent** was quite strong, so I had to listen carefully. _____accent_____

27. My father is of Scottish **decent**, but my mother is not. _____descent_____

28. Scotsmen wear kilts when they are **formerly** attired. _____formally_____

Name _____

Grab Bag

Read and Discover

a. Some visitors say that there isn't no country friendlier than Thailand.

b. My aunt says that she never encountered an unfriendly person there.

Which sentence uses too many negative words? __a.__

Which uses negatives correctly? __b.__

A **negative** is a word that means "no" or "not." The words *no, not, nothing, none, never, nowhere,* and *nobody* are negatives. The negative word *not* is found in contractions such as *don't* and *wasn't*. Use only one negative in a sentence to express a negative idea. Use the contraction **doesn't** with singular subjects, including *he, she,* and *it*. Use the contraction **don't** with plural subjects, including *we* and *they*. Use *don't* with *I* and *you,* too. **Remember to use this information when you speak, too.**

See Handbook Section 26

Part 1

Underline the correct expression in parentheses to complete each sentence.

1. Because they value harmony, Thai people try not to make (no one/<u>anyone</u>) feel uncomfortable.

2. Traditionally a stranger (isn't never/<u>isn't ever</u>) treated as an intruder.

3. Even if a family has very little food, they will (<u>never</u>/ever) let a visitor go hungry.

4. Most Thai residents practice Buddhism, which in general does not encourage (no/<u>any</u>) conflict.

5. Friendships are very important in this nation; a Thai person (won't/<u>will</u>) let nothing stand in the way of helping a close friend.

6. In Thai village life especially, nothing (<u>is</u>/isn't) more important than family.

7. It isn't (<u>unusual</u>/not unusual) for several generations of a family to live together in adjacent homes.

8. Young family members must (<u>never</u>/ever) be disrespectful of their elders.

9. Even among brothers and sisters, younger ones aren't (never/<u>ever</u>) permitted to disobey older ones.

10. Don't be surprised to see (no/<u>a</u>) young child leading a huge buffalo out of the village to graze.

11. In general, children in the United States do not have (no/<u>any</u>) responsibilities as significant as those that Thai children of the same age have.

12. Many Thai babies aren't given Thai official names by (no/<u>a</u>) parent; they receive a name from the village's religious leader.

13. Soon, though, the baby will be given a nickname, and family and friends will use this name, (<u>not</u>/not never) the official one.

14. Because so many Thai people are friendly and speak English, you shouldn't have (no/<u>any</u>) trouble learning more about Thai customs if you visit that nation.

Grab Bag

Part 2 Possible answers appear below. Accept all reasonable responses.

Rewrite each sentence so that it uses negatives correctly. There is more than one way to change each one.

15. No shopping mall isn't as interesting as the floating markets of Thailand. __No shopping mall is as interesting as the floating markets of Thailand.__

16. A friend told my dad and me that we shouldn't never pay the first price mentioned by no salesperson. __A friend told my dad and me that we should never pay the first price mentioned by a salesperson.__

17. Neither of us hadn't never gone shopping in a boat before. __Neither of us had ever gone shopping in a boat before.__

18. There isn't no space on neither bank of the canal that isn't occupied by no shop. __There isn't a space on either bank of the canal that isn't occupied by a shop.__

19. I didn't want to buy no more than one purse or handbag, but the shops had so many cool ones that I couldn't never make up my mind. __I didn't want to buy more than one purse or handbag, but the shops had so many cool ones that I couldn't make up my mind.__

20. We didn't feel no hunger, because we kept buying snacks from vendors with cookstoves on their boats! __We didn't feel hunger, because we kept buying snacks from vendors with cookstoves on their boats!__

Part 3 Possible answers appear below. Accept all reasonable responses.

Write a positive answer and a negative answer to each question about a Thai tourist experience.

21. Would you like to ride on an elephant for an hour?

    (positive) __I would like to ride on an elephant for an hour.__

    (negative) __I wouldn't like to ride on an elephant for an hour.__

22. Are vegetables with flames leaping from them your idea of a great meal?

    (positive) __Vegetables with flames leaping from them are my idea of a great meal.__

    (negative) __Vegetables with flames leaping from them aren't my idea of a great meal.__

23. Do you have any desire to sample very spicy food?

    (positive) __I have a strong desire to sample very spicy food.__

    (negative) __I don't have any desire to sample very spicy food.__

Name _____

Grab Bag

said
I ~~go~~, "Did you know that in Chinese folklore, dragons are helpful creatures?"
said
Max ~~is like~~, "What? I thought dragons terrorized villages."
said
So then Jenna ~~is all~~, "Those are video game dragons, Max!"

Has this conversation been written in formal language or informal language?
___informal___ Cross out the words that indicate that someone is speaking.
Write *said* above the words you crossed out.

> *Go* and *went* mean "move(d)." *Is like* means "resembles something." *All* means "the total of something." In your written work and in polite conversation, avoid using *goes, went, (is) all,* or *(is) like* to mean "said." Also be careful not to insert the word *like* where it doesn't belong, as in the sentence *This is, like, the best day ever.* **Remember to use this information when you speak, too.**
>
> **See Handbook** Section 32

Part 1

Cross out *go, went, all,* or *like* if these words are used incorrectly. (If a form of the verb *be* is part of the incorrect expression, cross it out also.) (1–13)

My sister and I were telling Max about our trip to Hong Kong. I ~~go~~,

"Would you like to hear about the dragon boat races?"

And Max ~~is all~~, "What are the boats like?"

Jenna ~~is like~~, "The boats are so impressive! Some of them

are ~~, like,~~ one hundred feet long! They have a dragon head

at the front of the boat and a tail at the end. A big one

may carry ~~, like,~~ fifty paddlers, plus an oarsman,

and a drummer who sets the pace."

Some dragon boats are one hundred feet long.

Then Max ~~goes~~, "Who do the boats belong to—sports teams?"

~~I was all~~, "I think each boat belongs to a particular village or organization."

Jenna ~~went~~, "People say that the boat races are held to remember a man named Qu Yuan who lived

more than 2,000 years ago. He was ~~, like,~~ a great poet and also an advisor to the emperor. He tried to get the

emperor to reform the government in order to bring peace to China."

And I ~~went~~, "The emperor not only rejected Qu Yuan's advice but also told him to leave the kingdom

forever! This made Qu Yuan very sad, so he went to the river to write. That was ~~, like,~~ the last time anyone

saw him."

Then Max ~~is all~~, "But what does that have to do with dragon boat races?"

Jenna ~~went~~, "When Qu Yuan disappeared, people raced around in their boats looking for him. Today the

dragon boats race around as if looking for Qu Yuan."

Part 2 Possible answers appear below. Accept all reasonable responses.

Rewrite each sentence to eliminate incorrect expressions. There is more than one way to rewrite each sentence.

14. Jenna was like, "Let's have our own dragon boat race!" __Jenna exclaimed, "Let's have our own dragon boat race!"__

15. I go, "What do you mean?" __"What do you mean?" I asked.__

16. Jenna goes, "We'll get some friends together and rent canoes at the lake." __"We'll get some friends together and rent canoes at the lake," Jenna answered.__

17. Max was like, "Canoes don't look like dragon boats!" __"Canoes don't look like dragon boats!" Max snorted.__

18. But she goes, "We'll make dragon heads and tails out of papier-mâché. __"We'll make dragon heads and tails out of papier-mâché," Jenna told him.__

19. Immediately Max was like, "I'll be the drummer in our canoe!" __Max immediately announced, "I'll be the drummer in our canoe!"__

20. I shook my head and went, "We need you to help row the boat!" __I shook my head and replied, "We need you to help row the boat!"__

Part 3 Answers will vary.

Many verbs, including *asked, answered, replied, added, exclaimed, remarked, suggested, began, continued, cried, whispered, grumbled,* and *yelled,* may be used to tell how a character is speaking. Using a variety of verbs for this purpose not only makes writing more interesting, it also has a dramatic effect on the mood of a direct quotation.

Choose verbs from the word bank to complete the sentence frame in six different ways. Notice how each verb gives the sentence a different mood.

| muttered | shouted | gasped | boomed | wailed | sighed | mumbled | breathed |
| growled | thundered | hissed | grumbled | whispered | giggled | screeched | sniffed |

21. "I know," he _____.   24. "I know," he _____.

22. "I know," he _____.   25. "I know," he _____.

23. "I know," he _____.   26. "I know," he _____.

Name _____

Grab Bag

Before a Japanese tea ceremony, the Tea Master carefully **sets** out utensils.

The guests will **sit** on mats, not in chairs.

I should **lie** down before the ceremony. I'm tired!

Would you hand me my guidebook? I **laid** it on the chair.

Which boldfaced word means "move your body into a chair"? ___sit___

Which means "recline"? ___lie___

Which boldfaced words mean "place or put something somewhere"?

___sets___ ___laid___

Lie and *lay* are different verbs. *Lay* takes a direct object and *lie* does not. *Lie* means "to recline." *Lay* means "to put something down somewhere." The past tense form of *lie* is *lay,* and the past participle form is *lain.* The past tense form of *lay* is *laid,* and the past participle form is also *laid.* *Set* and *sit* are different verbs, too. *Set* takes a direct object and *sit* does not. If you're about to use *set,* ask yourself, "Set what?" If you can't answer that question, use *sit.* Also, remember that you can't sit anything down—you must set it down. The past tense form of *sit* is *sat,* and the past participle form is also *sat.* *Set* is one of the few verbs that does not change in past or past participle form. **Remember to use this information when you speak, too.**

See Handbook Section 32

Part 1

Underline the word in parentheses that correctly completes each sentence.

1. Get up, Miki! You have (laid/<u>lain</u>) in bed all morning.

2. I'm going to (sit/<u>set</u>) your breakfast here to entice you to get up.

3. The tea ceremony starts at noon, so we can't (<u>sit</u>/set) around all day!

4. Did you see where I (sit/<u>set</u>) the pamphlet about the ceremony?

5. I think I (lay/<u>laid</u>) it on the dresser.

6. It says that everyone at a tea ceremony must follow a strict

    etiquette; even where and how guests (<u>sit</u>/set) is important.

7. Before the ceremony, the host, or Tea Master, (sits/<u>sets</u>) out tea utensils.

8. The Tea Master will hand you a bamboo ladle of water; use it to wash

    your hands and rinse your mouth and then carefully (lie/<u>lay</u>) it down.

9. When guests arrive, they politely remove their shoes and (sit/<u>set</u>) them outside the door.

10. Remember, you can't just (<u>lie</u>/lay) down on the *tatami* mat.

11. You must (<u>sit</u>/set) with your legs folded neatly beneath you.

12. When the Tea Master (sits/<u>sets</u>) your *matcha,* or traditional powdered tea, before you,

    you must turn the bowl in this way in order to admire it.

In a Japanese tea ceremony, a skilled Tea Master prepares a powdered green tea.

Part 2   Possible answers appear below. Accept all reasonable responses.

Rewrite each sentence using a form of *sit, set, lie,* or *lay.* There is more than one way to rewrite each sentence.

13. Miki placed her shoes outside the door.   Miki set her shoes outside the door.

14. She bowed to the host and took a seat on the tatami mat.   She bowed to the host and sat on the tatami mat.

15. Her sister had told her to admire the food that was placed before her.   Her sister had told her to admire the food that was laid before her.

16. The Tea Master placed the tea on a lacquered table.   The Tea Master set the tea on a lacquered table.

17. Miki wanted to recline on the mats, but I had warned her not to.   Miki wanted to lie on the mats, but I had warned her not to.

18. Miki put her bowl down too quickly, and it knocked against the tray.   Miki set her bowl down too quickly, and it knocked against the tray.

19. She wished that she had placed it on the tray silently.   She wished that she had laid it on the tray silently.

20. On the bus back to the Tokyo Hotel, Miki told me to take a seat by the window.   On the bus back to the Tokyo Hotel, Miki told me to sit by the window.

Part 3

Even professional writers sometimes make mistakes with word choices. Look at the following examples from published works. Correct each sentence by replacing the boldfaced word.

21. From a book review: "Rosa roams afield while Julie **lays** and writes."   lies

22. From a story about basketball players: "...they **laid** on the floor."   lay

23. From an ad for swimsuits: "Choose from one or two pieces in all these exciting styles for the beach or **laying** in the sun."   lying

24. From a *National Geographic Adventure* mailer: "A croc hits you with his tail, then drags you to the bottom and **lays** on you until you are drowned."   lies

25. From an Associated Press report: "The six participants **laid** down on the hogan's earthen floor to sleep around 4 A.M."   lay

Name _____

Grab   Bag

Read and Discover

The Spanish ~~brang~~ many things from the New World back to Europe. They **took** many fruits and vegetables that they had never **seen** before.

Cross out the boldfaced word that is an incorrect verb form.

Many commonly used verbs are **irregular;** they do not add *-ed* in the past tense. Here are some of the verbs:

Present	Past	With *has, have,* or *had*
take	took	taken
see	saw	seen
grow	grew	grown
spring	sprang	sprung
bring	brought	brought
make	made	made

Remember to use this information when you speak, too.

See Handbook Section 18d

Part 1

Circle the correct verb form in parentheses in each sentence.

1. Many foods enjoyed in Mexico today are foods that the Aztecs (eaten/**ate**) long ago.

2. Corn, or maize, (**grew**/growed) in abundance in the New World.

3. The Aztecs prepared it in a number of the same ways it is (ate/**eaten**) today.

4. They (beated/**beat**) it into flour and then used it to make tortillas and tamales.

5. Much as Mexicans do today, the Aztecs ate or (**drank**/drunk) *atole,* a corn flour porridge flavored with fruit or chilies.

6. Whole corn also (**went**/gone) into many Aztec dishes.

7. The Aztecs (**took**/taken) seeds from pumpkins and squash and used them in sauces.

8. Many travelers to Mexico have (saw/**seen**) *pipian verde* on menus.

9. This dish is (maked/**made**) with pumpkin seeds and another Aztec food, tomatillos, which are cousins of the tomato.

10. Another food that grew in the Americas was cacao, the plant from which chocolate is made; the Aztecs (**put**/putted) cacao to good use.

11. The Aztecs (grinded/**ground**) up cacao beans and used them to prepare a cold chocolate drink.

12. Sugar was not (knowed/**known**) to the Aztecs, so they flavored this thick, rich drink with vanilla and various spices.

13. Many years later, a Mexican dish (brang/**brought**) together chocolate, chili, and spices: *mole poblano,* a rich dark sauce served over chicken.

Maize has been a staple food in Mexico for hundreds of years.

Grab Bag

Part 2

Fill in the blank with a past tense form of the verb in parentheses.

14. I _____**brought**_____ *mole poblano* to Victor's birthday party. (bring)

15. My friend Raul _____**took**_____ tamales. (take)

16. Because our arms were full, Ana _____**held**_____ the door open for us. (hold)

17. We _____**heard**_____ music blasting in the backyard. (hear)

18. As we stepped onto the patio, we _____**saw**_____ brightly colored streamers everywhere. (see)

19. Victor's mother _____**lit or lighted**_____ colored lanterns. (light)

20. We _____**laid**_____ the food and gifts on a big table. (lay)

21. When Victor arrived, we all _____**sang**_____ a birthday song, *Las mañanitas*. (sing)

22. Victor _____**became**_____ embarrassed from all the attention. (become)

23. The party _____**went**_____ quite late. (go)

24. We waved *adiós* when we _____**left**_____ the party. (leave)

Part 3

Use forms of the verbs in the word bank to complete the crossword puzzle.

build	write	steal	drink	bring	take	know

Across
4. I ___ chocolate in Mexico last year.
5. English settlers ___ imported chocolate to the colonies.
6. I never ___ that the Aztecs drank chocolate.
7. The Spanish ___ Aztec gold and chocolate.

Down
1. The conquistadors ___ chocolate back to Europe.
2. I have just ___ a report on the Aztecs.
3. Last month I ___ a paper on the Maya.
5. The Aztecs ___ many impressive pyramids.

Crossword solution:
- 1 Down: TOOK
- 2 Down: W...
- 3 Down: WROTE
- 4 Across: DRANK
- 5 Across: BROUGHT
- 5 Down: BUILL
- 6 Across: KNEW
- 7 Across: STOLE

Name _____

 Grab Bag

See Handbook Section 40

Diagraming Prepositions and Prepositional Phrases

You have learned that many adverbial prepositional phrases tell *when, where,* or *how.* You have also learned that most adjectival prepositional phrases describe nouns. Note how the adverbial prepositional phrase is diagramed in the first example. Then observe how the adjectival prepositional phrase is diagramed in the second example.

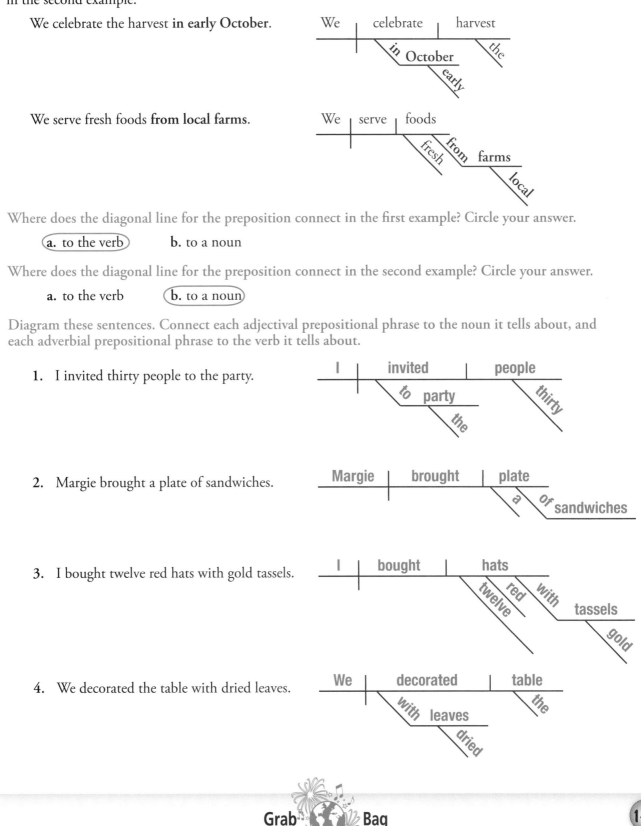

We celebrate the harvest **in early October**.

We serve fresh foods **from local farms**.

Where does the diagonal line for the preposition connect in the first example? Circle your answer.

a. to the verb   **b.** to a noun

Where does the diagonal line for the preposition connect in the second example? Circle your answer.

a. to the verb   **b.** to a noun

Diagram these sentences. Connect each adjectival prepositional phrase to the noun it tells about, and each adverbial prepositional phrase to the verb it tells about.

1. I invited thirty people to the party.

2. Margie brought a plate of sandwiches.

3. I bought twelve red hats with gold tassels.

4. We decorated the table with dried leaves.

Diagraming Indirect Objects

You have learned where to place a direct object in a sentence diagram. Here's how to diagram an indirect object. (The indirect object is in boldfaced type in this example.)

I sent my **cousin** an invitation.

Try diagraming these sentences.

5. Giselle brought me a huge pumpkin.

6. I lent Giovanni my binoculars.

7. He gave me some lettuce seeds.

8. Colleen gave the muddy puppy a good bath.

Diagraming Sentences with *There*

When the word *there* is used to begin a sentence, place it on a separate line above the subject.

There are ripe tomatoes on the vine.

Diagram these sentences.

9. There are apples in the orchard.

10. There is a bee on your watermelon!

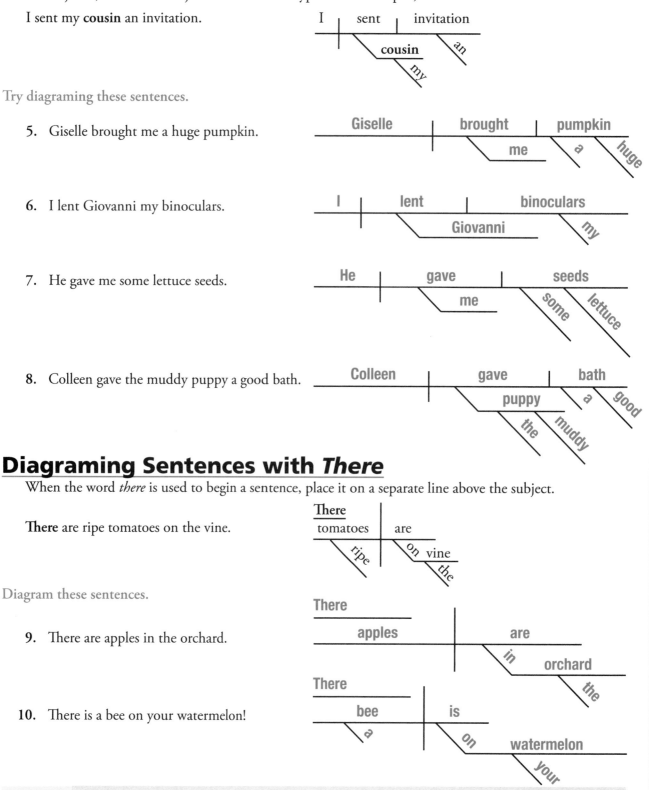

Name _____

Grab Bag

Writing Sentences

These sentences need your help. Rewrite each one so that homophones, problem words, and irregular verbs are used correctly.

1. Its no surprise that many celebrations of the Hopi people focus on rain and fertility.

   It's no surprise that many celebrations of the Hopi people focus on rain and fertility.

2. No large rivers or lakes furnish water to they're high desert homeland. **No large rivers or lakes furnish water to their high desert homeland.**

3. According to traditional Hopi beliefs, *kachinas* bring good health and rain with them; no year can be a good year without these too things. **According to traditional Hopi beliefs, kachinas bring good health and rain with them; no year can be a good year without these two things.**

4. In some Hopi ceremonies, dancers wear costumes and masks representing sacred spirits that are knowed as kachinas. **In some Hopi ceremonies, dancers wear costumes and masks representing sacred spirits that are known as kachinas.**

5. The kachina ceremonies show that the Hopi are a people who's harsh environment has affected their culture. **The kachina ceremonies show that the Hopi are a people whose harsh environment has affected their culture.**

6. Without rain, this people of the American Southwest wouldn't be able to raise no crops. **Without rain, this people of the American Southwest wouldn't be able to raise any crops.**

An informative paragraph's purpose is to inform readers. It should contain several important facts about a particular topic. The paragraph begins with an introductory sentence and ends with a concluding sentence. In between are sentences providing more information about the topic. Read this informative paragraph.

introductory sentence ——————

sentences that give more information about the topic ——————

concluding sentence ——————

The short days and cold weather of winter seem to require special ceremonies. The ancient Druids in Britain built huge bonfires and danced around them on the shortest day of the year. Members of the Iroquois people put on masks and shook rattles outside their neighbors' homes for their midwinter ceremony. In the state of Oaxaca, in Mexico, people carve sculptures out of odd-shaped radishes each winter. **These are only a few of the unusual winter traditions various cultures have developed.**

Writing a Paragraph

A suggested answer appears below. Accept all reasonable responses.

The sentences you repaired on page 151 can be reordered to make an informative paragraph. Decide which sentence is the introductory sentence, which sentences provide more information, and which sentence is the concluding sentence. Reorder the sentences, and write the paragraph below.

It's no surprise that many celebrations of the Hopi people focus on rain and fertility. Without rain, this people of the American Southwest wouldn't be able to raise any crops. No large rivers or lakes furnish water to their high desert homeland. In some Hopi ceremonies, dancers wear costumes and masks representing sacred spirits that are known as kachinas. According to traditional Hopi beliefs, kachinas bring good health and rain with them; no year can be a good year without these two things. The kachina ceremonies show that the Hopi are a people whose harsh environment has affected their culture.

Write an informative paragraph about a culture you read about in Unit 5 or another culture that interests you.

Answers will vary.

Reread your paragraph. Use this checklist to make sure it is complete and correct.

- ❏ My paragraph contains an introductory sentence and a concluding sentence.
- ❏ My paragraph provides several interesting facts about a topic.
- ❏ I have used homophones and problem words correctly.
- ❏ I have used irregular verbs correctly.
- ❏ I have used negatives correctly.

Name _____

Grab Bag

Proofreading Practice

Read this passage about Mongolia. Use the proofreading marks below to show how each mistake should be fixed.

Proofreading Marks

Suggested answers appear below. Accept all reasonable responses.

Mark	Means	Example
ℛ	delete	Mongolia's steppes ~~they~~ are grass-covered plains.
∧	add	Mongolia's steppes are grass-covered. ∧plains
≡	make into a capital letter	mongolia's steppes are grass-covered plains.
ⓢⓟ	fix spelling	Mongolia's steps are grass-covered plains.
⊙	add a period	Mongolia's steppes are grass-covered plains⊙
⌄	add an apostrophe	Mongolias steppes are grass-covered plains.
╱	make into a lowercase letter	Mongolia's Steppes are grass-covered plains.

Mongolian Cultural Traditions

Mongolia ~~lays~~ **lies** between Russia and china. The country's landscape ranges from steep mountains to flat grassland. For thousands of years, Mongolians lived as nomads, Guiding herds of horses, sheep, camels, oxen, and goats to different grazing areas⊙ In the past century, cities and towns ~~has~~ **have** sprouted throughout the country, and many Mongolians have sought jobs their. Others have ~~chose~~ **chosen** to settle on farms. Some Mongolians, however, are still nomadic. They're portable homes are called *gers* or *yurts*.

Mongolians celebrate there nomadic warrior culture in ∧**an** annual festival called *Naadam*. The festival is ~~holded~~ **held** in the capital city of Ulan Bator, which is in the north central part of the country. The festival features three sports: horse racing, wrestling, and archery.

The Naadam Festival features another distinctive Mongolian tradition, "throat" singing. According to Mongolian Tradition, the oldest music was created by shepherds in western Mongolia. There isn't nothing like the music that comes from that region. Its also ~~knowed~~ **known** in English as overtone singing because it requires the singer to produce too or more tones at the same time.

Mongolia is certainly a country who's cultural traditions are, ~~like,~~ distinctive!

Proofreading Checklist

You can use the list below to help you find and fix mistakes in your own writing. Write the titles of your own stories or reports in the blanks at the top of the chart. Then use the questions to check your work. Make a check mark (✓) in each box after you have checked that item.

Answers will vary.

Proofreading Checklist for Unit 5

	Titles			
Have I used *your* and *you're* correctly?				
Have I used *their, they're,* and *there* correctly?				
Have I used *its* and *it's* correctly?				
Have I used *who's* and *whose* correctly?				
Have I used *to, too,* and *two* correctly?				
Have I used *than* and *then* correctly?				
Have I used correct forms of irregular verbs?				
Have I used *go, went, like,* and *all* correctly?				
Have I used negatives correctly?				

Also Remember . . .

Does each sentence begin with a capital letter?				
Have I spelled each word correctly?				
Have I used commas correctly?				

Your Own List

Use this space to write your own list of things to check in your writing.

Name _____

Grab Bag

Review

(Numbers in parentheses identify related lessons.)

Your and *You're*; *Their*, *They're*, and *There*; *Its* and *It's*; *Who's* and *Whose*; *To*, *Too*, and *Two*; *Than* and *Then*

Circle the word in parentheses that correctly completes each sentence.

1. If (your/**you're**) looking for interesting ways to celebrate the beginning of spring, here are some ideas. **(41)**

2. If you go (**to**/too/two) India in the spring, you might see a Hindu festival called *Holi.* **(45)**

3. Everyone (whose/**who's**) participating throws water and brightly colored powder. **(44)**

4. Soon (their/there/**they're**) all covered with the colors of spring. **(42)**

5. Those of you (**whose**/who's) relatives live in Egypt may know about the holiday called *Sham al-Neseem,* which means "Smell the Spring Day." **(44)**

6. People in Egypt have celebrated this festive holiday for more than (to/too/**two**) thousand years. **(45)**

7. Many people go to the countryside and have picnics (their/**there**/they're). **(42)**

8. People in many parts of Europe show (**their**/there/they're) joy at the coming of spring by celebrating May Day on the first day of May. **(42)**

9. Each community puts up (it's/**its**) own maypole and decorates it, and then people dance around the pole. **(43)**

10. Many people decorate their homes with flowers on this day, (to/**too**/two). **(45)**

11. The Japanese holiday called *Setsubun* is more (**than**/then) just a celebration of spring. **(46)**

12. According to tradition, (**it's**/its) also a day to drive away evil spirits. **(43)**

13. If you want to follow tradition, you put sardine heads and branches on (**your**/you're) door on this day. **(41)**

14. (Than/**Then**) you throw beans in every corner of the house. **(46)**

15. (Their/**There**/They're) are also several significant holidays that are celebrated near the end of spring. **(42)**

16. (Your/**You're**) probably familiar with Memorial Day, which traditionally is celebrated on May 30. **(41)**

17. (Its/**It's**) a legal holiday in most states and territories of the United States. **(43)**

18. This holiday has special meaning for people (**whose**/who's) relatives and ancestors lost their lives fighting for the United States. **(44)**

19. (Whose/**Who's**) going to fly an American flag on Memorial Day? **(44)**

20. If people fly a flag on Memorial Day, (their/there/**they're**) likely to fly it on June 14 as well. **(42)**

21. They will fly the flag (**then**/than) because that day is Flag Day. **(46)**

22. Let's buy a larger flag; this one is (to/two/**too**) small to be seen by passersby. **(45)**

Negatives   Possible answers appear below. Accept all reasonable responses.

Circle each error. Write *C* on the line if the sentence is written correctly.

23. The Fourth of July is nearly here, and I haven't made (no) plans to celebrate yet. _____   **(47)**

24. I (haven't) never had as much fun as I did at last year's celebration. _____   **(47)**

25. I hope nobody gets hurt by fireworks this year. __C__   **(47)**

Words Often Misused   Possible answers appear below. Accept all reasonable responses.

Cross out each incorrect use of *go, went, like,* and *all.* (If the word *was* is part of the incorrect expression, cross that out also.) Write a correct word to replace the incorrect expression if a replacement is needed. Try not to use a word more than once as a replacement.

26. My brother Ali ~~was like~~, "We need some new holidays. The ones we have are all really old."
     _____said_____   **(48)**

27. I ~~was all~~, "They're not all old. Presidents Day is only about 40 years old." _____replied_____   **(48)**

28. Then Ali ~~went~~, "Presidents Day is not a new holiday. It's a combination of two old holidays, Washington's Birthday and Lincoln's Birthday." _____argued_____   **(48)**

29. I was ~~, like,~~ surprised to learn that Washington's Birthday has been celebrated as a holiday for ~~, like,~~ more than 200 years. _____   **(48)**

Lie and *Lay, Set* and *Sit*

Circle the correct word in parentheses to complete each sentence.

30. Last year Osamu (sat/(set)) up a snow cave for *Kamakura,* the Snow Cave Festival in Yohoto, Japan. **(49)**

31. After he had finished, he (lay/(laid)) a straw mat on the floor.   **(49)**

32. He invited his friends and family to ((sit)/set) inside and talk with him.   **(49)**

33. After they left, he ((lay)/laid) on the mat, covered himself with blankets, and went to sleep.   **(49)**

Irregular Verbs

Circle the correct form of the verb in parentheses.

34. *Loy Krathong,* or the Festival of the Floating Leaf Cups, has been ((held)/holden) in Thailand for more than six thousand years.   **(50)**

35. Tiny boats called *krathongs* are ((built)/builded) out of banana leaves, lotus, or paper.   **(50)**

36. Inside the boats people place candles, incense, coins, or gardenias they have (brung/(brought)) to the river's edge.   **(50)**

37. Then people launch the boats, (litten/(lit)) by candles, on the river.   **(50)**

38. It is ((thought)/thinked) that a wish will come true if the krathong disappears before the candle goes out.   **(50)**

Name _____

Grab   Bag

Community Connection

In Unit 5 of *G.U.M.* students learned how to **use words that are easily confused** when writing. The content of these lessons focuses on the theme **Cultural Snapshots**. As students completed the exercises, they learned about people in many parts of the world who have developed distinctive cultures. These pages offer a variety of activities that reinforce skills and concepts presented in the unit. They also provide opportunities for the student to make connections between the material in the lessons and the community at large.

Festival Calendar

Use the entertainment section of a local newspaper, fliers posted around your community, and other sources to find out what cultural events are happening in your community this season. Then create a calendar of cultural events to organize the information. If possible, arrange to go to one of the events with a friend or family member. You may also want to display your calendar in your school or community center for others to see.

Traditions

Interview an elderly person in your community who came to the United States from another country. Use his or her responses to write a report to summarize one or more important traditions in that culture. Make sure you correctly use words that are easily confused, such as *their* and *there*.

Party Time

Think about what kind of cultural celebration you would like to see in your community, and make a plan for organizing one. Try to answer these questions when making your plan.

- What culture or cultures will this event celebrate?
- What kinds of entertainment would the celebration feature? What individuals or groups would you invite to participate?
- Would the celebration have food, arts and crafts, or anything else? Whom would you have provide these things?
- When and where would the celebration be held?
- How would you advertise the celebration? Be specific.
- How much would you need to charge to offset the costs of putting on the event?

When you have finished working out your plan, develop a flier you could use to advertise the event. Include the important details about the event on the flier.

The Planning Stage

To hold a celebration, planners must make sure they follow local laws governing community events. Research the laws and rules you would need to comply with in order to hold a cultural celebration in your community. Make sure you also find out about any permits you would need. Use the Event Planner on the next page to help you organize what you learn.

Grab Bag

Event Planner   Answers will vary.

Phone number of City Hall: _____

Other numbers to call: Whom to speak to:

_____   _____

_____   _____

_____   _____

_____   _____

_____

Permits needed:

_____

_____

_____

_____

Other laws/regulations to follow:

_____

_____

_____

_____

Notes:

_____

_____

_____

_____

_____

_____

_____

_____

_____

_____

_____

_____

Name _____

Grab   Bag

a. Laluah and Bonsu tricked Anansi.
b. **They** tricked **him**.

Which boldfaced word replaces the word *Anansi?* _____him_____

Which boldfaced word replaces the phrase *Laluah and Bonsu?* _____They_____

Which pronouns would you use in sentence b. if Anansi tricked Laluah and Bonsu? _____He_____ _____them_____

Subject pronouns include *I, he, she, we,* and *they.* (Subject pronouns are in the *nominative case.*) Subject pronouns can be the subject of a clause or sentence. **Object pronouns** can be used after an action verb or a preposition. Object pronouns include *me, him, her, us,* and *them.* (Object pronouns are in the *objective case.*) The pronouns *it* and *you* can be either subjects or objects. **Remember to use this information when you speak, too.**

See Handbook Section 17b

Part 1

Circle the correct pronoun in parentheses. Write *S* if you circled a subject pronoun. Write *O* if you circled an object pronoun.

1. My aunt used to tell (I/**me**) stories about Anansi. _____O_____

2. (**She**/Her) says Anansi is the central folktale character of the Ashanti people of West Africa. _____S_____

3. The stories (**they**/them) tell about (he/**him**) teach moral lessons. _____S_____ _____O_____

4. In some stories Anansi is a spider, and in others (**he**/him) is a man. _____S_____

5. Anansi is called a trickster character because (**he**/him) is always trying to swindle others. _____S_____

6. Anansi is sometimes clever and sometimes foolish, but either way, another character usually gets the better of (he/**him**). _____O_____

7. (**I**/Me) remember a story in which Anansi says (**he**/him) wants to start a business but not do any work. _____S_____ _____S_____

8. Anansi's wife tells her friend Laluah about Anansi's plan, and (**she**/her) tells her husband, Bonsu. _____S_____

9. Bonsu tells (she/**her**) that (**he**/him) will trick Anansi into doing all the work instead. _____O_____ _____S_____

10. It's not surprising that (**he**/him) succeeds in tricking Anansi. _____S_____

11. Anansi's wife tells (he/**him**) at the end of the story that when (**he**/him) digs a hole for someone else, (**he**/him) will fall into it himself. _____O_____ _____S_____ _____S_____

12. My friend Vanessa and I have started telling stories about Anansi when (**we**/us) baby-sit. _____S_____

13. (**We**/Us) think (**they**/them) help kids learn the consequences of trying to cheat others. _____S_____ _____S_____

14. Telling these stories is fun for (we/**us**), too. _____O_____

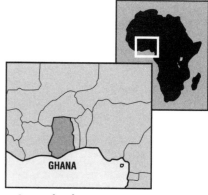

Anansi tales are popular in the West African nation of Ghana.

Part 2

Rewrite each sentence. Replace each boldfaced phrase with a pronoun. Circle the subject pronouns you write. Draw a box around the object pronouns.

15. **Anansi tales** have been carried all over the world by people of African descent. _(They) have been carried all over the world by people of African descent._

16. As new storytellers have told **Anansi tales, the tales** have changed in some ways. _As new storytellers have told [them], (they) have changed in some ways._

17. For example, **Anansi** has had his name changed to "Aunt Nancy" in some Caribbean countries. _For example, (he) has had his name changed to "Aunt Nancy" in some Caribbean countries._

18. **The plants and animals in a story** might change from African ones to those found in the Caribbean or in North or South America. _(They) might change from African ones to those found in the Caribbean or in North or South America._

19. **The message of the stories** has remained the same, however. _(It) has remained the same, however._

20. **Anansi** always tries to take advantage of **other people or animals in the forest,** but **others** usually teach **Anansi** a lesson in the end. _(He) always tries to take advantage of [them], but (they) usually teach [him] a lesson in the end._

Part 3

Forms of personal pronouns in English have changed over the years. Until the sixteenth century, the word *thou* was used as a subject pronoun to indicate the person being spoken to, and the word *thee* was used as the object form. Since that time, people have used the word *you* as both a subject and an object pronoun to indicate the person being spoken to. Yet many writers continued to use *thou* and *thee* well into the eighteenth century.

Read the following passage. Circle each pronoun that is no longer commonly used. Then write the modern English pronoun that would be used instead of each of these archaic pronouns.

ROMEO: By a name
I know not how to tell (thee) who I am:
My name, dear saint, is hateful to myself,
Because it is an enemy to (thee;)
Had I written it, I would tear the word.

JULIET: My ears have not yet drunk a hundred words
of (thy) tongue's uttering, yet I know the sound:
Art (thou) not Romeo, and a Montague?

ROMEO: Neither, fair maid, if either (thee) dislike.
—William Shakespeare, from *Romeo and Juliet*

21. _____ you
22. _____ you
23. _____ your
24. _____ you
25. _____ you

Name _____

Timeless Tales

Read and Discover

a. Carmen and I learned about Brer Rabbit in school.
b. My grandfather told Carmen and I stories about this folktale character.

If you delete "Carmen and" from each sentence, which sentence sounds correct? __a.__

Use a **subject pronoun** in a compound subject. Use an **object pronoun** in a compound direct object, a compound indirect object, or a compound object of a preposition. If you are unsure which pronoun form to use, say the sentence with only the pronoun part of the compound. For example, *He told stories to Carmen and I.* becomes *He told stories to I.* You can hear that *I* should be replaced with *me*.
📣 **Remember to use this information when you speak, too.**

See Handbook Section 17b

Part 1

Circle the correct pronoun in each pair. Write *S* if you chose a subject pronoun and *O* if you chose an object pronoun.

1. Last week Carmen, Bobby, and (**I**/me) visited my grandparents. __S__

2. Bobby had asked me to arrange the visit because (**he**/him) and Carmen hoped Grandfather would tell them about Brer Rabbit for their school folklore project. __S__

3. Carmen knows a lot about Anansi the Spider, and our teacher had told Bobby and (she/**her**) that Brer Rabbit stories are similar to Anansi stories. __O__

4. (**She**/Her) and Bobby explained that enslaved African Americans developed the Brer Rabbit stories. __S__

5. Grandfather told Grandmother and (we/**us**) that he heard Brer Rabbit stories when he was little. __O__

6. (**He**/Him) and Grandmother talked about the ways Brer Rabbit outsmarts more powerful animals. __S__

7. Grandfather told Carmen, Bobby, and (I/**me**) that these stories helped enslaved people think about outsmarting slaveholders. __O__

8. Carmen asked Grandfather to tell a Brer Rabbit story that (**she**/her) and Bobby had never heard. __S__

9. Grandfather told Grandmother and (we/**us**) about Brer Rabbit and Brer Fox. __O__

10. (**He**/Him) and Brer Rabbit were always trying to trick one another. __S__

11. Bobby took notes as Grandfather told Carmen and (he/**him**) that Fox caught Rabbit with some tar. __O__

12. Grandmother and (**I**/me) said we had heard this story many times before. __S__

13. Everyone listened to Grandmother and (I/**me**) as we told how Brer Rabbit got stuck to the Tar Baby. __O__

14. Grandfather turned to Carmen and asked Bobby and (she/**her**) what Brer Fox did to Brer Rabbit. __O__

15. Grandmother and (**I**/me) said Brer Rabbit tricked Brer Fox into throwing him into the briar patch. __S__

16. Carmen laughed and said (**she**/her) and Bobby could guess the ending: Brer Rabbit got away easily since he had been born and raised in the briar patch. __S__

Part 2

Rewrite these sentences. Substitute a pronoun for each boldfaced noun. Circle the subject pronouns you write. Draw a box around the object pronouns.

17. **Bobby** and Carmen collected stories about Brer Rabbit. (He) and Carmen collected stories about Brer Rabbit.

18. Grandmother and Grandfather told Bobby and **Carmen** most of the stories. Grandmother and Grandfather told Bobby and [her] most of the stories.

19. Ramona and **Carmen** read other stories in a book. Ramona and (she) read other stories in a book.

20. Ramona discovered lots of stories about Brer Fox and **Brer Rabbit**. Ramona discovered lots of stories about Brer Fox and [him].

21. Bobby, Carmen, and **Ramona** gave an oral report on folktales to the class. Bobby, Carmen, and (she) gave an oral report on folktales to the class.

22. **The students** and the teacher were especially interested in the Tar Baby. (They) and the teacher were especially interested in the Tar Baby.

23. The story of how **the Tar Baby** and **Brer Rabbit** met made everyone burst out laughing. The story of how (it) and (he) met made everyone burst out laughing.

24. Bobby and **Carmen** acted out a few stories. Bobby and (she) acted out a few stories.

25. Everyone gave **Bobby** and Carmen a big round of applause. Everyone gave [him] and Carmen a big round of applause.

Part 3

When *I* and *me* are used in a pair with a noun or another pronoun, the pronouns *I* and *me* should always come last (*Grandfather and me,* NOT *me and Grandfather*).

Circle the choice that completes each sentence correctly.

26. (I and Carmen/Carmen and I) presented what we had learned about Brer Rabbit to the class.

27. The class had lots of questions for (Carmen and me/me and Carmen).

28. (Me and Carmen/Carmen and I) answered all the questions we could.

29. The questions we couldn't answer gave (Carmen and me/me and Carmen) a great idea.

30. (Bobby, I, and Carmen/Carmen, Bobby, and I) are going to start up a folktales club at school.

Name _____

Timeless Tales

Read and Discover

Scheherazade is a mythical Arabian queen. **She** narrates the stories of *The Thousand and One Nights*.

Circle the proper noun that the boldfaced pronoun replaces. Draw an arrow from the pronoun to that name.

An **antecedent** is the word or phrase a pronoun refers to or takes the place of. The antecedent always includes a noun. When you write a pronoun, be sure its antecedent is clear. A pronoun must also **agree** with its antecedent. An antecedent and pronoun agree when they have the same number (singular or plural) and gender (male or female). For example, *women,* a plural noun naming females, would never be the antecedent of *he,* a singular masculine pronoun.
📣 **Remember to use this information when you speak, too.**

See Handbook Section 17c

Part 1

Circle the antecedent of each boldfaced pronoun.

1. The Thousand and One Nights is a famous piece of Arabic literature. **It** was written around A.D. 1500.

2. There are about 200 folktales in this collection. **They** originally came from Arabia, Egypt, India, Persia, and other countries.

3. The first story tells of a cruel king. **He** does not trust women.

4. Each evening the king marries a new bride. Then, the next morning, he executes **her**.

5. The wise and beautiful Scheherazade volunteers to marry the king. **She** has a plan to stop his cruelty.

6. On the night of the wedding, Scheherazade's sister asks the king if Scheherazade can tell a story. **He** gives his permission.

7. Scheherazade begins telling the king a story, but she does not finish **it**.

8. The king has to spare Scheherazade's life if **he** wants to find out how the story ends.

9. The next night, Scheherazade finishes the story. Then right away **she** tells the beginning of another story.

10. Scheherazade's stories tell about genies, princesses, and talking animals. **They** are wonderful fairy tales.

11. Every night, Scheherazade tells stories to her husband, and every morning **he** lets her live so that she can finish it.

12. Scheherazade tells stories for one thousand and one nights. By this time, the king has fallen in love with **her**.

13. Scheherazade's stories are so entertaining that **they** save her life.

14. Jean Antoine Galland made it possible for people in France to enjoy *The Thousand and One Nights*. **He** translated **it** into French in the early 1700s.

15. English translations of these tales were not generally available until the 1880s. **They** were prepared by Sir Richard Francis Burton, who was a famous explorer as well as a skillful translator.

The story of Aladdin's lamp is in *The Thousand and One Nights*.

Part 2

Write the pronoun that could take the place of each phrase in boldface. Capitalize a word that begins a sentence.

16. **The stories in *The Thousand and One Nights*** are hundreds of years old, but people still enjoy telling and listening to ____them____ today.

17. One of the most popular stories tells of **a poor boy named Aladdin.** ____He____ finds a genie in a magic lamp.

18. When Aladdin rubs the lamp, **the genie** appears. ____It____ grants Aladdin's wishes.

19. Aladdin later meets **a princess** and falls in love with ____her____.

20. **A cartoon film version of Aladdin's tale** was released in the early 1990s. ____It____ quickly became one of the most popular films ever shown.

21. **Sinbad the Sailor** also appears as a character in some of these stories. Incredible things happen to ____him____ during seven long sea voyages.

22. **Real Arab sailors** regularly sailed as far as China in the Medieval period (about A.D. 500–1500). Some scholars think the character of Sinbad was based on ____them____.

23. Another popular character in *The Thousand and One Nights* is **Ali Baba.** ____He____ finds a sealed cave filled with treasure.

24. To open **the treasure-filled cave,** Ali Baba stands in front of ____it____ and says the magic words.

25. Unfortunately, the treasure belongs to **forty thieves.** ____They____ will do anything to protect it.

Part 3   A possible answer appears below. Accept all reasonable responses.

Ante means "before." A pronoun's antecedent should come before the pronoun so that the reader knows for sure what noun the pronoun replaces. Rewrite the paragraph below so that every pronoun has a clear antecedent. There is more than one correct way to do this. You'll want to replace some pronouns with nouns, but remember that using pronouns with clear antecedents helps the flow of your writing.

She tells about him in the story "Ali Baba and the Forty Thieves." In it, Ali Baba hides from them. While hidden in the tree, he overhears them opening it with the password "open sesame." He later says the password himself and is able to enter their treasure cave and take it for himself. They try to kill him, but he gets away with it in the end. It has remained a favorite tale for centuries, and several exciting movie versions of it have been made.

Scheherazade tells about Ali Baba in the story "Ali Baba and the Forty Thieves." In it, Ali Baba hides from the thieves. While hidden in the tree, he overhears them opening the treasure cave with the password "open sesame." Ali Baba later says the password himself and is able to enter their treasure cave and take the treasure for himself. The thieves try to kill Ali Baba, but he gets away with the treasure in the end. The tale has remained a favorite for centuries, and several exciting movie versions of it have been made.

Name _____

Timeless Tales

Read and Discover

Some folk heroes are based on people **who** actually lived. ___subject___

John Henry was a real African American worker about **whom** many folk songs and stories have been written. ___object___

Underline the clause in each sentence that includes *who* or *whom*. Which boldfaced word is a subject? ___who___ Which boldfaced word begins a clause that is the object of a preposition? ___whom___ After each sentence, write whether *who* or *whom* is a subject or an object.

Use *who* as the **subject** of a sentence or a clause. Use *whom* as the **object** of a verb or a preposition. **Remember to use this information when you speak, too.**

See Handbook Sections 17b, 17h

Part 1

Underline the clause in each sentence that includes the words in parentheses. Decide whether the word in parentheses will be a subject or an object. Circle *who* or *whom* to complete each sentence correctly.

1. John Henry is a folk hero (*who*/whom) is legendary for his strength of body and will.
2. He was one of a group of workers (who/*whom*) a railroad company had hired to dig a tunnel in the 1870s.
3. The workers, (*who*/whom) had to be very strong, used heavy sledgehammers to pound drills into solid rock.
4. They were followed by other workers (*who*/whom) put sticks of dynamite into the holes to blast a tunnel through the rock.
5. John Henry could swing a hammer harder and faster than any of the other men with (who/*whom*) he worked.
6. One day a man came (*who*/whom) had built a steam-powered drill.
7. He claimed it could dig a hole faster than twenty workers (*who*/whom) used regular hammers.
8. The workers were worried: if the steam drill was so fast, (*who*/whom) would need workers to pound drills anymore?
9. To (who/*whom*) could they turn?
10. John Henry was the only one (*who*/whom) was willing to accept the challenge of competing against the steam drill driver.
11. The winner would be the one (*who*/whom) drilled a hole faster.
12. (*Who*/Whom) won the contest? John Henry did, but he died soon after.
13. According to legend, John Henry died of exhaustion, but the people (*who*/whom) witnessed the contest said he was crushed by falling rock.
14. The workers made a hero of John Henry, (who/*whom*) they buried with a hammer in his hand.
15. John Henry, (*who*/whom) came to symbolize the workers' struggle against machinery that could replace them, has been the subject of both stories and songs.

John Henry beat a machine in a race.

Part 2   Possible answers appear below. Accept all reasonable responses.

Complete a question to go with each statement. Be sure to end each sentence with a question mark.

16. The folktale character John Henry was based on a real person. On whom _**was the folktale character John Henry based?**_

17. The real John Henry was an African American worker. Who _**was the real John Henry?**_

18. He was working with other laborers to build the Big Bend Tunnel and the Ohio Railroad. Who _**was working with other laborers to build the Big Bend Tunnel and the Ohio Railroad?**_

19. Songs and stories have been written about him. About whom _**have songs and stories been written?**_

20. John Henry was given the task of competing with a mechanical steam drill. To whom _**was the task given of competing with a mechanical steam drill?**_

21. John Henry won the race. Who _**won the race?**_

22. Workers especially admired him. Who _**especially admired him?**_

23. For many, he is an important American hero. For whom _**is he an important American hero?**_

Part 3

Circle *who* or *whom* to complete each quotation correctly.

No man is an island . . . never send to know
for (who/(whom)) the bell tolls; it tolls for thee.

       —John Donne

He ((who)/whom) learns but does not think,
is lost. He ((who)/whom) thinks but does not learn
is in great danger.

       —Kong Qiu (Confucius)

I am only a public entertainer ((who)/whom)
has understood his time.

       —Pablo Picasso

If your lips would keep from slips,

Five things observe with care:

To (who/(whom)) you speak; of (who/(whom)) you
   speak;

And how, and when, and where.

       —William Edward Norris

No! the two kinds of people on earth that I mean

Are the people ((who)/whom) lift and the people
   ((who)/whom) lean.

       —Ella Wheeler Wilcox

Now write your own saying using *who* or *whom*.

24. _**Answers will vary.**_

Name _____

Timeless Tales

Read and Discover

Jewish (tales) of a helpful **monster** <u>have</u> been told and retold for centuries.

Circle the boldfaced noun that is the simple subject of this sentence. Is this noun singular or plural? _____plural_____ Underline the helping verb that agrees with the subject. What form of this verb would be used if the simple subject of this sentence was *tale*? _____has_____

The **subject** and its **verb must agree.** Add *s* or *es* to a verb in the present tense when the subject is a singular noun or *he, she,* or *it.* Do not add *s* or *es* to a verb in the present tense when the subject is a plural noun or *I, you, we,* or *they.* The verb *be* is irregular. Singular forms of *be* are *is, am, was.* Plural forms are *are* and *were.* Be sure the verb agrees with its subject and not with the object of a preposition that comes before the verb. 📢 **Remember to use this information when you speak, too.**

See Handbook Section 18f

Part 1

Circle the simple subject in each sentence. Then underline the correct form of the verb in parentheses.

1. (Stories) about the golem (is/<u>are</u>) still told and read today.

2. According to legend, the (body) of a golem (<u>is</u>/are) made of clay and dust.

3. Only a (person) very learned in the ways of magic (<u>is</u>/are) able to bring the clay golem to life.

4. These (monsters,) human in form, (is/<u>are</u>) very strong but unable to speak.

5. (One) of the most famous golem stories (<u>is</u>/are) "The Golem of Prague."

6. At the time in which this tale is set, the sixteenth century, Jewish (people) (was/<u>were</u>) terribly persecuted in many parts of eastern Europe.

7. In the story, the (rabbi) of Prague, a religious leader known for his great knowledge, (<u>creates</u>/create) a golem to guard his people.

8. This (protector) of the Jews (<u>roams</u>/roam) the streets of the city at night, stopping crime.

In legends of the golem, a clay figure comes to life.

9. Some (parts) of the story (is/<u>are</u>) humorous.

10. The (wife) of the rabbi (<u>asks</u>/ask) the golem to carry water from the well to fill a washtub.

11. The obedient (golem) (<u>carries</u>/carry) buckets of water so fast that the tub is soon overflowing.

12. (<u>Is</u>/Are) the (persecutors) of the Jews brought to justice with the help of the golem?

13. Yes, a (plot) to make false accusations against the Jewish residents (<u>is</u>/are) revealed by the golem, who has been disguised as a night watchman.

14. The (king,) hearing news of the cruel plot, (issue/<u>issues</u>) an order protecting the Jewish people.

15. When the help of the golem is no longer needed, the (rabbi) (<u>turns</u>/turn) the giant back into clay.

16. According to legend, the clay (form) of the golem still (<u>lies</u>/lie) hidden, waiting to be brought to life if needed.

Timeless Tales

Part 2

Circle the simple subject in each sentence. Then write the correct form of the verb in parentheses to complete the sentence.

17. A (book) of folktales _____**has**_____ the power to entertain adults as well as children. (have)

18. A favorite (story) of my parents _____**is or was**_____ "Strongheart Jack and the Beanstalk," an early version of the story we know as "Jack and the Beanstalk." (be)

19. In this version, a hot (desert) filled with cactus plants _____**is**_____ the first thing Jack sees when he reaches the top of the beanstalk. (be)

20. Then a yellow (turtle) in a pond _____**challenges**_____ Jack to answer a riddle. (challenge)

21. A calico (cat) named Octavia _____**helps**_____ Jack defeat the giant. (help)

22. The (prisoners) in the giant's castle _____**are**_____ very happy to be free. (be)

23. Any (story) about giants _____**scares**_____ my brother. (scare)

24. (One) of my assignments in art class this week _____**is**_____ to mold a clay figure. (be)

25. _____**Is**_____ the (name) "golem" a good one for a large clay figure? (be)

Part 3   Possible answers appear below. Accept all reasonable responses.

Folktales are one way wisdom has been passed from one generation to the next. *Aphorisms,* **brief truths about human behavior, are another.**

Read these three aphorisms from Benjamin Franklin. Underline the correct verb form in each. Then write a brief explanation of each saying's message.

26. The cat in gloves (catch/<u>catches</u>) no mice. <u>You can't get the job done if you're not properly</u> <u>prepared for the work.</u>

27. A word to the wise (<u>is</u>/are) enough, and many words won't fill a bushel. <u>A wise person hears and</u> <u>understands quickly, but even a lot of words won't make sense to an unwise person.</u>

28. They that can give up essential liberty to obtain a little temporary safety (<u>deserve</u>/deserves) neither liberty nor safety. <u>Anyone who is willing to trade an important freedom just to be safe for a</u> <u>while doesn't deserve to be either free or safe.</u>

Name _____

Timeless Tales

a. Neither the wolf's big eyes nor its big mouth makes Red Riding Hood suspicious.

b. Fortunately, Red and her grandmother escape from the wolf in the end.

Circle the compound subject in each sentence. Underline the verb in each sentence. Which sentence has a verb that goes with a singular subject? **a.**

A **compound subject** and its verb must agree. If a compound subject includes the conjunction *and*, the subject is plural and needs a plural verb. If a compound subject includes *or* or *nor*, the verb must agree with the last item in the subject.
Remember to use this information when you speak, too.

See Handbook Sections 11, 18f

Part 1

Look at the compound subject in each sentence. Draw a box around the conjunction. Then underline the correct verb in parentheses.

1. Lin and Rick (collect/collects) information about wild canine characters in folktales.

2. Wolves, foxes, and coyotes (is/are) all closely related to dogs.

3. A wolf or a coyote (act/acts) more like a dog than a fox does.

4. Native American cultures and European cultures (has/have) very different ideas about wild canine characters.

5. When a fox or a wolf (appears/appear) in a European fairy tale, it is usually the villain.

6. "Little Red Riding Hood" and "The Three Little Pigs" (is/are) two good examples.

7. Neither Red Riding Hood nor the pigs (regrets/regret) the evil wolf's death.

8. Although the real animals may be similar, the evil fairy tale wolf and the coyote of Native American tales (is/are) totally different from one another.

9. Native American stories and a favorite Mexican folktale of mine (portrays/portray) Coyote as a lovable trickster figure.

10. Greed, arrogance, or selfishness (gets/get) Coyote into trouble.

11. Fox, Bear, or other animals (laughs/laugh) at his misadventures.

12. But neither injury nor even death (stops/stop) Coyote.

13. The power to come back from the dead and the power to create anything he can imagine (belongs/belong) to Coyote.

14. This laughable fool or powerful creator (is/are) one of the most complicated characters in Native American folklore.

The Coyote character lived in a legendary time before humans.

Part 2

Write the correct present tense form of the verb in parentheses to complete each sentence.

15. Lin and Alvin, a friend of hers, _____ **like** _____ the story of Coyote's name best. (like)

16. The Great Spirit, or Spirit Chief, _____ **decides** _____ to rename all the animals. (decide)

17. Coyote and all the other animals _____ **agree** _____ to line up first thing the next morning for their new names. (agree)

18. *Grizzly Bear* or *Salmon* _____ **appeals** _____ to Coyote as a new name. (appeal)

19. Coyote's ambition and cunning _____ **help** _____ him think of a scheme for being first in line: he'll stay up all night. (help)

20. Boasts and selfish wishes _____ **pour** _____ from the mouth of Coyote almost all that night. (pour)

21. Finally, either laziness or just plain exhaustion _____ **overwhelms** _____ Coyote, and he falls asleep. (overwhelm)

22. While Coyote sleeps, the real Grizzly Bear and the real Salmon _____ **choose** _____ their own names. (choose)

23. By the time the tired Coyote wakes up, neither *Grizzly Bear* nor *Salmon* _____ **remains** _____ a possibility for a new name. (remain)

24. Coyote and his old name _____ **have** _____ to stick together. (have)

Part 3

Use information in this lesson and in earlier lessons in this unit to fill in the puzzle. Each answer will be part of a compound subject. Then circle the correct verb in parentheses to complete each clue.

Across
3. Aladdin, Ali Baba, and __ the Sailor (is/**are**) all characters in *The Thousand and One Nights*.
4. Either the steam drill driver or John __ (**wins**/win) the race.
5. The *Great Spirit* and the *Spirit* __ (is/**are**) both Native American names for the same deity.
6. Wolves and __ (is/**are**) often villains in European fairy tales.

Down
1. Bonsu and __ the Spider (goes/**go**) fishing together, and they try to trick each other.
2. Brer Rabbit and the Tar __ (sticks/**stick**) to each other.
5. Either Brer Rabbit, Anansi, or __ (**makes**/make) a good example of a trickster character.

Timeless Tales

The Folkways Club meets on Thursdays. "Cinderellas from Many Cultures" is the title of this week's discussion. Everybody has a different version of the story to read.

Look at the boldfaced subjects of these sentences. Circle the proper noun that refers to a group of people but does not end in *s*. Underline the story title. Draw a box around the indefinite pronoun. Do the verbs that follow these subjects agree with singular subjects or with plural subjects? **singular**

The **subject** and its **verb must agree**. There are special rules for certain kinds of subjects. **Titles** of books, movies, stories, or songs are considered singular even if they end in *-s*. (*"The Three Little Pigs" is my little brother's favorite story.*) A **collective noun,** such as *collection, group, team, country, kingdom, family, flock,* and *herd,* names more than one person or object acting together as one group. These nouns are almost always considered singular. (*Katie's team wins every game.*) Most **indefinite pronouns,** including *everyone, nobody, nothing, something,* and *anything,* are considered singular. (*Everyone likes pizza.*) A few indefinite pronouns, such as *many* and *several,* are considered plural. (*Many like spaghetti.*) **Remember to use this information when you speak, too.**

See Handbook Sections 17f, 18f

Part 1

Underline the simple subject in each sentence. Then circle the correct form of each verb in parentheses.

1. "Cinderella and the Little Glass Slipper" (**is**/are) a story with a fascinating history.

2. Almost every culture (**has**/have) a collection of folktales it passes from generation to generation.

3. Many (seems/**seem**) to have their own version of a Cinderella story, in which a poor, mistreated girl wins the love of a prince.

4. My favorite folktale collection (include/**includes**) versions of this tale from Russia, Appalachia, Egypt, and Vietnam.

5. "Mufaro's Beautiful Daughters" (**is**/are) a version from Zimbabwe.

6. "Boots and the Glass Mountain" (**comes**/come) from Norway.

7. Something (**is**/are) unique about each version of the story.

The footwear in the Cinderella stories reflects different cultures.

8. Cinderella's footwear (**is**/are) sometimes made of glass, sometimes of fur, and sometimes of gold.

9. In some versions Cinderella makes friends with the birds, and a flock (**helps**/help) her with difficult chores.

10. *Grimm's Fairy Tales* (**includes**/include) the grisly German version, in which Cinderella's sisters cut off their toes to try to fit into her shoe.

11. But everyone easily (**recognizes**/recognize) each of these stories as a Cinderella story.

12. In almost every version, Cinderella's family (**mistreats**/mistreat) her.

13. A prince finds the slipper of a beautiful, mysterious woman, and the whole kingdom (**tries**/try) it on for size.

14. Nobody (**fits**/fit) into the slipper but Cinderella.

15. When the prince and Cinderella marry, the whole country (**rejoices**/rejoice)—except Cinderella's family.

Part 2

Write the correct present tense form of the verb in parentheses to complete each sentence.

16. An ancient Chinese story collection _____**includes**_____ the earliest known version of the Cinderella story. (include)

17. The beautiful Yeh-hsien's wicked stepmother _____**makes**_____ her dress in rags and do dangerous chores. (make)

18. Yeh-hsien has a magic fish who _____**lives**_____ in a nearby pond, but her stepmother kills the fish. (live)

19. The pile of magic fish bones _____**grants**_____ Yeh-hsien's wishes, giving her gorgeous clothes to wear to a festival. (grant)

20. "Wishbones" _____**is**_____ one title for the story. (be)

21. Unlike many versions of the Cinderella story, no royal men _____**attend**_____ the festival. (attend)

22. But, just as in other versions, one of Yeh-hsien's golden slippers _____**gets**_____ lost as she hurriedly leaves the festival. (get)

23. The richest merchant in the land _____**finds**_____ Yeh-hsien's lost golden slipper after the festival. (find)

24. No one _____**looks**_____ more beautiful than Yeh-hsien when she tries on the slipper. (look)

25. In the end, the beautiful Yeh-hsien _____**marries**_____ the merchant. (marry)

Part 3

Flock and *herd* are not the only collective nouns that can refer to a group of animals. Groups of certain kinds of animals can be named by special collective nouns. Some of these nouns may be familiar to you, but others are used very rarely.

Match the collective nouns below with the animal groups they refer to. Write the correct letter in the blank.

a. cats
b. lions
c. seals or whales
d. zebras
e. dogs or wolves
f. fish
g. jellyfish
h. bees
i. grasshoppers
j. ants

26. school __f__
27. cloud __i__
28. pride __b__
29. swarm __h__
30. zeal __d__
31. fluther __g__
32. army __j__
33. clutter __a__
34. pack __e__
35. pod __c__

Now use one of these collective nouns in a sentence. Remember that a collective noun is singular even when it is followed by a prepositional phrase. (*A herd of horses is coming toward us.*)

36. **Answers will vary.** _____

_____

Name _____

Timeless Tales

Read and Discover

a. Always getting into trouble, Juan Bobo is a classic "noodlehead" character.

b. When telling stories to children, Juan Bobo tales are popular in Puerto Rico.

Who is getting into trouble in sentence a.? ___Juan Bobo___

Does sentence b. say exactly who is telling stories? ___no___

Verbal phrases must always refer to, or modify, a noun or a pronoun in the main part of a sentence. **Dangling modifiers** are phrases that do not clearly refer to any particular word in the sentence. Dangling modifiers make your writing unclear, so avoid them. When you begin a sentence with a verbal phrase such as "When telling stories to children," make sure that the question "<u>Who</u> is telling?" is answered clearly in the first part of the rest of the sentence.

See Handbook Sections 25, 31

Part 1

Underline the verbal phrase that begins each sentence. If the phrase is a dangling modifier, write *dangling* on the line. If the phrase is used correctly, circle the word it modifies and write *C* on the line.

1. While doing the housework, (Mama) often calls Juan Bobo to help her with the chores. ___C___

2. Needing his help, Juan Bobo only wants to play. ___dangling___

3. Doing everything wrong, even easy tasks spell disaster. ___dangling___

4. Needing water for the dishes, (Mama) asks Juan Bobo to fill buckets of water at the stream. ___C___

5. Not wanting to carry heavy buckets, baskets are chosen instead. ___dangling___

6. Woven from strips, the (baskets) are not waterproof. ___C___

7. Dripping through holes in the baskets, Juan Bobo walks home. ___dangling___

8. Arriving at the house, no water is left. ___dangling___

9. When leaving for church, (Mama) asks Juan Bobo to stay home and take care of the pig. ___C___

10. Listening to the pig's squealing, (Juan Bobo) thinks it must want to go to church, too. ___C___

11. Dressing the pig in Mama's new dress, the sight is hilarious. ___dangling___

12. Letting the pig go free, the people laugh or shriek. ___dangling___

13. Rolling in the mud with its snout in the air, Mama's dress is ruined. ___dangling___

14. Seeing the pig in her dress and shoes, (Mama) could not have been angrier. ___C___

15. Reading a Juan Bobo story, laughter is unavoidable. ___dangling___

Juan Bobo creates chaos and produces laughter in stories.

Timeless Tales

Part 2 Possible answers appear below. Accept all reasonable responses.

Use the noun in parentheses to rewrite each sentence correctly and avoid the dangling modifier. There is more than one way to rewrite each sentence.

16. While creating chaos for everyone else, trouble is sometimes made for himself as well. (Juan Bobo) **While creating chaos for everyone else, Juan Bobo sometimes makes trouble for himself as well.**

17. Warning him to be polite, Juan Bobo is taken to Señora Soto's house for lunch. (Mama) **Warning him to be polite, Mama takes Juan Bobo to Señora Soto's house for lunch.**

18. Trying not to sneeze, his head shakes from side to side. (Juan Bobo) **Trying not to sneeze, Juan Bobo shakes his head from side to side.**

19. Seeing Juan Bobo shake his head, it is assumed that he doesn't want any beans and rice. (Señora Soto) **Seeing Juan Bobo shake his head, Señora Soto assumes he doesn't want any beans and rice.**

20. Not wanting to scratch an itchy mosquito bite, a squeal of frustration is heard. (Juan Bobo) **Not wanting to scratch an itchy mosquito bite, Juan Bobo squeals in frustration.**

21. Hearing the squeal, the assumption is made that Juan Bobo doesn't like fried bananas, either. (Señora Soto) **Hearing the squeal, Señora Soto assumes that Juan Bobo doesn't like fried bananas, either.**

22. Going home hungry, it is very disappointing. (Juan Bobo) **Going home hungry, Juan Bobo is very disappointed.**

Part 3

> Introductory verbal phrases delay the message a sentence has to communicate. A writer might avoid introductory verbal phrases in a business letter in order to make the message more direct. Sometimes, though, writers want to delay the message of a sentence while they create an image or give important information.

Read the passage below; notice how the long introductory verbal phrase evokes Johnny Appleseed's long journey and the trees he planted.

Planting the trees that would march and train
On, in his name to the great Pacific,
Like Birnam Wood to Dunsinane,
Johnny Appleseed swept on.
  —Vachel Lindsay, from "In Praise of Johnny Appleseed"

Now look for a sentence beginning with a long verbal phrase in a book you are reading. On another sheet of paper, explain why the writer might have decided to construct the sentence this way. **Answers will vary.**

Name _____

Tall tales are **more exaggerated** than folktales. In fact, tall tales are the **most exaggerated** stories of all.

Circle the boldfaced words that compare tall tales with one other type of story. Underline the boldfaced words that compare tall tales with more than one other type of story.

The **comparative form** of an **adjective** or **adverb** compares two people, places, things, or actions. Add *-er* to short adjectives or adverbs to create the comparative form. Use the word *more* before long adjectives and adverbs (generally three or more syllables) to create the comparative form (*more exaggerated*). The **superlative form** compares three or more people, places, things, or actions. Add *-est* to create the superlative form. Use the word *most* before long adjectives and adverbs to create the superlative form (*most exaggerated*). Use *better* and *less* to compare two things. Use *best* and *least* to compare three or more things.

📢 **Remember to use this information when you speak, too.**

See Handbook Section 27

Part 1

Think about how many things are being compared in each sentence. Then underline the correct form of the adjective or adverb in parentheses.

1. (More often/Most often) than not, folktale characters have qualities that make them different from others.

2. Rapunzel's hair grows (longer/longest) than any ordinary person's hair ever grows.

3. Snow White's troubles arise from the fact that she is "the (fairer/fairest) of them all."

4. Tom Thumb gets his name because he is (shorter/shortest) than his father's thumb.

5. Thumbelina is the (smaller/smallest) of all: she is only half as big as a thumb.

6. Folktale giants, of course, are (taller/tallest) than normal.

7. In one English story, the (meaner/meanest) giant in the land captures three sisters and plans to eat them.

8. Molly Whuppie, the (younger/youngest) of the three, is very clever.

9. She is (smarter/smartest) than the giant, and she tricks him and steals his gold.

10. After Molly tricks him, the giant keeps watch (more carefully/most carefully) than before.

11. He captures her when she returns to steal his ring, but she tricks him again, even (more cleverly/most cleverly) than the first time.

12. The folktale giant known (better/best) is Paul Bunyan, the legendary North American lumberjack.

13. Stories about Paul Bunyan's adventures on the frontier are the (more outrageous/most outrageous) tall tales I have ever heard.

14. According to legend, Bunyan cleared all the trees from North Dakota and South Dakota, and, even (more incredible/most incredible) than that, he created all five Great Lakes.

15. He dug the lakes to provide water for his blue ox, Babe, who was much (larger/largest) than any real ox.

Timeless Tales

Part 2

Write the correct form of the adjective or adverb in parentheses. (You may need to add *more* or *most*.)

16. Is Goldilocks the _____ **rudest** _____ character in any folktale? (rude)

17. She may be the _____ **clumsiest** _____ of all: she breaks the baby bear's chair. (clumsy)

18. She wants her porridge to be _____ **cooler** _____ than the father bear's porridge. (cool)

19. She wants her porridge to be _____ **hotter** _____ than the mother bear's porridge. (hot)

20. She eats all of the baby bear's porridge because she thinks it is the _____ **best** _____ of all. (good)

21. If I were a bear in a folktale, I would lock my cottage _____ **more carefully** _____ than those bears did! (carefully)

Part 3   Possible answers appear below. Accept all reasonable responses.

> Some adjectives are *absolute*: either they describe a thing or they do not. They cannot properly be put into the comparative form. For example, a plant is either dead or alive; it does not make sense to say "That plant is the *deadest*."

Read each of the sentences below. Think about the italicized adjectives. Decide whether putting that adjective in the comparative or superlative form in which it appears is logical and correct. If it is not logical and correct, rewrite the sentence so it gives accurate information.

22. Paul Bunyan is the *most unique* character in American folklore. **Paul Bunyan is the most unusual character in American folklore.**

23. Snow White's stepmother seems even *more wicked* than Cinderella's stepmother. _____

24. The clothes made for the emperor in Hans Christian Andersen's tale "The Emperor's New Clothes" are the *most invisible* clothes any emperor has ever worn. **The clothes made for the emperor in Hans Christian Andersen's tale "The Emperor's New Clothes" are the only invisible clothes any emperor has ever worn.**

25. "Rumpelstiltskin" is one of the *most difficult* fairy tale names to spell. _____

26. Goldilocks thought that the baby bear's bed was the *most perfect*. **Goldilocks thought that the baby bear's bed was best of all.**

Name _____

Read and Discover

I **will** (tell) you about Mother Goose.
She **might** (be) the best-known nursery rhyme character.

Circle the main verb in boldface in each sentence. Underline the auxiliary verb in boldface that works with each main verb.

An **auxiliary verb,** or **helping verb,** works with a main verb. Auxiliary verbs have a variety of purposes. Some auxiliary verbs, such as *could, should, might,* and *may,* show how likely it is that something will happen. Some auxiliary verbs, such as *did, is, will,* and *would,* indicate the tense of the main verb.

See Handbook Sections 18c, 18e

Part 1

Underline the auxiliary verb or verbs in each sentence.

1. No rhyme or story <u>has</u> ever <u>been</u> written about Mother Goose.

2. But for many years nursery rhyme collections <u>have</u> displayed the name of Mother Goose on their covers. Why?

3. Some scholars think Mother Goose <u>may</u> <u>have</u> <u>been</u> inspired by a real storyteller.

4. Some say the original Mother Goose <u>might</u> <u>have</u> been Queen Bertha of France.

5. This ancient queen <u>was</u> often called "Goose-Footed Bertha."

6. Others say Mother Goose <u>could</u> <u>have</u> been an American invention.

7. A woman named Elizabeth Goose, who lived in colonial Boston, <u>may</u> <u>have</u> collected stories in a book called *Mother Goose's Melodies.*

8. Nowadays most experts <u>do</u> not believe this explanation.

9. They say that if this were true, someone <u>would</u> <u>have</u> found the book by now, but no such book <u>has</u> ever <u>been</u> found.

10. Many say Mother Goose <u>did</u> not exist in real life; they say she is a made-up character.

11. No one <u>can</u> say for sure how Mother Goose began.

12. Even though she seems to be a fictitious character, she <u>has</u> had a consistent and recognizable appearance for generations.

13. Most illustrators <u>have</u> drawn Mother Goose as an old woman in a pointed hat.

14. In many pictures she <u>is</u> riding on a huge goose.

15. She <u>can</u> often be seen reading to a group of children, too.

We may never know if Mother Goose was a real person.

Timeless Tales

Part 2   Possible answers appear below. Accept all reasonable responses.

Complete each sentence with an auxiliary verb or verbs. Some sentences have more than one correct answer.

16.   The Mother Goose rhyme "Rock-a-Bye-Baby" _____**could**_____ have been inspired by a Native American custom.

17.   At one time, some Native Americans _____**would**_____ hang babies' cradles safely from trees.

18.   Some historians believe the rhyme's writer _____**may**_____ have been a pilgrim who came to North America on the *Mayflower*.

19.   This rhyme _____**may**_____ be the earliest poem written in English on the North American continent.

20.   The rhyme that mentions "four-and-twenty blackbirds baked in a pie" _____**was**_____ probably inspired by real-life recipes.

21.   Sixteenth-century chefs _____**would**_____ sometimes hide live birds in "pies" as an amusing surprise.

22.   "Little Miss Muffet" _____**was**_____ written in the 1500s by a scientist who studied spiders.

23.   Perhaps he _____**would**_____ be surprised to discover how long his poem has lasted.

24.   Many modern readers _____**may have**_____ been confused by the rhyme's reference to a "tuffet."

25.   That's because most people today _____**do**_____ not know that *tuffet* was a name for a three-legged stool.

26.   You _____**might**_____ be surprised to learn that *curds and whey* was a name for a type of custard.

27.   Some of our modern expressions _____**will**_____ probably sound just as odd to people in the future.

28.   If you want to learn more about Mother Goose rhymes, you _____**can**_____ read an annotated Mother Goose collection.

Part 3

Find eight helping verbs in the puzzle and circle them.

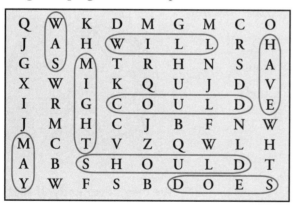

Now imagine how the story of "Little Miss Muffet" would have been different if Miss Muffet were not arachnophobic (afraid of spiders). On another sheet of paper, write two sentences about the story, using helping verbs you found in the puzzle.   **Answers will vary.**

Name _____

See Handbook Section 40

Diagraming Subject and Object Pronouns

You have learned how to diagram the simple subject and the direct object in a sentence.

Paul Bunyan liked fluffy **pancakes**.

Subject and object pronouns are placed in the same places in a sentence diagram as the nouns they stand for would be placed.

He liked **them**.

He | liked | them

Diagram these sentences. Refer to the models if you need help.

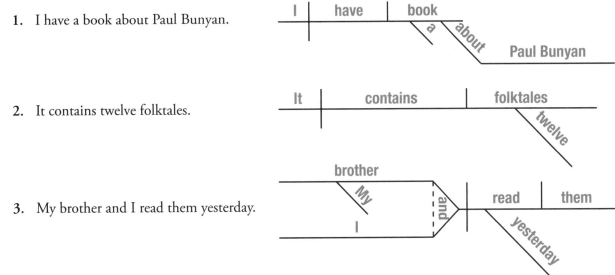

1. I have a book about Paul Bunyan.

2. It contains twelve folktales.

3. My brother and I read them yesterday.

Diagraming Adjective Clauses

You have learned that an adjective clause is a dependent clause that describes a noun or pronoun and begins with a relative pronoun such as *who, that,* or *which*. Notice the way an adjective clause is diagramed. In this sentence, the relative pronoun *that* is the direct object of the verb *found*.

The huge ox **that Paul Bunyan found** was blue.

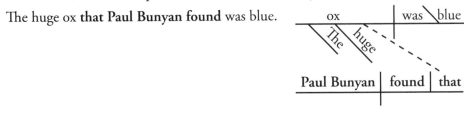

4. What sentence elements does the dashed slanted line connect? __**c.**__
   a. the two verbs in the sentence   b. the direct object and the relative pronoun *that*
          c. the relative pronoun *that* and the noun to which it refers

In this example, the relative pronoun *that* is the subject of the adjective clause.

An ox **that is blue** attracts attention.

ox | attracts | attention
An
that | is \ blue

Try diagraming these sentences. Be sure to decide whether the relative pronoun is the *subject* of the adjective clause or the *direct object* of its verb.

5. Babe had a body that resembled a blue mountain.

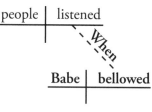

6. The strength that this ox possessed was tremendous.

Diagraming Adverb Clauses

You have learned that an adverb clause is a dependent clause that tells about a verb, an adjective, or an adverb and that an adverb clause often begins with a subordinating conjunction such as *although, because, when,* or *where.* Here's how to diagram a sentence that contains an adverb clause:

When Babe bellowed, people listened.

7. Where is the subordinating conjunction *when* placed in this diagram? __b.__
   a. on a slanted line below the simple subject
   b. on a slanted dotted line connecting the verb in the clause to the word the clause modifies
   c. on a slanted dotted line connecting two subjects

Diagram these sentences. Refer to the model if needed.

8. Although Babe was powerful, he obeyed Paul's commands.

9. Whenever Paul called, Babe appeared.

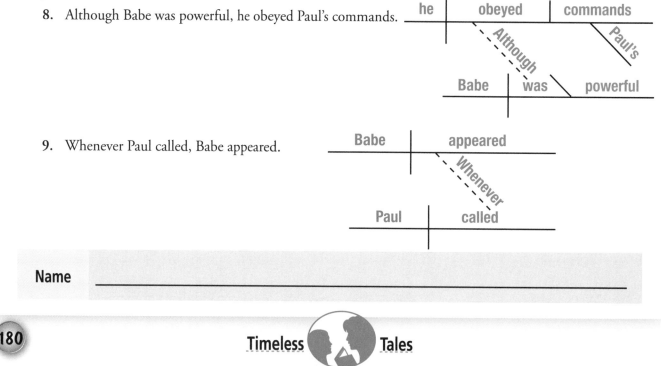

Name _____

Timeless Tales

Writing Sentences

These sentences need your help. Rewrite each one so that the subject and verb agree.

1. Nobody are sorry when the wolf falls into the soup pot as he is climbing down the chimney to eat the pigs.
   Nobody is sorry when the wolf falls into the soup pot as he is climbing down the chimney to eat the pigs.

2. Attitudes toward canine characters is more favorable in Native American tales than in European ones.
   Attitudes toward canine characters are more favorable in Native American tales than in European ones.

3. Thoughts of a wonderful new name makes Coyote drift off to sleep, however, and he ends up last of all.
   Thoughts of a wonderful new name make Coyote drift off to sleep, however, and he ends up last of all.

4. "The Three Little Pigs" are a good example of a European folktale with a villainous wolf. **"The Three Little Pigs" is a good example of a European folktale with a villainous wolf.**

5. When a fox or a wolf appear in a European fairy tale, that animal is usually the villain. **When a fox or a wolf appears in a European fairy tale, that animal is usually the villain.**

6. "Coyote Gets His Powers" tell how Coyote tries to stay awake all night in order to be first in line on the day all the animals are to be given names. **"Coyote Gets His Powers" tells how Coyote tries to stay awake all night in order to be first in line on the day all the animals are to be given names.**

7. In contrast, Native American folklore portray Coyote as a rascal, not a villain. **In contrast, Native American folklore portrays Coyote as a rascal, not a villain.**

A piece of writing comparing two characters may be divided into two paragraphs. The first paragraph describes how the characters are alike. The second paragraph might describe the characters' differences. Each paragraph should have a topic sentence stating its main idea. Notice this structure in this model.

　　At first glance, the character Sleeping Beauty and the character Beauty from "Beauty and the Beast" might seem to be very similar. Both are young and beautiful. Magic spells cause problems for both: Sleeping Beauty is put under a spell that makes her sleep endlessly, while Beauty meets a prince who has had a spell cast on him that makes him appear to be a monster. Also, both characters fall in love.

　　A closer look shows these characters to be very different, however. Sleeping Beauty is completely helpless. She must wait for someone else to break the spell she is under. In contrast, Beauty herself bravely breaks the spell that traps the Beast. While Sleeping Beauty falls in love at first sight with a handsome prince, Beauty falls in love slowly over time. She recognizes the inner goodness of the ugly Beast. She does not know until after she has fallen in love with him that the Beast is actually a handsome prince. Sleeping Beauty is weak and superficial; Beauty is brave and wise.

The sentences you repaired on page 181 can be reordered to make one paragraph describing differences between Coyote and Wolf. Decide which sentence is the topic sentence and which sentences are the supporting sentences. Reorder the sentences, and write the paragraph on the lines below.

> **Attitudes toward canine characters are more favorable in Native American tales than in European ones. When a fox or a wolf appears in a European fairy tale, that animal is usually the villain. "The Three Little Pigs" is a good example of a European folktale with a villainous wolf. Nobody is sorry when the wolf falls into the soup pot as he is climbing down the chimney to eat the pigs. In contrast, Native American folklore portrays Coyote as a rascal, not a villain. "Coyote Gets His Powers" tells how Coyote tries to stay awake all night in order to be first in line on the day all the animals are to be given names. Thoughts of a wonderful new name make Coyote drift off to sleep, however, and he ends up last of all.**

Write two paragraphs of your own in which you compare two folktale characters. In the first paragraph, tell how the characters are alike. Be sure to use a topic sentence and supporting examples. In the second paragraph, describe differences between the characters. Use the model paragraph on page 181 as a guide. Continue writing on a separate sheet of paper if you need more space.

Answers will vary.

_____

_____

_____

_____

_____

_____

_____

_____

Read your paragraphs again. Use this checklist to make sure they are complete and correct.

- ❏ My composition has a topic sentence.
- ❏ Each paragraph contains a topic sentence and supporting details.
- ❏ I have described both similarities and differences.

- ❏ The subject and verb in each sentence agree.
- ❏ My composition has a concluding sentence.

Name _____

Proofreading Practice

Read this passage about Hans Christian Andersen and find the mistakes. Use the proofreading marks below to show how each mistake should be fixed.

Proofreading Marks

Mark	Means	Example
℘	delete	Hans Christian Andersen's fairy tales are famous throughout the the world.
∧	add	Hans Christian Andersen's fairy tals are famous throughout the world.
≡	make into a capital letter	Hans Christian andersen's fairy tales are famous throughout the world.
∨	add apostrophe	Hans Christian Andersens fairy tales are famous throughout the world.
ⓢⓟ	fix spelling	Hans Christian Andersen's phary tales are famous throughout the world.
/	make into a lowercase letter	Hans Christian Andersen's fairy tales are Famous throughout the world.

A Master Storyteller

Before the invenshin of the printing press, Folklore were passed from generation to generation orally. Once the printing press made it possible for storys to be shared and preserved in print, writers began setting these tales down on paper. some writers proved to be most skillful storytellers than others. perhaps the more skillful of all was the Danish writer Hans Christian Andersen, whom took characters and plots from folktales and developed them into long, complecks storys.

Andersens lively tales is full of beautiful images noble characters and inspiring triumphs. It captures some of the best elements of the human spirit. Yet andersen's own life was filled with hardships and sadness. Born too poor parents in Odense, Denmark, Andersen lost his father when he was 11 years old. At the age of 14 he left home and moved to the capital, copenhagen, to try to make a life for him. After finishing school, Andersen began writing Poems, Plays, and Novels. He enjoyed some success, but life remained difficult. Hoping to add to his meager income, stories for children, which he called "trifles," were written. Them proved to be extremly poplar, but for a long time he considered these less importanter than his writings for adults.

Andersen eventually wrote and publish more than 160 tails for children. Many of his storys continues to be popular today, More than a century after his death. In fact, some is now been translated into more than one hundred languages.

Proofreading
Checklist

You can use the list below to help you find and fix mistakes in your own writing. Write the titles of your own stories or reports in the blanks at the top of the chart. Then use the questions to check your work. Make a check mark (✓) in each box after you have checked that item.

Answers will vary.

Titles

Proofreading Checklist for Unit 6

Have I used the correct subject and object pronouns?				
Have I made sure that all pronouns agree with their antecedents in number and gender?				
Does every verb agree with its subject?				
Have I avoided dangling modifiers?				

Also Remember . . .

Does each sentence begin with a capital letter?			
Have I spelled each word correctly?			
Have I used commas correctly?			

Your Own List

Use this space to write your own list of things to check in your writing.

Name

Timeless Tales

Review

Subject and Object Pronouns

Circle each boldfaced word that is a subject pronoun. Underline each boldfaced word that is an object pronoun.

1. **I** am doing a report on animal characters in folktales. **(51)**

2. Keesha is working with **me** on the report. **(51)**

3. **We** are going to act out some stories. **(51)**

Pronouns in Pairs

Circle the correct pronoun or pronouns in parentheses.

4. Keesha and (**I**/me) are going to act out the story of Coyote and Horned Toad. **(52)**

5. (Her and I/**She and I**) have made masks for our performance in the school folktale contest. **(52)**

6. I hope first prize will go to Keesha and (I/**me**). **(52)**

Antecedents

Underline the antecedent or antecedents of each boldfaced pronoun.

7. The story tells about an argument between <u>Coyote</u> and <u>Horned Toad</u> and explains why **they** don't like each other. **(53)**

8. Coyote gets mad at <u>Horned Toad</u> and swallows **him** whole. **(53)**

9. Trapped inside <u>Coyote</u>, Horned Toad begins kicking and scratching **him**. **(53)**

10. <u>Keesha</u> is playing Horned Toad, so **she** will hide behind me and pretend to be inside my stomach. **(53)**

Who and *Whom*

Write *who* or *whom* to complete each sentence correctly.

11. I made up my own folktale character, _____who_____ is a talkative squirrel named Slim. **(54)**

12. Slim tells predators _____who_____ plan to eat him long, boring stories. **(54)**

13. The animals to _____whom_____ Slim tells his stories fall asleep, and he gets away. **(54)**

Verbs

Circle the correct form of each verb in parentheses.

14. "The Bremen Town Musicians" (**is**/are) a terrific animal folktale. **(57)**

15. This story about four old animals (**makes**/make) me smile every time I read it. **(55)**

16. An old donkey no longer able to carry heavy loads (**goes**/go) off to make his fortune. **(55)**

17. He thinks he (**might**/has) be able to get a job as a musician in the town of Bremen. **(60)**

18. A dog, a cat, and a rooster (joins/**join**) the donkey along the road to Bremen. **(56)**

19. Nobody (**wants**/want) these animals anymore, so they must take care of themselves. **(57)**

20. Neither the donkey, nor the dog, nor the cat, nor the rooster (**sings**/sing) very well. **(56)**

21. But the group (makes/make) music that saves the day.   **(57)**

22. A gang of robbers (is/are) hiding out in a house in the forest along the way to Bremen.   **(57)**

23. All the animals sing together, and the robbers are convinced the racket (must/is) be made by a scary ghost. **(60)**

24. The sound of the animals (frightens/frighten) the robbers away, and the animal musicians live

happily ever after in the little house in the forest.   **(55)**

Dangling Modifiers

Underline the verbal phrase that begins each sentence. If the phrase is a dangling modifier, write *dangling* on the line. If the phrase is used correctly, circle the word it modifies and write *C* on the line.

25. <u>Traveling to Bremen</u>, the (animals) discover robbers hiding out in a little house. ____C____ **(58)**

26. <u>Crowing, barking, and making a big racket</u>, the robbers are driven out of the house. ___dangling___ **(58)**

27. <u>Relaxing and eating the robbers' food</u>, it is a perfect home. ___dangling___ **(58)**

Adjectives and Adverbs

Circle the correct form of the adjective or adverb in parentheses.

28. Those animals are the (noisier/noisiest) musicians I have ever heard.   **(59)**

29. The donkey sings even (worse/worst) than the cat.   **(59)**

30. The rooster is the (louder/loudest) singer of all.   **(59)**

Revising Sentences   Possible answers appear below. Accept all reasonable responses.

Rewrite each sentence so it is correct.

31. In the tale "bremen Town musicians," the dog the cat the rooster and the donkey makes an unusual entourage. __In the tale "Bremen Town Musicians," the dog, the cat, the rooster, and the donkey__ __make an unusual entourage.   (56)__

32. The four of them becomes friends in their quest for a happy life, and allies. __The four of them__ __become friends and allies in their quest for a happy life.   (55)__

33. A band of robbers are frightened by the terrible sounds of their music, who run away. __The terrible__ __sounds of their music frighten a band of robbers, who run away.   (55, 58)__

34. The story of how they outsmart the robbers prove that talent isn't everything. __The story of how__ __they outsmart the robbers proves that talent isn't everything.   (55)__

35. Coyotes, foxes, and wolves is all popular folktale characters. __Coyotes, foxes, and wolves are all__ __popular folktale characters.   (56)__

36. Wolfes in real life is smart, but they usually is the losers in Folktales. __Wolves in real life are smart,__ __but in folktales they usually are the losers.   (55)__

37. Kindness in folktales from most cultures, and cleverness generally wins out over greed. __Kindness and__ __cleverness generally win out over greed in folktales from most cultures.   (56)__

Name _____

Community Connection

In Unit 6 of *G.U.M.* students learned more about **grammar,** and they used what they learned to improve their own writing. The content of these lessons focuses on the theme **Folktale Characters.** As students completed the exercises, they learned about some traditional folktale characters from different parts of the world. These pages offer a variety of activities that reinforce skills and concepts presented in the unit. They also provide opportunities for students to make connections between the content of the lessons and the community at large.

The Storyteller's Craft

Invite a local storyteller to your class to share some of the stories he or she has collected over time. After the storyteller has finished, identify and evaluate different methods the storyteller used to help bring the stories to life for the listeners.

Sharing Stories

Many people who find it difficult to read for themselves enjoy listening to stories read aloud. Share your storytelling skills by volunteering as a reader at a nearby library, children's hospital, or nursing home. You may want to ask your listeners whether they liked each story you read and why. Use their responses to create a list of appropriate stories for that type of audience.

Community Tales

Talk to several people of different ages and cultural backgrounds about traditional folktales their families tell. Ask each person to tell one story to you. You may wish to tape-record the stories people tell and transcribe them (write them down) later. Use the stories to create a community folktale collection. Make notes that indicate the origin of each story you have collected, the name of the storyteller, and the date the story was recorded. Share the completed collection with your classmates. You may wish to donate your collection to the school library or to a public library in your community.

New Directions

Select one of the folktale characters you read about in Unit 6. Write an original tale in which that character plays the leading role. Adapt the setting so that the story takes place in the modern day in your own community. Make sure you follow all the rules of grammar you learned in Unit 6 when writing the story. Read the completed story aloud to your class or to a group of friends. You may want to submit it to a magazine or local newspaper for publication.

A Storied Event

Plan a storytelling festival for younger children in your school or community. Begin by making these decisions:

- Where and when will the festival be held?
- What stories will be included in the festival?
- Who will tell each story?
- What children will you invite to the festival?
- How will you announce the event?

Use the Storytelling Festival Planner on the following page to help you organize your ideas and plan the event.

Storytelling Festival Planner   Answers will vary.

When the festival will take place:

_____

Where it will take place:

_____

What stories will be included:

_____

_____

_____

_____

_____

Who will tell each story:

_____

_____

_____

_____

_____

Whom to invite to the festival:

_____

_____

_____

_____

How to advertise the event:

_____

_____

_____

_____

Things to bring (props, food, books):

_____

_____

_____

_____

Notes:

_____

_____

_____

_____

_____

Name _____

When tourists think about the (island) of <u>Jamaica</u>, most of them picture sun-drenched beaches and an aqua sea. Many people do not know that this [Caribbean] nation is home to a unique mix of cultures.

Circle the boldfaced word that names any body of land surrounded by water.
Underline the boldfaced word that names one specific island.
Draw a box around the boldfaced word that is an adjective.

A common noun names a person, place, thing, or idea. A **proper noun** names a specific person, place, thing, or idea. The important words in proper nouns are **capitalized**. **Proper adjectives** are descriptive words formed from proper nouns. They must be capitalized. A **title of respect,** such as *Mr.* or *Judge,* is used before a person's name. This title is also capitalized. The names of the months, the names of the days of the week, and the first word of every sentence are always capitalized.

See Handbook Sections 1, 15

Part 1

Draw three lines (≡) under each lowercase letter that should be capitalized. (1–35) Then circle each proper noun and draw a box around each proper adjective.

The (caribbean sea) is part of the (atlantic Ocean). Dozens of islands lie in the (Caribbean). (Trinidad) and (tobago) are two separate islands that form one country. (Haiti) and the (dominican republic) are two countries that share the same island. other [caribbean] island countries include (Jamaica), (barbados), (antigua), and (grenada).

The region's first inhabitants were the (Carib), (arawak), and (warahuns). in (october) 1492, (columbus) landed on an island in the (Caribbean) that he named (san salvador). During the decades that followed, [spanish] explorers established colonies on many of the islands. Most of the native peoples died as a result of diseases brought by the (europeans). Many others perished in wars waged against these invading colonial powers.

By 1750, the (English), (dutch), (swedish), and (french) had settled in parts of the (caribbean). (Barbados), (jamaica), and (haiti) became sugar plantation colonies. Sugar cane thrived in the fertile volcanic soil. Workers from (Africa) were forced into labor on the plantations. Laborers from (china) and (india) were also brought to the (Caribbean). In the 1800s, slavery was abolished in most [european] countries. During that century, the islands fought for their independence, one by one.

Today's [caribbean] islanders are the proud descendants of [Carib], [african], [European], [east indian], [middle Eastern], and [chinese] cultures. These cultures have combined to create a vibrant mix of traditions found nowhere else.

Great Getaways

Part 2

Draw three lines (⹀) under each lowercase letter that should be capitalized. Draw a line (/) through each capital letter that should be lowercase. (36–52)

The celebration of Carnival is perhaps the most famous caribbean festival. carnival has its roots in the traditions of african tribal celebrations and european religion. In some areas, Carnival takes place before easter. music, dancing, parades, and costumes are part of the celebration. In other areas, it is held in late Summer.

Paraders wear colorful and elaborate Costumes made of feathers, mirrors, animal horns, shells, and beads. Modern-day costumes might include beach balls, colored light bulbs, and headdresses shaped like satellite dishes. Traditional Characters such as moco jumbie, Midnight Robber, and Pitchy Patchy appear at Carnival festivals throughout the Caribbean. During Carnival, the sound of Steel Drums fills the air as dancers fill the street. The celebration continues nonstop for days and Nights. Carnival celebrations also occur in london, toronto, and New york City.

Part 3

> A character called "archy the cockroach" was created in the 1920s by American humorist Donald Robert Perry Marquis. The character archy was a very talented insect; he typed out wise sayings and poems by hopping from one key to another on Don Marquis's typewriter. With his method of typing, though, archy could not capitalize words because he could not use the shift key. He also could not punctuate sentences.

Read this passage by archy. Then rewrite it with correct capitalization and punctuation. Afterward, discuss with a partner the effect you think the absence of capitalization and punctuation has on the reader.

> i have noticed that when chickens quit quarreling over their food they often find that there is enough for all of them i wonder if it might not be the same with the human race
> —*archys life of mehitabel*
> random thoughts by archy

53. **I have noticed that when chickens quit quarreling over their food, they often find that there is**

enough for all of them. I wonder if it might not be the same with the human race.

—Archy's Life of Mehitabel

Random Thoughts by Archy

Name _____

Great Getaways

Dr. James L. Waihee, an expert on Hawaii, visited our class. Our teacher, Mr. Yamaguchi, invited him to speak about Hawaii and show us slides. Mr. Yamaguchi posted a sign that said: "Tues., Jan. 26—Dr. Waihee."

Underline a short way to write Doctor. *Draw a square around a short way to write* Mister. *Circle short ways to write* Tuesday *and* January. *Underline a letter that stands for a name.*

An **abbreviation** is a shortened form of a word. **Titles of respect** are usually abbreviated. So are words in **addresses,** such as *Street* (*St.*), *Avenue* (*Ave.*), and *Boulevard* (*Blvd.*). The names of **days,** the names of some **months,** and certain words in the names of **businesses** are often abbreviated in informal notes. These abbreviations begin with a capital letter and end with a period. An **initial** can replace a person's or a place's name. It is written as a capital letter followed by a period.

See Handbook Section 2

Part 1

Draw three lines (≡) under each lowercase letter that should be a capital letter. Draw a line (/) through each capital letter that should be a lowercase letter. Add periods where they are needed. (1–20)

Dr. James l. Waihee described the eight main islands of Hawaii. He discussed them in order from east to west. The largest Island is Hawaii, which is often called the *Big Island*.

West of Hawaii is a cluster of four islands. Maui, the largest of these, is called the *Valley Island* because much of its land lies in a fertile valley between two large volcanoes. Nearby is Molokai, called the *Friendly Island* because of the hospitality of its people. South of Molokai is Lanai, the *Pineapple Island*. Castle & Cooke, inc. grows and processes pineapples on Lanai. The Company owns 98 percent of the island. Kahoolawe, the smallest of the Main islands, is now dry, windy, and uninhabited. In the early part of the century it was used for raising cattle.

The island of Oahu, which lies to the northwest of the cluster of four islands, is sometimes called the *Gathering Place*. More than 75 percent of the state's people live there. Dr. Waihee said that his brother, mr. Merrill k. Waihee, lives on Oahu. He has a house on Ulukani st. in the Town of Kailua.

Because of its many colorful gardens and beautiful greenery, the island of Kauai is called the *Garden Island*. Mt. Waialeale, near the center of Kauai, is one of the world's rainiest places, with an average rainfall of 460 inches a year!

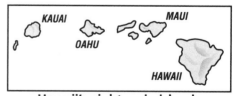

Hawaii's eight main islands

Niihau, the westernmost main island, is called the *Forbidden Island*. No one can visit Niihau without the permission of its owners, the Robinson Family. The Robinson family is descended from mrs. Elizabeth Sinclair, who bought the island in 1864. Most of Niihau's Residents are native Hawaiian people.

Great Getaways

Part 2

Rewrite each item below, using abbreviations and initials for the underlined words.

21. <u>Doctor</u> <u>Helen</u> <u>Marie</u> Kealoha   Dr. H.M. Kealoha

22. <u>Mount</u> Kaala   Mt. Kaala

23. <u>Mister</u> <u>David</u> <u>Glenn</u> Ariyoshi   Mr. D.G. Ariyoshi

24. <u>Mistress</u> Ellen <u>Claire</u> Takai   Mrs. Ellen C. Takai ⓞⓡ Miss Ellen C. Takai

25. 19 Lahaina <u>Street</u>   19 Lahaina St.

26. 212 Kalakaua <u>Avenue</u>   212 Kalakaua Ave.

27. The Koele <u>Company, Incorporated</u>   The Koele Co., Inc.

28. <u>Thursday, February</u> 14   Thurs., Feb. 14

29. 2222 Bradley <u>Boulevard</u>   2222 Bradley Blvd.

30. Haleakala <u>Drive</u>   Haleakala Dr.

31. <u>Monday, March</u> 22   Mon., Mar. 22

32. <u>Mistress</u> <u>Ellen</u> <u>Mae</u> Kanata   Mrs. E.M. Kanata ⓞⓡ Miss E.M. Kanata

33. Tropic Isles, <u>Incorporated</u>   Tropic Isles, Inc.

34. <u>Friday, October</u> 30   Fri., Oct. 30

35. The White Sands <u>Corporation</u>   The White Sands Corp.

36. <u>Wednesday, January</u> 20   Wed., Jan. 20

37. <u>Doctor</u> <u>Ralph</u> <u>Peter</u> Shuster   Dr. R.P. Shuster

Part 3

Use information from Part 1 to fill in the puzzle.

Across
1. The Gathering Place
6. The Valley Island
7. The Garden Island
8. The Pineapple Island

Down
2. The Big Island
3. Smallest main island
4. The Friendly Island
5. The Forbidden Island

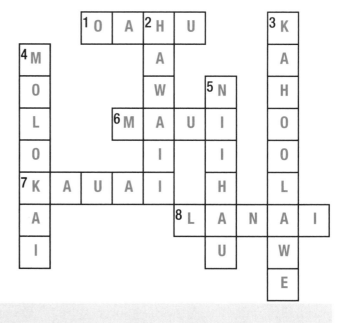

Name _____

Read and Discover

In class we saw a movie titled Hawaii: The 50th State. We also read a poem called "A Hawaiian Memory."

Circle the movie title. Draw a box around the title of the poem. How are they written differently? **The movie title is underlined. The title of the poem is in quotation marks.**

Underline the titles of books, magazines, newspapers and movies (or videos). These are written in italics in printed text. Use quotation marks around the titles of **songs, stories,** and **poems**. Capitalize the first word and the last word in titles. Capitalize all other words except articles, short prepositions, and coordinating conjunctions. Remember to capitalize short verbs, such as *is* and *are*.

See Handbook Section 3

Part 1

Draw three lines (≡) under each lowercase letter that should be a capital letter. Underline or add quotation marks to titles.

1. The state song of Hawaii is "hawaii ponoi," which means "Hawaii's Own."

2. Last night we watched a movie called the wettest place on Earth.

3. I just finished reading a book titled kings and queens of hawaii.

4. My sister can play a Hawaiian song called "the new hawaiian blues."

5. I learned a lot of Hawaiian words from a book titled you can speak hawaiian.

6. After visiting Hawaii, I wrote a poem called "aloha hawaii."

7. We watched a short movie in class called lanai: the pineapple island.

8. My mother is reading a book called the mystery of the sleeping volcano.

9. Last night she rented a musical comedy titled honolulu holiday.

10. She bought a travel book called from hawaii to maui in twenty days.

11. Bethany wrote a short story about Hawaii titled "the big hurricane."

12. She hopes that a magazine called the voice of hawaii will print her story.

13. She is working on another story titled "the sea turtles are gone."

14. I think a great title for a book about Hawaii would be the islands of sunshine and rain.

15. The poem "let's save the nene" is about Hawaii's state bird.

16. The video Habits of the hawaiian goose shows the nene in its natural environment.

17. Have you seen the movie islands of light?

18. The theme song for the movie is titled "rain song."

The nene, or Hawaiian goose, is Hawaii's state bird.

Part 2   Suggested answers appear below. Accept all reasonable responses.

Read the titles of the works on the library shelf and then answer each question by writing a complete sentence. Use correct capitalization and punctuation.

19. Which book probably contains information about Hawaii's natural environment? <u>Hawaii's Tropical</u> <u>Splendor</u> <u>tells about Hawaii's natural environment.</u>

20. Which book might give historical information about ancient Hawaii? <u>The History of Ancient</u> <u>Hawaii</u> <u>gives historical information about ancient Hawaii.</u>

21. Which book would likely be a good place to find traditional tales about Hawaii? <u>The book Legends</u> <u>of Hawaii</u> <u>has traditional tales about Hawaii.</u>

22. Which book would probably give information about surfing? <u>You can learn about surfing in The</u> <u>Waves Are Calling.</u>

23. Which movie might be a humorous mystery? <u>The Missing Pineapple Caper sounds funny.</u>

24. Which video would probably give information about Hawaiian history during the last fifty years? <u>Hawaii: 1958–2008</u> <u>tells about the last fifty years of Hawaiian history.</u>

25. Which video might show viewers how to make mango salsa? <u>The video Cooking with Tropical Fruit</u> <u>shows how to make mango salsa.</u>

26. Which book might inform visitors of the best places to go snorkeling? <u>Maui Snorkeling Guide</u> <u>names good places to go snorkeling.</u>

27. Which video probably describes the process of growing, harvesting, and shipping mangos? <u>The</u> <u>Mango: From Tree to Table</u> <u>tells all about mangos.</u>

Part 3   Answers will vary.

A famous Hollywood producer is interested in turning your book about Hawaii into a major motion picture. On another sheet of paper, write a paragraph to convince her to do so. Include the title of the book and create an exciting movie title. Use correct capitalization and punctuation.

Name _____

Read and Discover

Ellis Island in New York Harbor was the first stop for many of **America's** immigrants between 1892 and 1924. Those immigrants **couldn't** enter the United States until they had passed several inspections there.

Which boldfaced word shows possession or ownership? ____America's____
Which boldfaced word is a combination of two words? ____couldn't____

To form the possessive of a singular noun, add an apostrophe and s (*girl's shoe*). For plural nouns that end in *s*, add an apostrophe (*birds' nests*) to form the possessive. For plural nouns that do not end in *s*, add an apostrophe and s (*children's boots*). Apostrophes are also used in contractions, two words that have been shortened and combined.

See Handbook Sections 7, 26, 28, 30

Part 1

Underline the correct word in parentheses. If the answer is a possessive, write *possessive*. If the answer is a contraction, write the two words from which the contraction was made.

1. In the early nineteenth century, Samuel Ellis was the (island's/islands') owner. ____possessive____

2. The United States government bought the island from Mr. Ellis in 1808 but (did'nt/didn't) start using it as an immigrant station until 1892. ____did not____

3. More than 12 million people entered the United States through (Ellis Island's/Ellis Islands') elegant Main Building, which opened in 1900. ____possessive____

4. The dining room seated 1,200 people, but pleasing that many (wasn't/was'nt) easy. ____was not____

5. The dietary preferences of various (country's/countries') emigrants differed greatly. ____possessive____

6. The (immigrant's/immigrants') journeys by ship took weeks or months. ____possessive____

7. Some passengers (weren't/were'nt) in good health when they arrived in America. ____were not____

8. The (stations'/station's) Contagious Disease Hospital had eleven wards. ____possessive____

9. They were usually filled with immigrants who had contracted diseases in a (ships'/ship's) damp, crowded quarters. ____possessive____

10. Persons with infectious diseases (couldn't/couldnt') enter the United States. ____could not____

11. In addition to undergoing medical exams, newcomers had to answer immigration (inspector's/inspectors') questions. ____possessive____

12. Inspectors wanted to make sure applicants (wouldn't/would'nt) be a burden to society. ____would not____

13. The restrictions did not spoil (newcomer's/newcomers') dreams: only about two percent of all people processed at Ellis Island were refused admission to the United States. ____possessive____

14. Those who (didn't/did'nt) pass inspection were detained, often for weeks. ____did not____

15. Detainees stayed in big dormitories; (mens'/men's) and (women's/womens') areas were separate.
____possessive____   ____possessive____

Great Getaways

Part 2

Rewrite these sentences. Replace boldfaced words with possessives or contractions.

16. In 1924 the **passage of the immigrants** through Ellis Island started to decrease. In 1924 the immigrants' passage through Ellis Island started to decrease.

17. In 1954 the **buildings of the station** were closed completely. In 1954 the station's buildings were closed completely.

18. Sadly, the government **did not** maintain the elegant old buildings. Sadly, the government didn't maintain the elegant old buildings.

19. The historic structures **could not** withstand the damp, salty air, and they decayed. The historic structures couldn't withstand the damp, salty air, and they decayed.

20. In the 1980s, the National Park Service began major repairs on the **buildings of the island**. In the 1980s, the National Park Service began major repairs on the island's buildings.

21. Today Ellis Island is a museum honoring all **the immigrants of America**. Today Ellis Island is a museum honoring all of America's immigrants.

Part 3

> Writers sometimes use apostrophes to change the spellings of certain words to reflect the way the words are actually pronounced in informal speech. This technique is used quite often in representing a *dialect*, or regional speech pattern, in writing.

With a partner, read aloud this stanza of a poem about the famous explorer Sir Francis Drake. Circle the words for which the poet created new spellings, either by changing letters or by replacing letters with apostrophes, to make the words mirror the way they would have been spoken. Then, on another sheet of paper, write the words correctly. (22–44)

Drake he's in his hammock an' a thousand miles away,	and
(Capten, art tha sleepin' there below?)	Captain/thou/sleeping
Slung atween the round shot in Nombre Dios Bay,	between
An' dreamin' arl the time o' Plymouth Hoe.	And/dreaming/all/of
Yarnder lumes the Island, yarnder lie the ships,	Yonder/looms/yonder
Wi' sailor lads a-dancin' heel-an'-toe,	With/dancing/and
An' the shore-lights flashin', an' the night-tide dashin',	And/flashing/and/dashing
He see et arl so plainly as he saw et long ago.	sees/it/all/it

—Sir Henry Newbolt, from "Drake's Drum"

Name _____

a. Manhattan Island, the legend goes, was purchased by Dutch settlers in 1626.
b. The settlers paid a group of Native Americans cloth, beads, and small trinkets worth about $24.00.
c. Today Manhattan is the center of the teeming, bustling city known as New York.

Circle the commas in sentence a. Circle the commas in sentence b.
In which sentence do the commas separate three items in a series? **b.**
Circle the comma in sentence c. What kind of words does it separate? **adjectives**

A **series** is a sequence of three or more words, phrases, or clauses. A **comma** is used to **separate items in a series**. The last comma in a series goes before the conjunction (*and, or*). A comma is also used to separate **pairs of similar adjectives** (*teeming, bustling city*). To decide whether to put a comma between adjectives, read the sentence with the word *and* inserted between the adjectives. If the word *and* sounds natural, use a comma. Commas are also used to set off **appositives**.

See Handbook Sections 8, 16, 24

Part 1

Add commas where they are needed in these sentences.

1. New York City is a great center of culture, finance, entertainment, and trade.

2. Central Park, Times Square, and the Empire State Building are world famous.

3. These and other landmarks are on the busy, crowded island of Manhattan.

4. Manhattan is the smallest of New York City's five boroughs.

5. The other boroughs are the Bronx, Queens, Brooklyn, and Staten Island.

6. Ferries, tunnels, and bridges connect Manhattan to the other boroughs.

7. Many thousands of clerks, secretaries, executives, laborers, professionals, and job-seekers commute to Manhattan every day.

8. Some work in sunny, spacious offices high in the sky.

9. Others labor in dark, windowless rooms.

10. Manhattan is home to the Rockefeller Center, the New York Stock Exchange, and the United Nations headquarters.

The Empire State Building was once the world's tallest skyscraper.

11. Several of America's largest publishing companies and banks have headquarters there.

12. Harlem, a district in Manhattan, has been a center of African American business and culture for more than a century.

13. Duke Ellington, a suave, cosmopolitan bandleader, made his home in Harlem.

14. Many musicians, actors, and dancers come to New York City with high hopes.

15. Some seek experience, some want to study, and some hope to find work in the theater.

16. Only a few are able to achieve all their goals in this wealthy, worldly city.

17. Many others spend years on this glittering island chasing bright, elusive dreams.

Part 2

Suggested answers appear below. Accept all reasonable responses.

Rewrite each group of sentences as a single sentence. Use *and* or *or* to join the last two items in a series. Add commas where you need them.

18. New York's Greenwich Village is home to poets. Greenwich Village is home to artists. Many dancers live there, too. __New York's Greenwich Village is home to poets, artists, and dancers.__

19. Greenwich Village is known for its trendy boutiques. It is known for its charming restaurants and art galleries. __Greenwich Village is known for its trendy boutiques, charming restaurants, and art galleries.__

20. We could go shopping. We could see a play. We could visit the Museum of Modern Art. __We could go shopping, see a play, or visit the Museum of Modern Art.__

21. Central Park has a large skating pond. The pond is picturesque. __Central Park has a large, picturesque skating pond.__

22. Noisy subway trains whisk people from place to place on Manhattan Island. These subway trains are crowded. __Noisy, crowded subway trains whisk people from place to place on Manhattan Island.__

Part 3

Skillful public speakers often use items in a series to emphasize points they wish to make and to stir listeners' emotions. Read each quotation below. Circle the commas that set off items in a series. Then, with a partner, choose one quotation and explore its meaning.

…government of the people, by the people, for the people, shall not perish from the earth.
— Abraham Lincoln, from his address at Gettysburg

We shall not flag or fail. We shall go on to the end. We shall fight in France, we shall fight on the seas and oceans, we shall fight with growing confidence and growing strength in the air, we shall defend our island, whatever the cost may be, we shall fight on the beaches, we shall fight on the landing grounds, we shall fight in the fields and in the streets, we shall fight in the hills; we shall never surrender.
— Winston Churchill, from Speech on Dunkirk

Let every nation know, whether it wishes us well or ill, that we shall pay any price, bear any burden, meet any hardship, support any friend, oppose any foe to assure the survival and the success of liberty.
— John F. Kennedy, from Inaugural Address

Given what you know about each speaker quoted above, what would you say the three quotes have in common?

23. __Answers will vary but may include reference to defending and protecting democracy, independence, and liberty.__

Name _____

Great Getaways

"(Mariko), will you tell us about Japan?" Mrs. Harris asked.
"Yes, I'd be happy to, but I don't know where to start," she answered.

Circle the name of the person being spoken to in the first sentence.
What punctuation mark comes after it? __comma__

Draw a line under the word that introduces the second sentence.
What punctuation mark follows it? __comma__

Draw a box around the conjunction that joins the two parts of the second
sentence. What punctuation mark comes before it? __comma__

Commas tell a reader where to pause. A comma is used to separate an **introductory word,** such as *yes* or *well,* from the rest of a sentence. It is also used to separate **independent clauses** in a **compound sentence** and to separate a **noun of direct address** from the rest of a sentence. A noun of direct address names a person who is being spoken to.

See Handbook Sections 8, 13, 14, 23

Part 1

Add the missing comma to each sentence. Then decide why the comma is needed. Write *I* for introductory word, *C* for compound sentence, *D* for direct address, or *S* for items in a series.

1. "Well, Japan is made up of four large islands and thousands of smaller ones," Mariko began. __I__

2. "Honshu is the biggest island, and most of Japan's people live there." __C__

3. "Japan isn't one of the biggest countries in the world, but it is one of the most crowded," Raj added. __C__

4. "Yes, Japan has 11 cities with a population of over a million," Mariko said. __I__

5. "Mrs. Harris, is it true that Tokyo has 50 million people?" Raj asked. __D__

6. "No, that's an exaggeration. Tokyo has more than eight million people," she said with a smile. __I__

7. "Japan's cities are crowded, but even big cities have many peaceful gardens," Mariko continued. __C__

8. "Raj, would you hold up this picture?" she asked. __D__

9. "This traditional garden is hundreds of years old, and it's right in the middle of Tokyo!" she said. __C__

10. "Mrs. Harris, is it true that Japan has few natural resources?" Julie asked. __D__

11. "Yes, Japan must import most of the raw materials it uses in industry," she answered. __I__

12. "Nonetheless, Japan is one of the world's leading industrial nations," Mariko said. __I__

13. "Mariko, what does Japan export besides cars?" Mrs. Harris asked. __D__

14. "Well, optical equipment, electrical machinery, and other machines are made in quantity," she replied. __I__

15. "Julie, can you name Japan's other three major islands?" asked Mrs. Harris. __D__

16. "They are Hokkaido, Kyushu, and Sakhalin," replied Julie. __S__

17. "No, Sakhalin is not part of the nation of Japan," replied Mrs. Harris. __I__

18. "The correct answer is Shikoku, Hokkaido, and Kyushu," she continued. __S__

Part 2 Suggested answers appear below. Accept all reasonable responses.

Rewrite the sentences, adding the words in parentheses. Be sure to use commas correctly.

19. Is it true that raw fish is popular in Japan? (Mariko) __Mariko, is it true that raw fish is popular in Japan?__

20. Many people like sashimi. (yes) __Yes, many people like sashimi.__

21. I like sea urchin eggs. (but I also like hamburgers) __I like sea urchin eggs, but I also like hamburgers.__

22. Yellowfin tuna is delicious in sushi. (and shrimp is also excellent) __Yellowfin tuna is delicious in sushi, and shrimp is also excellent.__

23. The green paste in the little bowl is really hot! (wow) __Wow, the green paste in the little bowl is really hot!__

24. That paste is called *wasabi*. (Raj) __Raj, that paste is called wasabi.__ or __That paste is called wasabi, Raj.__

25. It's made from horseradish. (and it's traditionally served with sushi and sashimi) __It's made from horseradish, and it's traditionally served with sushi and sashimi.__

Part 3 Suggested answers appear below. Accept all reasonable responses.

An *interjection* is a word used to express strong or sudden feeling. Interjections are sometimes used as introductory words. (The word *wow*, which you have encountered in this lesson, is an interjection.) If an interjection is said with force or strong feeling, it is followed by an exclamation mark; if a sentence follows it, the first word of the sentence begins with a capital letter. If an interjection is not said with force or strong feeling, it is followed by a comma, and the word after the comma is not capitalized.

Choose an interjection from the word bank to complete each item. Add appropriate punctuation. Draw three lines (≡) under the first letter of any word that should be capitalized.

| Alas | Bravo | Eureka | Hooray | Ahoy | Ugh | Halt | Shh |

26. __Shh,__ the baby is asleep!
27. __Halt!__ this area is closed to the public!
28. __Ugh,__ this soup tastes terrible.
29. __Ahoy!__ who's in command of this ship?
30. __Bravo!__ what a magnificent performance!
31. __Alas,__ I'm afraid that book is no longer available.
32. __Eureka!__ we've struck gold!
33. __Hooray!__ we're all done!

Name _____

    a. The Galápagos Islands are located 600 miles west of Ecuador, they lie along the equator.
    b. These isolated islands are home to many unusual creatures: penguins, giant tortoises, and swimming iguanas are just a few of these.
    c. Scientists have studied Galápagos wildlife for centuries; they study not only the habits of certain species but also the interactions among them.

In which sentence are two independent clauses separated incorrectly with only a comma and no conjunction?   **a.**

What punctuation marks are used to separate the independent clauses in the other two sentences?   **:**   **;**

A **semicolon** (;) can be used instead of a comma and conjunction to separate the independent clauses in a **compound sentence**. A **colon** (:) can be used to separate two independent clauses when the second explains the first. It can also be used to introduce a list at the end of a sentence, to separate parts of references in a bibliography, and to separate hours and minutes in an expression of time.

See Handbook Sections 8, 13

Part 1

Write a colon or a semicolon to separate the clauses in each sentence. Note: Four sentences require a colon.

1. About five million years ago the Galápagos Islands rose from the sea; they are thought to be the result of volcanic explosions deep under the water.

2. These volcanic islands are barren and harsh; initially they were lifeless.

3. Scientists have a theory about how wildlife came to the Galápagos: creatures from South America rode there on "sea rafts" of vegetation.

4. These creatures were undisturbed for centuries; over time they adapted to the environment in unique ways.

5. The marine iguana is quite unusual: it swims in the rough surf.

6. Adult marine iguanas can dive forty feet; they can stay underwater for thirty minutes.

7. Hundreds of years ago pirates stopped in the Galápagos; some hid treasure there.

8. Whalers and seal hunters filled their ships with giant tortoises; they used them for food during long voyages.

9. The Spanish name for the tortoises is *galápagos*; the islands got their name from this word.

10. The tortoises are huge; they can weigh up to 600 pounds.

11. At one time there were 250,000 tortoises in the Galápagos; today there are fewer than 15,000.

12. Predators are responsible for much of this decrease: they have eaten tortoise eggs and killed adult tortoises.

13. Human beings have caused animal predation; we are now trying to protect the remaining tortoises.

14. Humans introduced dogs, pigs, and rats to the islands; these animals prey on the tortoises' eggs.

15. Scientists have taken action to save the tortoises from extinction: they have built a captive-breeding station.

Great   Getaways

Part 2   Possible answers appear below. Accept all reasonable responses.

Draw a line from each sentence on the left to a sentence on the right to make a compound sentence. Then rewrite each pair of sentences as one sentence. Use a semicolon or a colon to separate independent clauses.

Cormorants first flew to the Galápagos many centuries ago.

According to scientists, these birds' bodies changed over time.

Swimming became more important than flying.

Their feet became stronger, and their bodies became more streamlined.

In time, they lost their flying skills.

They adapted to island life.

16. **Cormorants first flew to the Galápagos many centuries ago; they adapted to island life.**

17. **According to scientists, these birds' bodies changed over time: their feet became stronger, and their bodies became more streamlined.**

18. **Swimming became more important than flying; in time, they lost their flying skills.**

Part 3

The colon has many uses in writing. Think about how the colon is used in these examples. Then draw a line from each example to the rule it matches.

RAMÓN: Look at that iguana!
CARLO: It's coming closer!

The game will begin at 7:15 P.M.

Remember the first rule of the Wildlife Observation Club: "Never touch a wild animal."

O'Dell, Scott. *Cruise of the Arctic Star*. Boston: Houghton Mifflin, 1973.

We saw fourteen iguanas: three adult males, six adult females, and five juveniles.

Use a colon to introduce a list or series at the end of a sentence.

Use a colon after the speaker's name in a play.

Use a colon to separate the place of publication and the name of the publisher in a book reference in a bibliography.

Use a colon to separate hours and minutes in an expression of time.

Use a colon to introduce a quotation.

Now write an example of your own to match each rule.

19. **Answers will vary.**

20.

21.

22.

23.

Name

Great Getaways

Read and Discover

a. Gibraltar (pronounced juh BRAHL ter) is not an island, but it is like an island in many ways. Gibraltar is on the southwestern tip of Spain. A barren strip of no-man's-land separates Gibraltar from Spain.

b. Gibraltar-pronounced-juh BRAHL ter is not an island, but it is like an island in many ways. Gibraltar is on the southwestern tip (of Spain). A barren strip of no man's land separates Gibraltar from Spain.

In which paragraph are parentheses ( ) correctly used to enclose information that explains a word in the sentence? __**a.**__ In which paragraph are hyphens correctly used to link words that form a compound word? __**a.**__

Hyphens and **parentheses** are used to make writing clearer. Use a **hyphen** to
- separate syllables in a word when you must break the word at the end of a line of text
- link the parts of some compound words, such as *no-man's-land*
- link some word pairs or groups of words that precede a noun and act as an adjective, such as *best-known attraction*
- link the parts of numbers (written as words) between twenty-one and ninety-nine.

Use **parentheses** to set off an explanation or example.

See Handbook Section 9

Part 1

Write *C* beside each sentence in which hyphens and parentheses are used correctly. Cross out hyphens and parentheses that are used incorrectly. If you are unsure whether a hyphen should be used to link parts of a compound word or adjective phrase, check a dictionary.

1. Gibraltar's inhabitants (who call themselves *Gibraltarians*) are citizens of Great Britain. __C__

2. The government of Spain believes that (because Gibraltar is physically attached to Spanish soil), it should be part of Spain. _____

3. In 1967 Gibraltarians were asked whether they wanted to become part of Spain; only forty-four people out of twelve thousand voted in favor of the idea. __C__

4. The Rock of Gibraltar is 1,398 feet (426 meters) tall; it rises almost vertically from the sea. __C__

5. The Rock is one of the (world's) most recognizable and visually-arresting-natural features. _____

6. The ancient Romans named the rock *ne plus ultra* (go "no more beyond" this point). __C__

7. The Moors (people from North Africa) captured Gibraltar from Spain in-the-700s. _____

8. Since then, this two-and-a-half-square-mile outcropping of land has undergone 14 sieges. __C__

9. In 1779 the Spanish and the French began a four-year siege. __C__

10. This attempt, which was unsuccessful, led to the expression ("safe as the Rock of Gibraltar"). _____

11. Gibraltar is also a real-life classroom for archaeologists. __C__

12. The Gorham Cave is more than 100 feet (30 meters) deep. __C__

13. Neanderthals (humanlike creatures who lived 100,000 years ago) (once inhabited the cave). _____

14. Speleologists (scientists who study caves) have been fascinated with it since its discovery in 1907. __C__

Great Getaways

Part 2

Add hyphens or parentheses where they belong.

15. Despite its rich and unique history, Gibraltar has a less-than-certain future.

16. Many residents are Anglophiles (people who love Britain and English things) who want to continue to live under British rule.

17. In 2002, Spain and Great Britain discussed sharing control over this cave-filled area.

18. To prevent this plan from becoming law, the people of Gibraltar held a referendum (a popular vote on an issue) in late 2002.

19. In an all-but-unanimous vote, the residents rejected joint control.

20. Gibraltarians (inhabitants of Gibraltar) remained under British rule.

Part 3

A dash is a punctuation mark used to signal a pause. A dash is longer than a hyphen. Think about how dashes are used in the sentences in the left-hand column. Then draw a line from each sentence to the rule it matches.

I'd like to visit Gorham Cave, but I—

Use a dash to stress a word or words at the end of a sentence.

The hike back up the Rock—all the guide books warn visitors about this—is exhausting.

Use dashes to set off a phrase or independent clause that interrupts an otherwise complete sentence.

I fear one thing more than anything else—heights.

Use a dash to mark an interrupted or unfinished sentence.

On the lines below, write your own example for each rule about the use of dashes.

21. _Answers will vary._ _____

_____

_____

22. _____

_____

_____

23. _____

_____

_____

Name _____

Read and Discover

Brigid asked, "Is Australia a continent or an island?"
Arthur explained that it is both.

Underline the sentence that shows a speaker's exact words. Circle the marks that begin and end this quotation. Circle the first letter of the quotation.

A **direct quotation** is a speaker's exact words. Use **quotation marks** at the beginning and end of a direct quotation. Use a comma to separate the speaker's exact words from the rest of the sentence. Begin a direct quotation with a capital letter. Add end punctuation (period, question mark, exclamation point, or comma in place of a period) before the last quotation mark. An **indirect quotation** is a retelling of a speaker's words. Do not use quotation marks when the words *that* or *whether* come before a speaker's words.

See Handbook Sections 4, 6

Part 1

Write *I* after each indirect quotation and *D* after each direct quotation. Then add quotation marks, commas, and end marks to direct quotations. Draw three lines (≡) under lowercase letters that should be capitalized.

1. "Australia is the smallest continent," said Arthur. __D__

2. Ms. Wetzel added that Australia is the only continent that is also a country. __I__

3. "look at Australia on the map," she said. __D__

4. She asked, "why do you think Australia is called *the land down under*?" __D__

5. "It's in the Southern Hemisphere," Ramón replied. __D__

6. Ms. Wetzel explained that many unusual creatures live in Australia. __I__

7. "Wallabies, wombats, and bandicoots are three you may have heard of," she said. __D__

8. Andre asked, "what's a wallaby?" __D__

9. Ramón explained that a wallaby is a marsupial similar to a kangaroo. __I__

10. He added, "the wombat is also a marsupial, but you might mistake it for a bear cub." __D__

11. "A bandicoot looks something like a rat," he continued. __D__

The platypus has a bill like a duck and fur like a beaver.

12. Ms. Wetzel said that the Australian emu is one of the world's largest birds. __I__

13. "I read that the platypus is a mammal that lays eggs," Randall said. __D__

14. "This ability makes the platypus unique among mammals," Ms. Wetzel replied. __D__

15. Randall asked whether any living animals are related to the platypus. __I__

16. "The platypus is a monotreme, a primitive mammal," said Ms. Wetzel, "and so is the echidna, a spiny anteater that lives in Australia, Tasmania, and New Guinea." __D__

Great Getaways

Part 2 Possible answers appear below. Accept all reasonable responses.

Rewrite each indirect quotation as a direct quotation. Rewrite each direct quotation as an indirect quotation. (There is more than one right way to do this.) Be sure to use punctuation marks correctly.

17. Ramón asked whether Australia was once used as a penal colony. _Ramón asked, "Was Australia once used as a penal colony?"_

18. Ms. Wetzel explained that for almost a century, large numbers of British convicts were sent to Australia to serve their prison sentences. _Ms. Wetzel explained, "For almost a century, large numbers of British convicts were sent to Australia to serve their prison sentences."_

19. Randall asked what the Australian outback is like. _Randall asked, "What is the Australian outback like?"_

20. Arthur said, "It's dry and mostly flat." _Arthur said that it's dry and mostly flat._

21. "Many children who live in the outback get their education via the Internet," he explained. _He explained that many children who live in the outback get their education via the Internet._

22. Brigid asked, "Who decided that Australia should be considered a continent?" _Brigid wondered who decided that Australia should be considered a continent._

23. Ms. Wetzel suggested that she do some research to find out. _Ms. Wetzel suggested, "Why don't you do some research to find out?"_

Part 3

Each clue describes an Australian animal. Write the answers in the puzzle. Use information in Part 1 or an encyclopedia if you need help.

Across
4. Small marsupial that resembles a rat
7. Large bird similar to an ostrich
8. Small marsupial similar to a kangaroo

Down
1. Mammal that hatches its young from eggs
2. Spiny anteater
3. Furry tree-dwelling marsupial
5. Wild dog (rhymes with *bingo*)
6. Marsupial that resembles a bear cub

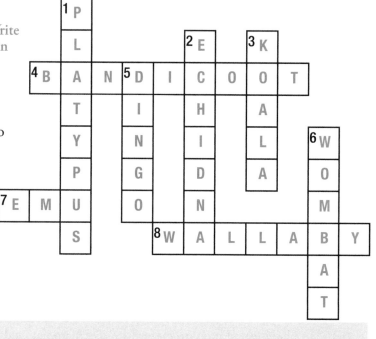

Name _____

Great Getaways

Coney Island Beach Chalet
Coney Island, New York 11235
August 15, 2008

(Dear Carmen,)

Today my cousins took me to the Boardwalk at Coney Island. Wow! There must have been fifty thousand people there! I rode the roller coaster, which is large and really scary. Aren't you proud of me? This used to be a real island, but the land was filled in to form a peninsula. Now Coney Island is part of Brooklyn, New York. I think it's a really neat place!

Your friend,
Rosie

There are five parts of this letter. Two have already been circled. Circle the other three.

A **friendly letter** has five parts: the **heading,** the **greeting,** the **body,** the **closing,** and the **signature**. A friendly letter may include informal language. A **business letter** is a formal letter written to an employer or a business. It has the same parts as a friendly letter, but it also includes the address of the person to whom the letter will be sent. Use a colon after the greeting in a business letter. An **e-mail** should also include five parts. Like a letter, it contains a greeting, a body, a closing, and your name. An e-mail header contains your **e-mail address,** the e-mail address of the person you are writing to, the date, and a **subject line**.

See Handbook Sections 2, 34, 35

Part 1

Use the appropriate boldfaced words in the rule box above to label the five parts of this friendly letter.

1. _____heading_____

425 Winters Street
Augusta, Georgia 30903
August 25, 2008

Dear Rosie, _____greeting_____ 2.

Our camping trip in Minnesota was really fun. We hiked thirty miles in two days. Have you ever hiked that far? I saw a moose and went trout fishing. I have plenty of great pictures to show you.

3. _____body_____

4. _____closing_____ Your friend,

5. _____signature_____ Carmen

Part 2

Rewrite this business letter correctly on the lines below. (Hint: The sender's address and the date go on the right. The business's, or receiver's, address goes on the left.)

<u>Brooklyn Gazette</u> 4005 Fifth Avenue New York, New York 10002 Dear Sir or Madam September 18, 2008 Please send me the September issue of your magazine. I am enclosing seven dollars to cover the cost of the issue and the mailing expense. Sincerely Arthur Aiken 6323 Rose Street Detroit, Michigan 48231

6323 Rose Street

Detroit, Michigan 48231

September 18, 2008

Brooklyn Gazette

4005 Fifth Avenue

New York, New York 10002

Dear Sir or Madam:

Please send me the September issue of your magazine. I am enclosing seven dollars to cover the cost of the issue and the mailing expense.

Sincerely,

Arthur Aiken

Part 3   Answers will vary.

See Handbook Section 37

Think of a place you would like to visit. (This could be an island, but it doesn't have to be.) Find the e-mail address of the chamber of commerce for that place or the e-mail address of a travel agent. On another sheet of paper write an e-mail to the chamber or the travel agent asking for information about the place you would like to visit. You may want to ask about travel options and costs, places to stay, sights to see, and special events. Be sure to use correct e-mail form.

Name _____

Great Getaways

See Handbook Section 40

Look at each model sentence diagram below. Then diagram the numbered sentences on another sheet of paper. Look back at the lessons on diagraming sentences if you need help, or see Handbook Section 40.

Diagraming Subjects, Verbs, Adjectives, Articles, and Direct Objects (pages 29–30)

A distant rumble filled the air.

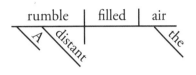

Answers appear on page T71.

1. The mountain belched black smoke.
2. Frightened residents left the area.
3. The eruption surprised scientists.

Diagraming Compound Subjects, Compound Predicates, and Compound Sentences (pages 59–60)

Goats and sheep pawed the ground and bleated.

Answers appear on page T71.

4. The mountain trembled and made loud noises.
5. An explosion rocked the village, and a strong odor filled the air.
6. Sulfur and other gases were released.

Diagraming Understood *You*, Possessive Pronouns, Demonstrative Pronouns, and Indefinite Pronouns (pages 89–90)

Cover your eyes!

Answers appear on page T72.

7. The villagers gathered their belongings.
8. Someone grabbed a flashlight.
9. That was a good idea!
10. Leave the village!

Diagraming Linking Verbs, Predicate Nouns, Predicate Adjectives, and Adverbs (pages 119–120)

Molten lava moves slowly.

The villagers were very courageous.

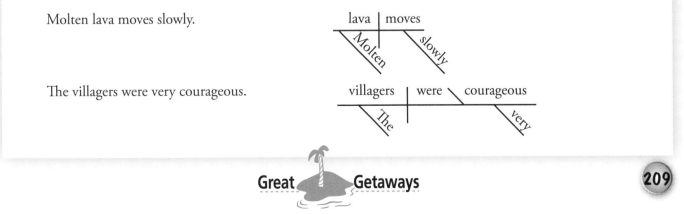

11. One woman quickly gathered the children.
12. The children were frightened, but most were quite brave.
13. A volcanic eruption is an awesome sight.

Answers appear on page T72.

Diagraming Prepositional Phrases, Indirect Objects, and *There* (pages 149–150)

There was one man with a small infant.

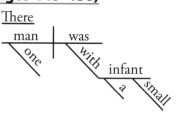

A woman handed her older son a camera.

Answers appear on page T72.

14. The boy put the camera in his pocket.
15. There was a family in a small truck.
16. They offered their neighbors a ride.
17. The driver drove quickly toward the highway.

Diagraming Subject and Object Pronouns, Adjective Clauses, and Adverb Clauses (pages 179–180)

Although some villagers feared the worst, everyone reached the safety of the distant hills.

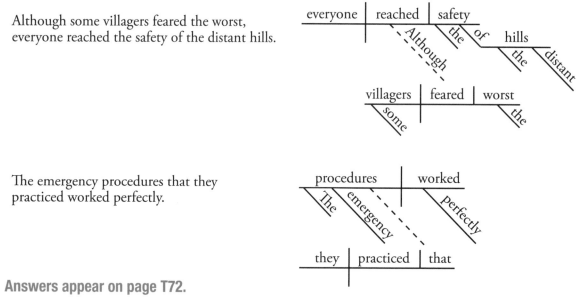

The emergency procedures that they practiced worked perfectly.

Answers appear on page T72.

18. Because a sudden rainstorm drenched the area, fires from the lava were quickly extinguished.
19. Ash that spewed from the mountain covered everything.
20. It blanketed trees and houses.

Name _____

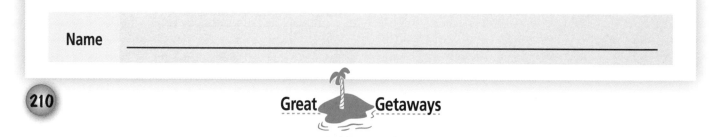

Great Getaways

Writing Sentences

Possible answers appear below. Accept all reasonable responses.
Rewrite each sentence so it makes sense. Make each one easier to understand by using correct punctuation and capitalization.

1. Nantucket is an island off the coast of Massachusetts: with an area of fifty seven square miles.
   Nantucket (with an area of fifty-seven square miles) is an island off the coast of Massachusetts.

2. She told me that "it's a Native American word meaning *faraway island*." She told me that it's a Native American word meaning faraway island.

3. Now I'm reading a book called nightbirds on Nantucket, by J R Aiken; I'll lend it to you as soon as I get home. Now I'm reading a book called Nightbirds on Nantucket by J.R. Aiken. I'll lend it to you as soon as I get home.

4. Visiting my aunt my uncle (and my cousins) in Nantucket, and I'm having a great time. I've been visiting my aunt, my uncle, and my cousins in Nantucket, and I'm having a great time.

5. I thought the island's name sounded interesting, I asked my aunt what does *Nantucket* mean? I thought the island's name sounded interesting, so I asked my aunt, "What does Nantucket mean?"

A friendly letter has a heading, greeting, body, closing, and signature. A well-written letter has a friendly tone, includes specific information, uses description to create pictures in the mind of its reader, and asks the reader questions to give him or her ideas for writing a letter in return. As you read the model letter below, notice the use of specific details and questions to the reader.

24 Coral Drive
Key Largo, Florida 33037
July 7, 2008

Dear Lin,

I can't believe it's already been a whole month since school let out! I've been having a good summer. For a few weeks I babysat the neighbors' three kids. It was hard work! I had fun taking them to the swimming pool, though. I even helped the youngest one learn how to swim.

Now I'm visiting my grandparents in Key Largo. It's one of the Florida Keys, a chain of little islands off the southern tip of Florida. Key Largo is famous because an old Humphrey Bogart movie called Key Largo was filmed there.

The best part of my vacation so far has been the glass-bottom boat ride we took over John Pennekamp Coral Reef State Park. Through the bottom of the boat we could see beautiful tropical fish and lots of scuba divers. I can see why Key Largo is called the Diving Capital of the World! I really want to take some scuba lessons while I'm here.

I hope your summer is going well. How do you like your job as a camp counselor? Please write back and tell me all about it!

Your friend,
Lakeesha

Writing a Paragraph

The sentences you revised on page 211 can be used as the body of a friendly letter. Decide what order the sentences should be in. Write them on the lines below. Then add a heading, greeting, closing, and signature.

Answers will vary. Accept all reasonable responses.

_____

_____

_____

_____

_____

_____

_____

_____

_____

_____

_____

Imagine that you have just spent five days on an island you've always wanted to visit. Write an e-mail to a friend back home. Include facts, descriptions, and questions. Make up e-mail addresses for you and your friend.

From: <your e-mail address> _____

To: <your friend's e-mail address> _____

Date: _____

Subject: _____

_____

_____

<closing> _____

<your name> _____

Reread your e-mail. Use this checklist to make sure your letter is complete and follows the correct form.

- ❏ Does my e-mail have all five parts?
- ❏ Have I punctuated the sentences correctly?
- ❏ Have I included specific information?
- ❏ Have I used abbreviations correctly?

- ❏ Have I capitalized proper nouns?
- ❏ Have I asked questions my reader will want to answer in a return e-mail?
- ❏ Have I used commas and semicolons correctly?

Name _____

Proofreading Practice

Read this passage about the island of Tahiti. Use the proofreading marks below to show how each mistake should be fixed.

Proofreading Marks

Mark	Means	Example
ℒ	delete	Papayas, coconuts, and and bananas grow on Tahiti.
∧	add	Papayas, coconuts, and bananas grow on Tahiti.
≡	make into a capital letter	papayas, coconuts, and bananas grow on Tahiti.
⊙	add a period	Papayas, coconuts, and bananas grow on Tahiti⊙
⋏	add a comma	Papayas⋏ coconuts, and bananas grow on Tahiti.
(sp)	fix spelling	Papayas, cocconuts, and bananas grow on Tahiti.
/	make into a lowercase letter	Papayas, Coconuts, and bananas grow on Tahiti.

A Paradise Island

For 200 years, the lush tropical, island of Tahiti has been a dream destination for those who wish to return to a simpler life. Tahiti was first settled by polynesians who arrived by see from Asia. In 1767, a british explorer named samuel wallis visited the Island and claimed it for Great britain. Wallis was'nt the only european explorer to take notice of this South Pacific jewel. The following year a french navagator, Louis Antoine Bougainville, claimed the island for france. Today Tahiti is a French overseas territorie.

tahiti gained fame as a tropicle paradise in the late 1800s. The french painter paul gaugin made the island his home in 1891 he lived there for most of his later life. Gaugins' powerfull paintings illustrate the lush beauty of the island. Gaugin wrote about his life in Tahiti in the book Noa Noa which was published in 1897. At least three notable writers have also spent time in Tahiti James Michener herman melville and Robert louis Stevenson.

Tahiti is 402 square miles (1,041 square kilometers) in size. The interior of the island is steep, rugged terrain covered by thick vegetation. Most of tahitis residents live in villages near the coast or in papeete (pah pee AY tee), it's largest city. Not surprisingly, the islands' cheif industry is Tourism.

Proofreading
Checklist

You can use the list below to help you find and fix mistakes in your own writing. Write the titles of your own stories or reports in the blanks at the top of the chart. Then use the questions to check your work. Make a check mark (✓) in each box after you have checked that item.

Answers will vary.

Titles

Proofreading Checklist for Unit 7

Have I capitalized proper nouns and proper adjectives?				
Have I used commas correctly to punctuate items in a series and after introductory words?				
Have I used apostrophes correctly in possessives and contractions?				
Have I used colons and semicolons correctly?				
Have I used hyphens and parentheses correctly?				
Have I punctuated direct quotations correctly?				

Also Remember . . .

Does each sentence begin with a capital letter?				
Have I spelled each word correctly?				
Have I used the correct end marks at the end of sentences?				

Your Own List

Use this space to write your own list of things to check in your writing.

Name _____

Great Getaways

Review

(Numbers in parentheses identify related lessons.)

Capitalization

Draw three lines (≡) under each letter that should be capitalized.

1. great britain is the largest european island. **(61)**

2. On this island are the countries of england, scotland, and wales. **(61)**

3. The full name of the british nation is the United kingdom of great Britain and northern Ireland. **(61)**

4. the head of britain's monarchy is queen elizabeth II. **(61)**

Initials, Abbreviations, and Titles

Draw three lines under each letter that should be capitalized. Add underlines, quotation marks, and periods where they are needed.

5. The game of golf may have been invented in scotland. **(61)**

6. The most famous golf courses in the world are in st. andrews, scotland. **(61, 62)**

7. I am reading a book titled golf for the enthusiastic beginner. **(63)**

8. It was written by Dr. p. j. gordon of Aberdeen, Scotland. **(61, 62)**

9. The movie Wuthering Heights takes place on the windy Scottish moors. **(63)**

10. One of Scotland's best-known artists is w. y. Macgregor. **(62)**

11. Robert burns is the national poet of Scotland; he wrote the poem "O My Luv's Like a Red, Red Rose."
    (61, 63)

Apostrophes

Underline the correct word in each pair. Write *C* if the word is a contraction or *P* if the word is a possessive.

12. (Londons'/London's) most famous museum is the British Museum. _P_ **(64)**

13. Some of the (worlds'/world's) most valuable artifacts are on display there. _P_ **(64)**

14. I (didn't/did'nt) know that in Britain, soccer is called *football*. _C_ **(64)**

15. (It's/Its) by far the most popular spectator sport in Britain. _C_ **(64)**

16. Professional football in Britain is no longer just a (mens'/men's) sport; women now play football professionally. _P_ **(64)**

Commas, Semicolons, and Colons

Add commas, semicolons, and colons where they are needed. (One item requires a colon.)

17. England, Scotland, Wales, and Northern Ireland are all part of Great Britain. **(65)**

18. The people of Northern Ireland are industrious and proud; some wish for freedom from British rule, but others want to remain part of Great Britain. **(67)**

19. Yes, conflicts continue to occur in Northern Ireland. **(66)**

20. Despite the violent actions of a few, there is hope for peace: large numbers of people on both sides of the issue want the children of Northern Ireland to grow up in a more peaceful world. **(67)**

Great Getaways

Hyphens and Parentheses

Add hyphens and parentheses where they are needed.

21. The Scottish *lochs* (lakes) are world famous. **(68)**

22. Loch Ness is the site of a real-life mystery. **(68)**

23. Dozens of people have claimed to have seen a dinosaur-like creature swimming in the lake. **(68)**

24. The monster is said to be as much as seventy-five feet (twenty-three meters) in length. **(68)**

Quotations

Write *D* after each direct quotation and *I* after each indirect quotation. Add quotation marks and other marks where they are needed. Draw three lines (≡) under each letter that should be capitalized.

25. "Have you ever visited Great Britain, Mr. Drake?" asked Roger. __D__ **(69)**

26. Mr. Drake answered, "yes, I toured England and Northern Ireland." __D__ **(69)**

27. Roger said that he would like to see the Scottish Highlands. __I__ **(69)**

28. Andrea exclaimed, "I'd like to see the Loch Ness monster!" __D__ **(69)**

29. Roger said, "bring a camera with you." __D__ **(69)**

Business Letter

Rewrite this business letter correctly on the blanks.

30. Dear Sir or Madam Island Marvels Travel Company 8835 Bison Avenue Omaha Nebraska 68005 Please send me some travel brochures about Great Britain. Sincerely yours, Lito Gaston 216 Cook **(70)** Street Grand Island Nebraska 68802 October 14, 2008

216 Cook Street

Grand Island, Nebraska 68802

October 14, 2008

Island Marvels Travel Company

8835 Bison Avenue

Omaha, Nebraska 68005

Dear Sir or Madam:

Please send me some travel brochures about Great Britain.

Sincerely yours,

Lito Gaston

Name

Great Getaways

Community Connection

In Unit 7 of *G.U.M.* students learned about **capitalization, punctuation, and other aspects of writing mechanics** and used what they learned to improve their writing. The content of these lessons focuses on the theme **Islands and Near-Islands**. As students completed the exercises, they learned about islands around the world and what makes each one distinctive. These pages offer a variety of activities that reinforce skills and concepts presented in the unit. They also provide opportunities for the student to make connections between the materials in the lessons and the community at large.

Friendly Skies

Have you ever wondered what it's like to work 30,000 feet above the ground? Invite a flight attendant who lives in your community to visit your class and describe his or her job. Before the visit, compile a list of questions to ask during the interview. You might want to find out about the training required to become a flight attendant, what responsibilities the job entails, or learn more about emergency procedures designed to keep airline passengers safe.

Passports

The United States requires its citizens to carry a passport when they are traveling to most international destinations. Find out about the process of obtaining a passport, the requirements for receiving a passport, the differences among the three kinds of passports issued in the United States, and the reasons why passports are required for international travel. Also find out which nations require American visitors to apply for a visa. Use what you learn to create a passport guide for potential travelers.

Careers on the Go

Find out more about careers related to travel and the tourist industry. You may want to explore one of these careers:

- travel agent
- cruise ship captain or navigator
- airline pilot
- wilderness guide
- hotel manager
- air tower control operator

Try to arrange an interview with a person in your community who is in the profession that interests you. Find out what the job is like and about the qualifications and training required. If possible, arrange to accompany that person on a tour of his or her workplace.

Hometown Attractions

Think about and list the things you think make your community an enjoyable place to visit. Then produce a brochure that advertises your community to potential visitors and helps them get the most out of a trip to your area. If you need any additional information to complete your brochure, contact the local tourist information center or the chamber of commerce.

Big Plans

Create an itinerary for a trip to any island in the world. You can obtain travel information about the island in travel books, at an embassy or consulate, at a travel agency, or on the Internet. When making your travel plans, consider these issues:

- when you will go on the trip and what the weather will be like during that season
- how you will get to your destination and the cost of the airfare or boat ticket
- where you will stay and the cost of lodging
- how much money you will need for expenses and in what form you will bring it
- what travel documents (such as a passport or visa) you will need
- what inoculations (if any) you will need to remain healthy in this part of the world
- what you will pack

Use the planner below to help you organize the information you find.

Island Trip Planner   Answers will vary.

Destination: _____

Numbers to call for information:

_____

_____

Travel documents needed:

_____

_____

Transportation/travel dates:

Departure _____

Arrival _____

Departure _____

Arrival _____

Cost of transportation:

_____

_____

Additional costs:

_____

What to pack:

_____ _____ _____ _____

_____ _____ _____ _____

Inoculations needed:

_____

Expected weather:

_____

_____

Lodging/dates needed:

_____

_____

_____

_____

Cost of lodging:

_____

_____

Name _____

Great Getaways

Appendix Table of Contents

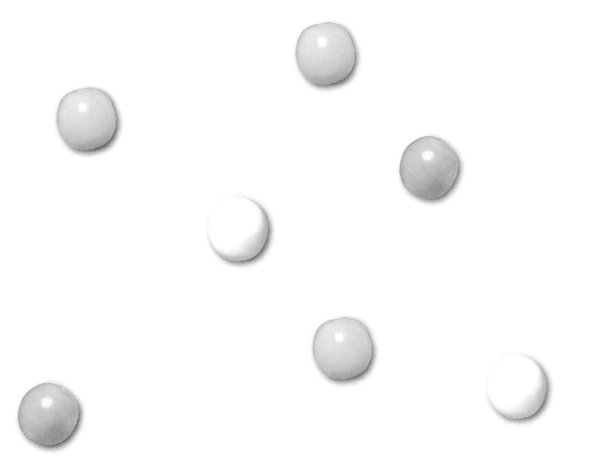

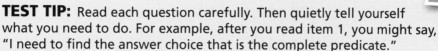

TEST TIP: Read each question carefully. Then quietly tell yourself what you need to do. For example, after you read item 1, you might say, "I need to find the answer choice that is the complete predicate."

(Numbers in parentheses identify related lessons.)

Read each item carefully. Select the best answer and fill in the circle on the answer sheet below.

1. Read this sentence.

   The ruins of the ancient city of Machu Picchu attract many visitors to Peru each year.

   What is the complete predicate of the sentence? (1)

   A   the ruins of the ancient city of Machu Picchu
   B   the ancient city of Machu Picchu
   C   attract many visitors
   D   attract many visitors to Peru each year

2. Read this sentence.

   A wall of stones surrounds this city in the clouds.

   What are the simple subject and the simple predicate of the sentence? (2)

   A   wall; stones
   B   wall; surrounds
   C   stones; surrounds
   D   surrounds; city

3. **Which of the following sentences has a compound subject?** (3)

   A   People of the Inca empire began the construction of Machu Picchu about 600 years ago.
   B   They built palaces for royal family members, and houses for workers and servants.
   C   Farmers and weavers produced goods for the royalty.
   D   The combination of steep cliffs and remote location protected the city from invaders.

4. Read this sentence.

   The ancient Inca built roads through the mountains and bridges across rivers.

   Which nouns are the direct objects in this sentence? (4)

   A   roads, mountains
   B   mountains, bridges
   C   roads, bridges
   D   bridges, rivers

5. Read this sentence.

   The high altitude of Machu Picchu can give visitors headaches for days.

   What is the indirect object of this sentence? (5)

   A   Machu Picchu
   B   visitors
   C   headaches
   D   days

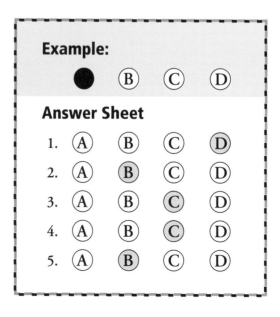

Example:

● Ⓑ Ⓒ Ⓓ

Answer Sheet

1. Ⓐ Ⓑ Ⓒ Ⓓ
2. Ⓐ Ⓑ Ⓒ Ⓓ
3. Ⓐ Ⓑ Ⓒ Ⓓ
4. Ⓐ Ⓑ Ⓒ Ⓓ
5. Ⓐ Ⓑ Ⓒ Ⓓ

Read each item carefully. Select the best answer and fill in the circle on the answer sheet below.

6. **Read the sentences.**

   The Inca empire was large and powerful at its height. Its fine system of roads was a key to the control of other Andes peoples.

   Which statement tells about the sentences? (6)

   A Both sentences contain predicate nouns. The first sentence contains a compound predicate noun.
   B Both sentences contain predicate adjectives. The first sentence contains a compound predicate adjective.
   C The first sentence contains a compound predicate noun. The second contains a predicate adjective.
   D The first sentence contains a compound predicate adjective. The second contains a predicate noun.

7. **Which sentence has a prepositional phrase underlined?** (7)

   A The Inca <u>did not use</u> wheeled vehicles.
   B They did not <u>write and solve</u> mathematical problems.
   C They did not <u>develop a written language</u>.
   D Nevertheless, the Inca ruled the largest empire <u>in the pre-Columbian Americas</u>.

8. **Read this sentence.**

   Inca buildings of carved stone have withstood earthquakes for five centuries and remain intact today.

   Which group of words is an adjectival prepositional phrase? (8)

   A of carved stone
   B have withstood earthquakes
   C for five centuries
   D remain intact today

9. **Read this sentence.**

   Teams of stone haulers moved blocks of tremendous weight to construction sites.

   Which group of words is an adverbial prepositional phrase? (9)

   A of stone haulers
   B moved blocks
   C of tremendous weight
   D to construction sites

10. **Which sentence has an appositive underlined?** (10)

    A Teams of stone haulers may have included 250 people <u>or more</u>.
    B A cobblestone road, <u>a path with a surface of small rocks</u>, made movement easier.
    C A carved rock <u>of 15 tons</u> could have been moved along a cobblestone path by a large team.
    D Carefully, <u>in a short period of time</u>, the Inca built hundreds of structures with huge stone blocks.

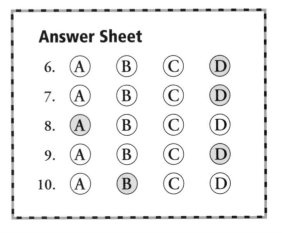

Answer Sheet

6. (A) (B) (C) **(D)**
7. (A) (B) (C) **(D)**
8. **(A)** (B) (C) (D)
9. (A) (B) (C) **(D)**
10. (A) **(B)** (C) (D)

Name _____

Read each item carefully. Select the best answer and fill in the circle on the answer sheet below.

11. **Read this sentence.**

    Ancient settlements of the Anasazi
    peoples fascinate both researchers and
    tourists.

    What is the complete predicate of the sentence? (1)

    A   ancient settlements of the Anasazi peoples
    B   of the Anasazi peoples fascinate both
        researchers and tourists
    C   fascinate both researchers and tourists
    D   both researchers and tourists

12. **Read this sentence.**

    Visitors to Mesa Verde National Park see
    remarkable cliff dwellings.

    What are the simple subject and the simple predicate of the sentence?   (2)

    A   visitors; see
    B   Mesa Verde National Park; see
    C   see; remarkable
    D   Mesa Verde National Park; dwellings

13. **Which of the following sentences has a compound subject?   (3)**

    A   Tall mesas are separated by narrow
        canyons in Mesa Verde.
    B   The first group of settlers established
        homes and farms on these flat-topped hills
        about A.D. 600.
    C   These first residents built underground
        homes and raised beans and grain.
    D   Roots, nuts, berries, and wild game were also
        important foods.

14. **Read this sentence.**

    The settlers on the mesas built dams
    and reservoirs for water collection
    and storage.

    Which nouns are the direct objects in this sentence?   (4)

    A   settlers, mesas
    B   dams, reservoirs
    C   reservoirs, water
    D   collection, storage

15. **Read this sentence.**

    Late summer rainstorms brought
    Anasazi farmers water every year.

    What is the indirect object of this sentence?   (5)

    A   summer
    B   farmers
    C   water
    D   year

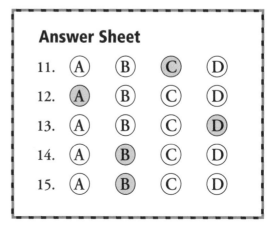

Answer Sheet

11. (A) (B) ●C (D)
12. ●A (B) (C) (D)
13. (A) (B) (C) ●D
14. (A) ●B (C) (D)
15. (A) ●B (C) (D)

223

Read each item carefully. Select the best answer and fill in the circle on the answer sheet below.

16. **Read these sentences.**

By A.D. 800 the Anasazi villages looked impressive and quite different from the first settlements. Houses were small aboveground structures.

Which statement tells about the sentences? (6)

A Both sentences contain predicate nouns. The first sentence contains a compound predicate noun.
B Both sentences contain predicate adjectives. The first sentence contains a compound predicate adjective.
C The first sentence contains a compound predicate noun. The second contains a predicate adjective.
D The first sentence contains a compound predicate adjective. The second contains a predicate noun.

17. **Which sentence has a prepositional phrase underlined?** (7)

A The bow and arrow had <u>replaced the spear</u> as a hunting device.
B Farmers now planted <u>squash, corn, and melons</u>.
C Farmers kept dogs <u>as lookouts</u>.
D Dogs typically bark furiously when they sense human <u>or animal intruders</u>.

18. **Read this sentence.**

In time, the Anasazi homes atop the mesas became taller and grander.

Which group of words is an adjectival prepositional phrase? (8)

A in time
B the Anasazi homes
C atop the mesas
D became taller and grander

19. **Read this sentence.**

Later, some kind of grave difficulty caused dramatic changes in these Anasazi communities.

Which group of words is an adverbial prepositional phrase? (9)

A later, some kind
B of grave difficulty
C caused dramatic changes
D in these Anasazi communities

20. **Which sentence has an appositive underlined?** (10)

A The villagers deserted the mesas and built new homes <u>on the steep canyon walls</u>.
B Perhaps winter weather atop the mesas <u>had become too cold</u>.
C Perhaps drought, <u>a lack of rainfall</u>, had made farming atop the mesas difficult.
D Most likely, <u>enemies had threatened</u>, and the Anasazi built the cliff dwellings as a refuge.

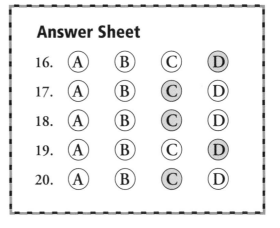

Answer Sheet

16. Ⓐ Ⓑ Ⓒ **Ⓓ**
17. Ⓐ Ⓑ **Ⓒ** Ⓓ
18. Ⓐ Ⓑ **Ⓒ** Ⓓ
19. Ⓐ Ⓑ Ⓒ **Ⓓ**
20. Ⓐ Ⓑ **Ⓒ** Ⓓ

Name _____

(Numbers in parentheses identify related lessons.)

Read each item carefully. Select the best answer and fill in the circle on the answer sheet below.

1. **Read this sentence.**

   Show me how to dig for clams.

   What type of sentence is it? (11)

   A   declarative
   B   interrogative
   C   imperative
   D   exclamatory

2. **Which of the following sentences is a compound sentence?** (12)

   A   Sea dragons live in the ocean near Australia; they are a type of sea horse.
   B   The leafy sea dragon has greenish flaps of flesh that grow out from its body.
   C   If you saw a leafy sea dragon, you might think it was dragging along pieces of seaweed.
   D   These creatures hide in clumps of seaweed and use their disguise to sneak up on prey.

3. **Read this sentence.**

   Individual humpback whales are easy to identify because each one has distinctive body marks and pigmentation.

   What types of clauses are in this sentence? (13)

   A   The first is an independent clause; the second is dependent.
   B   The first is a dependent clause; the second is independent.
   C   Both are dependent clauses.
   D   Both are independent clauses.

4. **Which of the following is a complex sentence?** (14)

   A   Have you had a chance to visit the National Aquarium in Baltimore?
   B   When you visit, you should spend time in the center of the Atlantic reef ring tank.
   C   You will be surrounded by fish, and you can watch them swim.
   D   Another interesting sight is the 63-foot-long skeleton of a humpback whale.

5. **Which sentence has an adjective clause underlined?** (15)

   A   The orca is a large marine mammal <u>with a huge appetite</u>.
   B   Another name <u>for this creature</u> is the killer whale.
   C   An adult orca may be 25 feet long <u>and weigh seven tons</u>.
   D   One orca <u>that is in captivity</u> eats more than 200 pounds of fish a day.

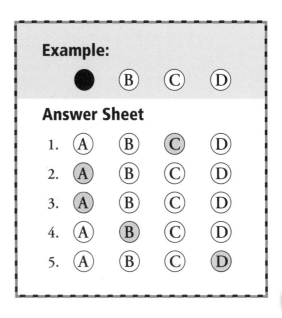

Example:

● Ⓑ Ⓒ Ⓓ

Answer Sheet

1. Ⓐ Ⓑ Ⓒ Ⓓ
2. Ⓐ Ⓑ Ⓒ Ⓓ
3. Ⓐ Ⓑ Ⓒ Ⓓ
4. Ⓐ Ⓑ Ⓒ Ⓓ
5. Ⓐ Ⓑ Ⓒ Ⓓ

Read each item carefully. Select the best answer and fill in the circle on the answer sheet below.

6. Which sentence has an adverb clause underlined? (16)

    A Orcas perform <u>at some wildlife theme parks</u>.
    B Trainers teach them <u>to perform stunts in a sequence</u>.
    C <u>When an orca performs its stunts well</u>, the trainer gives it food.
    D Many people <u>who work with orcas</u> consider them very intelligent.

7. Which sentence has an infinitive phrase underlined? (17)

    A Many orcas in captivity appear <u>to enjoy contact with humans</u>.
    B An orca may give a trainer <u>a ride on its back</u>.
    C One orca plays hide-and-seek with its trainer, <u>who looks through windows in the tank</u>.
    D Orcas respond <u>to eye contact with humans</u>.

8. Read this sentence.

    The creature staring at us from the tank is a giant Pacific octopus.

    Which of these phrases is a participial phrase in the sentence? (18)

    A the creature
    B from the tank
    C staring at us
    D a giant Pacific octopus

9. Which of these sentences has a gerund phrase underlined? (19)

    A Octopuses are invertebrates, <u>but they have eyes like vertebrates</u>.
    B The red Pacific octopus is <u>the largest</u> of all octopuses.
    C <u>Seeing its 15-foot-long arms</u> can be frightening.
    D An octopus <u>encountering an enemy</u> may eject an inky fluid to help itself escape.

10. Which of the following sentences is written correctly? (20)

    A Deep sea fishing, the most exciting type of fishing.
    B For me, the beach is the best place to have fun.
    C I dig for clams, I also collect mussels in rocky areas.
    D My uncle catches crabs in the winter months, and sometimes he takes me with him, and I help him set the traps and also haul them in, and I know how to be careful on the boat so I don't slip and go overboard.

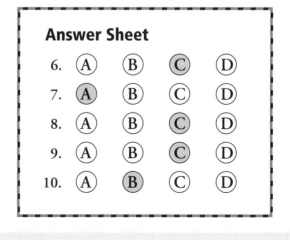

Answer Sheet

6. (A) (B) (C) (D)
7. (A) (B) (C) (D)
8. (A) (B) (C) (D)
9. (A) (B) (C) (D)
10. (A) (B) (C) (D)

Read each item carefully. Select the best answer and fill in the circle on the answer sheet below.

11. **Read this sentence.**

    What a huge creature that giant clam is!

    What type of sentence is it? **(11)**

    A declarative
    B interrogative
    C imperative
    D exclamatory

12. **Which of the following sentences is a compound sentence?** **(12)**

    A If you saw a thornback ray from the bottom, you might think you were in a science fiction movie.
    B This flat, broad fish is an eerie silver color, with shades of rose and blue.
    C You would see a yellow mouth and two dark, scary eyes.
    D Those "eyes" are actually nostrils; the thornback ray's real eyes are on its top side.

13. **Read this sentence.**

    When fiddler crabs tear leaves into tiny bits, they create an important element in the web of life in a red mangrove swamp.

    What types of clauses are in this sentence? **(13)**

    A The first is an independent clause; the second is dependent.
    B The first is a dependent clause; the second is independent.
    C Both are dependent clauses.
    D Both are independent clauses.

14. **Which of the following is a complex sentence?** **(14)**

    A My friend Ricardo did not like aquariums until he visited one.
    B He loved the tidepool exhibits, and the shark tank left him speechless.
    C Watching the otters crack open shellfish delighted him.
    D He was wise to visit on a weekday; the aquarium was not too crowded.

15. **Which sentence has an adjective clause underlined?** **(15)**

    A Humpback whales live in oceans throughout the world.
    B In summer they swim in deep, cold waters that teem with small fish and crustaceans.
    C In winter they live in warm tropical waters, and they breed there.
    D An adult humpback whale can be fifty feet long and weigh fifty tons.

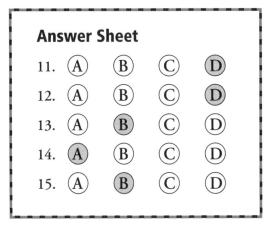

Answer Sheet

11.	Ⓐ	Ⓑ	Ⓒ	**Ⓓ**
12.	Ⓐ	Ⓑ	Ⓒ	**Ⓓ**
13.	Ⓐ	**Ⓑ**	Ⓒ	Ⓓ
14.	**Ⓐ**	Ⓑ	Ⓒ	Ⓓ
15.	Ⓐ	**Ⓑ**	Ⓒ	Ⓓ

Read each item carefully. Select the best answer and fill in the circle on the answer sheet below.

16. **Which sentence has an adverb clause underlined?** (16)

A Humpback whales produce <u>lengthy, varied songs</u>.

B The high notes sound like whistles, <u>and the low notes sound like rumbles</u>.

C <u>Although the songs are sung throughout the year</u>, they are sung most frequently in mating season.

D Whales <u>that are alone</u> sing these songs the most.

17. **Which sentence has an infinitive phrase underlined?** (17)

A Most humpbacks in the North Pacific swim <u>to Hawaii</u> in late fall.

B <u>Swimming in the warm water there</u>, they breed and care for their young.

C These huge creatures eat little or nothing <u>while in this region</u>.

D In late spring they return to cold ocean waters <u>to feed</u>.

18. **Read this sentence.**

Some tourists cruising through southeast Alaska are thrilled to see Steller's sea lions on rocky outcrops.

Which of these phrases is a participial phrase in the sentence? (18)

A cruising through southeast Alaska

B are thrilled

C to see Steller's sea lions

D on rocky outcrops

19. **Which of these sentences has a gerund phrase underlined?** (19)

A <u>Unlike some other sea lions</u>, Steller's sea lions avoid human beings.

B Some Steller's sea lions are permanent residents of <u>protected waters</u>.

C Many others move <u>between these waters and the open ocean</u>.

D <u>Photographing these marine mammals</u> may be easiest in late September.

20. **Which of the following sentences is written correctly?** (20)

A I am fascinated by sea creatures of all kinds, and I love to swim, and I have never gotten seasick, and my friends are scared of things like giant clams, but I'm not, and I hope to study them someday.

B My goal is to become a scuba diver.

C I have taken lessons in a pool, soon I will make my first ocean dive.

D If I ever get a chance to swim with a sea turtle!

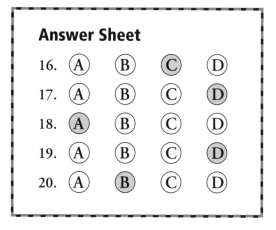

Answer Sheet

16. Ⓐ Ⓑ Ⓒ Ⓓ
17. Ⓐ Ⓑ Ⓒ Ⓓ
18. Ⓐ Ⓑ Ⓒ Ⓓ
19. Ⓐ Ⓑ Ⓒ Ⓓ
20. Ⓐ Ⓑ Ⓒ Ⓓ

Name _____

TEST TIP: Eliminate answer choices that you know are incorrect.

Standardized Test Format

(Numbers in parentheses identify related lessons.)

Read each item carefully. Select the best answer and fill in the circle on the answer sheet below.

1. Read this sentence.

   Charles Steinmetz helped the young General Electric Company become a success.

   Which of these choices is a common noun in this sentence? (21)

   A Charles Steinmetz
   B young
   C General Electric Company
   D success

2. Read this sentence.

   Steinmetz, a brilliant engineer, solved many problems having to do with electrical circuits.

   Which of these words is a singular noun in this sentence? (22)

   A engineer
   B problems
   C electrical
   D circuits

3. Read this sentence.

   This _____ spine was abnormally curved, but he did not let this disability affect his career.

   Which of these words would properly complete the sentence? (23)

   A genius'
   B genius's
   C geniuses'
   D geniuses's

4. Read this sentence.

   Helen Keller was born with sight and hearing, but <u>she</u> lost the ability to see and hear as the result of a childhood illness.

   What kind of personal pronoun is underlined? (24)

   A first person
   B second person
   C third person singular
   D third person plural

5. Read this sentence.

   Helen Keller's teacher was a woman named Anne Sullivan; she herself had limited vision.

   Which word from the sentence is a compound personal pronoun? (25)

   A teacher
   B woman
   C she
   D herself

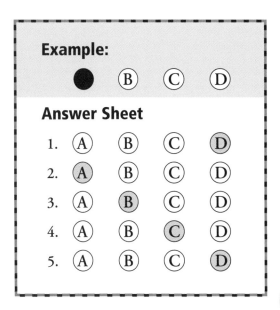

Example:

● ⒝ ⒞ ⒟

Answer Sheet

1. Ⓐ Ⓑ Ⓒ Ⓓ
2. Ⓐ Ⓑ Ⓒ Ⓓ
3. Ⓐ Ⓑ Ⓒ Ⓓ
4. Ⓐ Ⓑ Ⓒ Ⓓ
5. Ⓐ Ⓑ Ⓒ Ⓓ

Read each item carefully. Select the best answer and fill in the circle on the answer sheet below.

6. Read this sentence.

    Anne Sullivan taught young Helen signs for words, and Helen quickly began developing _____ language skills.

    Which of these is the correct pronoun form to use to complete this sentence? **(26)**

    A she
    B her
    C their
    D hers

7. **Read each sentence. Look at the underlined word in it. Which sentence is written** *incorrectly*? **(27)**

    A White water rafting is a sport <u>that</u> requires arm strength, cooperation, and good judgment.
    B People <u>who</u> cannot use their legs can become expert white water rafters.
    C People <u>what</u> have other disabilities can also enjoy this sport.
    D Environmental Traveling Companions, <u>which</u> is based in San Francisco, California, runs many river trips for disabled people.

8. **Read this sentence.**

    Almost all of the players in the National Basketball Association are taller than average height.

    Which word from the sentence is an indefinite pronoun? **(28)**

    A almost
    B all
    C taller
    D average

9. **Read this sentence. Look at the underlined word in it.**

    Tyrone "Muggsy" Bogues became <u>an</u> NBA star even though he was only 5 feet 3 inches tall.

    What kind of adjective is the underlined word? **(29)**

    A an adjective that tells what kind
    B an adjective that tells how many
    C an article
    D None of the above

10. **Read this sentence.**

    These players are stronger, but _____ players are quicker.

    Which of these words would correctly complete this sentence? **(30)**

    A this
    B that
    C these
    D those

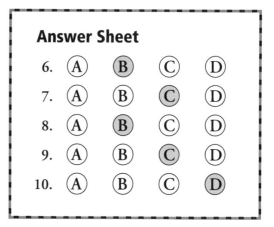

Answer Sheet

6. Ⓐ **Ⓑ** Ⓒ Ⓓ
7. Ⓐ Ⓑ **Ⓒ** Ⓓ
8. Ⓐ **Ⓑ** Ⓒ Ⓓ
9. Ⓐ Ⓑ **Ⓒ** Ⓓ
10. Ⓐ Ⓑ Ⓒ **Ⓓ**

Read each item carefully. Select the best answer and fill in the circle on the answer sheet below.

11. **Read this sentence.**

    Daniel Inouye, a resident of Hawaii, fought bravely for the United States in World War II.

    Which of these choices is a common noun in this sentence? (21)

    A Daniel Inouye
    B resident
    C the United States
    D World War II

12. **Read this sentence.**

    Many soldiers in Inouye's unit suffered terrible injuries; Inouye himself lost an arm.

    Which of these words is a singular noun in this sentence? (22)

    A soldiers
    B unit
    C injuries
    D himself

13. **Read this sentence.**

    This brave _____ injury did not prevent him from becoming a very successful politician.

    Which of these words would correctly complete the sentence? (23)

    A man's
    B mans'
    C men's
    D mens'

14. **Read this sentence.**

    After serving as a representative and a senator in Hawaii, <u>he</u> was elected to the U.S. House of Representatives and then to the Senate.

    What kind of personal pronoun is underlined? (24)

    A first person
    B second person
    C third person singular
    D third person plural

15. **Read this sentence.**

    Like most outstanding distance runners, Marla Runyan constantly pushes herself.

    Which word from the sentence is a compound personal pronoun? (25)

    A most
    B outstanding
    C runners
    D herself

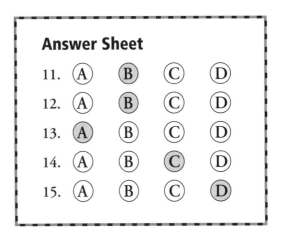

Answer Sheet

	A	B	C	D
11.	Ⓐ	**Ⓑ**	Ⓒ	Ⓓ
12.	Ⓐ	**Ⓑ**	Ⓒ	Ⓓ
13.	**Ⓐ**	Ⓑ	Ⓒ	Ⓓ
14.	Ⓐ	Ⓑ	**Ⓒ**	Ⓓ
15.	Ⓐ	Ⓑ	Ⓒ	**Ⓓ**

Read each item carefully. Select the best answer and fill in the circle on the answer sheet below.

16. **Read this sentence.**

    Although _____ vision is very poor, she made herself into an Olympic athlete.

    Which of these is the proper pronoun form to use to complete this sentence? (26)

    A   her
    B   their
    C   its
    D   hers

17. **Read each sentence. Look at the underlined word in it. Which sentence is written *incorrectly*?** (27)

    A   Neil Parry is an athlete <u>who</u> has overcome incredible adversity.
    B   A football wound <u>that</u> severed an artery caused him to have part of a leg amputated.
    C   Parry, <u>who</u> was a San José University varsity player, was fitted with an artificial leg.
    D   Two years after his injury, Neil Parry took the field again and became the first major college position player <u>which</u> competed with an artificial leg.

18. **Read this sentence.**

    Anyone who follows San José State football is likely to have heard Neil Parry on the radio; he became a broadcaster in 2005.

    Which word from the sentence is an indefinite pronoun? (28)

    A   anyone
    B   who
    C   likely
    D   he

19. **Read this sentence. Look at the underlined word in it.**

    Ralf Hotchkiss gained <u>international</u> fame as the designer of lightweight wheelchairs.

    What kind of adjective is the underlined word? (29)

    A   an adjective that tells what kind
    B   an adjective that tells how many
    C   an article
    D   None of the above

20. **Read this sentence.**

    _____ wheelchairs across the street were designed by him.

    Which of these words would correctly complete this sentence? (30)

    A   This
    B   That
    C   These
    D   Those

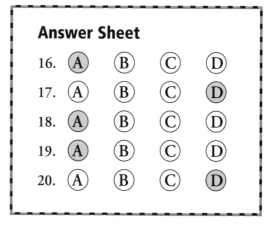

Answer Sheet

16. (A) B C D
17. A B C (D)
18. (A) B C D
19. (A) B C D
20. A B C (D)

Name _____

TEST TIP: Read every choice before deciding on an answer.

Format

(Numbers in parentheses identify related lessons.)

Read each item carefully. Select the best answer and fill in the circle on the answer sheet below.

1. **Read these sentences.**

   The summer sun bakes inland valleys in the Far West. However, the coastal lands remain cool.

   What kinds of verbs are in these sentences? (31)

   A first sentence—action verb; second sentence—linking verb
   B first sentence—linking verb; second sentence—action verb
   C both sentences—action verbs
   D both sentences—linking verbs

2. **Read each sentence. Which sentence has an intransitive verb?** (32)

   A The valley heat pulls ocean air inland.
   B Coastal mountains keep the cool, moist air out of the valleys.
   C Temperatures in the valleys soar above 100°F.
   D Fog blankets the lands along the coast day after day.

3. **Which sentence has a verb in the passive voice?** (33)

   A Silkworms spin cocoons of fine thread.
   B People in China have raised silkworms for many centuries.
   C Fine silk thread was produced from the cocoons by skilled workers.
   D China's emperors kept the process a secret from foreigners.

4. **Read this sentence.**

   The metamorphosis of that insect yielded a product more valuable than gold.

   In what tense is the underlined verb? (34)

   A past
   B present
   C future
   D None of the above

5. **Read the sentence.**

   That tarantula has shed its old skin.

   In what tense is the underlined verb? (35)

   A past perfect
   B present perfect
   C future perfect
   D None of the above

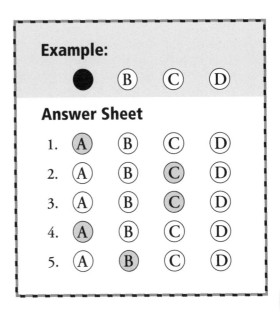

Example:

● Ⓑ Ⓒ Ⓓ

Answer Sheet

1. Ⓐ Ⓑ Ⓒ Ⓓ
2. Ⓐ Ⓑ Ⓒ Ⓓ
3. Ⓐ Ⓑ Ⓒ Ⓓ
4. Ⓐ Ⓑ Ⓒ Ⓓ
5. Ⓐ Ⓑ Ⓒ Ⓓ

Read each item carefully. Select the best answer and fill in the circle on the answer sheet below.

6. **Read the sentence.**

   A bird of prey <u>is eyeing</u> the tarantula hungrily.

   In what form is the underlined verb? (36)

   A past progressive
   B present progressive
   C future progressive
   D None of the above

7. **Read this sentence.**

   Until the tarantula's new skin hardens, the tarantula cannot effectively avoid predators.

   Which of these words is an adverb in the sentence? (37)

   A until
   B new
   C hardens
   D effectively

8. **Read the sentence.**

   Each of the moon's phases has its own name.

   Which of these words is a preposition in the sentence? (38)

   A each
   B of
   C its
   D own

9. **Read this sentence.**

   The waxing crescent moon appears after the new moon, and the waning crescent moon appears before the new moon.

   Which of these words is a coordinating conjunction in the sentence? (39)

   A appears
   B after
   C and
   D before

10. **Read each sentence. Which sentence has a pair of correlative conjunctions?** (40)

    A When you see the right half of the moon, you are seeing the first quarter moon.
    B When you see the left half, you are seeing the last quarter moon.
    C Neither the waxing gibbous moon nor the waning gibbous moon has the beauty of the full moon.
    D As you may have guessed, waxing means increasing, and waning means the opposite.

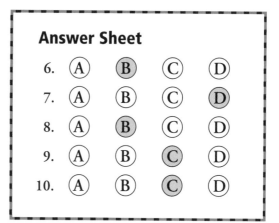

Answer Sheet

6. Ⓐ **Ⓑ** Ⓒ Ⓓ
7. Ⓐ Ⓑ Ⓒ **Ⓓ**
8. Ⓐ **Ⓑ** Ⓒ Ⓓ
9. Ⓐ Ⓑ **Ⓒ** Ⓓ
10. Ⓐ Ⓑ **Ⓒ** Ⓓ

Name _____

Read each item carefully. Select the best answer and fill in the circle on the answer sheet below.

11. **Read these sentences.**

    Maple trees lose their leaves in the fall. They are deciduous.

    What kinds of verbs are in these sentences? (31)

    A first sentence—action verb; second sentence—linking verb
    B first sentence—linking verb; second sentence—action verb
    C both sentences—action verbs
    D both sentences—linking verbs

12. **Read each sentence. Which sentence has an intransitive verb?** (32)

    A Many people visit New England each fall.
    B They love the splendor of the fall colors there.
    C Deciduous trees sense the diminishing length of days.
    D The color of their leaves changes from green to yellow or red.

13. **Which sentence has a verb in the passive voice?** (33)

    A The trees in the north change color first.
    B Visitors follow the changing colors south.
    C Hikers dress warmly because of the chilly temperatures.
    D Pictures are taken by many of the visitors.

14. **Read this sentence.**

    Each year a honey bee hive <u>produces</u> a new queen.

    In what tense is the underlined verb? (34)

    A past
    B present
    C future
    D None of the above

15. **Read the sentence.**

    Before the new queen has begun laying eggs, the old queen <u>will have left</u> the hive with a swarm of worker bees.

    In what tense is the underlined verb? (35)

    A past perfect
    B present perfect
    C future perfect
    D None of the above

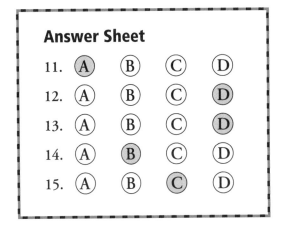

Answer Sheet

11. (A) B C D
12. A B C (D)
13. A B C (D)
14. A (B) C D
15. A B (C) D

Read each item carefully. Select the best answer and fill in the circle on the answer sheet below.

16. **Read the sentence.**

    Yesterday a swarm of bees <u>was hanging</u> from a branch in our yard.

    In what form is the underlined verb? (36)

    A past progressive
    B present progressive
    C future progressive
    D None of the above

17. **Read this sentence.**

    The swarm eventually will find a suitable location for a new hive.

    Which of these words is an adverb in the sentence? (37)

    A eventually
    B will
    C suitable
    D new

18. **Read the sentence.**

    A snake sheds its outer skin when that layer becomes worn from its activity.

    Which of these words is a preposition in the sentence? (38)

    A its
    B outer
    C when
    D from

19. **Read this sentence.**

    A molting snake loosens the skin around its head and then crawls out of the old skin.

    Which of these words is a coordinating conjunction in the sentence? (39)

    A around
    B and
    C then
    D out

20. **Read each sentence. Which sentence has a pair of correlative conjunctions?** (40)

    A Snakes in the tropics shed their skin more frequently than do snakes in other areas.
    B Some snakes molt six times a year, but others only shed their skin twice annually.
    C Young, active snakes shed their skin often.
    D Neither my sister nor I have ever seen a snake shed its skin.

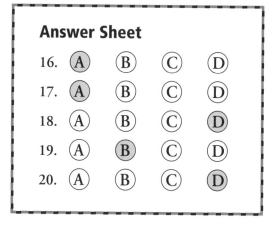

Answer Sheet

16. (A) (B) (C) (D)
17. (A) (B) (C) (D)
18. (A) (B) (C) (D)
19. (A) (B) (C) (D)
20. (A) (B) (C) (D)

236 **Name** _____

TEST TIP: Mark your answers neatly. If you erase, erase completely and clearly without smudging.

(Numbers in parentheses identify related lessons.)

Read each item carefully. Select the best answer and fill in the circle on the answer sheet below.

1. **Which of the following sentences has *your* or *you're* used *incorrectly*?** **(41)**

   A   You're going to enjoy your trip to Tuscany.
   B   The great museums of Florence should be on you're itinerary.
   C   Did any of your ancestors come to the United States from this part of Italy?
   D   When you reach Lucca, you're certain to appreciate its peacefulness.

2. **Read this sentence.**

   People expect to find good food in Italy, and _____ seldom disappointed.

   Which word would complete the sentence correctly? **(42)**

   A   their
   B   there
   C   they're
   D   theyre

3. **Which of the following sentences has *its* or *it's* used *incorrectly*?** **(43)**

   A   The Cyrillic alphabet is used in Bulgaria; it's also used in Russia and Serbia.
   B   Its name comes from Cyril, the name of one of the brothers who developed it.
   C   Bulgaria celebrates it's alphabet and culture with a holiday.
   D   It's called Slavic Script and Bulgarian Culture Day.

4. **Read each sentence. Look at the underlined word in it. Which sentence is written *incorrectly*?** **(44)**

   A   <u>Who's</u> visited Sofia, Bulgaria, on Slavic Script and Bulgarian Culture Day?
   B   Laura is one of the few Americans <u>who's</u> been in Sofia on May 24.
   C   <u>Who's</u> passport is this?
   D   A person <u>whose</u> passport is missing should contact his or her embassy.

5. **Read each sentence. Look at the underlined word in it. Which sentence is written *incorrectly*?** **(45)**

   A   A visitor <u>to</u> Malaysia should visit the state of Sarawak, on the Island of Borneo.
   B   Sarawak has outstanding cultural museums and beautiful natural areas, <u>too</u>.
   C   A bus leaves the city of Kuching for Kubah National Park every <u>two</u> hours.
   D   The park features beautiful waterfalls, many varieties of palms, and wild orchids, <u>to</u>.

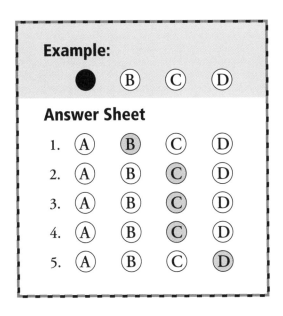

Example:

●   Ⓑ   Ⓒ   Ⓓ

Answer Sheet

1.   Ⓐ   Ⓑ   Ⓒ   Ⓓ
2.   Ⓐ   Ⓑ   Ⓒ   Ⓓ
3.   Ⓐ   Ⓑ   Ⓒ   Ⓓ
4.   Ⓐ   Ⓑ   Ⓒ   Ⓓ
5.   Ⓐ   Ⓑ   Ⓒ   Ⓓ

Read each item carefully. Select the best answer and fill in the circle on the answer sheet below.

6. Read each sentence. Look at the underlined word in it. Which sentence is written *incorrectly*? (46)

A Many visitors are more interested in Sarawak's indigenous peoples than in its natural wonders.
B If you are interested in unusual dwellings, then you should visit one of Sarawak's longhouses.
C These traditional dwellings of the Dayaks and the Orang Ulu are less common then in the past, but many are still in use.
D Some longhouses are more than one-half mile long.

7. Read each sentence. Which sentence is written *incorrectly*? (47)

A The Hopi Indians would not be able to raise crops without rain.
B No large rivers or lakes furnish water to their desert homeland.
C It shouldn't surprise nobody that many Hopi celebrations focus on rain and fertility.
D The celebrations can require stamina: it isn't easy to dance and sing for hours without stopping.

8. Read each sentence. Look at the underlined word in it. Which sentence is written *incorrectly*? (48)

A Tai's family likes attending Native American festivals.
B They went on a long trip to Arizona and New Mexico last year.
C The Hopi, Zuni, and Navajo peoples have reservations there; Tai's family visited reservations of all three peoples.
D On the way home, Tai went, "I'll probably never have a more interesting vacation!"

9. Read each sentence. Look at the underlined word in it. Which sentence is written *incorrectly*? (49)

A You have lain in bed all morning; we shouldn't waste the time we have in Cornwall.
B Come with me and lay flowers by the paths in the village of Padstow.
C May Day will be here soon, and we should not set in our room and miss the festivities.
D I have set a brochure about the Padstow 'Obby 'Oss celebration on the table.

10. Read each sentence. Look at the underlined word in it. Which sentence is written *incorrectly*? (50)

A My sister has taken a course in cultural anthropology.
B She has saw films about indigenous people in many regions.
C She ate foods from Kenya, Ethiopia, and Egypt last week.
D She has written papers on the customs of several peoples of Africa.

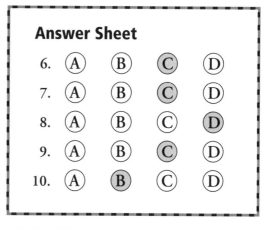

Answer Sheet

6. Ⓐ Ⓑ **Ⓒ** Ⓓ
7. Ⓐ Ⓑ **Ⓒ** Ⓓ
8. Ⓐ Ⓑ Ⓒ **Ⓓ**
9. Ⓐ Ⓑ **Ⓒ** Ⓓ
10. Ⓐ **Ⓑ** Ⓒ Ⓓ

Name _____

Read each item carefully. Select the best answer and fill in the circle on the answer sheet below.

11. **Which of the following sentences has *your* or *you're* used *incorrectly*?** (41)

   A You're fond of traveling, aren't you?
   B If you save your money, you can take a trip to Asia.
   C You're going to be surprised at how affordable a trip with a group can be!
   D Make sure to select a trip that will attract people with you're high energy level!

12. **Read this sentence.**

   The people of Japan welcome visitors to _____ colorful festivals.

   Which word would complete the sentence correctly? (42)

   A their
   B there
   C they're
   D theyre

13. **Which of the following sentences has *its* or *it's* used *incorrectly*?** (43)

   A Kyoto is famous for its Gion Matsuri festival.
   B This festival had it's beginnings more than 1,100 years ago.
   C It's an early summer event that features a parade.
   D Look at that float: its wheels are almost ten feet tall!

14. **Read each sentence. Look at the underlined word in it. Which sentence is written *incorrectly*?** (44)

   A <u>Who's</u> visited the European nation of Belgium?
   B Belgium, <u>whose</u> residents speak French or Flemish, is famous for its chocolate.
   C Bruges is a city <u>who's</u> canals make it picturesque.
   D Tourists <u>whose</u> interests include Renaissance art will particularly enjoy Bruges.

15. **Read each sentence. Look at the underlined word in it. Which sentence is written *incorrectly*?** (45)

   A New Zealand comprises <u>two</u> large islands.
   B Travelers <u>to</u> this nation can learn about Maori culture.
   C The Maoris lived in New Zealand long before the first Europeans came <u>to</u> settle.
   D In traditional Maori culture, when <u>to</u> people meet, they press their noses together.

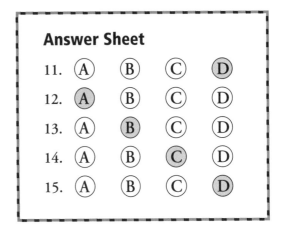

Answer Sheet

11.	Ⓐ	Ⓑ	Ⓒ	**Ⓓ**
12.	**Ⓐ**	Ⓑ	Ⓒ	Ⓓ
13.	Ⓐ	**Ⓑ**	Ⓒ	Ⓓ
14.	Ⓐ	Ⓑ	**Ⓒ**	Ⓓ
15.	Ⓐ	Ⓑ	Ⓒ	**Ⓓ**

Read each item carefully. Select the best answer and fill in the circle on the answer sheet below.

16. **Read each sentence. Look at the underlined word in it. Which sentence is written** *incorrectly*? **(46)**

   A   In older times Maoris were hunters and fishers; <u>then</u> some became farmers.
   B   Maori woodcarvers were more skillful <u>than</u> carvers on many other islands.
   C   World War II created both hardships and opportunities, and many Maoris moved to cities <u>then</u>.
   D   Maoris have their own language; they speak it far more <u>then</u> English at Maori gatherings.

17. **Read each sentence. Which sentence is written** *incorrectly*? **(47)**

   A   I haven't never heard anyone blow a wooden horn.
   B   Wooden horns aren't used in the Netherlands as musical instruments.
   C   Ancient people there didn't want evil winter spirits to bother them.
   D   Wouldn't the noise from that wooden horn frighten just about anything?

18. **Read each sentence. Look at the underlined word in it. Which sentence is written** *incorrectly*? **(48)**

   A   My grandparents <u>go</u> to Cape Breton Island every year.
   B   They both <u>like</u> the traditional fiddle music played there.
   C   This spring they were <u>all</u>, "Why don't you come with us this summer?"
   D   I told them yes, because of <u>all</u> instruments, the fiddle is my favorite.

19. **Read each sentence. Look at the underlined word in it. Which sentence is written** *incorrectly*? **(49)**

   A   When I was in Bangkok, I <u>set</u> on a bench and painted a picture of a temple.
   B   When I got back to my hotel, I <u>set</u> the painting on my bedside table.
   C   I <u>lay</u> my paintbrush down on the table and admired my painting.
   D   That night I <u>lay</u> on my bed and thought about what a great day it had been.

20. **Read each sentence. Look at the underlined word in it. Which sentence is written** *incorrectly*? **(50)**

   A   Many cultures have <u>held</u> festivals in the middle of winter.
   B   The ancient Druids of Britain <u>built</u> a bonfire on the shortest day of the year.
   C   They <u>singed</u> and danced around the fire.
   D   They <u>thought</u> that this ceremony ensured the return of spring.

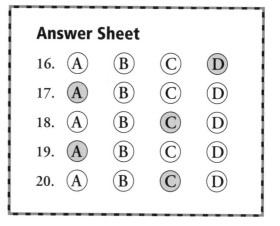

Answer Sheet

16. Ⓐ   Ⓑ   Ⓒ   Ⓓ
17. Ⓐ   Ⓑ   Ⓒ   Ⓓ
18. Ⓐ   Ⓑ   Ⓒ   Ⓓ
19. Ⓐ   Ⓑ   Ⓒ   Ⓓ
20. Ⓐ   Ⓑ   Ⓒ   Ⓓ

Name _____

Unit 6 Assessment

 TEST TIP: Change an answer only if you are sure that your first choice is wrong.

(Numbers in parentheses identify related lessons.)

Read each item carefully. Select the best answer and fill in the circle on the answer sheet below.

1. **Read this sentence.**

   Throughout Africa, people tell talking animal tales; they tell them to convey traditional values.

   Which word in the sentence is an object pronoun? (51)

   A throughout
   B people
   C they
   D them

2. **Read each sentence. Which sentence is written** *incorrectly*? (52)

   A Grandma told a tale about a lizard and a python to my sister and I.
   B My sister and I heard how Lizard stole a special drum from his friend Python.
   C Grandma described to my sister and me how Lizard then taunted Python.
   D Although she and we thought Python should punish Lizard, the snake saved Lizard's life.

3. **Read this sentence.**

   Animal stories such as this tale teach lessons, and <u>they</u> entertain listeners.

   Which is the antecedent for the underlined pronoun? (53)

   A stories
   B tale
   C lessons
   D listeners

4. **Read each sentence. Look at the underlined word. Which sentence is** *not* **correct?** (54)

   A Anyone <u>who</u> likes folktales is likely to enjoy "The Magic Pot."
   B A woodcutter <u>whom</u> fortune has treated poorly finds a brass pot.
   C He brings it home to his wife, <u>whom</u> is very happy with it.
   D She is the one <u>who</u> notices that the axe her husband put into it has turned into two axes.

5. **Read each sentence. Look at the underlined verb. Which sentence is** *not* **correct?** (55)

   A A pot with such magical powers <u>create</u> opportunities.
   B Any object dropped into the pot <u>becomes</u> two.
   C In folktales, of course, magic inevitably <u>causes</u> problems.
   D A wife who falls into a pot of this kind suddenly <u>becomes</u> two identical wives!

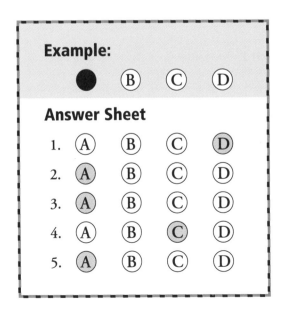

Example:

● Ⓑ Ⓒ Ⓓ

Answer Sheet

1. Ⓐ Ⓑ Ⓒ Ⓓ
2. Ⓐ Ⓑ Ⓒ Ⓓ
3. Ⓐ Ⓑ Ⓒ Ⓓ
4. Ⓐ Ⓑ Ⓒ Ⓓ
5. Ⓐ Ⓑ Ⓒ Ⓓ

Read each item carefully. Select the best answer and fill in the circle on the answer sheet below.

6. Read each sentence. Look at the underlined verb. Which sentence is *not* correct? **(56)**

   A Twilight or midnight <u>is</u> a good time to tell a scary story.
   B A big crocodile or a giant bear <u>is</u> certainly a scary character!
   C The smell or the noises of such an animal, when described vividly, <u>adds</u> to the fear.
   D Neither young storytellers nor an elderly tale teller <u>wants</u> listeners to become too frightened.

7. Read each sentence. Look at the underlined verb. Which sentence is *not* correct? **(57)**

   A "Goldilocks and the Three Bears" <u>has</u> many lessons to teach.
   B Almost everyone here <u>have heard</u> this very old tale.
   C A bear family <u>goes</u> for a walk before mealtime.
   D While the family <u>is</u> away from their home, someone enters it without permission.

8. Read each sentence. Which sentence is *not* correct because of a dangling modifier? **(58)**

   A Showing very bad manners, the bears' breakfast is tasted by the intruder.
   B Sampling Papa Bear's porridge, the intruder pronounces it too hot.
   C Discussing the intruder's behavior, our family decided that she deserved punishment.
   D Knowing how the story ends, we wondered if being badly frightened by bears is enough of a punishment.

9. Read this sentence.

   In "Goldilocks and the Three Bears," the animals behave _____ than the human does.

   Which choice would complete the sentence correctly? **(59)**

   A gooder
   B more good
   C better
   D more better

10. Read this sentence.

   In real life, bears would never behave politely.

   Which word in the sentence is an auxiliary verb? **(60)**

   A would
   B never
   C behave
   D politely

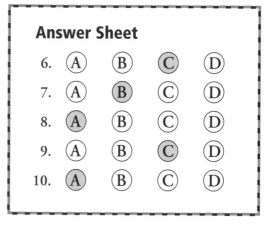

Answer Sheet

6. (A) (B) **(C)** (D)
7. (A) **(B)** (C) (D)
8. **(A)** (B) (C) (D)
9. (A) (B) **(C)** (D)
10. **(A)** (B) (C) (D)

Name _____

Read each item carefully. Select the best answer and fill in the circle on the answer sheet below.

11. Read this sentence.

The Little Mermaid is the main character in one of Hans Christian Andersen's fairy tales; you can see a statue of her in Copenhagen, Denmark.

Which word in the sentence is an object pronoun? (51)

A character
B you
C statue
D her

12. Read each sentence. Which sentence is written *incorrectly*? (52)

A My brother and I perform puppet shows for our friends.
B Our cousin Gretchen asked him and I to create a new show.
C She told him and me to perform Hans Christian Andersen's "Ugly Duckling."
D I showed my brother and her how to make duck puppets.

13. Read this sentence.

Hans Christian Andersen wrote stories for adults, too, but nowadays very few people read <u>them</u>.

Which is the antecedent for the underlined pronoun? (53)

A stories
B adults
C nowadays
D people

14. Read each sentence. Look at the underlined word. Which sentence is *not* correct? (54)

A <u>Whom</u> among your friends is the best storyteller?
B A person <u>who</u> can keep an audience fascinated just with words is a powerful person indeed.
C My cousin is a person to <u>whom</u> storytelling comes naturally.
D A 12-year-old <u>who</u> tells ancient tales is a rarity.

15. Read each sentence. Look at the underlined verb. Which sentence is *not* correct? (55)

A Either Homer or Aesop <u>was</u> the greatest ancient storyteller in my opinion.
B Homer's *Iliad*, a tale of the Trojan War, <u>thrills</u> people today.
C The fables of Aesop <u>contain</u> more useful wisdom than Homer's epics do.
D Which one of his fables do you think <u>teach</u> the most important lesson?

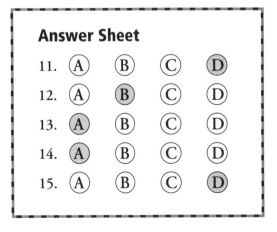

Answer Sheet

11.	Ⓐ	Ⓑ	Ⓒ	**Ⓓ**
12.	Ⓐ	**Ⓑ**	Ⓒ	Ⓓ
13.	**Ⓐ**	Ⓑ	Ⓒ	Ⓓ
14.	**Ⓐ**	Ⓑ	Ⓒ	Ⓓ
15.	Ⓐ	Ⓑ	Ⓒ	**Ⓓ**

Read each item carefully. Select the best answer and fill in the circle on the answer sheet below.

16. **Read each sentence. Look at the underlined verb. Which sentence is *not* correct?** (56)

    A My mother and my brother <u>believe</u> that "The Tortoise and the Hare" conveys great wisdom.
    B Neither she nor he ever <u>quits</u> before the end of a project.
    C My grandfather and I <u>value</u> the message of "The Boy and the Wolf" a lot.
    D One false cry or two false cries <u>ruins</u> a person's credibility.

17. **Read each sentence. Look at the underlined verb. Which sentence is *not* correct?** (57)

    A "The Town Mouse and the Country Mouse" <u>remind</u> us that we feel comfortable in familiar places.
    B This collection of fables <u>includes</u> "The Goose and the Golden Eggs."
    C Anyone who gives in to greed and impatience <u>risks</u> suffering the fate of the man in this fable.
    D An output of one golden egg a day <u>sounds</u> fine to me.

18. **Read each sentence. Which sentence is *not* correct because of a dangling modifier?** (58)

    A Laying one golden egg a day, the man's goose made him rich.
    B Wanting more wealth faster, the man decided on a plan.
    C Believing that he could get many golden eggs at once, the goose was slain by the man.
    D Looking inside the poor goose, the man found no golden eggs.

19. **Read this sentence.**

    In real life as in folktales, coyotes may be the _____ animals of all.

    Which choice would complete the sentence correctly? (59)

    A shrewder
    B more shrewd
    C shrewdest
    D most shrewd

20. **Read this sentence.**

    In many tales, though, coyote does not succeed with his tricks.

    Which word in the sentence is an auxiliary verb? (60)

    A does
    B not
    C succeed
    D with

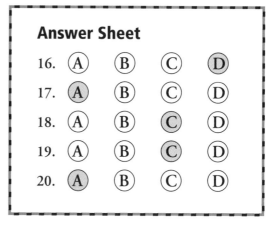

Answer Sheet

16. (A) (B) (C) (D)
17. (A) (B) (C) (D)
18. (A) (B) (C) (D)
19. (A) (B) (C) (D)
20. (A) (B) (C) (D)

Name _____

TEST TIP: Review your work. If you finish a test before time is up, go back and check your work.

(Numbers in parentheses identify related lessons.)

Read each item carefully. Select the best answer and fill in the circle on the answer sheet below.

1. Read this sentence.

   Trinidad is a large island in the Caribbean Sea near the Nation of Venezuela.

   Which term should not be capitalized? (61)

   A Trinidad
   B Caribbean Sea
   C Nation
   D Venezuela

2. Read this sentence.

   Mister George Maxwell Richards became president of Trinidad and Tobago in 2003.

   How should the boldfaced name be written with initials and abbreviations? (62)

   A Mr. G.M. Richards
   B Mr. GM. Richards
   C Mr G M Richards
   D Mr. GM Richards

3. Read each sentence. Which sentence has the title in it written correctly? (63)

   A My sister is reading a book titled "The Modern History of the Caribbean Islands."
   B The author also wrote a story titled <u>Mystery in the Caribbean</u>.
   C My sister has written a poem titled "My First Free Breath."
   D She dedicated it to our grandmother, who grew up in Jamaica and once wrote a song titled Dreams for My Grandchildren.

4. Read each sentence. Look at the underlined word. Which sentence is written *incorrectly*? (64)

   A Those <u>musician's</u> instruments were made from oil drums.
   B These <u>instruments'</u> tones are bright and resonant.
   C Steel drum music is an invention of <u>Trinidad's</u> people.
   D This <u>island's</u> Carnival celebrations feature the Calypso music of steel drum orchestras.

5. Read each sentence. Look at the commas. Which sentence is written correctly? (65)

   A Do you know which country comprises the islands of Hokkaido, Honshu, Shikoku, and, Kyushu?
   B Luzon, Mindanao, and Palawan, are major islands in what nation?
   C Which country in Southeast Asia includes the islands of, Java, Sumatra, and Sulawesi?
   D If you answered Japan, the Philippines, and Indonesia, you are correct!

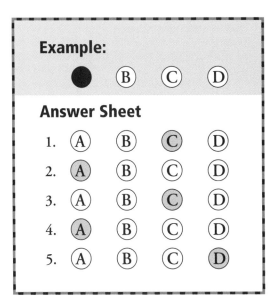

Example:

● Ⓑ Ⓒ Ⓓ

Answer Sheet

1. Ⓐ Ⓑ Ⓒ Ⓓ
2. Ⓐ Ⓑ Ⓒ Ⓓ
3. Ⓐ Ⓑ Ⓒ Ⓓ
4. Ⓐ Ⓑ Ⓒ Ⓓ
5. Ⓐ Ⓑ Ⓒ Ⓓ

Read each item carefully. Select the best answer and fill in the circle on the answer sheet below.

6. **Read this sentence.**

Yes Haiti was the first Caribbean country to gain its independence.

Where should a comma be placed in this sentence? (66)

A after yes
B after first
C after country
D after gain

7. **Read this sentence.**

The Shetland Islands are famous for two distinctive items their woolen sweaters and their ponies.

Where should a colon be placed in this sentence? (67)

A after Islands
B after famous
C after items
D after sweaters

8. **Read each sentence. Which sentence is *not* punctuated correctly?** (68)

A Rising sea levels—a result of global warming—threaten low-lying islands.
B Island nations in the southwest Pacific (Vanuatu is one) are losing land to sea.
C Many of these nations' islands are very small to-begin-with.
D If sea levels rise even another foot (a likely possibility, according to some scientists), some well-populated islands will become uninhabitable.

9. **Read each sentence. Which sentence is *not* punctuated correctly?** (69)

A Karl asked, "What country is building artificial islands?"
B Diana said that she thought Dubai was doing this.
C "Do the islands float, or are they built up from the sea floor?" Karl asked.
D I'm not sure; I'll need to do some research, said Diana.

10. **Read this friendly letter.**

1168 West Wind Ct.
Honolulu, HI 96820
April 3, 2008

Bradley, I can't wait to visit you, Melanie, Uncle Paul, and Aunt Iris! The Hawaiian Islands are great, but I'm ready for some time in the desert with you. Keep things nice and warm until I get there!

Your cousin,
Walter

Which part of the letter is missing? (70)

A heading
B greeting
C closing
D signature

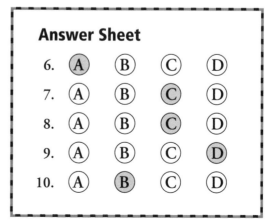

Answer Sheet

6. (A) B C D
7. A B (C) D
8. A B (C) D
9. A B C (D)
10. A (B) C D

Name _____

Read each item carefully. Select the best answer and fill in the circle on the answer sheet below.

11. **Read this sentence.**

    Reindeer Island is an island in a lake in Manitoba, a Province of Canada.

    Which term should not be capitalized? (61)

    A   Reindeer Island
    B   Manitoba
    C   Province
    D   Canada

12. **Read this sentence.**

    Our neighbor, **General David Julio Estaris,** is obsessed with that island.

    How should the boldfaced name be written with initials and abbreviations? (62)

    A   Gen. DJ Estaris
    B   Gen. D.J. Estaris
    C   Gen D J Estaris
    D   Gen D. J. Estaris

13. **Read each sentence. Which sentence has the title in it written correctly?** (63)

    A   He wants to film a movie called <u>Escape to Reindeer Island</u>.
    B   He has written a song called <u>Rudy, the Mayor of Reindeer Island</u>.
    C   Would you believe that he's written a poem titled You Won't Freeze If You Say Please?
    D   According to this book titled "Inland Islands in the Prairie Provinces," General Estaris may be a bit disappointed if he does visit Reindeer Island.

14. **Read each sentence. Look at the underlined word. Which sentence is written *incorrectly*?** (64)

    A   <u>Norway's</u> hikers flock to the Lofoten Islands in summer.
    B   These rocky <u>islands'</u> trails are challenging, but views from the trails are breathtaking.
    C   Several <u>postcard's</u> photos show hikers hopping from rock to rock.
    D   A <u>hiker's</u> boots must provide traction on the rugged rocks.

15. **Read each sentence. Look at the commas. Which sentence is written properly?** (65)

    A   Lahaina, Kahului, and Makawao, are towns on the island of Maui.
    B   On the island of Kauai are the towns of Kalaheo, Lihue, and Kapaa.
    C   The big island of Hawaii has Honokaa, Hilo, and, Mountain View.
    D   Honolulu, located on the island of Oahu, is Hawaii's largest city; other communities on that island include, Waipahu, Pearl City, and Kaneohe.

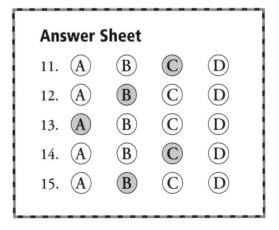

Answer Sheet

11. Ⓐ   Ⓑ   **Ⓒ**   Ⓓ
12. Ⓐ   **Ⓑ**   Ⓒ   Ⓓ
13. **Ⓐ**   Ⓑ   Ⓒ   Ⓓ
14. Ⓐ   Ⓑ   **Ⓒ**   Ⓓ
15. Ⓐ   **Ⓑ**   Ⓒ   Ⓓ

Read each item carefully. Select the best answer and fill in the circle on the answer sheet below.

16. **Read this sentence.**

    Yes the Republic of Singapore is an island nation at the tip of the Malay Peninsula.

    Where should a comma be placed in this sentence? (66)

    A after yes
    B after Singapore
    C after island
    D after tip

17. **Read this sentence.**

    The population density of Singapore is one of the highest of any nation more than 16,000 people per square mile.

    Where should a colon be placed in this sentence? (67)

    A after Singapore
    B after highest
    C after nation
    D after 16,000

18. **Read each sentence. Which sentence is *not* punctuated correctly?** (68)

    A Singapore—a separate nation since 1965—is very prosperous.
    B Its only natural resource is fish (a resource that every nation with a coastline has).
    C Its land area is only 267 square miles (693 sq. km.).
    D It has gained prosperity (primarily because of the skills, talents, and education of its residents).

19. **Read each sentence. Which sentence is *not* punctuated correctly?** (69)

    A "Many financial institutions have offices in Singapore," said Hiro.
    B Karishma said that chemicals are manufactured there.
    C Tam said that "his uncle manages an electronics plant in Singapore."
    D "I hope he gives you free cell phones," said Karishma, smiling.

20. **Read this friendly letter.**

    Dear Valerie,

    I am trying to memorize the names of 1,000 islands this summer. Since I managed to memorize the names of 1,000 rivers last summer, I don't think it will be that big of a challenge. What are your summer plans?

    Your pal,
    Edie

    Which part of the letter is missing? (70)

    A heading
    B greeting
    C closing
    D signature

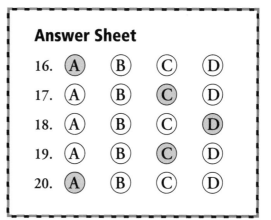

Answer Sheet

16. (A) B C D
17. A B (C) D
18. A B C (D)
19. A B (C) D
20. (A) B C D

Name _____

Lesson 1 Circle the complete subject in each sentence. Underline the complete predicate.

1. (I) am taking guitar lessons.
2. (My lessons) are on Thursdays.
3. (Some of the exercises) are difficult.
4. (I) practice really hard.
5. (My teacher) doesn't know any new songs.
6. (His favorite songs) are from the 1980s.
7. (Alternative music) is my favorite.
8. (I) took my teacher a tape of my favorite song.
9. (He) figured out the chords.
10. (Most of the chords) were actually very simple.
11. (I) learned them with no trouble.
12. (My love for the song) made practicing fun.
13. (We) played it together last week.
14. (My teacher) liked the song a lot.
15. (Our lessons) are teaching him about today's music.

Lesson 2 Circle the simple subject in each sentence. If the subject is understood *you,* write *you* on the line. Underline the simple predicate.

1. (Hummus) is a Middle Eastern dish. _____
2. My (sister) gave me the recipe. _____
3. Pour a can of garbanzo beans into a blender. __you__
4. Some (people) call garbanzo beans chick peas. _____
5. Squeeze one whole lemon over the beans. __you__
6. (I) use even more lemon sometimes. _____
7. Add crushed garlic, olive oil, salt, and tahini. __you__
8. (Tahini) is sesame seed paste. _____
9. The (action) of the blender squashes the beans. _____
10. (Hummus) on pita bread makes a great sandwich. _____
11. Slice the bread into two half-circles. __you__
12. Open the pita pocket carefully with your hand. __you__
13. This (bread) breaks sometimes. _____
14. Put hummus, lettuce, tomato, and anything else into the pocket. __you__
15. Many (people) simply dip the pita into the hummus. _____

Name _____

Lesson 3 Each sentence has a compound subject or a compound predicate. Circle the two or three simple nouns or pronouns that make up each compound subject. Underline the two verbs that make up each compound predicate.

1. (Marisa) and (Rachel) play on a soccer team together.

2. (Kelly), (Raph), and (I) watched one of their games.

3. Rachel <u>ran</u> down the field and <u>trapped</u> the ball.

4. The (goalie) and a defensive (player) ran towards her.

5. Rachel <u>saw</u> Marisa and <u>kicked</u> the ball to her.

6. Marisa <u>took</u> a shot and <u>scored</u> a goal.

7. (Raph) and (Kelly) cheered.

8. I <u>put</u> two fingers in my mouth and <u>whistled</u>.

9. We <u>shouted</u> and <u>clapped</u> for a long time.

10. (Marisa), (Rachel), and (I) went out for pizza after the game.

11. (Rachel) and (I) wanted pizza with mushrooms and pepperoni.

12. Marisa <u>dislikes</u> mushrooms and <u>suggested</u> olives instead.

13. I <u>went</u> to the counter and <u>ordered</u> a large pizza.

14. (Mushrooms) and (pepperoni) were on one half of the pizza.

15. The other half <u>was</u> for Marisa and <u>had</u> olives on it.

Lesson 4 Circle each direct object in the sentences below.

1. An artist painted a (mural) in my neighborhood.

2. I watched (her) every afternoon.

3. First she sketched a (plan).

4. She drew (dancers) at a carnival.

5. The artist chose bright (colors) at the paint store.

6. Then she mixed the (colors) together into new shades.

7. She built a (scaffold) next to the wall.

8. The scaffold raised (her) to the level of the mural.

9. The artist painted (masks) and (feathers) on the dancers.

10. One dancer in the mural carries a huge, colorful (umbrella).

11. Another juggles flaming (torches).

12. Some of the dancers resemble (people) in my neighborhood.

13. I recognized the (face) of my math teacher on the juggler.

14. One acrobat actually resembles (me)!

15. Everyone likes the new (mural).

Lesson 5 Circle the indirect object in each sentence below.

1. Charlie's uncle gave (Charlie) a ticket to a comic book convention.
2. Charlie's aunt gave (them) a ride to the convention center.
3. Inside, dealers offered (collectors) rare comic books.
4. Some collectors were paying (dealers) large sums for the best comics.
5. Charlie showed a (dealer) his prize old comic.
6. On the cover, a villain was giving a (superhero) a blast of supersonic cold rays.
7. The dealer offered (Charlie) a trade for another rare comic.
8. Charlie and his uncle gave the (trade) careful consideration.
9. They made the (dealer) an offer for two comics.
10. On the convention stage, a famous illustrator told the (audience) stories about his career.
11. The illustrator's friends had often given (him) ideas for comic book heroes.
12. An archaeologist friend had given (him) the inspiration for Dino-Woman.
13. She had told the (illustrator) many fascinating tales about dinosaurs.
14. The illustrator's talents had won (him) many awards.
15. Afterwards, the illustrator drew (Charlie) a picture and then signed it.

Lesson 6 Write *PN* if the boldfaced term is a predicate noun. Write *PA* if the boldfaced term is a predicate adjective. Circle the linking verb in each sentence.

1. The rafflesia (is) a **flower**. __PN__
2. Its home (is) the **rain forest**. __PN__
3. These blossoms (are) **huge**. __PA__
4. Some blossoms (are) three feet **wide**. __PA__
5. They (look) **beautiful**. __PA__
6. The thick, heavy petals (are) dark **red**. __PA__
7. Rafflesias (smell) **terrible,** however. __PA__
8. The flower's scent (is) the **smell** of rotten meat. __PN__
9. But this scent (smells) **wonderful** to flies. __PA__
10. Flies (are) the main **pollinators** of this rare plant. __PN__
11. Rafflesias (have become) **endangered**. __PA__
12. Rain forest logging and slash-and-burn agriculture (are) the main **threats** to the flower's survival. __PN__
13. The rafflesia (is) still so little **understood**. __PA__
14. Scientists (are) **hopeful** about future studies of this plant. __PA__
15. The extinction of this plant (would be) a **tragedy**. __PN__

Name _____

Extra Practice

Lesson 7 Underline each prepositional phrase. Circle the preposition that begins each phrase. Draw a box around the object of the preposition. There may be more than one prepositional phrase in each sentence.

1. (In) [July] my camp went (on) a rafting [trip].
2. Our bus drove (through) the [woods] and stopped (at) a [river].
3. We carried rubber rafts (from) the [bus] (to) the [water].
4. Soon we were floating (down) the [river].
5. Our paddles dipped (into) the [water].
6. (Across) the [river] a bird fished (with) its [beak].
7. (After) a calm [stretch], we paddled (through) some [rapids].
8. Foamy waves splashed (over) [us].
9. We held tightly (to) the [raft].
10. My friend Peg was swept (into) the [water].
11. (For) a [minute], we could only see her hat bobbing (on) the [waves].
12. Then we saw Peg drifting (down) the [rapids].
13. She floated (on) her [back] and kept her feet (above) the [water].
14. We did exactly what we'd learned (in) safety [class], and soon Peg was (in) the [boat] again.
15. (Before) [nightfall], we climbed (onto) the [bus] and returned (to) [camp].

Lesson 8 Underline each adjectival prepositional phrase. Circle the noun it tells about. Some sentences have more than one adjectival prepositional phrase.

1. Noel's summer job earns her (money) for CDs.
2. She washes the (windows) of her neighbors' houses.
3. First she gets a (bucket) of warm water.
4. Then she carefully adds one (capful) of ammonia.
5. The (fumes) from the ammonia sometimes make Noel's eyes water.
6. Noel next uses a wet (cloth) from the bucket.
7. Then a quick (wipe) with a squeegee removes the streaks.
8. The (sound) of the squeegee makes Noel giggle.
9. A (window) without streaks is a beautiful sight.
10. The (windows) in Noel's neighborhood sparkle.
11. Noel's job gave me an (idea) for my own summer job.
12. I have started mowing the (lawns) in (front) of my neighbor's houses.
13. The (smell) of the grass is wonderful.
14. A (cap) with a big brim keeps away the (glare) of the sun.
15. My (weekdays) in the mowing business leave my Saturdays free.

Name _____

Lesson 9 Underline each adverbial prepositional phrase. Circle the verb or verb phrase it modifies. There may be more than one prepositional phrase in a sentence.

1. I (like) making origami figures in my spare time.
2. This craft (originated) in Japan.
3. Origami paper (is folded) into elaborate shapes.
4. On Tuesday I (made) an origami frog.
5. I (folded) some green paper in half.
6. Then I (folded) the right side over the left.
7. For twenty minutes I carefully (made) more and more folds.
8. In the end, I (had) a little green paper frog.
9. If you (push) on its back, the frog (hops) across the table.
10. I (have placed) many origami figures around my room.
11. A boat, a giraffe, a spider, and three fish (sit) on my shelf.
12. With a hanger and ten origami cranes I (made) a mobile.
13. It (hangs) over my desk.
14. My friends (received) origami stars for the Fourth of July.
15. In my opinion, origami (is) a terrific hobby.

Lesson 10 Underline the appositive phrase in each sentence.

1. Miacis, a prehistoric weasel-like animal, was the ancestor of cats.
2. Ancient Egyptians, the first people to domesticate cats, considered the animal sacred.
3. Cats, excellent hunters of mice and rats, kept houses free of vermin.
4. In Medieval Europe, cats, supposedly "evil" animals, were killed in large numbers.
5. The resulting increase in rat populations helped spread the Black Death, a plague carried by the rats' fleas.
6. The Egyptian Mau, an ancient cat breed, has a striped and spotted coat and green eyes.
7. The Manx, a breed that originated on the Isle of Man in the Irish Sea, usually has no tail.
8. The Japanese bobtail, another breed with an unusually short tail, is considered good luck in Japan.
9. The Siamese is a breed with a colorpoint coat, a coat with contrasting patches of color on the face, ears, tail, and feet.
10. A tabby coat, one with patterns of dark stripes, is often found on American shorthair cats.
11. The Scottish fold, a breed with ears that fold down, originated in Scotland.
12. The largest breed, the Maine coon cat, resembles a raccoon.
13. Crossbreds, cats with characteristics from more than one breed, are often healthier than purebred cats.
14. Animal shelters, which are found in most communities, are excellent places to find a cat.
15. The cats at a shelter, crossbreds as well as cats of different breeds, need a good home.

Name _____

Lesson 11 Add the correct punctuation mark to each sentence. Then label each sentence *declarative, interrogative, imperative,* or *exclamatory.*

1. Do you want to see my new pet? _____ interrogative _____
2. What kind of animal is it? _____ interrogative _____
3. It's a common garter snake. _____ declarative _____
4. Wow, it's so thin and fast-moving! _____ exclamatory _____
5. May I hold it for a while? _____ interrogative _____
6. Support it gently with both hands. _____ imperative _____
7. Hey, it's wrapping around my arm! _____ exclamatory _____
8. Don't worry about being bitten. _____ imperative _____
9. What is its usual diet? _____ interrogative _____
10. I feed it earthworms and insects. _____ declarative _____
11. Would you like to see it eat? _____ interrogative _____
12. Yes, I'd like to. _____ declarative _____
13. Bring me that jar of grasshoppers. _____ imperative _____
14. Yeesh, it strikes so quickly! _____ exclamatory _____
15. Now it will lie quietly and digest its food for a while. _____ declarative _____

Lesson 12 Write *S* next to each simple sentence and *CD* next to each compound sentence. Circle the comma and conjunction or the semicolon in each compound sentence.

1. Some people avoid packaged prepared food, (but) I like it. __CD__
2. Those salty peanuts always taste delicious. __S__
3. I enjoy opening little packets of cheese and crackers. __S__
4. You can have lasagna, (or) you can try a rice bowl. __CD__
5. Washed and peeled baby carrots are the most perfect snack in the world. __S__
6. This salad comes with dressing on the side(;) it also comes with a fork. __CD__
7. The enchiladas sit invitingly in neat compartments. __S__
8. I love cooking, (but) I often don't have time. __CD__
9. Some companies offer tasty vegetarian meals. __S__
10. I've heard those meals are very good, (but) I have never tried them myself. __CD__
11. Some prepared foods contain large amounts of salt. __S__
12. Salt can make foods tastier, (but) too much salt can cause health problems. __CD__
13. Green, leafy vegetables are recommended for health. __S__
14. A serving of spinach can make any meal healthier, (and) a portion of broccoli can do the same. __CD__
15. A quick but healthy meal is a good thing! __S__

Lesson 13 Draw one line under each independent clause and two lines under each dependent clause. Circle the subordinating conjunction that begins each dependent clause.

1. (Because) Tim enjoys acting, he auditioned for the school play.
2. (Although) he wanted the part of the hero, he was cast as the bandit.
3. (If) he hadn't had a cold for his audition, he would have gotten a bigger part.
4. He had trouble with his lines at the audition (because) his nose was stuffed up.
5. He was still happy with this part (because) the bandit is a colorful character.
6. (As) the curtain rose, the bandit was pacing back and forth on the stage.
7. He was planning revenge (because) the hero had laughed at his science experiments.
8. (Although) the hero called him crazy, he was making fantastic discoveries about time travel.
9. He would have the last laugh (when) he committed the perfect crime!
10. The audience booed (when) he announced his evil scheme.
11. (While) the hero innocently ate dinner, Tim tied knots in his shoelaces.
12. The hero was saved (because) his sister warned him.
13. (Although) they were all nervous, the cast performed well on opening night.
14. (When) they took their bows, the audience gave them a standing ovation.
15. Tim will be a professional actor someday, (if) everything goes according to his plan.

Lesson 14 Write *CX* next to each complex sentence and *CD* next to each compound sentence.

1. Although diatoms are invisible to the naked eye, they may be the most important sea creatures. __CX__
2. Diatoms are microscopic one-celled plants; most drift in the top layer of the ocean. __CD__
3. Diatoms live in the top layer because sunlight penetrates the water there. __CX__
4. Although most diatoms drift with the currents, some can move independently. __CX__
5. Diatoms have glasslike silica shells, and they come in shapes similar to saucers, flowers, propellers, buttons, and beads. __CD__
6. Because the shapes are so beautiful, hobbyists have collected diatom shells since the 1700s. __CX__
7. Collectors must use one tiny hair for a tool as they place diatoms on microscope slides. __CX__
8. Diatoms may be small, but their huge populations feed countless marine animals. __CD__
9. Diatoms have been called the "grass of the sea" because they are food for huge schools of krill. __CX__
10. These schools of krill feed small fish; they are the base of the marine food chain. __CD__
11. Small fish aren't the only ones that eat krill; some of the biggest sea creatures like krill as well. __CD__
12. As a baleen whale swims through a school of krill, it filters them out of the water. __CX__
13. The whale shark is the largest fish in the world, but it uses a similar method for eating krill. __CD__
14. If diatoms were to die out, other life in the sea would probably die as well. __CX__
15. We land creatures depend on diatoms, too, because they produce much of our oxygen. __CX__

Name _____

Lesson 15 Underline the adjective clause in each sentence. Circle the noun it describes. Draw a box around the relative pronoun that begins the clause.

1. Last week I tried sea kayaking, which is an exciting sport.
2. Sea kayaks are large, stable boats that are hard to tip over.
3. The kayak paddle, which has two blades, allows kayakers to steer through the water.
4. Our instructor, who is an expert kayaker, showed us the best paddling methods.
5. We sat in the kayaks on the beach and waited for a wave which pulled us out into the bay.
6. My friend Matt, who came along with me, paddled fast.
7. We encountered marine animals that we had never seen up close before.
8. We passed an otter whose stomach was draped in kelp.
9. Matt saw a whiskered, large-eyed seal, which swam behind his kayak.
10. Kayakers may encounter seals that seem curious about humans.
11. Were we the ones who were being watched?
12. The government has passed laws that protect marine mammals.
13. The instructor who led our trip kept a wide space between our kayaks and the seals and otters.
14. People who get too close to seals or otters may face fines and other penalties.
15. Sea kayaking is a sport that I would like to try again sometime.

Lesson 16 Underline the adverb clause in each sentence. Draw a box around the subordinating conjunction that begins the clause.

1. Because oceans are so broad and so deep, they have always been mysterious.
2. People imagined gigantic sea monsters before they were able to explore the ocean's depths.
3. Scylla and Charybdis, two sea monsters of Greek myth, supposedly lived where the sea passed through a narrow channel.
4. Whenever Charybdis sucked water into her huge mouth, a perilous whirlpool formed.
5. Although Charybdis was dangerous, sailors feared Scylla even more.
6. As a boat passed between the two monsters, Scylla used her twelve tentacles to grab a meal of sailors.
7. One of the exciting parts of Homer's *Odyssey* comes when Ulysses encounters Scylla and Charybdis.
8. Ulysses steers his ship through the middle of the passage because he knows the dangers on both sides.
9. Although Ulysses tries his best, Scylla drags his boat towards her with her tentacles.
10. As everyone shrieks in horror, Scylla devours six sailors.
11. Ulysses somehow steers the boat past the monsters before any more of his crew are lost.
12. Wherever sailors took to the sea, people told tales of monsters.
13. When a Scottish sea serpent died, its coiled body became the island of Iceland, according to a legend.
14. After oceanographers were able to study deep-sea life, they discovered truths behind some legends.
15. Some real "sea monsters" like the giant squid are even stranger than the imaginary creatures were.

Name _____

Lesson 17 Underline the infinitive phrase in each sentence.

1. In art class I learned how to make a clay pot.

2. The clay must be soft enough to mold easily.

3. To make the clay soft, potters knead it with their hands.

4. This also helps to remove any air bubbles from the clay.

5. Now the potter is ready to shape the pot.

6. Some potters use their fingers to pinch the pot into shape.

7. Others coil strips of clay to form the pot's sides.

8. The coil method is an ancient way to make pottery.

9. Potters use slip, a mixture of clay and water, to join the coils together.

10. To smooth the surface of a coil pot, the potter rubs it gently.

11. My favorite way to make a pot is the potter's wheel.

12. As the lump of clay spins on the wheel, the potter uses his or her hands to press it into shape.

13. Potters are able to create a wide range of shapes and sizes on the wheel.

14. The heat of a kiln helps to harden the finished pot.

15. Many potters use brilliant glazes to color their pots.

Lesson 18 Underline the participial phrase in each sentence. Circle the participle.

1. Wrestling with each other, lion cubs learn important skills.

2. These skills, acquired in play, will make the lions effective hunters as adults.

3. My kitten moves forward silently, stalking a ball of string.

4. Pretending the ball of string is a mouse, she bats it with her paw and then pounces on it.

5. I often play with my kitten, swinging a toy on a string.

6. Attracted by the sudden movements, she attacks the toy.

7. Other kinds of young animals also play games, developing different types of skills.

8. Fetching balls or sticks, dogs play happily with humans.

9. Growling at each other, puppies learn protective skills.

10. Young goats play in the mountains, jumping from rock to rock.

11. Dolphins play together in the water, leaping in pairs through the foamy wake.

12. Young chimpanzees, known for their high intelligence, chase one another for fun.

13. Playing just for the fun of it, children and young animals prepare for adulthood.

14. Human children also learn through play, imitating older children and adults.

15. Social skills learned in play stay with a person throughout life.

Name _____

Lesson 19 Underline each gerund phrase. Draw a box around the gerund.

1. [Becoming] a triathlete is my dream.

2. A triathlon involves [competing] in three different events.

3. Triathletes compete without even [taking] a rest between events!

4. [Swimming] almost a mile is the first event of most triathlons.

5. [Bicycling] 25 miles comes next.

6. The hardest part, though, may be [running] six miles at the end.

7. [Finishing] a triathlon successfully is considered the ultimate athletic challenge.

8. Each week I spend some time on [training] for the triathlon.

9. I really enjoy [riding] my bike to and from school.

10. [Running] long distance is my best event in track.

11. I am not as good at [swimming] laps, however.

12. I plan to work on [swimming] long distances at the pool this summer.

13. A friend will help me by [timing] my laps.

14. The real trick will be [putting] all three events together.

15. [Training] for nine to twelve months should prepare me for the competition.

Lesson 20 Label each item *F* (fragment), *RO* (run-on), *CS* (comma splice), or *RA* (ramble-on).

1. The saguaro is often called the giant cactus it grows up to sixty feet tall. __RO__

2. Up to ten tons in weight. __F__

3. The saguaro's trunk is shaped like a thick column, a few branches point upward. __CS__

4. When I saw a saguaro cactus I thought that in my opinion the branches looked like the arms of a human person who was waving hello to somebody the person knew. __RA__

5. Found in Arizona, southern California, and parts of Mexico. __F__

6. Because the region receives very little rain. __F__

7. The saguaro soaks up rain, grooves in its trunk expand to hold the water. __CS__

8. When the rainstorms finally come. __F__

9. The saguaro's grooves expand and contract like an accordion, which is a musical instrument that has grooves that expand and contract in much the same way. __RA__

10. The saguaro has white, funnel-shaped flowers they bloom on summer nights. __RO__

11. State flower of Arizona. __F__

12. Bats drink the flowers' nectar, pollen is spread from flower to flower on the bats' wings. __CS__

13. Pollinated cacti produce reddish-purple fruit black seeds spill out when the fruit splits open. __RO__

14. The saguaro is an essential part of the ecosystem its fruit provides food for many desert animals. __RO__

15. People eat the fruit raw, they also use it to make jam and syrup. __CS__

Lesson 21 Underline each proper noun. Circle each common noun.

1. Liechtenstein is a very small (country).
2. It is about the (size) of Washington, D.C.
3. This (country) lies in the Alps, which are among the highest (mountains) in Europe.
4. (Trains) pass through Liechtenstein as they travel between Austria and Switzerland.
5. German is the official (language) of Liechtenstein.
6. This tiny (country) is ruled by a (prince).
7. Vaduz is the (capital) of Liechtenstein, and it is also the (location) of the royal (castle).
8. Surrounded by forested (mountains), Liechtenstein lies on the (banks) of the Rhine River.
9. The (region) was once controlled by Charlemagne, (king) of the Franks.
10. It later became a (part) of the Holy Roman Empire.
11. In 1712 Johann-Adam Liechtenstein became (ruler) of what would become Liechtenstein.
12. Liechtenstein has been independent since 1719, except for a short (time) when Napoleon conquered it.
13. (Tourists) from around the (world) visit this picturesque (country).
14. (Collectors) prize (stamps) from Liechtenstein.
15. The (stamps) are decorated with (paintings) by famous (artists) such as Rembrandt and Rubens.

Lesson 22 Write each noun in parentheses in its correct plural form.

1. Two (day) ago my (parent), my brother, and I moved to a new town. _____ days, parents _____
2. I heard the (echo) of the movers' (voice) in our empty new house. _____ echoes, voices _____
3. Everything was packed in (box) and (crate). _____ boxes, crates _____
4. My brother and I sat on the (step) and talked about our new (school). _____ steps, schools _____
5. My brother was scared to meet the (child) in his new second-grade class. _____ children _____
6. I wasn't looking forward to starting (class), either. _____ classes _____
7. Mom said, "Don't dwell on your (worry). Set up your new (room)." _____ worries, rooms _____
8. I unpacked my (book) and placed them on (shelf) in my room. _____ books, shelves _____
9. As I was changing my (shoe), I heard (noise) in the hall. _____ shoes, noises _____
10. I opened my door and saw two (puppy) wagging their (tail). _____ puppies, tails _____
11. I decided that not all the (surprise) in this new town would be bad. _____ surprises _____
12. One puppy was black with white (patch) on his paws, and the other was brown with black (fleck).
    _____ patches, flecks _____
13. We ran out into the garden, where the little dogs leaped like (fox) and howled like (wolf).
    _____ foxes, wolves _____
14. Then they ran off to chase (butterfly) and hide under (bush). _____ butterflies, bushes _____
15. My brother and I wrote about our new (pet) in our (diary). _____ pets, diaries _____

Name _____

Lesson 23 Write the possessive form of each noun in parentheses. Circle each plural possessive noun you write.

1. My (day) work begins with a ride on the bus. _____ day's _____

2. The bus hurries through the (city) traffic. _____ city's _____

3. The (wheels) rumbling is a relaxing sound. _____ (wheels') _____

4. (Passengers) minds wander as they ride. _____ (Passengers') _____

5. Some find entertainment in a (book) pages. _____ book's _____

6. I wonder if it is any (author) dream to be read on all the buses in the country. _____ author's _____

7. You can learn a lot from (riders) conversations. _____ (riders') _____

8. The sound of (children) giggling often fills the bus. _____ (children's) _____

9. I enjoy looking out the (bus) windows. _____ bus's _____

10. That's the best way to get a feel for a (city) character. _____ city's _____

11. (Shops) windows filled with interesting things can be seen all along the route. _____ (Shops') _____

12. You can watch different (pedestrians) walking rhythms. _____ (pedestrians') _____

13. The (leaves) shadows flicker on the sidewalk. _____ (leaves') _____

14. The (bus) engine wheezes as it climbs steep hills. _____ bus's _____

15. At the (ride) end, the doors swing open onto a new neighborhood. _____ ride's _____

Lesson 24 Circle each personal pronoun. Write *1* if it is a first person pronoun, *2* if it is second person, or *3* if it is third person.

1. (I) played handball with Marc yesterday. __1__

2. Is (he) a good player? __3__

3. (You) are just as good. __2__

4. Juan beat (him) in three games last week. __3__

5. (They) played at the park. __3__

6. Marc beat (me), though. __1__

7. (We) played twice yesterday. __1__

8. Did (you) play a good game? __2__

9. (I) was moving fast. __1__

10. (You) should play Marc. __2__

11. Have (you) played against Maria? __2__

12. (She) is surprisingly quick. __3__

13. Juan lost to (her) in an intense game. __3__

14. Marc said the two of (them) are the best players in the neighborhood. __3__

15. Maybe Juan and Maria will play doubles against (us) sometime. __1__

Name _____

Lesson 25 Circle each compound personal pronoun.

1. Shawn and I made (ourselves) a pizza for lunch.
2. Many people like pizza, but most never bake pizzas (themselves).
3. I (myself) was surprised to see how easy it is.
4. Shawn dressed (himself) in an apron before starting to mix and knead the dough.
5. I gave (myself) the task of chopping up the vegetable toppings.
6. As we waited, the rising dough puffed (itself) into a big ball.
7. Shawn twirled the ball of dough in the air above (himself) to flatten it out.
8. We arranged toppings on the surface of the pizza, placing one mushroom by (itself) in the center.
9. The pizza was just the way we like it because we made it (ourselves).
10. You should try it (yourself) sometime.
11. It's not very hard, but there is some work involved: pizzas don't make (themselves).
12. Clear (yourself) a big area for kneading dough and slicing toppings.
13. A friend of mine got (herself) a special stone to cook pizzas on.
14. I (myself) don't think that's necessary.
15. Just find (yourself) a cookie sheet large and sturdy enough to hold the crust.

Lesson 26 Circle each possessive pronoun.

1. (My) dog is bigger than Lia's dog.
2. (Hers) is a tiny, yappy dog.
3. I don't like it as much as I like (yours).
4. (Mine) is huge.
5. Most other dogs are afraid of (my) dog.
6. But he just wants to be (their) friend.
7. (His) tail thumps on the ground.
8. Soon the other dogs are wagging (theirs).
9. (Our) neighborhood has lots of dogs in it.
10. (Your) dog is the nicest.
11. Lia's dog may be small, but have you seen (her) cat?
12. "Kitty" is bigger than both of (my) cats put together.
13. (His) fur puffs out in all directions.
14. That cat's enormous tail has stripes all down (its) length.
15. Some cats' meows sound strangely human, but (his) sound more like a lion's roar.

Name _____

Lesson 27 Circle each relative pronoun and underline the noun it refers to. Draw a box around each interrogative pronoun.

1. [What] is a bobcat?

2. It is a wildcat (that) lives in North America.

3. The bobcat gets its name from its tail, (which) is short, or "bobbed."

4. You can also recognize bobcats by the long hairs on the sides of the face, (which) resemble sideburns.

5. [Who] has seen a bobcat?

6. These animals, (which) are shy and active mainly at night, are hard to observe.

7. [What] is a bobcat's habitat?

8. Bobcats live in areas (that) are wooded, swampy, or mountainous.

9. Mountain climbers (who) venture into the back country occasionally encounter bobcats.

10. For their dens, bobcats prefer small caves and hollow trees, (which) provide shelter and security.

11. Practically any animal (that) is not a predator can become a meal for a bobcat.

12. [Which] do bobcats hunt in the wild?

13. Rabbits, birds, mice, rats, and squirrels are some of the animals (that) make up a bobcat's diet.

14. [Who] must keep an eye out for bobcats on the prowl?

15. Farmers (who) keep chickens must protect their flocks from bobcats.

Lesson 28 Circle each indefinite pronoun.

1. (Everyone) in our family thinks that spaghetti is the best food on earth.

2. My dad knows (everything) there is to know about cooking spaghetti.

3. (Nothing) could taste better.

4. (Most) of us prefer spaghetti with marinara sauce.

5. My sister is the only (one) who likes carbonara sauce better.

6. (Both) are really delicious.

7. Would you prefer a spaghetti dish with meatballs or (one) with sun-dried tomatoes?

8. (Either) would make me happy.

9. (Few) enjoy spaghetti as much as I do.

10. (No one) could possibly be any hungrier than I am right now.

11. Won't (someone) bring me a plateful of spaghetti?

12. (Everybody) come to the table; it's dinnertime!

13. I can't think of (anything) I'd rather do.

14. (Somebody) pass the Parmesan cheese, please.

15. There's (none) left, so you'll have to eat your spaghetti plain.

Name _____

Lesson 29 Circle each adjective that *describes* or tells *what kind*. Underline each adjective that tells *how many*. Draw a box around each article (*a, an, the*).

1. An ancient oak leans over the bank of the lake.

2. Its numerous roots dip into the placid water.

3. A rope is tied to a high branch.

4. I have swung on it on many warm afternoons.

5. You should stand on the grassy bank and grab the thick rope.

6. Swing out over the deep, clear water.

7. Then let go and plunge in with a thunderous splash.

8. You may descend to a depth of ten feet.

9. Everything looks green under the glassy surface.

10. The cold water may make you feel breathless.

11. A few seconds of vigorous swimming will make you warm.

12. If you swim to shallow water, you can do impressive handstands.

13. You might even see a white egret fishing with its long beak in the slender reeds.

14. Then you can swim to shore and scramble up the slippery bank.

15. After a brief rest, you can catch the rope and swing again.

Lesson 30 Circle each demonstrative adjective. Underline each demonstrative pronoun.

1. This store sells loose beads for making jewelry.

2. I made this the last time I came here.

3. That is an interesting bracelet; how did you make it?

4. I strung these beads on wire and made loops to form flower petals.

5. What are those beads in the center of each flower?

6. Those are seeds with holes drilled through them.

7. These beads in the big jar are made out of old buttons.

8. Those beads over there are made of plastic.

9. This is a cowry shell.

10. People once used these shells as money.

11. Look at those colorful beads in the basket.

12. Craftspeople molded those out of multicolored glass.

13. That is my favorite one.

14. This wooden bead is carved in the shape of a turtle.

15. These would make a beautiful bead necklace.

Name _____

Lesson 31 Underline each action verb. Circle each linking verb.

1. Plants <u>make</u> sugar with the sun's energy.
2. A water molecule (is) a combination of hydrogen and oxygen.
3. Plants <u>obtain</u> water from the soil.
4. Their leaves <u>absorb</u> carbon dioxide from the air.
5. Plants (appear) green because of the substance chlorophyll.
6. With energy from sunlight, a plant's chlorophyll <u>splits</u> water molecules into hydrogen and oxygen.
7. A combination of this hydrogen and carbon dioxide <u>forms</u> sugar.
8. Fruit (tastes) sweet because of this sugar.
9. *Photosynthesis* (is) the name of this process.
10. Oxygen (is) a waste product of photosynthesis.
11. Animals <u>breathe</u> this oxygen.
12. Plants (are) an important food source for animals.
13. Inside animals, plant sugars and oxygen (become) energy.
14. Animals <u>exhale</u> carbon dioxide for the plants.
15. Plants and animals <u>depend</u> on each other for survival.

Lesson 32 Underline each transitive verb and draw a box around its direct object. Draw a circle around each intransitive verb.

1. Like all the planets in our solar system, the earth <u>orbits</u> the [sun].
2. It <u>completes</u> one [rotation] each year.
3. The earth's position in relation to the sun <u>causes</u> the [seasons].
4. The earth's axis (tilts) during its orbit.
5. In North America's winter, the North Pole (points) away from the sun.
6. Rain and snow (fall) frequently in the Northern Hemisphere.
7. The winter solstice <u>marks</u> the shortest [day] of the year in the Northern Hemisphere.
8. It (occurs) on December 21 or 22.
9. This day <u>marks</u> the first [day] of summer in the Southern Hemisphere.
10. For the next three months, the Southern Hemisphere <u>experiences</u> its summer [season].
11. The equator <u>divides</u> the earth's Northern and Southern [hemispheres].
12. The vernal equinox, the start of spring, (occurs) in March.
13. The autumnal equinox (happens) in September.
14. During the equinoxes, the sun (shines) directly on the equator.
15. At these times, the length of the day <u>equals</u> the [length] of the night.

Lesson 33 Write *A* if the verb in the sentence is in the active voice. Write *P* if the verb in the sentence is in the passive voice.

1. Seafood is eaten by people all over the world. __P__

2. Squid is called *calamari* by Italian chefs. __P__

3. They often fry calamari in batter. __A__

4. *Sashimi,* sliced raw fish, is offered as an appetizer in Japanese restaurants. __P__

5. In the Japanese dish *sushi,* rice and raw fish are carefully wrapped in seaweed by master chefs. __P__

6. Japanese chefs broil eels for another popular seafood dish. __A__

7. Many people enjoy raw oysters on the half shell. __A__

8. Sturgeon are caught by fishers in the Caspian Sea. __P__

9. Restaurants serve the eggs of these large fish as caviar. __A__

10. Chicken, sausage, rice, and several kinds of seafood are mixed together by skillful chefs in the Spanish dish *paella.* __P__

11. Soft-shell crabs have shed their hard exoskeletons. __A__

12. In Maryland these crabs are eaten whole by hungry diners. __P__

13. Lobsters from Maine are considered a delicacy by gourmets. __P__

14. These crustaceans have tender, sweet, pinkish meat inside their tough red shells. __A__

15. Lobster bibs are often worn by diners for this messy treat. __P__

Lesson 34 Circle each present tense verb. Underline each past tense verb. Draw a box around each future tense verb.

1. The monsoon cycle (controls) rainfall in parts of Asia, Africa, and Australia.

2. Temperature differences between sea air and inland air (cause) the monsoon.

3. Dry winds (blow) from the northeast in winter.

4. By midsummer, southwest winds [will bring] torrential rain to the parched land.

5. In July 2005, 37 inches of monsoon rain fell on Mumbai, India, in a single day.

6. With so much rain, the city streets became severely flooded.

7. A violent cyclone devastated Bangladesh during the 1991 monsoon season.

8. More than 138,000 people died in that storm.

9. The rains (bring) new life along with destruction, however.

10. Heavy monsoon rains (are) essential for healthy crops.

11. Every summer, people (watch) the weather reports anxiously for news of the monsoon.

12. Right now, no one accurately (predicts) the time or strength of the monsoon very far in advance.

13. Accurate predictions [will come] eventually, though.

14. In 1978 scientists began MONEX, a wide survey of the monsoon.

15. With more intensive study, we [will understand] this cycle better.

Name _____

Lesson 35 Circle the boldfaced verbs in present perfect tense. Underline the boldfaced verbs in past perfect tense. Draw a box around the boldfaced verbs in future perfect tense.

1. I <u>had liked</u> rubber bands since I was in kindergarten, but I had never collected them before last year.
2. My interest (has grown) even greater since then.
3. Every day, once I (have finished) my homework, I look for rubber bands to add to my collection.
4. As soon as I <u>had collected</u> twenty rubber bands, I began forming a rubber band ball.
5. The ball (has grown) much larger since then.
6. I (have added) rubber bands of all sizes and colors.
7. Once I had to knock my rubber band ball out of a tree; it <u>had bounced</u> up after I threw it at the sidewalk.
8. I began my collection several months ago; by March I [will have kept] it for one year.
9. The biggest rubber band ball weighs more than 4,000 pounds; I <u>had seen</u> a picture of it in a book.
10. By the time I graduate from high school, my rubber band ball [will have grown] even larger than that one.
11. I (have researched) some other rubber band records recently.
12. Surely you (have heard) about the longest rubber band in the world.
13. Students who <u>had tied</u> thousands of rubber bands together found that the chain measured more than 19 miles in length.
14. I (have thought) about starting a rubber band chain myself.
15. I will not rest until I (have broken) a rubber band record!

Lesson 36 Circle each boldfaced verb in a progressive form. Underline each boldfaced verb that is not in a progressive form.

1. I (am having) a bad day.
2. It (was raining) when I woke up.
3. My sister <u>had eaten</u> the last of my favorite cereal.
4. I still <u>have</u> not <u>forgiven</u> her for it.
5. Outside, a big gust of wind blew just as I (was opening) my umbrella.
6. Soon it <u>had turned</u> inside out; it was ruined.
7. I guess this weekend I (will be buying) a new umbrella.
8. As I got to the bus stop, the bus (was driving) away.
9. Since I <u>had missed</u> the bus, I had to walk to school.
10. I got very wet while I (was walking).
11. I <u>have been</u> on time every day this semester, but today I was late.
12. Just as I walked in, my teacher (was distributing) a pop quiz.
13. Now, however, my day (is getting) a little better.
14. My teacher announced that next week we (will be going) to the aquarium.
15. I <u>have decided</u> to put this terrible morning behind me.

Name _____

Lesson 37 Circle each adverb. Then tell whether the adverb explains *how, when, where,* or *to what extent.*

1. The dancers leaped (high) into the air. _____to what extent_____

2. They moved (gracefully). _____how_____

3. They balanced (daintily) on their toes to delicate music. _____how_____

4. (Then) the music changed to a loud, dramatic piece. _____when_____

5. The company stomped (thunderously) with their heels. _____how_____

6. They seemed to dance (effortlessly). _____how_____

7. It must be (extremely) difficult to learn and practice complicated dance steps. _____to what extent_____

8. One dancer performed a solo (beautifully). _____how_____

9. Another dancer tripped on some scenery (there). _____where_____

10. He fell (clumsily) to the floor. _____how_____

11. He had twisted his ankle (severely). _____to what extent_____

12. He was helped off the stage and his ankle was (immediately) examined. _____when_____

13. The ankle was (only) sprained. _____to what extent_____

14. (Afterwards), the dancer appeared for a curtain call. _____when_____

15. Everyone clapped (loudly) for the dedicated dancer. _____how_____

Lesson 38 Underline each prepositional phrase. Circle the preposition and draw a box around its object. There may be more than one prepositional phrase in a sentence.

1. The strangler fig grows (in) the rainforest.

2. Birds and bats drop its seeds (over) tall trees.

3. (In) the leafy canopy, a fig seed sprouts.

4. Long vines grow (from) that seed.

5. These strong vines encircle the trunk (of) a host tree.

6. The fig plant then drops roots (to) the forest floor.

7. (After) a while, the host tree dies and rots away.

8. The strong lacework (of) vines stands (on) its own.

9. You can climb (inside) the hollow strangler fig.

10. The interior (of) the hollow trunk towers (above) your head.

11. You could imagine you are (in) a deep well.

12. Then you grab (onto) the sturdy vines and climb (through) the hollow center.

13. The spaces (between) the vines resemble small windows.

14. You can see amazing sights (from) that vantage point.

15. The rainforest floor lies (beneath) you.

Name _____

Lesson 39 Underline each coordinating conjunction. Circle each subordinating conjunction.

1. (Before) my brother started playing the bagpipe, I had never heard the instrument.

2. The bagpipe is an ancient instrument, but no one knows its origins.

3. Scottish bagpipes are made of a leather bag and five pipes.

4. (When) a musician blows into the *blowpipe,* the bag inflates.

5. The musician presses the bag, and air flows out of the pipes.

6. Each of the three *drone* pipes makes one continuous note, but the musician plays tunes by covering holes on the *chanter* pipe.

7. (Although) Scottish bagpipes can only produce nine notes, many bagpipe tunes are challenging.

8. (Since) my brother started playing, he has learned ten tunes.

9. (Because) bagpipes are expensive, my brother started with a practice instrument called a chanter.

10. The chanter is basically a blowpipe and a chanter pipe combined.

11. (When) my brother had learned to play the chanter well, he bought a real bagpipe.

12. (If) you've ever heard a bagpipe, you know it sounds very different from most other instruments.

13. Its sounds make me think of a person humming, the ocean roaring, or a duck quacking.

14. I like my brother's music, but I wish his bagpipes weren't so loud.

15. He practices outside, (because) he would drive everyone in the house crazy otherwise.

Lesson 40 Circle each conjunction. If a sentence contains correlative conjunctions, write *CC* on the line.

1. My sister (and) I are identical twins. _____

2. We (not only) look alike (but also) sound alike. __CC__

3. (Both) our friends (and) our parents can tell us apart, however. __CC__

4. (Neither) my sister (nor) I like to wear identical clothes. __CC__

5. We may look alike, (but) our personalities are different. _____

6. After school, my sister is usually (either) playing sports (or) practicing ballet. __CC__

7. I prefer reading (and) acting in plays. _____

8. Still, my twin is (not only) my sister (but also) a good friend. __CC__

9. (Both) she (and) I enjoy hiking in the wilderness. __CC__

10. We often take hikes (or) just short walks together. _____

11. We joke around (and) talk about whatever is on our minds. _____

12. We share a sense of humor; often (either) she is playing a practical joke (or) I am telling a funny story. __CC__

13. Once we switched clothes (and) pretended to be each other. _____

14. Some of our friends were fooled at first, (but) after talking to us for a while they figured out the trick. _____

15. (Neither) our teachers (nor) our parents were fooled. __CC__

270   **Name** _____

Lesson 41 Fill in the blanks with *your* or *you're*. Remember to capitalize a word that begins a sentence.

1. What is ___your___ favorite sport?

2. Lucia told me that ___you're___ a fan of gymnastics.

3. Is becoming an Olympic gymnast ___your___ dream?

4. If ___you're___ planning to become a gymnast, be prepared to work very hard.

5. You will have to spend part of every day at ___your___ gym.

6. ___Your___ coach will teach you many new skills.

7. She will also help you build ___your___ strength.

8. ___You're___ going to need to eat lots of healthful foods to build up muscles.

9. Soon ___you're___ going to be doing flips and handstands.

10. ___Your___ safety is extremely important; a "spotter" will make sure you don't hurt yourself on difficult moves.

11. When ___you're___ ready, you can enter competitions.

12. You'll need to put together all ___your___ new skills into a smooth routine.

13. ___You're___ probably going to be nervous.

14. Still, try to keep ___your___ mind on the routine.

15. If you always do ___your___ best, you will be satisfied with whatever you accomplish.

Lesson 42 Fill in the blanks with *their*, *they're*, or *there*. Remember to capitalize a word that begins a sentence.

1. ___There___ are many European legends about elves.

2. ___They're___ imaginary creatures who are said to have magic powers.

3. Elves are said to tell people where ___there___ are rich veins of gold.

4. In some stories elves use ___their___ powers to help people.

5. For example, elves might help lost travelers find ___their___ way.

6. In other stories, though, ___they're___ mean and unpleasant.

7. Some stories tell about elves who kidnap humans and take them to ___their___ secret land.

8. When the humans return, ___they're___ old and gray.

9. A storyteller may point out a round hill and say, "Elves live under ___there___!"

10. ___They're___ also said to live on magical islands.

11. Time passes very slowly ___there___, so elves seem never to reach old age.

12. When elves ask humans for ___their___ help and the humans provide that help, the elves usually repay the humans handsomely.

13. Many authors have included elves in ___their___ stories.

14. You may have heard of Legolas, Elrond, or Galadriel; ___they're___ all elves in books by J.R.R. Tolkien.

15. You can read more about elves in the book over ___there___ by the clock.

Name _____

Lesson 43 Circle the correct word in parentheses.

1. (It's/Its) amazing how many different kinds of fish there are.

2. What is the largest fish in the world? (It's/Its) the whale shark, which can weigh more than 15 tons.

3. (It's/Its) diet is primarily made up of tiny aquatic organisms.

4. I was relieved to learn that (it's/its) harmless to people.

5. The black swallower can eat fish twice (it's/its) size.

6. It does this by unhinging (it's/its) jaw in the same way a boa constrictor does.

7. The flying hatchet fish can use (it's/its) pectoral fins as wings.

8. (It's/Its) actually able to take off from the water's surface and fly for up to ten feet.

9. The porcupine fish uses (it's/its) prickly spines for protection.

10. (It's/Its) also able to fill itself with water to appear larger than it actually is.

11. If someone asks you what fish has four eyes, tell her (it's/its) the anableps.

12. (It's/Its) eyes are divided in two, so it can swim just below the surface and see above and below the water.

13. A cave fish is adapted to life in total darkness; (it's/its) eyes may be small and sightless, or nonexistent.

14. An archerfish catches (it's/its) prey by spitting water through the air.

15. (It's/Its) an expert at catching small insects it knocks into the water.

Lesson 44 Circle the correct word in parentheses.

1. (Whose/Who's) interested in puppets?

2. I first became interested through a friend (whose/who's) mother is a puppeteer.

3. I know another puppeteer (whose/who's) going to teach me his craft.

4. He says that anyone (whose/who's) as interested as I am is sure to do well.

5. I made a puppet (whose/who's) head is a sock.

6. The puppet looks like the Cheshire Cat, (whose/who's) my favorite character.

7. I have a friend (whose/who's) working on a puppet of her own.

8. It's a paper bag puppet (whose/who's) hair is made of shredded newspaper.

9. We can't decide (whose/who's) puppet is funnier.

10. My hero is Mario Lamo Jiménez, (whose/who's) the author of the puppet play *Andar nas Nuvens*.

11. I've been reading about different kinds of puppets in a book (whose/who's) author is a famous puppeteer.

12. Marionettes are puppets (whose/who's) movements are controlled by strings or wires.

13. (Whose/Who's) familiar with the Japanese form of puppetry known as Bunraku?

14. A friend of mine (whose/who's) seen Bunraku told me that the puppeteers dress all in black but don't hide out of sight.

15. Some of the most popular entertainers in Indonesia are puppets (whose/who's) shadows are projected onto screens.

  Name _____

Lesson 45 Fill in each blank with *to, too,* or *two* to complete each sentence correctly.

1. Yesterday I went _____to_____ the African art museum.

2. I took the special tour on battles, which began at _____two_____ o'clock.

3. The tour took _____two_____ hours, but the time passed very quickly.

4. I learned about historic African weapons and armor and battle customs, _____too_____.

5. Many Central African throwing knives had _____two_____ points, one on each side.

6. The throwing method was similar _____to_____ that of throwing a boomerang.

7. Although some knives were only used in battle, others had ceremonial functions, _____too_____.

8. Some African cavalrymen rode _____to_____ battle wearing quilted cloth armor.

9. Their horses wore this kind of armor, _____too_____.

10. Fulani cavalrymen wore quilted battle coats, but they also protected their bodies from shoulder _____to_____ waist with heavy iron armor.

11. A Fulani warrior who fell off his horse in battle could not remount because the armor was _____too_____ heavy.

12. Often a soldier carried a sword and _____two_____ spears into battle.

13. Most of the soldiers used shields, _____too_____.

14. Beautiful silverwork often attached a lion's mane or tail _____to_____ an Ethiopian warrior's shield.

15. The Maasai and the Kikuyu peoples often held a duel between their _____two_____ best warriors before a battle.

Lesson 46 Fill in each blank with *than* or *then* to complete each sentence correctly.

1. Earthquakes happen almost every day in some part of California; now and _____then_____ one of them is strong enough for people to feel.

2. I think small earthquakes are more exciting _____than_____ frightening.

3. Some earthquakes begin more _____than_____ 400 miles below ground.

4. First the earth's crust starts moving deep below the surface; _____then_____ energy waves go through the ground.

5. Compressional, or primary, waves travel faster _____than_____ shear, or secondary, waves.

6. This is why compressional waves arrive first, and _____then_____ shear waves arrive.

7. Both of these waves travel faster deep inside the earth's crust _____than_____ they do near the surface.

8. If the ground continues to shake for a long time, buildings may shake apart and _____then_____ collapse.

9. If you're inside and feel an earthquake begin, take shelter right _____then_____ under a desk or table.

10. Wait until you are sure the quake is over; only _____then_____ should you come out.

11. When it comes to earthquakes, nothing is more important _____than_____ being prepared.

12. Schools and businesses practice emergency procedures; _____then_____ everyone knows what to do in a disaster.

13. Often more damage is caused by the by-products of earthquakes _____than_____ by the earthquakes themselves.

14. An undersea earthquake may cause a tsunami, which may _____then_____ roll toward land and do terrible damage.

15. Sometimes, fires started by ruptured gas lines cause more damage _____than_____ the earthquake.

Name _____

Lesson 47 Write *X* after each sentence that uses negatives incorrectly. Write *C* after each sentence that is written correctly.

1. I haven't never had a pet before, but my father says I can get one for my birthday. __X__
2. I can't decide what kind of pet I want. __C__
3. My dad doesn't want no cat in the house because he's allergic to them. __X__
4. Tropical fish are beautiful, but they don't do nothing but swim. __X__
5. You can't take them nowhere, neither. __X__
6. A friend of mine has a gerbil, and it never stops running on its exercise wheel. __C__
7. My dad doesn't like the idea of having a rat in the house. __C__
8. Snakes are cool, but I wouldn't want to feed them no live mice. __X__
9. Insects aren't really pets, in my opinion. __C__
10. An ant farm doesn't count, and neither does a beehive. __C__
11. Parrots are pretty, but my dad wouldn't never let me have such a noisy pet. __X__
12. Besides, birds aren't very cuddly, and you can't really play with them. __C__
13. I can't think of nothing wrong with dogs. __X__
14. My dad doesn't have any problems with dogs either. __C__
15. It won't be long before we have a new puppy in the family. __C__

Lesson 48 Cross out each incorrect usage of *go, went, like,* and *all.* (If the word *was* is part of the incorrect expression, cross that out also.) Write correct words to replace the crossed out words if a replacement is needed.

1. Jamal ~~was all~~, "My friend Tatiana is going to enter a math competition." ____said____
2. Then he ~~goes~~, "She is one of the smartest people I know." ____said____
3. He was, ~~like,~~ so insistent that she would win, ~~like,~~ no matter who else entered the contest. _____
4. Marjorie ~~was like~~, "What will happen if she does win?" ____asked____
5. Jamal said if she, ~~like,~~ *did* win locally, she'd go against students from, ~~like,~~ all over the state. _____
6. Then he ~~went~~, "All the winners of the state contest will form a team to compete with others from around the country." ____said____
7. So Marjorie ~~goes~~, "Do you think she'll get that far?" ____asked____
8. Jamal ~~was like~~, "She was on the winning team last year, and I think she can do it again." ____said____
9. Marjorie ~~was all~~, "Tatiana sounds like a very smart person. I'd like to meet her sometime." ____said____
10. Jamal said that he would, ~~like,~~ introduce us after school. _____
11. Then we, ~~like,~~ ran into Tatiana. _____
12. She ~~went~~, "Oh, hi, how are you?" ____said____
13. At first I thought she was kind of, ~~like,~~ shy. _____
14. Then she ~~goes~~, "I heard you guys are really good in math." ____said____
15. She, ~~like,~~ asked us to join her team for the competition! _____

Possible replacement words are given. Accept all reasonable responses.

Lesson 49 Circle the correct word in parentheses.

1. From where we (sit/set), we can see the pyramids of ancient Egypt on the west bank of the Nile River.

2. The mummified bodies of pharaohs once (lay/laid) in them.

3. Realistic statues showing a pharaoh (sitting/setting) on his throne were believed to help the pharaoh's spirit recognize the pyramid as its home.

4. Statues' eyes were often (sit/set) with quartz crystal to make them as lifelike as possible.

5. Some experts believe that the pyramids were built by farm laborers during the part of each year when Nile floodwaters (lay/laid) on the fields.

6. A major step in building the pyramids was to build ramps and (lie/lay) planks on them to reduce friction.

7. Then workers slid enormous blocks of limestone up the ramps and (sat/set) them in layers.

8. Archaeologists have calculated that the workers had to (sit/set) one block every two and a half minutes.

9. Finally, workers (lay/laid) a smooth coating of smaller stones over the top.

10. Once these smaller stones were (sat/set) in place, the pyramid looked like solid stone from a distance.

11. Archaeologists have made interesting discoveries about the lives of the workers who (lay/laid) the stones.

12. The remains of a bakery and of a workers' graveyard still (lie/lay) near the pyramids.

13. Some workers were (lay/laid) to rest under miniature pyramids made of mud bricks.

14. Ancient robbers looted the pharaohs' pyramids for the treasures that (lay/laid) inside them.

15. After about 1700 B.C., Egyptians (lay/laid) their pharaohs in secret tombs to hide them from robbers.

Lesson 50 Circle the correct word in parentheses.

1. I (thought/thinked) I saw a dog in the alley.

2. It turned and (shaked/shook) its tail at me.

3. I (threw/throwed) a rubber ball to it.

4. The next day I (bringed/brought) it some food.

5. Someone had (built/builded) a small shelter for it.

6. Unfortunately, the wind had (blew/blown) some of the boards apart.

7. I was glad I had (wore/worn) a scarf.

8. The alley was (lit/litten) by a rosy sunset.

9. As it (grew/grown) darker, I worried that I wouldn't see the dog again.

10. My heart (sang/singed) when I saw the dog come around the corner.

11. It (ate/eated) the food eagerly.

12. Then I (gone/went) home slowly.

13. At my door I turned and saw that the dog had (ran/run) after me, wagging its tail.

14. My parents (said/sayed) we could keep the dog if no one reported it as missing.

15. We (drived/drove) to the vet to make sure the dog was healthy and to get it its shots.

Name _____

Lesson 51 Circle each boldfaced word that is a subject pronoun. Underline each boldfaced word that is an object pronoun.

1. (You) won't believe what (we) got from Mildred.

2. (She) gave **us** a fruitcake.

3. (We) thanked **her** politely.

4. (It) was as hard as a rock.

5. Floyd told **me** that (he) likes fruitcake.

6. (I) sent the cake to **him**.

7. (He) could not eat **it**.

8. His cousins like sweets; (he) gave it to **them**.

9. (They) don't want **it** either.

10. Maybe (they) will send it to **you**.

11. (I) have thought of a gift that (we) all want.

12. (It) is useful to all of **us**.

13. (I) will give **you** a hint.

14. (You) write your thoughts in **it**.

15. (You) guessed **it**: a pocket notebook.

Lesson 52 Circle the correct pronoun in each pair. Write *S* if you chose a subject pronoun and *O* if you chose an object pronoun.

1. Brock and (I/me) met MacDougal at the scene of the crime. __S__

2. (He/Him) and Findley were dusting for fingerprints. __S__

3. I asked them to give Brock and (I/me) the lowdown. __O__

4. They said Lizzie had given the Tenth Precinct and (we/us) the slip. __O__

5. As Brock and (I/me) interviewed Mrs. Patel, the owner of the jewelry store, her son Billy came in. __S__

6. (He/Him) and Mrs. Patel got into an argument about whether Mrs. Patel had locked the door. __S__

7. (She/Her) and Billy were the last to leave the store before the robbery. __S__

8. They told Brock and (I/me) that everything had seemed normal that night. __O__

9. I told Brock and (they/them) that Lizzie and her accomplices always strike when you least expect it. __O__

10. I knew it would be hard to catch Lizzie and (they/them). __O__

11. Brock and (I/me) were determined to give it our best shot. __S__

12. There's an old score to settle between Lizzie and (I/me). __O__

13. (She and I/Her and me) worked together once, before she turned to the wrong side of the law. __S__

14. I knew Lizzie couldn't resist the lasagna served at the restaurant where (she and I/her and me) used to get lunch on our break. __S__

15. We staked out the restaurant, and, sure enough, the lasagna and (I/me) captured the master thief. __S__

Lesson 53 Circle the antecedent or antecedents of each boldfaced pronoun.

1. (Rachelle) and her (mother) and (brother) drove across the United States when **they** moved from Philadelphia to Los Angeles.

2. (Rachelle) kept a diary of everything **she** saw along the way.

3. In her diary, Rachelle wrote about the (Sears Tower) in Chicago; **it** is a very tall building.

4. (Rachelle's) mother pointed out the Mississippi River to **her,** and Rachelle wrote about that, too.

5. When the trip got boring, (Rachelle) played the license plate game to pass the time; **she** kept track of each new state's license plate she saw.

6. The (car) broke down somewhere near Denver, but a mechanic fixed **it.**

7. The (mechanic) was friendly, and Rachelle wrote about **him** in her diary.

8. Rachelle wrote about the (Rocky Mountains) when her mother drove through **them.**

9. In Utah, Rachelle's (brother) asked to visit Zion National Park; **he** had read that the park is beautiful.

10. (Rachelle), her (mother), and her (brother) parked the car so **they** could go hiking in the colorful canyons.

11. In some places, the canyon (walls) were so close together Rachelle could touch **them** both at the same time.

12. Back in the car, Rachelle wrote about (Zion); she said **it** was the most amazing place she had ever visited.

13. As Rachelle's (mother) navigated the streets of Las Vegas, **she** pointed out all the flashing signs.

14. (Rachelle) wrote in her diary that the lights looked like stars to **her.**

15. Finally, the (family) arrived at the Pacific Ocean, and **they** went for a swim.

Lesson 54 Circle the pronoun in parentheses to complete each sentence correctly.

1. (Who/Whom) is playing first base?

2. The player (who/whom) the league named MVP for last year is the first baseman.

3. (Who/Whom) or what is an "MVP"?

4. MVP stands for Most Valuable Player, a player without (who/whom) the team would be lost.

5. I have a cousin (who/whom) admires that player very much.

6. (Who/Whom) is that over there?

7. To (who/whom) are you referring?

8. I am referring to the person (who/whom) is sitting in the front row of the bleachers.

9. I still can't tell to (who/whom) you are pointing.

10. I mean that woman (who/whom) is eating a hot dog.

11. Oh, she is someone of (who/whom) you may have heard.

12. She's the one (who/whom) starred in that movie.

13. Do you mean the movie with the director (who/whom) won an Academy Award?

14. That's a person (who/whom) I would like to meet!

15. Let's find someone (who/whom) will introduce us.

Name _____

Lesson 55 Circle the simple subject in each sentence. Then underline the correct form of each verb in parentheses.

1. A new (set) of watercolors (<u>is</u>/are) what I want for my birthday.
2. (Tubes) of paint (works/<u>work</u>) best for my style of painting.
3. Mineral-based (pigments) (gives/<u>give</u>) the paints their colors.
4. (Paints) made with the pigment cadmium (looks/<u>look</u>) red.
5. (Cobalt), another pigment, (<u>turns</u>/turn) paints blue.
6. (Compounds) of chrome and lead (produces/<u>produce</u>) brilliant pigments.
7. The many (colors) of chrome (includes/<u>include</u>) red, yellow, orange, and bright green.
8. The health (risks) of lead (necessitates/<u>necessitate</u>) handling these pigments with great care.
9. A (mixture) of iron oxide, clay, and sand (<u>creates</u>/create) ocher, a yellowish-brown pigment.
10. A (material) called gum arabic (<u>holds</u>/hold) watercolors together.
11. (Blobs) of paint (dot/<u>dots</u>) my mixing palette.
12. A skillful (artist) always (<u>mixes</u>/mix) shades carefully.
13. (Drops) of water (lightens/<u>lighten</u>) a color; I add the drops slowly.
14. Long, quick (strokes) with a big brush (creates/<u>create</u>) a thin wash of color.
15. (Layers) of transparent color (overlaps/<u>overlap</u>) to make a new shade.

Lesson 56 Look at the compound subject in each sentence. Circle the conjunction. Then underline the correct verb.

1. My friends (and) my brother (likes/<u>like</u>) eating in the cafeteria.
2. Either Mr. Novak (or) Mrs. MacGee usually (<u>serves</u>/serve) us the entree.
3. The window table (or) the corner table (<u>is</u>/are) a good place to sit.
4. Fresh-baked bread (or) muffins often (appears/<u>appear</u>) on Mondays.
5. Jaia (and) Piper (likes/<u>like</u>) muffins a lot.
6. A vegetarian entree (and) a sugar-free dessert (is/<u>are</u>) always available.
7. On Tuesdays, hamburgers (or) vegetable lasagna (<u>is</u>/are) the featured entree.
8. Gerome (and) Garth always (chooses/<u>choose</u>) hamburgers.
9. Sometimes Gerome (or) Garth (<u>lets</u>/let) me have a few french fries.
10. Either baked ziti (or) fried chicken (<u>is</u>/are) served on Wednesdays.
11. Thursdays are my favorite because fajitas (and) black bean chili (is/<u>are</u>) on the menu that day.
12. Neither the fried chicken (nor) the hamburgers (tastes/<u>taste</u>) as good as the black bean chili.
13. Neither cake (nor) pie (<u>is</u>/are) ever served for dessert on Fridays.
14. Jaia (and) I usually (orders/<u>order</u>) bread pudding that day.
15. Today, a baked potato (and) a salad from the salad bar (sounds/<u>sound</u>) good to me.

Name _____

Extra Practice

Lesson 57 Circle the simple subject in each clause. Then underline the correct form of each verb in parentheses.

1. "Megatoaster" (**is**/are) the name of our band.
2. Dimitri and Damon (is/**are**) in the group with me.
3. The group (**sounds**/sound) really good now.
4. We always (plays/**play**) our own original music.
5. "Walls and Windows" (**is**/are) a new song I've just written.
6. The band (**plays**/play) at teen clubs and picnics.
7. Everyone (**dances**/dance) when we play.
8. "I Froze My Toes" (**is**/are) our most popular song.
9. The whole crowd (**cheers**/cheer) when we start playing it.
10. At that moment, everything (**seems**/seem) great.
11. My family (**does**/do) not come to hear us very often.
12. No one (**says**/say) the music is too loud, but all of them cover their ears when we play.
13. Earplugs (helps/**help**) protect our eardrums from the noise.
14. Nothing (**stops**/stop) us in the middle of a song.
15. Our sound equipment sometimes (**blows**/blow) fuses, but we keep playing.

Lesson 58 Underline the verbal phrase that begins each sentence. If the phrase is a dangling modifier, write *dangling* on the line. If the phrase is used correctly, circle the word it modifies and write *C* on the line.

1. Learning to knit, sweaters can be made. __dangling__
2. Wanting to try a new hobby, Maxine learned to knit. __C__
3. Never having knitted before, a simple pattern was chosen. __dangling__
4. Looping yarn around long needles, the project seemed easy. __dangling__
5. Glancing briefly at the instructions, Maxine began knitting very quickly. __C__
6. Knitting the front of the sweater, mistakes were made. __dangling__
7. Covered with holes and lumps in the stitches, the sweater was not wearable. __C__
8. Unraveling it stitch by stitch, disappointment was inevitable. __dangling__
9. Determined to learn, it was time to make a new start. __dangling__
10. Studying the instructions carefully, Maxine realized where she had gone wrong. __C__
11. Knitting carefully this time, the sweater grew slowly but steadily. __dangling__
12. Spaced evenly and neatly, the rows of stitches looked better. __C__
13. Taking her time, Maxine created a beautiful sweater. __C__
14. Made with her own two hands, she was very content. __dangling__
15. Having knit one sweater successfully, she is ready to begin another. __C__

Name _____

Lesson 59 Think about how many things are being compared in each sentence. Then underline the correct form of the adjective or adverb in parentheses.

1. Jamal runs (<u>faster</u>/fastest) than I do.

2. But Aya is the (faster/<u>fastest</u>) runner on the track team.

3. She runs even (<u>better</u>/best) than our coach.

4. Last month I started practicing (<u>harder</u>/hardest) than I ever had before.

5. I ate the (healthier/<u>healthiest</u>) foods I could find.

6. I spent (<u>longer</u>/longest) than usual warming up each day before races.

7. Yesterday was the (bigger/<u>biggest</u>) race of the season.

8. It was scheduled (<u>earlier</u>/earliest) than I had expected.

9. Still, I felt (<u>more ready</u>/most ready) than I feel before most races.

10. I also felt the (more nervous/<u>most nervous</u>) I had ever felt in my life.

11. I pushed myself (<u>more determinedly</u>/most determinedly) than anyone else in the race.

12. I almost ended up with a (<u>better</u>/best) time than Aya.

13. Even though I didn't win, I was the (prouder/<u>proudest</u>) one there.

14. She's still the (swifter/<u>swiftest</u>) runner of all.

15. But now no one will think of me as the (slower/<u>slowest</u>) on the team.

Lesson 60 Underline the correct helping verb in each sentence.

1. If you like mazes, you (have/<u>might</u>) be interested in learning about the Labyrinth of Minos.

2. This legendary building (did/<u>may</u>) have been the first maze.

3. The legend of the Labyrinth (<u>has</u>/should) been told for over two thousand years.

4. According to the Greek myth, King Minos (was/<u>had</u>) asked Daedalus to build the Labyrinth.

5. A bull-headed monster called the Minotaur (should/<u>was</u>) imprisoned inside.

6. Greeks of ancient Athens (<u>would</u>/may) sacrifice seven young men and women each year to the Minotaur.

7. The Greek hero Theseus felt that the sacrifices to the Minotaur (have/<u>must</u>) be stopped.

8. He said he (is/<u>would</u>) be one of the seven to enter the Labyrinth.

9. King Minos's daughter gave Theseus a ball of twine so that he (was/<u>could</u>) mark his path through the confusing passages of the Labyrinth.

10. After Theseus (<u>had</u>/should) killed the Minotaur, he escaped with King Minos's daughter.

11. The Labyrinth of legend (can/<u>might</u>) have been based on a real place.

12. Archaeologists (did/<u>may</u>) have found the original Labyrinth at the ancient palace of Knossos in Crete.

13. No Minotaur lived in the real Labyrinth, but, according to wall paintings young athletes (<u>did</u>/is) jump over bulls there.

14. Today visitors (had/<u>can</u>) tour the rebuilt palace at Knossos.

15. That tour (<u>would</u>/is) be fascinating to take.

Name _____

Lesson 61 Draw three lines (≡) under each lowercase letter that should be capitalized. Draw a line (/) through each capital letter that should be lowercase.

1. The country of fiji is in the South pacific.
2. more than 300 Islands and 500 reefs make up this tropical Nation.
3. viti levu, or Big Fiji, is the Largest island.
4. Smaller islands include Kandavu and vanua levu.
5. thousands of years ago, people migrated to fiji from indonesia.
6. Nearly 2,000 years ago, a group of polynesians settled there.
7. A dutch navigator named abel tasman was the first european explorer to visit the islands.
8. In 1774 captain james cook visited a southern Island called vatoa.
9. In the decades that followed, many european traders and Missionaries settled in Fiji.
10. Thousands of workers from india were brought to fiji to work on sugar plantations.
11. A few escaped convicts from australia also made fiji their home.
12. Many of today's Fijians are of indian, polynesian, Chinese, micronesian, and european descent.
13. Fiji has been an independent Nation since 1970.
14. The official language of fiji is english, but many island residents speak fijian or hindi.
15. Fiji's capital and largest City is suva, which lies along the southern coast of viti levu.

Lesson 62 Rewrite each item below. Use initials and abbreviations where you can.

1. Doctor Martha Jane Brown — **Dr. M.J. Brown**
2. Mister Miguel Garcia — **Mr. M. Garcia**
3. Stanyan Street — **Stanyan St.**
4. Mount Shasta — **Mt. Shasta**
5. Riverland Avenue — **Riverland Ave.**
6. Mistress Madeline Trimble — **Mrs. M. Trimble or Miss M. Trimble**
7. Castle Corporation — **Castle Corp.**
8. General Robert Edward Lee — **Gen. R.E. Lee**
9. Monterey Boulevard — **Monterey Blvd.**
10. Mister Gino Raffetto — **Mr. G. Raffetto**
11. Bonnview Road — **Bonnview Rd.**
12. Doctor Peter Murray — **Dr. P. Murray**
13. Cellular Network, Incorporated — **Cellular Network, Inc.**
14. Cassock Drive — **Cassock Dr.**
15. Mister Robert Elwood Jones — **Mr. R.E. Jones**

Name _____

Lesson 63 Draw three lines (≡) under the letters that should be capitalized. Underline or add quotation marks where they are needed in titles.

1. My family rented the movie <u>south pacific</u>, and we found it very entertaining.
2. Now I am writing an adventure story titled "lost in the south Pacific."
3. I found information about the region in the book <u>journeys in paradise</u>.
4. I also found information in a DVD titled <u>island escapes</u>.
5. I read a book called <u>in search of the coral reef</u>.
6. My favorite short story in the book was "shark escape."
7. I also enjoyed the story "marlin adventure."
8. My sister wrote a beautiful poem called "Reef dream."
9. She also wrote a silly song titled "the stingray's revenge."
10. Her poem was printed in a literary magazine called <u>fresh literary voices</u>.
11. If you plan to visit the South Pacific, you should read the book <u>basic canoeing tips</u>.
12. Bring a copy of the cookbook <u>Tropical island delights</u>.
13. You should also rent the video documentary <u>how to avoid electric eels</u>.
14. I saw a short film titled <u>exotic wildlife of Borneo</u>.
15. It was based on the book <u>wild creatures of Borneo</u>.

Lesson 64 Underline the correct word in parentheses. If the word is a possessive, write *possessive*. If the word is a contraction, write the two words it was made from.

1. In 1994 a group of adventurers traveled the length of (<u>Canada's</u>/Canadas') largest island, Baffin Island. ___possessive___
2. Baffin Island is the (<u>world's</u>/worlds') fifth largest island. ___possessive___
3. The majority of the (<u>island's</u>/islands') land mass lies above the Arctic Circle. ___possessive___
4. Most of Baffin Island (is'nt/<u>isn't</u>) accessible by car. ___is not___
5. The (<u>men's</u>/mens') journey required the use of skis, kayaks, and sleds. ___possessive___
6. The (explorer's/<u>explorers'</u>) goal was to travel 1,800 miles in six months. ___possessive___
7. They knew such a journey (<u>couldn't</u>/could'nt) be done during winter. ___could not___
8. They started in March, when (<u>winter's</u>/winters') icy grip had eased. ___possessive___
9. The travelers (<u>weren't</u>/were'nt) able to escape the cold weather entirely, however; they encountered temperatures of more than 40 degrees below zero. ___were not___
10. On the (<u>journey's</u>/journeys') first leg, they skied more than 1,000 miles. ___possessive___
11. Maps (<u>didn't</u>/did'nt) prepare them for the reality of the rugged terrain. ___did not___
12. The (mens'/<u>men's</u>) sleds weighed 200 pounds apiece, making travel slow and difficult. ___possessive___
13. Next the explorers paddled 600 miles in kayaks, but their journey (<u>wasn't</u>/was'nt) over. ___was not___
14. They hiked the final 230 miles to Baffin (<u>Island's</u>/Islands') southern tip. ___possessive___
15. The (<u>adventurer's</u>/adventurers') entire journey took 192 days. ___possessive___

Name _____

Lesson 65 Add commas where they belong. Use the delete mark (⌿) on commas that don't belong. Remember that a comma is not needed to separate two items, but it is needed to separate two adjectives of the same kind.

1. The three Aran Islands~~,~~ are called Inishmore, Inishmaan, and Innishneer.
2. They lie~~,~~ six miles off the coast~~,~~ of Ireland.
3. The islands are isolated, windswept, and barren.
4. The islands had no running water, electricity, or telephones until 1970.
5. Then the islands gained rapid~~,~~ popularity as a tourist destination.
6. Despite the damp, windy weather, people from Europe and America began choosing the Aran Islands as a destination.
7. Visitors were fascinated by the Iron Age structures, ancient monasteries, and quaint villages.
8. Soon restaurants, tour buses, and inns became part of life in the Aran Islands.
9. Tourists visit the islands today to hear the Gaelic language spoken and to get a sense of traditional~~,~~ Irish culture.
10. Permanent residents love the islands' ruggedness, solitude, and beauty.
11. Many islanders farm~~,~~ or fish for a living.
12. Lobster, crab, and mackerel are harvested from the icy Atlantic.
13. The limestone cliffs are studded with small, well-kept villages.
14. Aran Islanders keep traditions alive through music~~,~~ and dancing.
15. The lively, melodic music played by islanders is popular with natives and tourists alike.

Lesson 66 Add the missing comma to each sentence. Then decide why the comma is needed. Write *I* for introductory word, *C* for compound sentence, and *D* for direct address.

1. "Maya, please show us your pictures of Puget Sound," we asked. __D__
2. "I'd like to, but I have so many!" Maya replied. __C__
3. "Well, let's see all of them," Mike said. __I__
4. Maya cleared a space on the table, and then she took out her photographs. __C__
5. She spread out the photographs, and we crowded around. __C__
6. "Wow, this is you!" Sabrina said to Maya as she pointed to one photograph. __I__
7. "Yes, this picture shows me on our kayaking trip," Maya said. __I__
8. "Maya, weren't you scared out there in the sound?" Mike asked. __D__
9. "Well, we weren't exactly in the open sea," Maya responded. __I__
10. "Puget Sound is protected by islands and a peninsula, and the water is usually quite calm." __C__
11. "I was nervous at first, but I followed the leader's instructions," she continued. __C__
12. "A seal swam up to my kayak, and it looked right at me!" Maya said. __C__
13. "Well, weren't you at least a little frightened?" Mike asked. __I__
14. "No, the seal was just curious," Maya replied. __I__
15. "Seals often approach kayakers, and kayakers usually feel lucky to see them," she continued. __C__

Name _____

Lesson 67 Write a semicolon or a colon to separate the independent clauses in each sentence. Three sentences require a colon.

1. Sicily is the Mediterranean's largest island; it lies off mainland Italy's southern tip.

2. The Greeks first settled Sicily 2,800 years ago; they built temples and theaters.

3. Many peoples have claimed Sicily as their own: Romans, Arabs, and Normans are among them.

4. Each culture left its mark; Sicilian architecture reveals many influences.

5. Tourists may visit Norman castles and cathedrals; they can also explore Greek ruins.

6. Sicily is prone to earthquakes and volcanic activity; Mt. Etna, in northeastern Sicily, is Europe's tallest volcano.

7. Sicily's warm Mediterranean climate makes it possible for farmers to raise a variety of crops: pistachios, lemons, melons, and oranges are just a few of those.

8. Family is an important part of Italian culture; family members gather at mealtime.

9. Farmers produce much of the island's foods: fresh pasta, olives, and sheep's cheese are among the delicacies.

10. Many traditional values and customs persist in Sicily; some modern residents resist the old ways, though.

Write a colon where it should be in each item.

11. We brought home five souvenirs: a leather purse, three T-shirts, and a book of postcards.

12. The plane will arrive from Sicily at 1:45 P.M.

13. Martinez, Iris A. *Italy's Volcanic Island*. Rome: Dante Brothers, 1998.

14. The guide told us a good nickname for Sicily: "One Island, Many Cultures."

15. **Michel:** The view of the harbor is spectacular!

    Maria: I wish we could see Rome from here.

Lesson 68 Add parentheses and hyphens to these sentences where they are needed.

1. The island of New Guinea, which is in the western Pacific Ocean north of Australia, is the second largest island in the world.

2. In 1963 Indonesia claimed the island's western half and named it *West Irian* (victorious hot land).

3. After forty-five years of Indonesian rule, much of this territory (now known as Irian Jaya or Papua) remains unchanged.

4. Out-of-the-way villages are insulated from the modern world by dense forests and rugged mountains.

5. The highest mountain in Irian Jaya rises to a height of 16,503 feet (5,030 meters).

6. The tropical highlands are home to many native groups collectively called Papuans (PAP yuh wuhns).

7. The Asmat, a fierce swamp-dwelling people, are one of many native groups who face a huge dilemma.

8. Their age-old traditions are being challenged by the temptations and demands of the modern age.

9. Many Papuans still live as hunters or as sustenance farmers (farmers who grow only enough for their families).

10. Until fairly recently, many had never seen an honest-to-goodness modern vehicle.

11. Ready-to-wear clothing is a rarity in rural New Guinea.

12. For most people a visit to New Guinea would be an exotic vacation, a once-in-a-lifetime experience.

13. For many workers, though, a trip to New Guinea is made in search of better-than-average wages.

14. New Guinea's mineral wealth (copper, gold, petroleum) has attracted both international corporations and fly-by-night operators.

15. Mineral resources create jobs and wealth, but they often spell the end of long-established ways of life.

Name _____

Lesson 69 Write *I* after each indirect quotation and *D* after each direct quotation. Then add quotation marks and other punctuation to the direct quotations. Draw three lines (≡) under each lowercase letter that should be capitalized.

1. Rick said that he visited San Francisco with his family. __I__

2. "Rick, did you visit Alcatraz Island on your trip?" Jared asked. __D__

3. Rick said, "yes, my family took a tour of Alcatraz." __D__

4. Jared asked whether the island was still a federal prison. __I__

5. Rick replied, "no, it hasn't been used as a prison since 1963." __D__

6. "Now it is part of the Golden Gate National Recreation Area," he continued. __D__

7. Rick explained that the name *Alcatraz* comes from a Spanish word meaning "pelican." __I__

8. "More than a mile of cold, rough water separates Alcatraz from San Francisco," Rick said. __D__

9. "Some of America's most dangerous criminals were held at Alcatraz," he added. __D__

10. Jared asked, "who lives on the island now?" __D__

11. Rick said that the island is inhabited mostly by birds. __I__

12. He told us that the birds have become a real problem. __I__

13. Jared asked if the tour was spooky. __I__

14. "It was a little spooky, but it was also fascinating," Rick replied. __D__

15. Jared said, "when I visit San Francisco, I'm going to take the first ferry in the morning out to Alcatraz." __D__

Lesson 70 Rewrite this business letter in correct letter form.
Western Sporting Goods 143 Arkansas Way Nacogdoches, Texas 75961 Dear Sir or Madam I am interested in purchasing some snorkeling gear. Will you please send me a copy of your latest catalog? Sincerely yours Benjamin Ross 1434 Laughlin Road Derry, New Hampshire 03038 October 24, 2008

1434 Laughlin Road

Derry, New Hampshire 03038

October 24, 2008

Western Sporting Goods

143 Arkansas Way

Nacogdoches, Texas 75961

Dear Sir or Madam:

    I am interested in purchasing some snorkeling gear. Will you please send me a copy of your

latest catalog?

Sincerely yours,

Benjamin Ross

Name _____

Decide which word is the simple subject of each sentence. Fill in the circle that matches your answer.

1. Modern inventors register their ideas with the United States Patent Office.

   (a) ideas   (b) inventors   (c) understood *you*   (d) register

2. Many inventions in the patent record were never successful.

   (a) inventions   (b) patent   (c) record   (d) understood *you*

3. Imagine yourself in a pair of metal shoes.

   (a) shoes   (b) understood *you*   (c) Imagine   (d) yourself

Choose the answer that describes the underlined part of each sentence. Fill in the circle next to your answer.

4. <u>Thousands of other inventions</u> have been equally impractical.

   (a) complete subject   (b) complete predicate

5. <u>Someone</u> invented an unusual foot warmer.

   (a) simple predicate   (b) complete subject

6. This foot warmer <u>runs on breath power</u>.

   (a) simple predicate   (b) complete predicate

7. The wearer <u>breathes</u> into a funnel.

   (a) simple predicate   (b) simple subject

8. Tubes <u>carry the warm breath to the wearer's cold feet</u>.

   (a) complete subject   (b) complete predicate

9. <u>Housework</u> and <u>play</u> were combined in the Clean Swing.

   (a) compound subject   (b) compound predicate

10. The motion of the swing <u>turns</u> a crank and <u>runs</u> a washing machine.

    (a) compound subject   (b) compound predicate

11. With this invention, a person <u>swings</u> and <u>washes</u> clothes at the same time.

    (a) compound subject   (b) compound predicate

12. The Wood-Awake alarm clock is another odd <u>invention</u>.

    (a) direct object   (b) predicate noun

13. Its inventor was probably a heavy <u>sleeper</u>.

    (a) predicate noun   (b) predicate adjective

14. The owner hangs this <u>clock</u> over the bed.

    (a) direct object   (b) indirect object

15. Each morning, the clock gives its <u>owner</u> a wake-up alert.

    (a) direct object   (b) indirect object

> If you prefer to keep these Unit Tests in a separate file, remove them before you distribute the books (or have students carefully tear them out). Then distribute the tests when you are ready to administer them.

Name _____

16. It drops wooden <u>blocks</u> on the sleeper's head.

    (a) direct object   (b) indirect object

17. This device could awaken <u>anyone</u>!

    (a) predicate noun   (b) direct object

18. It might give its <u>owner</u> a headache, however.

    (a) direct object   (b) indirect object

19. Not surprisingly, the device has never been <u>popular</u>.

    (a) predicate adjective   (b) predicate noun

20. Which underlined phrase is an appositive phrase?
    Another invention, <u>the carry-all hat</u>, also may give its owner <u>a headache</u>.
                      a   b   (a) (b)

21. Which is a prepositional phrase?
    Makeup <u>and other small items</u> fit <u>inside this box-shaped hat</u>.
              a   b   (a) (b)

22. Which is a prepositional phrase?
    A strap <u>around the chin</u> secures <u>the hat</u> tightly.
            a   b   (a) (b)

23. Which is a prepositional phrase?
    It was once the custom <u>for men</u> to tip <u>their hats</u>.
           a   b   (a) (b)

24. Which is an appositive phrase?
    The Tipsy Derby, <u>an even stranger hat</u>, lifts up and <u>tips itself mechanically</u>.
           a   b   (a) (b)

25. Which is an adjectival prepositional phrase?
    The inventor <u>of the self-cleaning house</u> must have hated housework <u>for years</u>!
           a   b   (a) (b)

26. Which is an adverbial prepositional phrase?
    Each room <u>in the self-cleaning house</u> had a soap-and-water tank <u>on the ceiling</u>.
           a   b   (a) (b)

27. Which is an adjectival prepositional phrase?
    Jets <u>on the tank</u> would squirt soapy water <u>onto the walls and the floor</u>.
           a   b   (a) (b)

28. Which is an adverbial prepositional phrase?
    The dirt <u>in the room</u> would be washed away <u>by the soapy waterfall</u>.
           a   b   (a) (b)

29. Which is an adjectival prepositional phrase?
    <u>After the shower</u>, a hot-air blower <u>on the wall</u> would dry the room.
           a   b   (a) (b)

30. Which is an adverbial prepositional phrase?
    <u>In the future</u>, perhaps a new, improved version <u>of the self-cleaning house</u> will be invented.
           a   b   (a) (b)

31. Which is an adjectival prepositional phrase?
    Anyone <u>with this invention</u> will probably need waterproof furniture <u>in every room</u>!
           a   b   (a) (b)

Fill in the circle next to the choice that correctly describes each sentence.

1. Listen to these facts about undersea exploration.
   - (a) declarative
   - (b) interrogative
   - **(c) imperative**
   - (d) exclamatory

2. Ancient Greek skin divers held their breath underwater.
   - **(a) declarative**
   - (b) interrogative
   - (c) imperative
   - (d) exclamatory

3. Did you know that expert skin divers can hold their breath for more than five minutes?
   - (a) declarative
   - **(b) interrogative**
   - (c) imperative
   - (d) exclamatory

4. Wow, that's a long time!
   - (a) declarative
   - (b) interrogative
   - (c) imperative
   - **(d) exclamatory**

5. People used diving bells from ancient times until the early 1900s.
   - **(a) simple sentence**
   - (b) compound sentence
   - (c) complex sentence

6. These hulls were bell-shaped, and their undersides were open.
   - (a) simple sentence
   - **(b) compound sentence**
   - (c) complex sentence

7. Because the air inside the bell pressed down, water did not enter the bell.
   - (a) simple sentence
   - (b) compound sentence
   - **(c) complex sentence**

8. Diving bells were useful, but divers could not descend very deep in them.
   - (a) simple sentence
   - **(b) compound sentence**
   - (c) complex sentence

9. When the bathysphere was developed in 1930, deep-sea exploration became possible.
   - (a) simple sentence
   - (b) compound sentence
   - **(c) complex sentence**

10. This vehicle consisted of a hollow ball on a cable.
    - **(a) simple sentence**
    - (b) compound sentence
    - (c) complex sentence

11. Although the bathysphere was a breakthrough, scientists would later develop much more efficient exploration devices.
    - (a) simple sentence
    - (b) compound sentence
    - **(c) complex sentence**

12. Some oceanographers live underwater for short periods of time, research stations have been built on the sea floor.
    - (a) fragment
    - (b) run-on
    - **(c) comma splice**
    - (d) ramble-on

13. Leaving the station each day for exploration.
    - **(a) fragment**
    - (b) run-on
    - (c) comma splice
    - (d) ramble-on

14. One man spent almost 70 days in a submerged chamber in Florida he was studying the effects on humans of life underwater.
    - (a) fragment
    - **(b) run-on**
    - (c) comma splice
    - (d) ramble-on

15. In my opinion, I think living underwater would be difficult because there would be nothing but water around, and you would be living in the middle of it all the time, with no fresh air to breathe.
    - (a) fragment
    - (b) run-on
    - (c) comma splice
    - **(d) ramble-on**

Name _____

Fill in the circle next to the choice that correctly describes each underlined phrase.

16. Locating the wreck of the *Titanic* took oceanographer Robert Ballard many years.

    (a) infinitive phrase   (b) gerund phrase

17. After the initial discovery was made, Ballard decided to return to the site of the wreck inside *Alvin*.

    (a) gerund phrase   (b) infinitive phrase

18. Riding inside the tough little submersible, Ballard's crew could explore the wreck carefully.

    (a) infinitive phrase   (b) participial phrase

19. Although submersibles allow oceanographers to visit the depths, they are expensive to launch.

    (a) dependent clause   (b) independent clause

20. If modern oceanographers want to gather data, they no longer have to dive themselves.

    (a) dependent clause   (b) independent clause

21. There are now machines that will dive for them.

    (a) dependent clause   (b) independent clause

22. The term for these machines is *ROV*, which stands for "Remotely Operated Vehicle."

    (a) adjective clause   (b) adverb clause

23. An ROV records information and videotapes the ocean's depths while oceanographers control it from a ship on the surface.

    (a) adjective clause   (b) adverb clause

24. ROVs that have mechanical arms collect samples.

    (a) adjective clause   (b) adverb clause

25. Although ROVs are extremely effective, scientists are working to develop even more advanced robotic devices.

    (a) independent clause   (b) adverb clause

26. Submersibles are designed to carry scientists to the ocean's farthest depths.

    (a) gerund phrase   (b) infinitive phrase

27. The submersible *Alvin* allowed scientists to visit deep-sea rifts.

    (a) infinitive phrase   (b) participial phrase

28. Seeing giant clams and tube worms in the Galápagos Rift must have been a thrill for researchers.

    (a) infinitive phrase   (b) gerund phrase

29. Sent to the bottom of the ocean by an iceberg, the *Titanic* lay undisturbed for more than 70 years.

    (a) participial phrase   (b) gerund phrase

Fill in the circle next to the plural form that will complete each sentence correctly.

1. Ludwig von Beethoven, one of the greatest _____ of all time, began to go deaf at the age of thirty.

   (a) composers   (b) composeres

2. Soon he could hear only faint _____ of sound.

   (a) patches   (b) patchs

3. But he was able to compose brilliant _____ in his head.

   (a) symphonys   (**b**) symphonies

Choose the answer that correctly identifies the underlined item in each sentence. Fill in the circle next to your answer.

4. <u>Elizabeth Blackwell</u> was the first woman granted a medical degree in the United States.

   (a) common noun   (**b**) proper noun

5. Blackwell desperately wanted to be a <u>doctor</u>, but almost every medical school in the United States rejected her application because she was a woman.

   (**a**) common noun   (b) proper noun

6. Thinking her application was a joke, <u>Geneva Medical College</u> accepted Blackwell.

   (a) common noun   (**b**) proper noun

7. The <u>students'</u> scorn turned into respect as Blackwell succeeded in her studies.

   (a) singular possessive noun   (**b**) plural possessive noun

8. <u>Blackwell's</u> struggle was far from over when she received her medical degree in 1849.

   (**a**) singular possessive noun   (b) plural possessive noun

9. <u>She</u> found that no hospital would hire a woman doctor.

   (a) personal pronoun: first person   (b) personal pronoun: second person

   (**c**) personal pronoun: third person

10. Blackwell decided to open her own hospital, which would treat <u>women's</u> health problems.

    (a) singular possessive noun   (**b**) plural possessive noun

11. <u>I</u> have seen the building in New York where Blackwell founded her hospital.

    (**a**) personal pronoun: first person   (b) personal pronoun: second person

    (c) personal pronoun: third person

12. It is a small building; <u>you</u> would never guess that it was once a hospital.

    (a) personal pronoun: first person   (**b**) personal pronoun: second person

    (c) personal pronoun: third person

13. Blackwell also decided to open a medical school for women, since she had had so much trouble getting into medical school <u>herself</u>.

    (**a**) compound personal pronoun   (b) possessive pronoun   (c) indefinite pronoun

14. Blackwell is remembered because she dared to do what <u>no one</u> had done before.

    (a) relative pronoun   (b) interrogative pronoun   (**c**) indefinite pronoun

Name _____

15. Thor Heyerdahl, on the other hand, is remembered for doing <u>what</u> others may have done long ago.

   (a) relative pronoun   **(b)** interrogative pronoun   **(c)** indefinite pronoun

16. <u>Who</u> was Thor Heyerdahl?

   (a) relative pronoun   **(b)** interrogative pronoun   **(c)** indefinite pronoun

17. He was a researcher <u>who</u> studied the spread of ancient civilizations.

   (a) relative pronoun   **(b)** interrogative pronoun   **(c)** indefinite pronoun

18. Heyerdahl was convinced that ancient Inca sailors could have traveled across the Pacific, and he decided to prove that <u>his</u> theory was sound.

   (a) compound personal pronoun   **(b)** possessive pronoun   **(c)** indefinite pronoun

19. <u>What</u> did he do?

   (a) relative pronoun   **(b)** interrogative pronoun   **(c)** indefinite pronoun

20. Heyerdahl built <u>himself</u> a balsa wood raft, which he called the *Kon Tiki.*

   (a) compound personal pronoun   **(b)** possessive pronoun   **(c)** relative pronoun

21. <u>Few</u> would have dared sail across the Pacific Ocean on such a small and primitive craft, but Heyerdahl and five others set out from Peru in 1947.

   (a) relative pronoun   **(b)** interrogative pronoun   **(c)** indefinite pronoun

22. <u>Their</u> journey was long and hard.

   (a) compound personal pronoun   **(b)** possessive pronoun   **(c)** relative pronoun

23. But Heyerdahl achieved <u>his</u> goal: the *Kon Tiki* landed safely on an island 4,300 miles from Peru.

   (a) possessive pronoun   **(b)** relative pronoun   **(c)** indefinite pronoun

24. <u>Nobody</u> knows for sure whether the ancient voyages Heyerdahl imagined occurred, but we know they were possible.

   (a) compound personal pronoun   **(b)** interrogative pronoun   **(c)** indefinite pronoun

25. Ellen Craft faced <u>a</u> challenge of a very different kind.

   (a) adjective telling *what kind*   **(b)** adjective telling *how many*   **(c)** article

26. Born into slavery in nineteenth-century Georgia, she and her husband planned a <u>dangerous</u> escape to freedom.

   (a) adjective telling *what kind*   **(b)** adjective telling *how many*   **(c)** article

27. <u>This</u> was their strategy: Craft disguised herself as a white man and posed as her husband's owner.

   (a) demonstrative pronoun   **(b)** demonstrative adjective

28. During their 1,000-mile journey, there were <u>many</u> moments when Craft's identity was almost discovered.

   (a) adjective telling *what kind*   **(b)** adjective telling *how many*   **(c)** article

29. But despite <u>these</u> close calls, Craft never lost her courage.

   (a) demonstrative pronoun   **(b)** demonstrative adjective

30. <u>That</u> is the reason she and her husband made it to safety.

   (a) demonstrative pronoun   **(b)** demonstrative adjective

Identify the verb in each sentence. Fill in the circle that matches your answer.

1. Comets **follow** oval-shaped **paths around** the sun.
            a   b   c
       (a) (b) (c)

2. A few **comets are frequent** visitors to our sky.
                 a b   c
       (a) **(b)** (c)

3. Halley's Comet **is visible** to people on Earth **every** 76 years or so.
                         a   b   c
       (a) (b) (c)

4. Other comets **require more** than 400,000 years for the **completion** of a single orbit.
                            a   b   c
       (a) (b) (c)

Decide which word describes the boldfaced verb. Fill in the circle next to your answer.

5. Comets **are** actually huge balls of dirty ice.
   (a) action   **(b)** linking

6. A comet **may develop** a tail during its approach to the sun.
   (a) action   (b) linking

7. Some of the ice in its nucleus **evaporates**.
   (a) action   (b) linking

8. Evaporation **releases** many dust particles and gas molecules.
   (a) action   (b) linking

9. Many of these particles and molecules **remain** near the nucleus.
   (a) transitive   **(b)** intransitive

10. The pressure of the sun's light **pushes** particles and molecules away from the nucleus in a long stream, or tail.
    (a) transitive   (b) intransitive

11. In 1997 the Hale-Bopp Comet **was seen** by millions of people in North America.
    (a) active voice   **(b)** passive voice

12. That comet **shone** brightly for several weeks that spring.
    (a) active voice   (b) passive voice

Choose the correct verb or verb phrase to complete each sentence. Fill in the circle next to your answer.

13. Yesterday I ____ a bottle of iced tea.
    (a) buy   **(b)** bought   (c) have bought   (d) will have bought

14. I ____ this kind of tea many times before.
    (a) am buying   (b) will have bought   **(c)** have bought   (d) was buying

15. In the past I ____ empty tea bottles into the trash, but this time I wanted to make sure my bottle would be recycled.
    (a) had thrown   (b) throw   (c) will throw   (d) was throwing

16. Right now it ____ on my desk with a flower in it.
    (a) has sat   (b) sat   (c) will sit   **(d)** is sitting

17. Next Tuesday I ____ the bottle in a bin for the recycling truck.
    (a) will put   (b) will have put   (c) put   (d) had put

Name _____

18. I always ___ the bottles from the paper.

   (a) am separating   (b) separate   (c) was separating   (d) will have separated

19. After the truck driver finishes her route, she ___ the bottle to a recycling plant.

   (a) has taken   (b) took   (c) had taken   (d) will take

20. By the end of the week, a furnace ___ my bottle into liquid glass.

   (a) is melting   (b) melted   (c) will have melted   (d) melts

21. Soon someone else ___ from a new glass bottle made from the one I placed in my recycling bin.

   (a) drank   (b) drinks   (c) is drinking   (d) will be drinking

Decide which boldfaced word is an adverb. Fill in the circle that matches your answer.

22. Recyclers sort garbage **carefully** to sell as **reusable material**.
    a   b   c
    (a) (b) (c)

23. **Often** these materials are **made** into a completely **new** product.
    a   b   c
    (a) (b) (c)

24. **The** use of **recycled** materials can be **very** economical.
    a   b   c
    (a) (b) (c)

Decide which boldfaced word is a preposition. Fill in the circle that matches your answer.

25. Comfortable shoes **have** been produced **from** used grocery bags **and** coffee filters.
    a   b   c
    (a) (b) (c)

26. Plastic soft drink bottles **can** be made **into** carpets **and** pillow stuffing.
    a   b   c
    (a) (b) (c)

27. Perhaps **someday** you will live **in** a house made of old cans **and** tires.
    a   b   c
    (a) (b) (c)

Decide which boldfaced word is a conjunction. Fill in the circle that matches the answer.

28. The United States **now** recycles 65% of aluminum cans, **but** only 2% **of** plastic.
    a   b   c
    (a) (b) (c)

29. Aluminum cans **are** recycled **because** that is less **expensive** than mining aluminum.
    a   b   c
    (a) (b) (c)

30. **Although** recycling has grown, each American **still** wastes 3.6 pounds **per** day.
    a   b   c
    (a) (b) (c)

Decide whether each boldfaced word or phrase is a coordinating conjunction, a subordinating conjunction, or a correlative conjunction. Fill in the circle next to your answer.

31. Environmentalists work to make recycling **not only** right, **but also** cheaper than throwing trash away.

   (a) coordinating conjunction   (b) subordinating conjunction   (c) correlative conjunction

32. The U.S. produces 200 million tons of garbage per year, **and** that makes it the world's biggest trash producer.

   (a) coordinating conjunction   (b) subordinating conjunction   (c) correlative conjunction

33. We must **both** reduce the amount of trash we create **and** recycle more of that trash.

   (a) coordinating conjunction   (b) subordinating conjunction   (c) correlative conjunction

34. **If** we do these things, we will have more resources available for the future.

   (a) coordinating conjunction   (b) subordinating conjunction   (c) correlative conjunction

Decide which word completes each sentence correctly. Fill in the circle next to your answer.

1. ___ common all over the world to hold agricultural festivals.

   (a) Its   (b) It's

2. People ___ land gets very little rain often conduct rain dances or similar rituals.

   (a) who's   (b) whose

3. Rice farmers in Japan plant pine, chestnut, or bamboo trees in ___ fields for good luck.

   (a) there   (b) their   (c) they're

4. They plant rice seeds in February and ___ hold festivals when they transplant seedlings in June or July.

   (a) then   (b) than

5. The rhythmic way the farmers move can seem more like dancing ___ planting.

   (a) then   (b) than

6. Every year the Cuchumatan people of Guatemala go ___ a cliff where, according to tradition, frost lives.

   (a) to   (b) too   (c) two

7. Once they get ___, they lower one person over the cliff.

   (a) there   (b) their   (c) they're

8. ___ counting on him to seal the rock with cement so the frost won't ruin the corn plants.

   (a) There   (b) Their   (c) They're

9. ___ deities, Wuro and Dwo, are important in the farming traditions of the Bobo people of Burkina Faso.

   (a) To   (b) Too   (c) Two

10. According to legend, Wuro gave the world ___ balance of earth, rain, and sun, but people ruined the balance by farming.

    (a) its   (b) it's

11. Dwo is the deity ___ helping people restore the natural order.

    (a) who's   (b) whose

12. Each year the Bobo people ask Dwo for his help in keeping away evil and restoring order and in bringing the rains, ___.

    (a) to   (b) too   (c) two

13. If you study ethnology or anthropology, ___ going to learn about agricultural festivals around the world.

    (a) your   (b) you're

14. Does ___ community hold an agricultural festival?

    (a) your   (b) you're

Decide whether each sentence uses negatives correctly. Fill in the circle next to your answer.

15. My brother doesn't know nothing about Mayan culture.

    (a) correct   (b) incorrect

Name _____

16. He hasn't never seen photographs of the Mayan pyramids.

    (a) correct   (b) incorrect

17. He doesn't realize that Mayan people keep many traditions alive today.

    (a) correct   (b) incorrect

Decide whether each sentence uses *go, like, went,* or *all* correctly. Fill in the circle next to your answer.

18. Madeleine went, "Did you know Turkey has a holiday called Children's Day?"

    (a) correct   (b) incorrect

19. "On that day, children go to the national and local government offices and take them over," she continued.

    (a) correct   (b) incorrect

20. Fuad was all, "I would pass a law guaranteeing free ice cream forever!"

    (a) correct   (b) incorrect

21. Then Madeleine was like, "On Children's Day, children get free ice cream, movies, and transportation all day!"

    (a) correct   (b) incorrect

22. This festival indicates that children are, like, very important in Turkish culture.

    (a) correct   (b) incorrect

Decide which word completes each sentence correctly. Fill in the circle next to your answer.

23. Last Thanksgiving I ____ felt pads down on the dining room table and then spread out a green tablecloth.

    (a) lay   (b) laid

24. My brother ____ plates and glasses at each place.

    (a) sat   (b) set

25. When the turkey was ready, everyone ____ around the table.

    (a) sat   (b) set

26. Later I ____ on a soft rug in front of the fire and talked with my cousins.

    (a) lay   (b) laid

Decide which form of the verb completes each sentence correctly. Fill in the circle next to your answer.

27. Last year my relatives in Nice, France, ____ flowers for the Carnival celebration.

    (a) grown   (b) grew   (c) growed

28. They ____ the flowers to the parade.

    (a) brang   (b) brung   (c) brought

29. The ground ____ as the large floats thundered past.

    (a) shaken   (b) shaked   (c) shook

30. The best one had been ____ almost entirely out of flowers.

    (a) built   (b) build   (c) builded

31. When the signal was given, everyone ____ flowers at one another.

    (a) threw   (b) throwed   (c) thrown

Choose the correct pronoun to replace each boldfaced word or phrase. Fill in the circle next to your answer.

1. Alexandra's grandmother told Pilar and **Alexandra** a story about Baba Yaga.

   (a) she   (b) them   (c) her   (d) I

2. Pilar told the story to Shanna and **Jeremy**.

   (a) he   (b) him   (c) his   (d) them

3. Baba Yaga is a popular character in **Russian folktales**.

   (a) them   (b) it   (c) they   (d) her

4. **This old woman** lives in a house that walks on huge chicken legs.

   (a) Her   (b) They   (c) It   (d) She

5. **Baba Yaga** rides around in a magical stone bowl.

   (a) They   (b) She   (c) Her   (d) Them

6. Alexandra and **Pilar** decided to do research on Baba Yaga tales at the library.

   (a) her   (b) I   (c) she   (d) it

Decide which phrase the boldfaced word replaces in each sentence. Fill in the circle next to your answer.

7. In some tales Baba Yaga tries to capture Russian children because she likes to eat **them**.

   (a) Russian children   (b) Pilar and Alexandra   (c) Baba Yaga   (d) some tales

8. In one story, a girl escapes from Baba Yaga by dropping a magic comb; **it** turns into an impenetrable forest.

   (a) a girl   (b) one story   (c) a magic comb   (d) an impenetrable forest

9. Baba Yaga is not always a wicked character; in one story **she** helps a prince find his love.

   (a) a princess   (b) Baba Yaga   (c) a wicked character   (d) his love

Choose the word or phrase that completes each sentence correctly. Fill in the circle next to your answer.

10. One of folklore's greatest trickster characters ___ the Monkey King.

    (a) is   (b) are

11. Stories about the Monkey King ___ entertained people in China for centuries.

    (a) has   (b) have

12. He is a mischievous immortal ___ protects a monk on an important pilgrimage to India.

    (a) who   (b) whom

13. When the story begins, the Monkey King has been imprisoned under a mountain by the other immortals ___ he has annoyed with his mischief.

    (a) who   (b) whom

14. The wandering monk passes by the mountain prison of the Monkey King, ___ asks the monk to set him free.

    (a) who   (b) whom

15. The magic powers of the Monkey King ___ the monk a great deal on his journey.

    (a) helps   (b) help

Name _____

16. The Monkey King has a magic needle that he keeps tucked behind his ear; he can make it grow ___ than a log, to become a powerful weapon.

   (a) larger   (b) largest

17. Sandy and Pigsy ___ two monsters who turn good and join the Monkey King and the monk.

   (a) is   (b) are

18. Neither Sandy nor Pigsy ___ as effective as the Monkey King at defending the monk from the demons who live in the mountains.

   (a) is   (b) are

19. The Monkey King thinks Sandy and Pigsy ___ help out more.

   (a) should   (b) have

20. He exposes Pigsy's cowardice, and the shamefaced Pigsy begins to act ___ than before.

   (a) more bravely   (b) most bravely

21. Eventually the travelers must cross the ___ mountain of all, which is defended by thousands of demons.

   (a) higher   (b) highest

22. The Monkey King realizes that he ___ disguise himself as a demon and spy on the enemy to find out their weaknesses.

   (a) is   (b) must

23. He discovers that one of the head demons ___ suck enemies into his stomach in an instant.

   (a) has   (b) can

24. The Monkey King, ___ is a brilliant strategist, lets the demon swallow him whole and then threatens to eat the demon from the inside out.

   (a) who   (b) whom

25. The entire demon army ___ away because of the Monkey King's ingenious tricks.

   (a) runs   (b) run

26. No one ___ more clever than the Monkey King.

   (a) is   (b) are

27. *Folktales from Many Lands* ___ the book in which I found this story.

   (a) is   (b) are

Decide whether the boldfaced phrase is a dangling modifier or is used correctly. Fill in the circle next to your answer.

28. **Using a clever disguise,** the demons never suspect they are being tricked.

   (a) dangling modifier   (b) correct

29. **Tricking powerful enemies,** protection is given to the monk.

   (a) dangling modifier   (b) correct

30. **Containing ancient folktales,** *The Pilgrimage to the West* is a classic work of Chinese literature.

   (a) dangling modifier   (b) correct

Decide which boldfaced word needs to be capitalized. Fill in the circle with the letter that matches it.

1. My **uncle** sailed across the **pacific** Ocean.   ⓐ **ⓑ**
        a   b

2. **he** made the voyage in **summer**.   **ⓐ** ⓑ
     a   b

3. He reached the **island** of **maui** in August.   ⓐ **ⓑ**
                  a   b

4. He became a fan of **hawaiian** music and bought a **ukulele**.   **ⓐ** ⓑ
                 a   b

Choose the correct way to rewrite the boldfaced part of each sentence. Fill in the circle next to your answer.

5. **Mistress Mary Ellen Riley** is an expert sailor.
     ⓐ Mrs. M.E Riley   ⓑ Mss. M.E. Riley   **ⓒ** Mrs. M.E. Riley

6. She lives on **Edmonton Boulevard**.
     ⓐ Edmon. Blvd.   **ⓑ** Edmonton Blvd.   ⓒ Edmonton blvd.

7. She works for **Pacific Winds Corporation**.
     ⓐ Pacific Winds Corp. ⓑ Pacific W. Cor'tion ⓒ Pac Winds Cor

8. She wrote a book titled **Following the trade winds**.
     ⓐ <u>Following The Trade Winds</u> ⓑ "Following the Trade Winds" **ⓒ** <u>Following the Trade Winds</u>

9. I read her short story **escape from the volcano**.
     ⓐ "Escape from the Volcano" ⓑ Escape From The Volcano ⓒ <u>Escape from the Volcano</u>

10. Mrs. Riley **has not** answered my letter.
      ⓐ hasn't   ⓑ hasnt'   ⓒ has'nt

11. **The enthusiasm of her fans** is amazing.
      ⓐ Her fans' enthusiasm ⓑ Her fan's enthusiasm ⓒ Her fans enthusiasm

12. Every day **the mailbox of Mrs. Riley** is stuffed with fan mail.
      ⓐ Mrs. Riley's mailbox ⓑ Mrs. Rileys' mailbox ⓒ Mrs. Rileys mailbox

13. I **have not** read Mrs. Riley's latest book.
      ⓐ havent'   ⓑ have'nt   **ⓒ** haven't

14. It **is not** in the library yet.
      ⓐ isn't   ⓑ is'nt   ⓒ isnt'

Decide where the comma belongs in each sentence. Fill in the circle with the matching letter.

15. Rex saw manta rays, sharks and dolphins in Hawaii.   **ⓐ** ⓑ
                    a b

16. "Rex did you see any giant sea turtles?" asked Pete.   **ⓐ** ⓑ
         a   b

17. "Yes I saw one swimming in the ocean," Rex replied.   **ⓐ** ⓑ
       a   b

Name _____

18. "I swam up to it but it swam away," he said.   ⓐ ⓑ
            a   b

19. "Those big gentle animals are quite shy," said Pete.   ⓐ ⓑ
           a   b

Decide where the semicolon or colon is needed in each sentence. Fill in the circle next to your answer.

20. Centuries ago; volcanoes erupted in the Pacific; these became the Hawaiian islands. ⓐ **ⓑ**
             a   b

21. The islands are still volcanic; eruptions occur often; on the Big Island. **ⓐ** ⓑ
                   a   b

22. Volcanoes can cause great damage: entire communities have been destroyed by: lava. **ⓐ** ⓑ
                      a   b

23. Hawaii is not yet complete: volcanoes and ocean waves continually reshape: the islands. **ⓐ** ⓑ
               a   b

Decide whether each sentence is missing quotation marks or is correct as written. Fill in the circle next to your answer.

24. Anna asked Have you ever seen an extinct volcano?

    ⓐ needs quotation marks ⓑ correct as written

25. Bill said that he had visited the Haleakala Crater in Hawaii.

    ⓐ needs quotation marks **ⓑ** correct as written

Decide what kind of punctuation each sentence needs. Fill in the circle next to your answer.

26. The Haleakala Crater is 21 miles 34 kilometers in circumference.

    ⓐ needs parentheses   ⓑ needs a hyphen

27. Haleakala "house of the sun" is on the island of Maui.

    ⓐ needs parentheses   ⓑ needs a hyphen

28. Haleakala has been a national park for more than thirty five years.

    ⓐ needs parentheses   **ⓑ** needs a hyphen

29. The volcano imploded crashed inward to form a huge crater.

    ⓐ needs parentheses   ⓑ needs a hyphen

Find the part of the letter below that is the answer to each question. Fill in the circle next to your answer.

30. Which part of the letter is the greeting?   ⓐ **ⓑ** ⓒ ⓓ ⓔ

31. Which part of the letter is the body?   ⓐ ⓑ **ⓒ** ⓓ ⓔ

32. Which part of the letter is the closing?   ⓐ ⓑ ⓒ **ⓓ** ⓔ

              Haleakala National Park
ⓐ Pukalani, Maui, Hawaii 96788
              February 9, 2008

Dear Mark, ⓑ

  ⓒ The Haleakala Crater is awesome! The colors inside the crater are beautiful.

                  ⓓ Your friend,

                  ⓔ Liam

Grammar, Usage, and Mechanics Handbook
Table of Contents

(Continued on page 304)

Name _____

(Continued from page 303)

Usage

Letters and E-mails

Research

Guidelines for Listening and Speaking

(you) | Diagram | sentences

Mechanics

Section 1 Capitalization

- **Capitalize the first word in a sentence.**
  The kangaroo rat is an amazing animal.

- **Capitalize all *proper nouns*, including people's names and the names of particular places.**
  Gregory Gordon   Washington Monument

- **Capitalize titles of respect.**
  Mr. Alvarez   Dr. Chin   Ms. Murphy

- **Capitalize family titles used just before people's names and titles of respect that are part of names.**
  Uncle Frank   Aunt Mary   Governor Adamson

- **Capitalize initials of names.**
  Thomas Paul Gerard (T.P. Gerard)

- **Capitalize place names.**
  France   Utah   China   Baltimore

- **Capitalize *proper adjectives,* adjectives that are made from proper nouns.**
  Chinese   Icelandic   French   Latin American

- **Capitalize the months of the year and the days of the week.**
  February   April   Monday   Tuesday

- **Capitalize important words in the names of organizations.**
  American Lung Association   Veterans of Foreign Wars

- **Capitalize important words in the names of holidays.**
  Veterans Day   Fourth of July

- **Capitalize the first word in the greeting or closing of a letter.**
  Dear Edmundo,   Yours truly,

- **Capitalize the word *I.***
  Frances and I watched the movie together.

- **Capitalize the first, last, and most important words in a title. Be sure to capitalize all verbs, including *is* and *was.***
  Island of the Blue Dolphins   *Away Is a Strange Place to Be*

- **Capitalize the first word in a direct quotation.**
  Aunt Rose said, "Please pass the clam dip."

Section 2 Abbreviations and Initials

Abbreviations are shortened forms of words. Many abbreviations begin with a capital letter and end with a period.

- **You can abbreviate words used in addresses when you write.**
  Street (**St.**)   Avenue (**Ave.**)   Route (**Rte.**)   Boulevard (**Blvd.**)   Road (**Rd.**)   Drive (**Dr.**)

- **You can abbreviate the names of states when you address envelopes.**
  Note: State names are abbreviated as two capital letters, with no periods.

Alabama (AL)	Idaho (ID)	Missouri (MO)	Pennsylvania (PA)
Alaska (AK)	Illinois (IL)	Montana (MT)	Rhode Island (RI)
Arizona (AZ)	Indiana (IN)	Nebraska (NE)	South Carolina (SC)
Arkansas (AR)	Iowa (IA)	Nevada (NV)	South Dakota (SD)
California (CA)	Kansas (KS)	New Hampshire (NH)	Tennessee (TN)
Colorado (CO)	Kentucky (KY)	New Jersey (NJ)	Texas (TX)
Connecticut (CT)	Louisiana (LA)	New Mexico (NM)	Utah (UT)
Delaware (DE)	Maine (ME)	New York (NY)	Vermont (VT)
District of	Maryland (MD)	North Carolina (NC)	Virginia (VA)
Columbia (DC)	Massachusetts (MA)	North Dakota (ND)	Washington (WA)
Florida (FL)	Michigan (MI)	Ohio (OH)	West Virginia (WV)
Georgia (GA)	Minnesota (MN)	Oklahoma (OK)	Wisconsin (WI)
Hawaii (HI)	Mississippi (MS)	Oregon (OR)	Wyoming (WY)

- **You can abbreviate titles of address and titles of respect when you write.**
  Mister (**Mr.** Brian Davis)   Mistress (**Miss** or **Mrs.** Maria Rosario)   General (**Gen.** Robert E. Lee)
  Doctor (**Dr.** Emily Chu)   Junior (Everett Castle, **Jr.**)   Saint (**St.** Andrew)
  Note: *Ms.* is a title of address used for women. It is not an abbreviation, but it requires a period
  (**Ms.** Anita Brown).

- **You can abbreviate certain words in the names of businesses when you write.**
  Pet Helpers, Incorporated (Pet Helpers, **Inc.**)   River Corporation (River **Corp.**)

- **You can abbreviate days of the week when you take notes.**
  Sunday (**Sun.**)   Wednesday (**Wed.**)   Friday (**Fri.**)
  Monday (**Mon.**)   Thursday (**Thurs.**)   Saturday (**Sat.**)
  Tuesday (**Tues.**)

- **You can abbreviate months of the year when you take notes.**
  January (**Jan.**)   April (**Apr.**)   October (**Oct.**)
  February (**Feb.**)   August (**Aug.**)   November (**Nov.**)
  March (**Mar.**)   September (**Sept.**)   December (**Dec.**)
  (May, June, and July do not have abbreviated forms.)

- **You can abbreviate directions when you take notes.**
  North (**N**)   East (**E**)   South (**S**)   West (**W**)

An *initial* is the first letter of a name. An initial is written as a capital letter and a period. Sometimes initials are used in the names of countries or other places.

Michael Paul Sanders (**M.P.** Sanders)   United States of America (**U.S.A.**)
Washington, District of Columbia (Washington, **D.C.**)

Section 3 Titles

- **Underline titles of books, newspapers, TV series, movies, and magazines.**
  <u>Island of the Blue Dolphins</u>   <u>Miami Herald</u>   <u>I Love Lucy</u>
  Note: These titles are written in italics in printed text.

- **Use quotation marks around articles in magazines, short stories, chapters in books, songs, and poems.**
  "This Land Is Your Land"   "The Gift"   "Eletelephony"

- **Capitalize the first, last, and most important words in titles. Articles, short prepositions, and conjunctions are usually not capitalized. Be sure to capitalize all verbs, including forms of the verb** *be* (*am, is, are, was, were, been*).
  A Knight in the Attic   *My Brother Sam Is Dead*

Section 4 Quotation Marks

- **Put quotation marks (" ") around the titles of articles, short stories, book chapters, songs, and poems.**
  My favorite short story is "Revenge of the Reptiles."

- **Put quotation marks around a** *direct quotation,* **or a speaker's exact words.**
  "Did you see that alligator?" Max asked.

- **Do not put quotation marks around an** *indirect quotation,* **a person's words retold by another speaker. An indirect quotation is often signalled by** *whether* **or** *that.*
  Max asked Rory whether he had seen an alligator.

Writing a Conversation

- **Put quotation marks around the speaker's words. Begin a direct quotation with a capital letter. Use a comma to separate the quotation from the rest of the sentence.**
  Rory said, "There are no alligators in this area."

- **When a direct quotation comes at the end of a sentence, put the end mark inside the last quotation mark.**
  Max cried, "Look out!"

- **When writing a conversation, begin a new paragraph with each change of speaker.**
  Max panted, "I swear I saw a huge, scaly tail and a flat snout in the water!"
  "Relax," Rory said. "I told you there are no alligators around here."

Section 5 Spelling

Use these tips if you are not sure how to spell a word you want to write:

- Say the word aloud and break it into syllables. Try spelling each syllable. Put the syllables together to spell the whole word.
- Write the word. Make sure there is a vowel in every syllable. If the word looks wrong to you, try spelling it other ways.
- Think of a related word. Parts of related words are often spelled the same.

When you use the word processing function of a computer to write something, you can use the spell check feature to identify possible spelling errors. But a spell checker will not catch errors with homophones. For example, if you type *break* instead of *brake,* the spell checker will not catch the mistake, because the word is spelled correctly.

Section 6 End Marks

Every sentence must end with a period, an exclamation point, or a question mark.

- Use a *period* at the end of a statement (declarative sentence) or a command (imperative sentence).
  Dad and I look alike. (*declarative*)   Step back very slowly. (*imperative*)
- Use an *exclamation point* at the end of a firm command (imperative sentence) or at the end of a sentence that shows great feeling or excitement (exclamatory sentence).
  Get away from the cliff! (*imperative*)   What an incredible sight! (*exclamatory*)
- Use a *question mark* at the end of an asking sentence (interrogative sentence).
  How many miles is it to Tucson? (*interrogative*)

Section 7 Apostrophes

An apostrophe (') is used to form the possessive of a noun or to join words in a contraction.

- **Possessives show ownership. To make a singular noun possessive, add** *'s.*
  The bike belongs to Carmen. It is Carmen's bike.
- **To form a possessive from a plural noun that ends in** *s,* **add only an apostrophe.**
  Those books belong to my sisters. They are my sisters' books.
- **Some plural nouns do not end in** *s.* **To form possessives with these nouns, add** *'s.*
  The children left their boots here. The children's boots are wet.
- **Use an apostrophe to replace the dropped letters in a contraction.**   it's (it is)   hasn't (has not)

Section 8 Commas, Semicolons, and Colons

Commas in Sentences

- Use a comma after an introductory word in a sentence.
  Yes, I'd love to go to the movies.   Actually, we had a great time.
- Use a comma to separate items in a series. A series is a list of three or more items. Put the last comma before *and* or *or*. A comma is not needed to separate two items.
  Shall we eat cheese, bread, or fruit?   Let's eat cheese and fruit.
- Use a comma to separate a noun of direct address from the rest of a sentence.
  Akila, will you please stand up?   We would like you to sing, Akila.
- Use a comma to separate a direct quotation from the rest of a sentence.
  Joe asked, "How long must I sit here?"   "You must sit there for one hour," Vic said.
- Use a comma with the conjunction *and, or,* or *but* when combining independent clauses in a compound sentence.   Lisa liked the reptiles best, but Lyle preferred the amphibians.
- Use a comma to separate a dependent clause at the beginning of a sentence from the rest of the sentence.   Because Lisa likes reptiles, she is considering a career as a herpetologist.
- Use a comma to separate a pair of adjectives that are of a similar kind. To decide whether to put a comma between adjectives, try reading the sentence with the word *and* inserted between the adjectives. If the word *and* sounds natural there, you should use a comma.
  Reptiles have dry, scaly skin. (*needs a comma*)
  Look at that big green lizard! (*does not need a comma*)

- Use commas to set off a nonrestrictive adjective clause. A nonrestrictive clause is one that adds information about the word it modifies but is not essential to the meaning of the sentence.
Walt Jackson, **who sold me a turtle last year,** has a new pet gecko. (*The adjective clause just tells more about the noun it modifies. Because the information in the clause is not essential, the clause is nonrestrictive. Commas are needed.*)
The woman **who runs the pet store** offered me a job. (*The adjective clause tells which woman is being talked about. Because the information in the clause is essential, no commas are used.*)

Semicolons and Colons in Sentences

- You may use a semicolon in place of a comma and a conjunction when combining independent clauses.   Lisa likes reptiles; Lyle prefers amphibians.
- A colon can be used when the second clause states a direct result of the first or explains the first. Lisa owns reptiles: she has two pet snakes.
- Use a colon to introduce a list or series.   I like three kinds of cheese: cheddar, Swiss, and colby.
- Use a colon to introduce a quotation.
Cory always follows this motto: "A penny saved is a penny earned."
- Use a colon after the speaker's name in a play.
LOGAN: Where were you on the night of October 5th, when the gold bullion was stolen?
BLAKE: I was attending the opening night of *Carmen* at the opera house.
- Use a colon to separate hours and minutes in an expression of time.   8:15 P.M.   11:45 A.M.
- Use a colon between the city of publication and the publisher in a bibliographical reference.
O'Dell, Scott. *The Cruise of the Arctic Star*. Boston: Houghton Mifflin, 1973.

Commas with Dates and Place Names

- Use a comma to separate the day from the date and the date from the year.
We clinched the division championship on Saturday, September 20, 2008.
- Use a comma to separate the name of a city or town from the name of a state.
I visited Memphis, Tennessee.

Commas and Colons in Letters

- Use a comma after the greeting and the closing of a friendly letter.
Dear Reginald,   Your friend, Deke
- Use a colon after the greeting of a business letter. Use a comma after the closing.
Dear Ms. Brocklehurst: Sincerely,

Section 9 Hyphens and Parentheses

Hyphens in Sentences

- When you break a word at the end of a line, use a hyphen to separate the syllables.
There is no single "perfect food." Milk, for example, contains most of the nutri-ents needed by the human body, but it lacks enough iron.
- Use hyphens to link the parts of some compound words.   **son-in-law**   **city-state**
- Use hyphens to link some pairs or groups of words that precede a noun and act as an adjective.
a **family-style** meal   a **horse-drawn** carriage   an **up-to-date** schedule
- Use hyphens to link the parts of numbers between twenty-one and ninety-nine.
eighty-two   fifty-seven   seventy-six   thirty-five

Parentheses in Sentences

- Use parentheses to set off an explanation.
I interviewed my uncle (**he raises goats for a living**) for my report on animal husbandry.
Rolf and Dana's farm is 100 miles (**160 km**) outside of Chicago.
- Use parentheses to set off an example.
Many types of cheese (**chèvre, for example**) are made with goats' milk.

Sentence Structure and Parts of Speech

Section 10 The Sentence

A *sentence* is a group of words that tells a complete thought. A sentence has two parts: a *subject* and a *predicate*.

- The subject tells *whom* or *what* the sentence is about.　　　<u>The swimmers</u> race.
- The predicate tells what the subject *is* or *does*.　　　The judges <u>watch carefully</u>.

There are four kinds of sentences: *declarative, interrogative, imperative,* and *exclamatory.*

- A *declarative sentence* makes a statement and ends with a period.
  Jake swam faster than anyone.
- An *interrogative sentence* asks a question and ends with a question mark.
  Did Sammy qualify for the finals?
- An *imperative sentence* gives a command and usually ends with a period; a firm command can end with an exclamation point.
  Keep your eyes on the finish line.　　　Watch out for that bee!
- An *exclamatory sentence* ends with an exclamation point.　　　Jake has won the race!

Section 11 Subjects

The *subject* of a sentence tells whom or what the sentence is about.

- A sentence can have one subject.　　　<u>Mary</u> wrote a book.
- A sentence can have a *compound subject,* two or more subjects that are joined by a conjunction (*and, or*) and that share the same predicate.
  <u>Alex and Mark</u> have already read the book.
- Imperative sentences have an unnamed *understood subject,* the person being spoken to. This subject is referred to as "understood *you.*"　　　Give me the book, please.

The *complete subject* includes all the words that name and tell about the subject.

　　　<u>Many students</u> have borrowed the book.

The *simple subject* is the most important noun or pronoun in the complete subject.

　　　Many <u>students</u> have borrowed the book.　　　<u>They</u> discussed the book yesterday.

Note: Sometimes the simple subject and the complete subject are the same.　　　<u>Ricardo</u> is writing a book.

Section 12 Predicates

The *predicate* of a sentence tells what happened. The *complete predicate* includes a verb and all the words that tell what happened, or tell more about the subject.

- A complete predicate can include an action verb to tell what the subject of the sentence did.
  Mary <u>*won an award*</u>.
- A complete predicate can include a linking verb to tell more about the subject.
  Mary <u>*is a talented writer*</u>.

The *simple predicate* is the verb that goes with the subject. It generally tells what the subject did, does, or will do.

　　　Celia <u>won</u> an award for her performance.
　　　She <u>will receive</u> a trophy next week.

A *compound predicate* is two or more predicates that share the same subject. Compound predicates are often joined by the conjunction *and* or *or.*

　　　Ramon <u>sang</u> and <u>danced</u> in the play.
　　　Mary <u>wrote</u> the play and <u>directed</u> it.

A *predicate noun* follows a linking verb and renames the subject.

　　　Mary is a <u>writer</u>.　　　　　　Ramon is a <u>singer</u>.

A *predicate adjective* follows a linking verb and describes the subject.

　　　Mary is <u>talented</u>.　　　　　　Ramon is <u>clever</u>.

Section 13 Simple, Compound, and Complex Sentences

A *simple sentence* tells one complete thought.

> Arthur has a rock collection.

A *compound sentence* is made up of two simple sentences (or *independent clauses*) whose ideas are related. The clauses can be joined by a comma and a conjunction (*and, or, but*).

> Arthur has a rock collection, **and** Mary collects shells.

The two independent clauses in a compound sentence can also be joined by a semicolon.

> Arthur collects rocks; Mary collects shells.

Two clauses in a compound sentence can be separated by a colon when the second clause is a direct result of the first clause.

> Arthur enjoys visiting new places: he can hunt for rocks to add to his collection.

A *complex sentence* is made up of one independent clause and at least one dependent clause. A *dependent clause* is a group of words that has a subject and a predicate, but it cannot stand on its own.

Dependent Clause:	when Arthur visited Arizona
Independent Clause:	He learned a lot about desert plants.
Complex Sentence:	When Arthur visited Arizona, he learned a lot about desert plants.

A *compound-complex sentence* includes two or more independent clauses and at least one dependent clause.

Independent Clauses:	Arizona is proud of its saguaro cactus.
	The saguaro cactus can grow up to sixty feet tall.
Dependent Clause:	which is also called the giant cactus
Compound-complex Sentence:	Arizona is proud of its saguaro cactus; the saguaro, which is also called the giant cactus, can grow up to sixty feet tall.

An *adjective clause* is a dependent clause that describes a noun or pronoun. An adjective clause always follows the word it describes and begins with a relative pronoun such as *who, whom, whose, which,* or *that.*

> My cousin Arthur, **who has a rock collection,** visited the Arizona desert. (*describes* Arthur)
> He studied the interesting rock formations **that rise above the desert floor.** (*describes* formations)

An *adverb clause* is a dependent clause that tells more about a verb, an adjective, or an adverb. Adverb clauses tell *where, when, why,* or *how much.* They often begin with a subordinating conjunction such as *after, since, where, than, although, because, if, as, as if, while, when,* or *whenever.*

> **Whenever Arthur came across an unfamiliar rock,** he took a photograph of it.
> (*tells* when Arthur *took a photograph*)
> Arthur didn't take any rocks away **because the desert environment is fragile.**
> (*tells* why Arthur *didn't take* rocks away)

Section 14 Fragments, Run-ons, Comma Splices, and Ramble-ons

A *fragment* is an incomplete sentence that does not tell a complete thought.

> Sumi and Ali. (*missing a predicate that tells what happened*)
> Went hiking in the woods. (*missing a subject that tells who went hiking*)

A *run-on sentence* is two complete sentences that are run together. To fix a run-on sentence, use a comma and a conjunction (*and, or, but*) to join the two sentences. (You may also join the sentences with a semicolon.)

Incorrect:	Sumi went hiking Ali went swimming.
Correct:	Sumi went hiking, **but** Ali went swimming.

A *comma splice* is two complete sentences that have a comma between them but are missing a conjunction (*and, or, but*). To fix a comma splice, add *and, or,* or *but* after the comma.

Incorrect:	Sumi went hiking yesterday, Ali went swimming.
Correct:	Sumi went hiking yesterday, **and** Ali went swimming.

A *ramble-on sentence* is grammatically correct but contains extra words that don't add to its meaning.

Incorrect: Hiking through the wilderness to enjoy nature is my favorite outdoor sports activity, probably because it is so enjoyable and such good exercise, and because I enjoy observing wild animals in the wilderness in their natural environment.

Correct: Hiking through the wilderness to enjoy nature is my favorite outdoor sports activity. I enjoy observing wild animals in their natural environment.

Try not to string too many short sentences together when you write. Instead, combine sentences and take out unnecessary information.

Incorrect: I stared at him and he stared at me and I told him to go away and he wouldn't so then I called my big sister.

Correct: We stared at each other. I told him to go away, but he wouldn't. Then I called my big sister.

Section 15 Nouns

A *common noun* names any person, place, thing, or idea.

Ira visited an auto **museum** with his **friends**. Ira has always had an **interest** in **cars**.
He likes that blue **convertible**.

A *proper noun* names a certain person, place, thing, or idea. Proper nouns begin with a capital letter. A proper noun that is made up of two or more words is considered one noun.

Ira wants to visit the **Sonoran Desert** in **Mexico** in **April 2009**.
He is reading a guidebook about the region entitled *The Undiscovered Desert*.

A *collective noun* names a group of people or things that act as one unit.

jury   family   committee   audience   crowd

Section 16 Adjectives

An *adjective* is a word that tells more about a noun or a pronoun.

- Some adjectives tell what kind.
  Jim observed the **huge** elephant. The **enormous** beast towered above him.

- Some adjectives tell how many.
  The elephant was **twelve** feet tall. It weighed **several** tons.

- A *predicate adjective* follows a linking verb and describes the subject.
  Jim was **careful** not to anger the elephant. He was **happy** when the trainer led it away.

- *A, an,* and *the* are special kinds of adjectives called *articles*. Use *a* and *an* to refer to any person, place, thing, or idea. Use *the* to refer to a specific person, place, thing, or idea. Use *a* before a singular noun that begins with a consonant sound. Use *an* before a singular noun that begins with a vowel sound.
  An elephant is heavier than **a** rhino. **The** elephant in this picture is six weeks old.

- A *demonstrative adjective* tells which one. *This, that, these,* and *those* can be used as demonstrative adjectives. Use *this* and *these* to talk about things that are nearby. Use *that* and *those* to talk about things that are farther away.

  This book is about rhinos.   **These** rhinos just came to the zoo.
  That rhino is enormous!   **Those** funny-looking creatures are wildebeests.
  Note: Never use *here* or *there* after the adjectives *this, that, these,* and *those.*

- A *proper adjective* is made from a proper noun. Capitalize proper adjectives.
  Italian cooking   **Democratic** convention   **Apache** legend

Section 17 Pronouns

A *pronoun* can replace a noun.

17a Personal Pronouns

Personal pronouns include *I, me, you, we, us, he, she, it, they,* and *them.* Personal pronouns can be used to stand for the person speaking, the person spoken to, or the person spoken about.

- *First person pronouns* refer to the speaker (*I, me*) or include the speaker (*we, us*).
  Let **me** know when **I** am next at bat.   It took **us** hours, but **we** managed to get to the stadium.

- *Second person pronouns* refer to the person or people being spoken to (*you*).
  Are **you** going to the game?   I asked Marisa to give the bases to **you**.
- *Third person pronouns* refer to the person, people, or thing(s) being spoken about (*he, him, she, her, it, they, them*).
  They played well.   Pass the ball to **him**.   Kick **it** to **her**.
- The third person pronoun *he* (with *him* and *his*) was once accepted as a universal pronoun that could refer to anyone, male or female, if a generalization about people was being made. Now most writers try to avoid the use of universal *he*.

  One solution to this pronoun problem is to make the pronoun and the word it refers to plural. When a chef cooks, **he** displays creativity. **becomes:** When chefs cook, **they** display creativity. Each player should bring **his** own racket. **becomes:** Players should bring **their** own rackets.

  Another solution is to replace *he* **with** *he or she,* **or replace** *his* **with** *his or her.*
  Each player should bring **his** own racket. **becomes:** Each player should bring **his or her** own racket.

17b Subject and Object Pronouns

A *subject pronoun* takes the place of the subject of a sentence. Subject pronouns are said to be in the *nominative case*. Subject pronouns include *I, you, he, she, it, we,* and *they.*

>   Incorrect: Rita is an excellent soccer player. **Rita she** made the team.

>   Correct: Rita plays goalie. **She** never lets the other team score.

An *object pronoun* replaces a noun that is the object of a verb or a preposition. Object pronouns are said to be in the *objective case*. Object pronouns include *me, him, her, us,* and *them.*

>   Rita's team played the Bobcats. Rita's team beat **them**.

The pronouns *it* and *you* can be either subjects or objects.

>   **It** was a close game. (*subject pronoun*)   The Bobcats almost won **it**. (*object pronoun*)

- Use a subject pronoun as part of a compound subject. Use an object pronoun as part of a compound object. To test whether a pronoun is correct, say the sentence **without** the other part of a compound subject or object.
  Incorrect: Rita told Ellen and **I** it was a close game. (Rita told **I** it was a close game.)
  Correct: Rita told Ellen and **me** it was a close game. (Rita told **me** it was a close game.)
- When the pronouns *I* and *me* are used in a compound with a noun or another pronoun, *I* or *me* always comes second in a pair or last in a series of three or more.
  Incorrect: The coach gave the Most Improved Players awards to **me and Carlos**.
  Correct: The coach gave the Most Improved Players awards to **Carlos and me**.

17c Pronoun Antecedents

An *antecedent* is the word a pronoun refers to. The antecedent is almost always a noun.

>   The **Bobcats** are excellent players. (They) won every game last season.

- A pronoun must agree with its antecedent. An antecedent and a pronoun agree when they have the same *number* (singular or plural) and *gender* (male or female).
  Nick's **mother** cheered. **She** was very excited.

17d Possessive Pronouns

Possessive pronouns show ownership.

- The possessive pronouns *my, your, his, her, its, their,* and *our* replace possessive nouns.
  Those skates belong to **my** brother Jorge.
  Those are **his** kneepads, too. (*the pronoun* his *replaces the possessive noun* Jorge's)
- The possessive pronouns *mine, ours, yours, hers, his, its,* and *theirs* replace both a possessive noun and the noun that is possessed.
  Alisha's kneepads are blue. **Mine** are red, and **hers** are blue.
  (*The possessive pronoun* hers *replaces both the possessive noun* Alisha's *and the noun* kneepads.)
- *Whose* is the possessive form of the relative pronoun *who*. It is also used as the possessive form of the relative pronoun *which*.
  The skaters **whose** parents cannot pick them up at 6 P.M. must wait inside the office.
  (Whose *indicates that the parents belong to the skaters.*)

17e Compound Personal Pronouns

A *compound personal pronoun* contains the word *self* or *selves*. Compound personal pronouns include *myself, herself, himself, itself, yourself, ourselves,* and *themselves.*

- **They often show that the action of a sentence is reflecting back to the subject.**

  My brother bought <u>himself</u> a new puck.   We cheered for <u>ourselves</u>.

- **Compound personal pronouns can also be used to show emphasis.**

  She made the winning goal <u>herself</u>.   I <u>myself</u> thought it was a terrific game.

17f Indefinite Pronouns

Indefinite pronouns refer to persons or things that are not identified as individuals. These pronouns include *all, anybody, both, anything, few, most, no one, either, nothing, everyone, one, several, none, everybody, nobody, someone, everything, something, anyone,* and *somebody.*

<u>Somebody</u> lost the ball.   We can't play <u>anything</u> until we find it.

17g Relative Pronouns

When the pronouns *who, whom, whose, which,* and *that* are used to introduce an adjective clause, they are called *relative pronouns.* A relative pronoun always follows the noun it refers to.

The player <u>who brought the volleyball</u> can serve first.
I joined the team <u>that chose me</u>.
This net, <u>which I found in my closet,</u> will be perfect for our volleyball game.

Note: For more information on using *who, whom, which,* and *that,* see Section 32, Problem Words.

17h Interrogative Pronouns

When the pronouns *who, whom, which,* and *what* are used to begin a question, they are called *interrogative pronouns.*

<u>Who</u> has brought the volleyball?   <u>What</u> is a wicket used for?
<u>Which</u> is the net for volleyball?   To <u>whom</u> did you hit the ball?

17i Demonstrative Pronouns

This, that, these, and *those* can be used as *demonstrative pronouns.*

- **Use *this* and *these* to talk about one or more things that are nearby.**

  <u>This</u> is a soft rug.   <u>These</u> are sweeter than those over there.

- **Use *that* and *those* to talk about one or more things that are far away.**

  <u>That</u> is where I sat yesterday.   <u>Those</u> are new chairs.

Section 18 Verbs

18a Action and Linking Verbs

An *action verb* shows action.

Scientists <u>study</u> the natural world.   They <u>learn</u> how the laws of nature work.

A *linking verb* does not show action. It connects the subject of a sentence to a word or words in the predicate that tell about the subject. Linking verbs include *am, is, are, was, been,* and *were. Seem, appear,* and *become* can be used as linking verbs, too.

Explorers <u>are</u> brave.   That route <u>seems</u> long and dangerous.

Some verbs, such as *appear, look, smell, feel, grow, sound,* and *taste,* can be either action verbs or linking verbs. You can test whether a verb is a linking verb by substituting a form of the verb *be* (*am, is, are, was,* or *were*) in its place. If the form of *be* makes sense, the verb is probably a linking verb.

I <u>looked</u> at the bear. (*"I was at the bear" does not make sense:* looked *is an action verb.*)
The bear <u>looked</u> hungry. (*"The bear was hungry" makes sense:* looked *is a linking verb.*)

18b Transitive and Intransitive Verbs

A *transitive verb* is an action verb that transfers its action to a direct object.

The polar bear <u>watched</u> a seal's air hole in the ice.   The polar bear <u>caught</u> the seal.

An *intransitive verb* does not have a direct object. An intransitive verb shows action that the subject does alone.

The bear **waited** patiently.   Suddenly the bear **struck**.

Many verbs can be either transitive or intransitive, depending on whether or not there is a direct object.

The bear **ate** the seal. (*Seal* is the direct object: *ate* is a transitive verb.)
The bear **ate** hungrily. (*Hungrily* is an adverb, and there is no direct object: *ate* is an intransitive verb.)

18c Main Verbs and Auxiliary Verbs

A *main verb* is the most important verb in a sentence. An *auxiliary verb*, or helping verb, comes before the main verb to help it show action. Auxiliary verbs such as *had, are,* and *will* indicate the tense of the main verb. Others, such as *could, might,* and *may,* show how likely it is that something will happen.

Scientists ***are* studying** glaciers.   The studies ***may* help** us learn more about Earth.

18d The Principal Parts of a Verb

Each verb has three *principal parts:* its *present form,* its *past form,* and its *past participle form.*

- Most verbs add *-ed* to the present form to create both the past form and the past participle form. These verbs are called *regular verbs.*
- *Irregular verbs* form their past and past participle forms in other ways. The chart below shows the principal parts of several common irregular verbs.

Present	Past	Past Participle
arise	arose	arisen
(be) is	was	been
blow	blew	blown
bring	brought	brought
build	built	built
cut	cut	cut
drive	drove	driven
eat	ate	eaten
fall	fell	fallen
fly	flew	flown
give	gave	given
go	went	gone
grow	grew	grown
have	had	had
hear	heard	heard
hide	hid	hidden
hold	held	held
know	knew	known
lay	laid	laid
leave	left	left
lie	lay	lain
light	lit	lit
make	made	made
ring	rang	rung
run	ran	run
say	said	said
see	saw	seen
shake	shook	shaken
sing	sang	sung
swim	swam	swum
take	took	taken
tell	told	told
think	thought	thought
throw	threw	thrown
wear	wore	worn
write	wrote	written

- Almost all verbs add *-ing* to the present form to create the *present participle* form: *sing/singing; talk/talking.*

18e Verb Tense

Verb tense places an action in time.

- The *present tense* is used to show that something happens regularly or is true now.
  Squirrels <u>bury</u> nuts each fall.

  Add *s* to most verbs to show present tense when the subject is *he, she, it,* or a singular noun. Add *es* to verbs ending in *s, ch, sh, x,* or *z.* Do not add *s* or *es* if the subject is a plural noun or *I, you, we,* or *they.*

  add *s*   add *es*   change *y* to *i*
  speak/speak<u>s</u>   reach/reach<u>es</u>   carry/carr<u>ies</u>

- The *past tense* shows past action. Add *-ed* to most verbs to form the past tense. Verbs that do not add *-ed* are called *irregular verbs.*   reach/reach<u>ed</u> (regular)   speak/<u>spoke</u> (irregular)

- The *future tense* shows future action. Use the verb *will* to form the future tense.
  Mom <u>will visit</u> Antarctica next year.   She <u>will photograph</u> penguins.

- The *present perfect tense* shows action that began in the past and may still be happening. To form the present perfect tense, add the helping verb *has* or *have* to the past participle of a verb.
  Mom <u>has studied</u> Antarctica for years.   Her articles <u>have appeared</u> in science journals.

- The *past perfect tense* shows action that was completed by a certain time in the past. To form the past perfect tense, add the helping verb *had* to the past participle of a verb.
  Before she visited Antarctica, Mom <u>had imagined</u> it as a wasteland.

- The *future perfect tense* shows action that will be complete by a certain time in the future. To form the future perfect tense, add the helping verbs *will have* to the past participle form of a verb.
  By the end of next year, Mom <u>will have published</u> a book on Antarctic wildlife.

- *Progressive forms* of verbs show continuing action. To form a *present progressive* verb, add *am, is,* or *are* to the *present participle* of a verb (usually the present form + *-ing*). To form the *past progressive* verb, add *was* or *were* to the present participle. To form a *future progressive* verb, add *will be* to the present participle.
  Scientists <u>are learning</u> new facts about Antarctica every day. (*present progressive*)
  When Mom <u>was traveling</u> in Antarctica, she saw its beauty. (*past progressive*)
  Someday soon I <u>will be visiting</u> Antarctica with Mom. (*future progressive*)

18f Subject and Verb Agreement

The subject and its verb must agree in number. Be sure that the verb agrees with its subject and not with the object of a preposition that comes before the verb.

An Antarctic explorer needs special equipment.
(*singular subject:* **An Antarctic explorer;** *singular verb* [*verb + s or es*]: **needs**)
Explorers in Antarctica carry climbing tools and survival gear.
(*plural subject:* **Explorers;** *plural verb* [*verb without s or es*]: **carry**)

A *compound subject* and its verb must agree.

- **Compound subjects joined by *and* are plural.**   Snow and ice <u>make</u> exploration difficult.
- **If a compound subject is joined by *or,* the verb must agree with the last item in the subject.**
  Either the helpers or the leader <u>checks</u> the weather report.

There are special rules for agreement with certain kinds of subjects.

- **Titles of books, movies, magazines, newspapers, stories, and songs are always considered singular, even if they end in *s.***
  The Secret Life of Penguins is the title of Mom's book.
  "Ice and Darkness" is the name of a poem I wrote.
- **A collective noun, such as *collection, group, team, country, kingdom, family, flock,* and *herd,* names more than one person or object acting as a group. These nouns are usually considered singular.**
  My <u>family</u> lives in southern Australia.   A <u>flock</u> of seagulls is flying overhead.
- **Most indefinite pronouns, including *everyone, nobody, nothing, everything, something,* and *anything,* are considered singular.**
  <u>Somebody</u> has left the tent flap open.   Is <u>anything</u> missing?   <u>Everything</u> is fine.
- **Some indefinite pronouns that clearly refer to more than one, such as *many, most, few,* and *both,* are considered plural.**
  <u>Many</u> are interested in Antarctica, but <u>few</u> are able to make the journey there.

18g Active and Passive Voice

A verb is in *active voice* if its subject performs an action. A verb is in *passive voice* if its subject is acted upon by something else. Many sentences in the passive voice have a prepositional phrase that begins with the word *by* and follows the verb.

> Explorers **plan** trips months in advance. (*active voice*)
> Trips **are planned** by explorers months in advance. (*passive voice*)

The active voice can communicate action briefly and powerfully. In most cases, the active voice is stronger and clearer than the passive voice. Try to write most of your sentences in the active voice.

> **Strong active voice:** The penguin **snapped** up the fish.
> **Weak passive voice:** The fish was **snapped up** by the penguin.

Some writers believe that the passive voice should be used only when an action is done by an unknown or unimportant agent.

> The tent flap **was left** open. (*The agent who left the tent flap open is unknown.*)

Section 19 Adverbs

An *adverb* describes a verb, an adjective, or another adverb. Adverbs tell how, when, where, or to what extent.

- **Many adverbs end in *-ly*.** Some adverbs do not end in *-ly*. These include *now, then, very, too, often, always, again, sometimes, soon, later, first, far, now,* and *fast*.
  Andrew approached the snake cage **slowly**. He knew that snakes can move **fast**.

- **Some adverbs tell *how*.**
  She spoke **confidently**.   He **eagerly** bit into the sandwich.

- **Some adverbs tell *when*.**
  Then the bell rang.   School ended **yesterday**.   I eat pizza **only** on Friday.

- **Some adverbs tell *where*.**
  We went **inside**.   They built a house **there**.   Come **here**.

- **Some adverbs tell *to what extent*.**
  It is **very** quiet.   I am **almost** finished.

Section 20 Prepositions

A *preposition* shows a relationship between a word in a sentence and a noun or pronoun that follows the preposition. Prepositions tell when, where, what kind, how, or how much.

- Prepositions include the words *after, in front of, without, above, down, among, with, of, from, for, about, such as, throughout, into, onto, inside, in, at, under, over, on, through, to, across, around, by, beside, during, off,* and *before*.
  Jeff left the milk **on** the table.   He knew it belonged **in** the refrigerator.

- A *prepositional phrase* is a group of words that begins with a preposition and ends with its object. The object of a preposition is a noun or a pronoun. A prepositional phrase can be at the beginning, middle, or end of a sentence.
  Jeff's mom would be home **in five minutes**. **Within three minutes** he had put it away.

- Prepositional phrases that modify (or tell more about) nouns or pronouns are called *adjectival prepositional phrases*. An adjectival prepositional phrase usually comes after the noun or pronoun it modifies. Adjectival prepositional phrases often tell *which*.
  The milk **in the refrigerator** is spoiled. (*modifies the noun* milk *and tells* which milk)
  I can't stand the odor **of spoiled milk**! (*modifies the noun* odor *and tells* which odor)

- *Adverbial prepositional phrases* modify a verb, an adverb, or an adjective. Many adverbial prepositional phrases tell *when, where, how,* or *how long* something was done.
  Jeff usually drinks orange juice **before breakfast**. (*modifies the verb* drinks *and tells* when)
  He says his mom's fresh-squeezed orange juice is the best **in the world**.
  (*modifies the adjective* best *and tells* where)
  Late **in the evening** I heard a knock at my door. (*modifies the adverb* late *and tells* when)

Section 21 Direct Objects and Indirect Objects

A *direct object* is the noun or pronoun that receives the action of the verb. Direct objects follow action verbs. To find the direct object, say the verb and then "Whom?" or "What?"

> Jacques painted a **picture**. (Painted whom or what? Picture. *Picture* is the direct object.)

- A *compound direct object* occurs when more than one noun receives the action of the verb.
  He used a **brush** and oil **paints**. (*Brush* and *paints* comprise the compound direct object.)

A sentence with a direct object may also have an *indirect object*. An indirect object is a noun or pronoun and usually tells to whom something is given, told, or taught.

> Jacques gave his **mom** the painting.

Section 22 Conjunctions

The words *and, or,* and *but* are *coordinating conjunctions*.

- **Coordinating conjunctions may be used to join words within a sentence.**
  My favorite reptiles are snakes **and** lizards.   Najim doesn't like snakes **or** lizards.

- **A comma and a coordinating conjunction can be used to join two or more simple sentences. (The conjunction *and* does not need a comma if both sentences are short.)**
  I like snakes, **but** he says they're creepy.   We can get a snake, **or** we can get a lizard.

A *subordinating conjunction* relates one clause to another. Dependent clauses begin with a subordinating conjunction. Subordinating conjunctions include *because, so, if, although, when, where, as, while, though, than, as if, whenever, since, wherever, after, often, over,* and *before.*

> **Before** his mom left, Bo cleaned his room. He had a favor to ask, **so** he vacuumed, too.

Correlative conjunctions always appear in pairs. They connect words or groups of words and provide more emphasis than coordinating conjunctions. Some common correlative conjunctions are *both—and, either—or, neither—nor, not only—but (also),* and *whether—or.*

> She is **not only** a good singer **but also** an excellent athlete.
> **Neither** Raj **nor** Chris came to the concert.

Section 23 Interjections

An *interjection* expresses emotion and is not part of any independent or dependent clause.

> **Wow!** This bread is delicious.   **Mmmm,** this bread tastes good!

Section 24 Appositives

An *appositive* is a phrase that identifies a noun.

> My favorite snack, **cornbread with honey,** is easy to make.

- **Most appositives are separated from the rest of a sentence by commas. These appositives just give more information about the nouns they describe.**
  Tara, **my friend who figure-skates,** is traveling to Dallas for a competition.

- **Some appositives should not be set off by commas. If an appositive is vital to the meaning of the sentence, it should not be set off by commas.**
  His book *The Basics of Automobile Maintenance* tells how to take care of a car.
  My sister **Katie** likes to read on the porch.

Section 25 Verbals and Absolutes

25a Verbals

Sometimes a verb does not act as a predicate. *Verbals* are forms of verbs that play other roles in sentences.

- One type of verbal, a *participle,* acts as an adjective. A participle may be the present participle or the past participle form of a verb. (See Handbook Section 18d.)
  George heard the bell <u>ringing</u>. (*acts as an adjective describing the noun* bell)
  A <u>shivering</u> child stood at the door. (*acts as an adjective describing the noun* child)

  A *participial phrase* is made up of a participle and other words that complete its meaning.
  <u>Filled</u> with pride, Angela accepted her medal. (*acts as an adjective modifying the noun* Angela)
  Matt noticed a skunk <u>waddling</u> <u>through the bushes</u>. (*acts as an adjective modifying the noun* skunk)

- An *infinitive* is a phrase made up of the word *to* followed by the present form of a verb (*to defend*).
  Infinitives may act as adjectives, adverbs, or nouns. An *infinitive phrase* is made up of an infinitive and other words that complete its meaning.
  I like <u>to walk</u> in the woods. (*acts as a noun; the direct object of the verb* like)
  This is a good way <u>to appreciate</u> nature. (*acts as an adjective modifying the noun* way)
  I listen carefully <u>to hear</u> the sounds of woodland creatures. (*acts as an adverb modifying the verb* listen)

- A *gerund* is a verbal that acts as a noun. All gerunds are present participles. (See Handbook Section 18d.)
  My brother enjoys <u>swimming</u>. (*acts as a noun; the direct object of the verb* enjoys)

  A *gerund phrase* is made up of a gerund and the other words that complete its meaning.
  <u>Riding</u> the waves on a surfboard is his great ambition. (*acts as the subject of the sentence*)

25b Absolutes

An *absolute phrase* consists of a noun or noun phrase followed by a descriptive word or phrase.

- An absolute phrase may contain a present or past participle.
  <u>Her face</u> <u>**glowing**</u>, Sue looked as happy as she felt. (*noun phrase plus a present participle*)
  The general, <u>his army</u> <u>**defeated**</u>, prepared to surrender. (*noun phrase plus a past participle*)

- An absolute phrase may also contain an adjective, a noun, or a prepositional phrase.
  Teri woke from a deep sleep, <u>her mind and body</u> <u>**alert**</u>. (*noun phrase plus an adjective*)
  Melissa, <u>good grades</u> <u>**her prime objective**</u>, never went out on a school night. (*noun phrase plus a noun phrase*)
  Teri rode home, <u>her guitar</u> <u>**across her back**</u>. (*noun phrase plus a prepositional phrase*)

Usage

Section 26 Negatives

A *negative word* means "no" or "not."

- The words *no, not, nothing, none, never, nowhere,* and *nobody* are negatives.
  The notebook was **nowhere** to be found.   **Nobody** wanted to miss the party.

- Often negatives are in the form of contractions.
  Do **not** enter that room.   **Don't** even go near the door.

- In most sentences it is not correct to use two negatives.

  Incorrect
  We **can't** see **nothing**.
  We **haven't** got **no** solution.

  Correct
  We **can't** see anything.
  We **haven't** got a solution.

- Some sentences express ideas that require the use of two negative words.
  No one will work for you for **nothing**. (*In other words, anyone who works will expect to be paid.*)
  I **couldn't** *not* say hello to her. (*In other words, the speaker had to say hello, even if the speaker might not have wanted to.*)

- Do not use the word *ain't*.

Section 27 Comparisons

- The *comparative form* of an adjective or an adverb compares two people, places, or things.
  The comparative form is often followed by "than." To compare two people, places, or things,
  add *-er* to short adjectives and adverbs.
  An elephant is **tall**. A giraffe is **taller** than an **elephant**. (*Giraffe is compared with* elephant.)
  A lion runs **fast**. A cheetah runs **faster** than **any other land animal**. (*Cheetah is compared with* any other land animal.)

- The *superlative form* of an adjective or an adverb compares three or more people, places, or things. The article *the* usually comes before the superlative form. To compare three or more items, add *-est* to short adjectives and adverbs.
  The giraffe is the **tallest** land animal.   The cheetah runs the **fastest** of any land animal.

- When comparing two or more persons, places, or things using the ending *-er* or *-est,* never use the word *more*.

  Incorrect
  She is **more faster** than he is.

  Correct
  She is **faster** than he is.

- The word *more* is used with longer adjectives to compare two persons, places, or things. Use the word *most* to compare three or more persons, places, or things.
  Mario is **excited** about the field trip.
  Duane is **more excited** than Mario.
  Kiki is the **most excited** student of all.

- Sometimes the words *good* and *bad* are used to compare. These words change forms in comparisons.
  Mario is a **good** athlete.   The basketball court is in **bad** shape.
  Kiki is a **better** athlete.   The tennis court is in **worse** shape than
  the basketball court.
  Bill is the **best** athlete of all.   The ice rink is in the **worst** shape of all.
  Note: Use *better* or *worse* to compare two things. Use *best* or *worst* to compare three or more things.

Section 28 Contractions

When two or more words are combined to form one word, one or more letters are dropped and replaced by an apostrophe. These words are called *contractions*. For example, when *he will* becomes the contraction *he'll*, the apostrophe replaces *wi*.

- Here are some other common contractions.
  can't (cannot)   **haven't** (have not)   **she'd** (she would)
  couldn't (could not)   **I'll** (I will)   **they've** (they have)
  doesn't (does not)   **it's** (it is, it has)   **we're** (we are)

Section 29 Plural Nouns

- A *singular noun* names one person, place, thing, or idea.
  girl   pond   arrow   freedom
- A *plural noun* names more than one person, place, thing, or idea. To make most singular nouns plural, add *s*.
  girl<u>s</u>   pond<u>s</u>   arrow<u>s</u>   freedom<u>s</u>
- For nouns ending in *sh, ch, x,* or *z,* add *es* to make the word plural.
  bush/bush<u>es</u>   box/box<u>es</u>
  lunch/lunch<u>es</u>   quiz/qui<u>zzes</u>
- For nouns ending in a consonant and *y,* change the *y* to *i* and add *es*.
  penny/penn<u>ies</u>   army/arm<u>ies</u>
- For some nouns that end in *f* or *fe,* replace *f* or *fe* with *ves* to make the noun plural.
  shelf/shel<u>ves</u>   wife/wi<u>ves</u>   (Exceptions: cliff/cliff<u>s</u>; reef/reef<u>s</u>; cafe/cafe<u>s</u>)
- Some words change spelling when the plural is formed.
  man/m<u>e</u>n   woman/wom<u>e</u>n   mouse/m<u>ic</u>e   goose/g<u>ee</u>se
- Some words have the same singular and plural form.
  deer   sheep   offspring   scissors

Section 30 Possessive Nouns

A *possessive* shows ownership.

- To make a singular noun possessive, add an apostrophe and *s*.
  John<u>'s</u> bat   the girl<u>'s</u> bike
- When a singular noun ends in *s,* add an apostrophe and *s*.
  Ross<u>'s</u> project   James<u>'s</u> glasses
- To make a plural noun that ends in *s* possessive, add an apostrophe.
  the soldiers<u>'</u> songs   the girls<u>'</u> bikes
- When a plural noun does not end in *s,* add an apostrophe and *s* to show possession.
  the men<u>'s</u> ideas   the children<u>'s</u> shoes

Section 31 Dangling Modifiers

A verbal phrase acting as an adjective must modify, or refer to, a specific word in the main part of a sentence. A *dangling modifier* is a phrase that does not refer to any particular word in the sentence.

> Incorrect: <u>Walking down the street</u>, deep thoughts come to mind.
> (*Are deep thoughts walking down the street? No. This verbal phrase does not refer to any particular word in the main part of the sentence: it is a dangling modifier.*)

Dangling modifiers make your writing unclear, so avoid them. When you begin a sentence with a verbal phrase such as "Walking down the street," make sure that the question "Who is walking down the street?" is answered clearly in the first part of the rest of the sentence.

> Correct: <u>Walking down the street</u>, I often think deep thoughts.
> (<u>*Who*</u> *is walking down the street? I am. This verbal phrase clearly relates to the pronoun* I.)

These words are often misused in writing.

sit	*Sit* means "rest or stay in one place." **Sit** down and relax for a while.
sat	*Sat* is the past tense of *sit*. I **sat** in that chair yesterday.
set	*Set* is a verb meaning "put." **Set** the chair here.
lay	*Lay* means "to put something down somewhere." It takes a direct object. The past tense form of *lay* is *laid,* and the past participle form of *lay* is also *laid*. Each day I **lay** a tablecloth on the table. Yesterday I **laid** the yellow tablecloth. I had never **laid** that one on the table before.
lie	*Lie* means "to recline." It can also mean "to occupy a certain place." *Lie* does not take a direct object. The past tense form of *lie* is *lay,* and the past participle form of *lie* is *lain*. Most mornings I **lie** half awake just before the alarm rings. Early this morning I **lay** with my eyes open, waiting for the alarm. I had **lain** there for a few minutes before I realized that it was Saturday. Ohio **lies** east of Indiana.
may	*May* is used to ask permission or to express a possibility. **May** I have another hot dog? I **may** borrow that book someday.
can	*Can* shows that someone is able to do something. I **can** easily eat three hot dogs.
learn	*Learn* means "to get knowledge." Who will help you **learn** Spanish?
teach	*Teach* means "to give knowledge." Never use *learn* in place of *teach*. Incorrect: My sister will **learn** me to speak Spanish. Correct: My sister will **teach** me to speak Spanish.
is	Use *is* to tell about one person, place, or thing. Alabama **is** warm during the summer.
are	Use *are* to tell about more than one person, place, or thing. Also use *are* with the word *you*. Seattle and San Francisco **are** cool during the summer. You **are** welcome to visit me anytime.
doesn't	The contraction *doesn't* is used with the singular pronouns *he, she,* and *it*. He **doesn't** like sauerkraut. It **doesn't** agree with him.
don't	The contraction *don't* is used with the plural pronouns *we* and *they*. *Don't* is also used with *I* and *you*. They **don't** like Swiss cheese. I **don't** care for it, either.
I	Use the pronoun *I* as the subject of a sentence. When using *I* or *me* with another noun or pronoun, always name yourself last. **I** am going to basketball camp. Renée and **I** will ride together.
me	Use the pronoun *me* after action verbs. Renée will call **me** this evening. Also use *me* after a preposition, such as *to, at,* and *with*. Pass the ball to **me**. Come to the game with Renée and **me**.
good	*Good* is an adjective.
well	*Well* is an adverb. These words are often used incorrectly. Incorrect: Renée plays **good**. Correct: Renée is a **good** basketball player. She plays **well**.

raise	*Raise* must be followed by a direct object. I **raise** the flag every morning.
rise	*Rise* is not used with a direct object. I **rise** at dawn every morning.
like	*Like* means "similar to" or "have a fondness for." Do not use *is like* to indicate a pause or to mean "says." Incorrect: I enjoy, **like**, all kinds of water sports. He was **like**, "Swimming is fun." Correct: I **like** swimming and water polo. He said, "I **like** the water."
go	*Go* means "move from place to place." Don't use *go* or *went* to mean "says" or "said." Incorrect: She **went**, "The swim meet was yesterday." Correct: She said, "I **went** to the swim meet."
all	*All* means "the total of something." Avoid using *was all* to mean "said." Incorrect: He **was all**, "Everyone likes swimming." Correct: He said, "Everyone likes swimming."
you know	Use the phrase *you know* only when it helps a sentence make sense. Try not to use it in places where it does not belong. Incorrect: We can, **you know**, go canoeing. Correct: Did **you know** that my family has a canoe?
let	*Let* is a verb that means "allow." Please **let** me go to the mall with you.
leave	*Leave* is a verb that means "go away from" or "let stay." We will **leave** at noon. **Leave** your sweater here.
was	*Was* is a past tense form of *be*. Use *was* to tell about one person or thing. Hana **was** sad yesterday.
were	*Were* is also a past tense form of *be*. Use *were* to tell about more than one person or thing. Also use the word *were* with *you*. Hana and her friend **were** both unhappy. **Were** you home yesterday?
has	Use *has* to tell about one person or thing. Rory **has** a stamp collection.
have	Use *have* to tell about more than one. Also use *have* with the pronoun *I*. David and Lin **have** a rock collection. I **have** a bottle cap collection.
who	*Who* is in the nominative case and should be used as the subject of a clause. Use *who* to refer to people. The man **who** picked me up is my father.
whom	*Whom* is in the objective case and should be used as a direct or indirect object or as the object of a preposition. Use *whom* to refer to people. To **whom** am I speaking?
which	Use *which* to refer to things. His rear tire, **which** was flat, had to be repaired.
that	*That* can refer to people or things. Use *that* instead of *which* to begin a clause that is necessary to the meaning of the sentence. The picture **that** Stephen drew won first prize.
very	*Very* is an adverb. It means "extremely." I was **very** tired after the hike.
real	*Real* is an adjective. It means "actual." Never use *real* in place of *very*. Incorrect: The hike was **real** long. Correct: I used a **real** compass to find my way.

Homophones sound alike but have different spellings and meanings.

are	*Are* is a form of the verb *be*.	We <u>are</u> best friends.
our	*Our* is a possessive pronoun.	<u>Our</u> favorite color is green.
hour	An *hour* is sixty minutes.	Meet me in an <u>hour</u>.

its	*Its* is a possessive pronoun.	The horse shook <u>its</u> shaggy head.
it's	*It's* is a contraction of *it is* or *it has*.	<u>It's</u> a beautiful day for a ride.

there	*There* is an adverb that usually means "in that place." It can also be used in the expressions "there is" and "there are." Please put the books <u>there</u>. <u>There</u> is an aquarium nearby.	<u>There</u> are three books on the table.
their	*Their* is a possessive pronoun. It shows something belongs to more than one person or thing. <u>Their</u> tickets are in my pocket.	
they're	*They're* is a contraction made from the words *they are*. <u>They're</u> waiting for me inside.	

two	*Two* is a number.	Apples and pears are <u>two</u> fruits I like.
to	*To* can be a preposition meaning "toward." *To* can also be used with a verb to form an infinitive. I brought the pot <u>to</u> the stove. (*preposition*)	I like <u>to</u> cook. (*infinitive*)
too	*Too* means "also." *Too* can mean "more than enough."	I'd like some lunch, <u>too</u>. That's <u>too</u> much pepper!

your	*Your* is a possessive pronoun. Where are <u>your</u> socks?
you're	*You're* is a contraction made from the words *you are*. <u>You're</u> coming with us, aren't you?

whose	*Whose* is a possessive pronoun. It can refer to people or things. <u>Whose</u> raincoat is this?	The raincoat <u>whose</u> buttons are blue is mine.
who's	*Who's* is a contraction made from the words *who* and *is* or *who* and *has*. <u>Who's</u> at the front door?	<u>Who's</u> taken my book?

than	*Than* is a subordinating conjunction used to make comparisons. We waited for more <u>than</u> an hour.	She is taller <u>than</u> you.
then	*Then* can be an adverb that tells about time. It can also mean "therefore." <u>Then</u> I went home. If you like mangoes, <u>then</u> you should try this mango ice cream.	

principal	A *principal* is a person with authority. The <u>principal</u> made the rule.
principle	A *principle* is a general rule or code of behavior. He lived with a strong <u>principle</u> of honesty.

waist	The *waist* is the middle part of the body. She wore a belt around her <u>waist</u>.
waste	To *waste* something is to use it in a careless way. She would never <u>waste</u> something she could recycle.

aloud	*Aloud* means out loud or able to be heard.	He read the poem <u>aloud</u>.
allowed	*Allowed* is a form of the verb *allow*.	We were not <u>allowed</u> to swim after dark.

Letters and E-mails

Section 34 Letters

A *friendly letter* is an informal letter written to a friend or a family member.

In a friendly letter, you might send a message, invite someone to a party, or thank someone for a gift. A friendly letter has five parts.

- The *heading* gives your address and the date.
- The *greeting* includes the name of the person you are writing to. It begins with a capital letter and ends with a comma.
- The *body* of the letter gives your message.
- The *closing* is a friendly or polite way to say good-bye. It ends with a comma.
- The *signature* is your name.

> 35 Rand Street
> Chicago, Illinois 60606
> July 15, 2008
>
> Dear Kim,
>
> Hi from the big city. I'm spending the summer learning to skateboard. My brother Raj is teaching me. He's a pro.
>
> I have one skateboard and hope to buy another one soon. If I can do that, we can practice together when you come to visit.
>
> Your friend,
> Art

A *business letter* is a formal letter.

You would write a business letter to a company, an employer, a newspaper, or any person you do not know well. A business letter looks a lot like a friendly letter, but a business letter also includes the name and address of the business you are writing to. The *greeting* of a business letter begins with a capital letter and ends with a colon (:).

> 35 Rand Street
> Chicago, Illinois 60606
> July 15, 2008
>
> Swenson Skateboard Company
> 10026 Portage Road
> Lansing, Michigan 48091
>
> Dear Sir or Madam:
>
> Please send me your latest skateboard catalog. I am particularly interested in your newest models, the K-7 series.
> Thank you.
>
> Sincerely yours,
> Arthur Quinn
> Arthur Quinn

The envelope below shows how to address a letter. A friendly letter and a business letter are addressed the same way.

> Arthur Quinn
> 35 Rand St.
> Chicago, IL 60606
>
> Kim Lee
> 1555 Montague Blvd.
> Memphis, TN 38106

An *e-mail* is a note sent from one person to another person, a group, or a company through a computer network. Today, many people use e-mail to stay in touch with friends and family. An e-mail should contain five parts, like a letter does.

- An e-mail contains a *greeting*, a *body*, a *closing*, and your *name*.
- An e-mail *header* contains your e-mail address, the e-mail address of the person you are writing to, the date, and a subject line.

Send	Save as a Draft	Cancel

From:	arthur_quinn@communicago.net
To:	info@swenskate.com
Date:	July 15, 2008
Subject:	Skateboard catalog

Attach Files

Dear Sir or Madam:

Please send me your latest skateboard catalog. I am particularly interested in your newest models, the K-7 series.

My address is 35 Rand Street, Chicago, IL 60606. Thank you.

Sincerely,
Arthur Quinn

Research

Section 36 Library Research

You can find information for a report or a project in a library.

- Many libraries have an information desk. The person at the desk can help you look for information.
- Libraries have many reference books, including dictionaries, thesauruses, and encyclopedias. You can use these to find information about words and basic information about topics.
- Libraries have nonfiction books about all kinds of subjects. You can find books on a particular subject by entering that subject into a computer connected to the library's database. This database lists all the publications in the library. The computer will usually list several books on the subject you entered. Each listing will have a code that tells where in the library that book can be found.

You can use online dictionaries, thesauruses, and encyclopedias to find basic information about words and topics. You can also find information for a report or a project by using an Internet *search engine*.

- Think of **key words** that describe what you are looking for. For example, if you need information on animals that live in the rainforest, you might use the key words **rainforest animals**. Type these words into the search engine's text box.

- The search engine will provide you with links to **Web sites**. You can click on a link to visit a Web site.

- When you get to the Web site, you need to judge whether it will be a good source of information.
  - Notice the last three letters of the Web site's Internet address. Sites with **.gov** and **.edu** are usually more reliable than sites with **.com**.
  - Think about who has written the information. Is the writer an expert on the topic? Is the writer giving facts, or just expressing opinions?
  - Check to see if the information is up-to-date. The site should tell you when it was last updated.

Internet Safety

Be sure to follow safety rules whenever you use the Internet. These rules will help you keep personal information private.

- When you log on to a school computer, you may type your own name as a username. However, when you go on the Internet, you use a screen name. That should never be your real name or nickname. You will also use a password, a secret word or symbol that identifies who you are. Keep your password safe. Do not share it with anyone. Never use your address, birthday, phone number, or pet's name as a password. Those are too easy for someone else to figure out.

- Have you ever received e-mail with an attachment? Usually you must click the attachment to load it into your computer. Never download attachments from strangers. These may harm your computer.

Guidelines for Listening and Speaking

These steps will help you be a good listener:

- **Listen carefully** when others are speaking.
- **Keep in mind your reason for listening.** Are you listening to learn about a topic? To be entertained? To get directions? Decide what you should get out of the listening experience.
- **Look directly at the speaker.** Doing this will help you concentrate on what he or she has to say.
- **Do not interrupt** the speaker or talk to others while the speaker is talking.
- **Ask questions** when the speaker is finished talking if there is anything you do not understand.

Section 39 Speaking

Being a good speaker takes practice. These guidelines can help you become an effective speaker:

Giving Oral Reports

- **Be prepared.** Know exactly what it is that you are going to talk about and how long you will speak. Have your notes in front of you.
- **Speak slowly** and **clearly.** Speak **loudly** enough so everyone can hear you.
- **Look** at your audience.

Taking Part in Discussions

- **Listen** to what others have to say.
- **Disagree politely.** Let others in the group know you respect their point of view.
- **Try not to interrupt** others. Everyone should have a chance to speak.

(you) | Diagram | sentences

Section 40 Diagraming Sentences

A sentence diagram is a map of a sentence. It shows how the parts of a sentence fit together and how the individual words in a sentence are related. Sentence diagrams can represent every part of speech and every type of sentence. The models below demonstrate how to create sentence diagrams, beginning with the simplest kinds of sentences.

- In a sentence consisting of a subject and an action verb, the subject and the verb are separated by a vertical line that bisects the horizontal line.

  Rain fell.

  Rain | fell

- An adjective (or article) that modifies a noun or pronoun belongs on a slanted line below the word it modifies.

  A cold rain fell.

- An adverb that modifies a verb belongs on a slanted line below the verb it modifies.

  A cold rain fell **steadily.**

- A direct object is placed on a horizontal line to the right of the verb. It is separated from the verb by a short vertical line that does not bisect the horizontal line.

  The downpour drenched the **land.**

- An indirect object goes below the verb to show *who* or *what* receives something.

  It gave the **crops** a welcome soaking.

  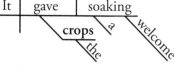

- Two separate horizontal lines show a compound predicate. The conjunction joins the verbs.

  Seedlings **uncurled** and **grew**.

  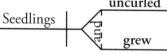

- A compound subject is placed on two horizontal lines with a conjunction joining the subjects.

  Leaves and **flowers** glistened.

- A compound sentence is diagramed as two sentences with a conjunction joining them.

  The rain stopped and the sun appeared.

  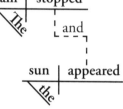

- A demonstrative pronoun takes the place of a noun. It belongs wherever the noun it replaces would go in the diagram.

  This prompted a collective cheer.

  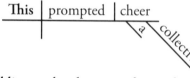

- A possessive pronoun belongs on a slanted line under the noun that is the possession.

  The children left **their** homes gleefully.

- An indefinite pronoun, a subject pronoun, or an object pronoun also belongs wherever the noun it replaces would go.

  Someone started a soccer game.

  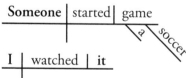

  I watched **it**.

- The understood *you* belongs where the subject of the sentence would go. It is written in parentheses.

  Remove your muddy shoes.

  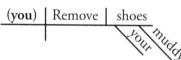

- A linking verb has the same position in a diagram that an action verb has, but the linking verb is separated from the predicate adjective or predicate noun by a diagonal line instead of by a vertical line.

  Your clothes **are** incredibly muddy.

  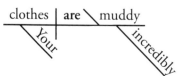

Soccer **is** a rough sport.

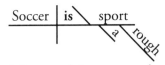

- An adverbial prepositional phrase that modifies a verb is connected to that verb.
Leave your shoes **on the porch**.

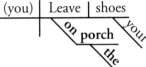

- An adjectival prepositional phrase that modifies a noun is connected to that noun.
The mud **in the field** is quite deep.

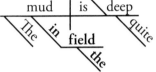

- When *there* begins a sentence, it is placed on a separate line above the rest of the diagram.
There are fresh towels inside the house.

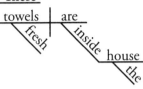

- An adjective or an adverb is written on a slanted line and is connected to the word it modifies.
The **bright** green towel is mine.

You must clean your shoes **very** carefully.

- To diagram a sentence containing an adjective clause, first identify the independent clause and diagram it. Then place the dependent clause below the first diagram. Connect it to the first diagram with a slanted, dashed line that joins the clause to the noun it modifies. Write the subordinating conjunction on the dashed line.
The new shoes **that you bought** are very wet.

- Diagram a sentence containing an adverb clause in a similar way, but connect the dependent clause to the independent clause with a slanted, dashed line connecting to the verb.
They looked nice **until you wore them in the mud**.

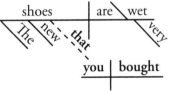

Topic Index

Language Index